THE *LAIS* OF MARIE DE FRANCE

broadview editions
series editor: Martin R. Boyne

THE *LAIS* OF MARIE DE FRANCE

TEXT AND TRANSLATION

edited and translated by Claire M. Waters

broadview editions

BROADVIEW PRESS – www.broadviewpress.com
Peterborough, Ontario, Canada

Founded in 1985, Broadview Press remains a wholly independent publishing house. Broadview's focus is on academic publishing; our titles are accessible to university and college students as well as scholars and general readers. With over 600 titles in print, Broadview has become a leading international publisher in the humanities, with world-wide distribution. Broadview is committed to environmentally responsible publishing and fair business practices.

Library and Archives Canada Cataloguing in Publication

Marie, de France, active 12th century, author
    The Lais of Marie de France : text and translation / edited and translated by Claire M. Waters.

Includes bibliographical references.
Text in Old French with English translation.
ISBN 978-1-55481-082-6 (softcover)

    1. Marie, de France, active 12th century—Translations into English. 2. Lays—Translations into English. I. Waters, Claire M., editor, translator II. Marie, de France, active 12th century. Lais. III. Marie, de France, active 12th century. Lais. English. IV. Title.

PQ1494.L3E5 2018   841'.1   C2017-907023-1

Broadview Editions
The Broadview Editions series is an effort to represent the ever-evolving canon of texts in the disciplines of literary studies, history, philosophy, and political theory. A distinguishing feature of the series is the inclusion of primary source documents contemporaneous with the work.

Advisory editor for this volume: Michel Pharand

Broadview Press handles its own distribution in North America:
PO Box 1243, Peterborough, Ontario K9J 7H5, Canada
555 Riverwalk Parkway, Tonawanda, NY 14150, USA
Tel: (705) 743-8990; Fax: (705) 743-8353
email: customerservice@broadviewpress.com

Distribution is handled by Eurospan Group in the UK, Europe, Central Asia, Middle East, Africa, India, Southeast Asia, Central America, South America, and the Caribbean. Distribution is handled by Footprint Books in Australia and New Zealand.

Broadview Press acknowledges the financial support of the Government of Canada through the Canada Book Fund for our publishing activities.

Canada

Typesetting and assembly: True to Type Inc., Claremont, Canada
Cover Design: Aldo Fierro

PRINTED IN CANADA

Contents

Acknowledgements

Translating Marie de France has taken me back almost to my earliest roots as a medievalist when, after studying modern and medieval Welsh and realizing that I wanted to study the Middle Ages, I found myself in a tutorial with Laurence de Looze and learning Old French, as so many others have, by way of William W. Kibler's *An Introduction to Old French*. I am grateful to Laurence and to subsequent teachers—Jill Mann, Bill Paden, Tilde Sankovitch, and Barbara Newman—who encouraged and forwarded my interests in Old French literature. In more recent years, I owe a debt to the colleagues who welcomed my translations of a handful of Marie's *Lais* in the *Broadview Anthology of British Literature* and suggested that I should undertake the rest, and to the many who have supported the project along the way, especially Don LePan, Marjorie Mather, Martin Boyne, Tara Lowes, and Michel Pharand at Broadview. Matilda Bruckner and anonymous readers for the press gave detailed and incisive feedback on the translations and Introduction and improved both; I appreciate their time and expertise.

Particular and emphatic thanks go to Noah Guynn and Amy Ogden for their kind willingness to respond to queries and, especially, for test-driving the translations with their students and making many valuable suggestions and corrections. Geoff Rector has been generous in sharing his knowledge of Old French and Anglo-French and in discussing all things Marie. Elizabeth Allen, Seeta Chaganti, Sally Poor, and Cathy Sanok offered helpful comments on the Introduction. Numerous graduate and undergraduate students have, over the years, enriched my understanding of the *Lais*. In fall 2013, I was especially fortunate to have the opportunity to teach the translations in a senior seminar, whose participants were wonderful interlocutors throughout the quarter. I relish the memory of the final creative projects in which each devised a response to one of the *Lais* in a non-literary medium; I regret that I cannot reproduce here Fwjchim Thaoxaochay's cartoon version of *Le Fresne*. Among this group, Jillian Kern deserves special thanks for her insightful responses to the text and for suggesting certain nuances that contributed to the final version. I am grateful to Sara Petrosillo and Cordelia Ross for sharing their expertise on hawks and werewolves and making suggestions for the Appendices. In the late stages, Jessica

Hanselman Gray did a painstaking read-through that caught many errors and infelicities—but inevitably some remain that are my responsibility alone. I look forward to being alerted to them by readers.

Introduction

Some time in the second half of the twelfth century, a lady (*dame*) named Marie composed some lais—short narratives that centrally feature a love affair and often have otherworldly elements—that were warmly received by an aristocratic audience. Roughly a century later, a scribe copied a Prologue and twelve lais, in the first of which, the lai of *Guigemar*, the author calls herself Marie; he also copied, into the same manuscript, a collection of Aesopic *Fables* (also known as the *Ysopë*, or "little Aesop") in whose epilogue the author says, "I will name myself for the sake of remembrance: Marie is my name, I am from [or 'of'] France." While the figure usually referred to as "Marie de France" has traditionally been regarded as the author of both these works and possibly two others, we know very little about her.[1] Nevertheless, the strong appeal of her texts to modern as well as medieval audiences, and the unusualness, in this time period, of a female author who not only gives but highlights her name, have made her works some of the best known of the European Middle Ages.

What we know or can deduce about Marie and her works is discussed below, but while for the sake of both tradition and convenience I will treat her as the author of the *Lais*, it is worth remembering that it is the thirteenth-century manuscript mentioned above—London, British Library, Harley MS 978—that offers the main grounds for seeing the *Lais* as a deliberate collection and for considering them as the work of the person we call Marie de France.[2] This manuscript, which serves as the basis for the French text edited below, is the only manuscript containing all twelve of the *Lais* traditionally attributed to Marie, though eleven of them and the Prologue also appear, in a different order and interspersed with other lais, in an Old Norse translation compiled for the king of

---

1 Claude Fauchet (1530–1602), in a work of 1581, seems to have been the originator of this designation, though it gained popularity in the early nineteenth century and later thanks to the work of the Abbé la Rue (1751–1835). On post-medieval reception and criticism of Marie's works, see Maréchal. The extensive scholarship on Marie is detailed in the invaluable volumes by Glyn S. Burgess, *Marie de France: An Analytical Bibliography* and the three *Supplements* published so far, the third with the assistance of Giovanna Angeli. For the *Fables*, see Appendices B3 and C1.
2 Taylor (76–136) offers an extensive account of the manuscript's history and contents.

Norway, Hákon Hákonarson (r. 1217–63), in the mid-thirteenth century. Nine of them are contained in Paris, Bibliothèque nationale de France, nouv. acq. fr. 1104, again among a number of other lais, and a few appear singly or in small groups in other manuscripts.[1] The Norse collection and BnF nouv. acq. fr. 1104, while not attributing these particular works to a named author, suggest that they were recognizably part of a genre of lais, since in both cases they are presented in the context of other works categorized as such.[2]

All twelve of the stories that are collected in Harley 978 are quite brief, ranging from 118 lines (*Chevrefoil*) to 1184 (*Guildelüec et Guilliadun*, also known as *Eliduc*). Each one involves a love relationship that takes place in an aristocratic milieu— though the nature of those relationships and the extent to which they dominate the narrative vary greatly—and all of the narratives are set in northern France or the British Isles.[3] The *Lais* as presented in Harley 978 thus have an internal coherence of theme, genre, and setting. Though the scribe of the manuscript does not attribute the *Lais* and the *Fables* he copied to the same person, nor assert that all the *Lais* were written by one author, the fact that he presented these twelve lais together, following a Prologue, and copied them in close proximity to the *Fables* has encouraged the view that both collections were the work of the same author.

There are, in fact, four works in French octosyllabic couplets from the later twelfth or early thirteenth century whose author calls herself "Marie": *Guigemar*, the first lai in the Harley collection; the *Fables*; an account of a purgatorial journey (*L'Espurgatoire seint Patriz* or *St. Patrick's Purgatory*; see Appendix C2); and the life of an Anglo-Saxon saint (*La vie seinte Audree*, *The Life of St. Audrey*; see Appendix C3). While the *Fables*, *Espurgatoire*, and *Vie seinte Audree* are not a primary concern of the present book, the grounds for linking them to the Marie who authored the *Lais* can nonetheless shed some light on central features of the latter. A key element these works share, and one that may strengthen the suggestion that they are the work of the same author, is their consistent conjunction, in their pro-

---

1 A discussion of the Old Norse manuscript and an edition and English translation of the lais it contains can be found in Cook and Tveitane; the contents of BnF nouv. acq. fr. 1104 can most efficiently be viewed at http://www.arlima.net. See the Note on the Text for details.

2 The collection by Koble and Séguy gives a sense of the genre more broadly.

3 Burgess, *Lais* 1–34 gives an extensive account of the settings of the *Lais* and what this may suggest about their order of composition.

logues or epilogues, of authorial self-naming and memory.[1] Neither of these emphases is unusual in medieval texts (though there was likely some pressure on women authors to leave their work anonymous, given concerns about women exercising authority), but their persistent presence in these four texts is nevertheless striking.

Most famously, in the Epilogue of the *Fables* the author writes, "At the end of this text, which I have composed and told in French, I shall name myself for the sake of remembrance: Marie is my name, I am from France" (Al finement de cest escrit, / Que en romanz ai treité e dit, / me numerai pur remembrance: / Marie ai num, si sui de France).[2] The prologue to *Guigemar*, the first of the *Lais*, urges, "Listen, lords, to what Marie says, who does not forget her duty in her time" (Oez, seignurs, ke dit Marie, / Ki en sun tens pas ne s'oblie, ll. 3–4; p. 52).[3] *L'Espurgatoire seint Patriz* emphasizes remembrance of the text, rather than the author, but again links the two closely: "I, Marie, for the sake of memory, have put into French the book of the *Purgatory*" (Jo(e), Marie, ai mis en memoire / le livre de l'Espurgatoire / en romanz, ll. 2297–99).[4] Finally, the epilogue of the *Vie seinte Audree* reads, "One is indeed foolish who forgets herself: here I write my name 'Marie' so that I may be remembered" (Mut par est fol ki se oblie. / Ici escris mon non Marie, / Pur ce ke soie remembree, ll. 4624–25).[5] To have two

---

1 On naming and memory in the *Lais*, see Bruckner, *Shaping* 157–206, and Whalen, *Marie*.

2 Spiegel, Epilogue ll. 1–4 (p. 156); my translation. This and the other prologues discussed here are included more fully in the Appendices below.

3 The precise meaning of "Ki en sun tens pas ne s'oblie" is ambiguous: it could also be translated "who is not forgotten in her time" or "who does not forget herself." While this prologue to *Guigemar* does not mention concern about remembering the story (as opposed to the author), several other lais in the Harley group do so, as does the Prologue to the collection: "Plusurs en ai oï conter, / Ne voil laisser ne oblier" (I have heard many of them told; I do not wish to leave them aside or forget them, ll. 39–40; p. 50).

4 Pontfarcy, *L'Espurgatoire* 278; my translation and I have modified the punctuation. See Appendix C2, p. 392.

5 McCash and Barban 246. A few lines earlier, the author says that she has translated the life and miracles from Latin into French, adding, "Ne voil nul mettrë en obli" (I do not wish to let anything be forgotten, l. 4616; see Appendix C3, p. 393). The Epilogue to the *Fables* echoes the idea of self-forgetting when Marie writes that others may try to claim her work, but should not do so, saying, "il fet que fol ki sei ublie" (she acts foolishly who forgets herself, l. 8; see Appendix C1, p. 390).

(or more) women authors with the same name and the same insistence on commemoration of both authorship and text writing in the same period seems unlikely, especially at a time when it was common for women writers, if they did acknowledge their gender, to apologize for it, something none of these Maries does. Most scholars consider the *Fables*, *Lais*, and *Espurgatoire* to be the work of the same person, and many have begun, in recent years, to include the *Vie seinte Audree* as well.[1]

The four works have other points of contact, though these are less consistently marked than their emphasis on naming and remembrance. As noted above, they generally share a courtly milieu; all but the *Fables* have main characters of chivalric or aristocratic (or, indeed, royal) background, and even the *Fables* engage with concerns about governance and loyalty that were of deep interest in the world of the political elite. Both the *Fables* and the *Lais* incorporate English words; the *Fables* claims to be a translation of a work by the Anglo-Saxon King Alfred (r. 871–99), while the *Vie seinte Audree* is the story of a royal Anglo-Saxon woman. Several of the *Lais*, as well as the *Vie* and the *Espurgatoire*, are set in the British Isles, and the latter two are based on Latin works composed in England. All four works present themselves as translations, though only in the cases of the *Vie* and the *Espurgatoire* do we have the originals. And the *Vie seinte Audree*, despite its more centrally religious focus, concerns itself with a woman's self-definition and ability to direct her own life in a way reminiscent of many of the *Lais*.

The Prologue to the *Lais* shows Marie's careful attention to the transmission of writings over time, the *translatio studii* or cultural transfer that brings material from one tradition or time to a new land or audience and that is in keeping with her attention to remembrance in all her works. Her consistent interest in translation in its linguistic sense is marked in the *Lais* as a whole by her careful provision of different languages' words for key terms in a given lai.[2] The beginnings and ends of several of the lais empha-

---

1   This recent acceptance is primarily based on the detailed case made by June Hall McCash in "*La vie seinte Audree:* A Fourth Text by Marie de France?"; scholars such as Rupert Pickens, Logan Whalen, and Carla Rossi, among others, have accepted this attribution, though it is not universally endorsed. Kinoshita and McCracken sound a note of caution, pointing to the questions such an attribution raises rather than choosing one side or the other (2–3, 110–12).

2   Scholars have also connected this interest in translation to Marie's fascination with the "translation" of human and animal in various forms; see for example McCracken; Bruckner, "Speaking."

size the stories' origins in the culture and language of the "bretuns" (Bretons or Britons), while references to classical figures such as Semiramis or Octavian and the Prologue's evocation of a learned tradition, as well as echoes of biblical narratives and figures, show Marie to be of her time in her conjoining of classical Latin authorities, Christian culture, and Celtic narrative for dissemination in French verse. Like her contemporaries, Marie worked to integrate the learned culture of biblical and classical works with the rich and varied indigenous traditions of twelfth-century Britain and Ireland and to present these to a noble class committed to literary and cultural patronage.

Multicultural England in the Twelfth Century

The date of the *Lais* is uncertain: the earliest manuscripts that contain them are from the mid-thirteenth century, but the linguistic evidence suggests that they were composed much earlier, and, as we will see below, there is external evidence that assures us that lais by Marie were known in the late twelfth century. In addition, the *Lais* contain echoes of the continental *Roman d'Eneas*, whose composition is usually placed around 1160 (see Appendix B1), and do not seem to draw on the slightly later romances of Chrétien de Troyes (c. 1130–c. 1190), probably from the 1170s–80s. This suggests that they were almost certainly composed during the reign of Henry II Plantagenet (r. 1154–89), who came to the throne after a period of unsettled rule, and probably relatively early in his reign, though of course they may have been composed over a period of time, most likely in the 1160s–70s.[1]

Following the Norman Conquest of 1066, when William, Duke of Normandy, defeated the English king Harold Godwinsson (r. 1066), England came under the rule of French-speaking

---

1 A reference to the anonymous *Proverbes au vilain* in Marie's *Fables* makes it likely that the latter were composed after the *Proverbes*' date of 1180. The *Book of Ely* (*Liber eliensis*) that was one of Marie's sources for the *Vie seinte Audree* dates to the 1170s, indicating that the text must be later than that, while the *Tractatus de Purgatorio Sancti Patricii* from which the *Espurgatoire* derives probably dates from around 1185. In addition, Marie's mention of St. Malachi, who was canonized in 1190, may imply that the *Espurgatoire* was translated after that date; but since saintly individuals could be referred to as saints even before canonization, this is not definitive.

aristocrats. William ruled England for twenty years, dying in 1087, and had the good fortune to leave three sons who could inherit his lands in the British Isles and in Normandy. His eldest son, Robert, became Duke of Normandy (r. 1087–1106), while William II, known as William Rufus, inherited his father's lands in Great Britain and Ireland (though the latter were not securely under Norman rule) and reigned from 1087 until he died in a hunting accident in 1100, leaving no heir.[1] At that point his younger brother, Henry I (b. c. 1068), known as Henry Beauclerc, took the throne; but when Henry died in 1135, he left a daughter, Matilda (c. 1102–67), as his sole heir, since his only legitimate son, William, had predeceased him in 1120.

Although there was no law against a woman ruling, the French barons resisted Matilda's accession and instead offered the throne to Stephen of Blois (r. 1135–54), grandson of William the Conqueror through his mother, Adela (c. 1067–1137). Matilda contested this, leading to a period of civil war from 1135 to 1153, sometimes known as "the anarchy," although Stephen held the kingship for most of this time. A resolution was eventually reached whereby Matilda's son, Henry, would inherit the kingdom after the death of his uncle, which took place in 1154.[2] Henry's father, Geoffrey Plantagenet, held lands in Anjou, so while England passed out of strictly Norman hands after the death of Stephen, its rulers continued to come from French-speaking lands. Henry II, an Angevin (that is, from Anjou), and his queen, Eleanor of Aquitaine (1122–1204), whom he had married in 1151, thus strengthened and indeed extended the ties between the British Isles and the francophone world.[3]

Henry and Eleanor presided over the expansion of a cultural flowering already underway, and Marie's works are part of a great wave of literary composition and translation in Britain in the twelfth century.[4] While already during the reigns of Henry I and Stephen texts had been composed for the Norman aristocracy in

---

1 An account of this event is provided in Appendix D.
2 On the vexed and violent transmission of power in the British Isles between the Norman Conquest and 1216, see Bartlett 4–11.
3 Henry II was, of course, not "purely" Angevin; he was also of (Anglo-)Norman descent through his grandfather Henry I, and of Anglo-Saxon and Scots descent through his grandmother Edith/Matilda; see below.
4 Simon Meecham-Jones addresses the role of literary production in relation to Henry II's political situation and aims, 1–24. See also Short, "Patrons and Polyglots," 229–49.

Latin and, increasingly, in Old French, the production of works in French for aristocratic patrons increased greatly during their rule. The emergence of French as a literary language in this period is evident in the many works composed by francophone authors from the continent writing in Great Britain and by authors who originated in the Channel Islands or in the British Isles, writing in the high-status language of the rulers. Thus a substantial part of the early history of French literature is based in the British Isles as well as in what is now France.

It is important to note that French, though of great cultural prestige in the British Isles for the next three hundred years (and beyond), never became the primary language of the population as a whole.[1] While for the first century and a half after the Norman invasion the kings of England maintained very strong cultural ties to France, and most of them married women from the francophone areas of the Continent, the first wife of Henry I was Edith (c. 1080–1118, also known as Matilda or Maud, a very popular name in this period), the daughter of King Malcolm of Scotland (r. 1058–93) and his wife Margaret (c. 1045–93), a descendant of the royal Anglo-Saxon line. Anglo-Norman and Anglo-Angevin noblemen were very likely to marry women whose families had been in England prior to the Conquest, leading to a mixed English and Norman/Angevin aristocracy.[2] The precise extent of the aristocracy's knowledge of French over time is a complex and disputed topic, but it is clear that bilingualism in French and English was increasingly the norm for them, even as the main population remained primarily monolingual in English. During Henry and Eleanor's time the court language, at least, was firmly and solidly French—both they and most of their court were native speakers of continental forms of French—but the knowledge of certain English and Celtic words that Marie shows in her *Lais* aptly reflects the Anglo-French awareness of the contemporary multilingualism of the islands.

At the same time, there was an acknowledgement in this period that French itself was changing in its new environment; a number of authors born in the British Isles speak apologetically or defen-

---

1 For an overview of the complex history of "French" (itself not a single, coherent language in this period, though I use the term for convenience) in England, see Butterfield 53–65, and "England and French," in Wogan-Browne, Fenster, and Russell 401–13; the variety of French writing in the British Isles is evident in the latter volume and in the essays collected in Wogan-Browne.
2 On the influence of intermarriage on bilingualism, see Crane 36–37.

sively of the ways in which their French usage or spelling (and, probably, pronunciation) failed to adhere to continental norms. It is worth noting that Marie makes no such apologies, and indeed her language is generally considered very "correct" in its use of meter and rhyme by contemporary continental standards; this makes sense in view of her claim to be "from France." She has therefore been considered a key figure in the history of both French and English literatures, even as the *Lais*, with their attention to Celtic storytelling traditions and their settings in both northern France and the British Isles, especially the western parts of Great Britain, reflect the Anglo-Normans' and, in Marie's period, Anglo-Angevins' strong interest in the topography and traditions of their adopted country.

While francophone rulers and cultural connections provide the most obvious historical context for Marie's *Lais*, both their Celtic debts and their placement in a broader northern European setting are also significant for their composition and reception. Marie is emphatic in attributing the origins of her lais to the "bretuns" and their musical and storytelling traditions. *Bretuns* is usually translated as "Bretons," that is, the Celts of northern France (Brittany), but for Marie the term seems to encompass British Celtic peoples as well. The various Celtic inhabitants of France and the British Isles had migrated there before the advent of the Romans, probably in the late centuries BCE, and thus formed a longstanding and influential part of the culture of these areas. The arrival in Great Britain of the Angles, Saxons, and Jutes in the fifth and sixth centuries CE—first as mercenaries, later as settlers and rulers—overlaid the Celtic presence in the eastern parts of the island, but Brythonic Celtic culture retained a substantial role in the west and southwest (roughly, modern Wales and Cornwall) as did the Goidelic Celts in the north (now Scotland).[1] Goidelic Celts also remained predominant in Ireland and continued to be a potential threat, as well as a potential ally, for the Anglo-Saxons. The Brythonic Celts' history of opposition to the Anglo-Saxons gave them a natural appeal for the Normans, who had defeated the Anglo-Saxons and wanted to

---

1 The threat recorded in, for example, *Lanval*, where Arthur is in northern England due to the "Scots and Picts who were ravaging the country" (ll. 7–8; p. 163), makes it clear that Marie (following Geoffrey of Monmouth and others) did not conflate all groups of Celtic origin.

establish the legitimacy of their claims to Britain; stories of ancient British rulers, such as, for example, those offered by Geoffrey of Monmouth (c. 1100–55) in his influential *Historia regum Britanniae* or *History of the Kings of Britain*, were therefore of political as well as cultural interest to the Normans.[1] Continental writers, too, drew on this heritage; the romances of Chrétien de Troyes, composed probably in the 1170s–80s, make use of many Brythonic Celtic names, characters (primarily Arthur and his court), and motifs, and helped to disseminate the "matter of Britain"—that is, the legendary history of the island—to a wide audience. Marie's use of the terms "bretun" and "Britaine" may sometimes have particular geographic reference, but often it can as usefully be thought of as evoking a "Brittonic" world whose precise location is less important than its connection to marvels.

If the Brythonic inheritance was strongly influential on the literary side, Anglo-French political reckoning had to deal not only with various Celtic peoples but also with the defeated Anglo-Saxons and another group with a persistent though less dominant presence in the British Isles: the Scandinavian groups loosely known as Vikings. While the Normans were, by the time of their conquest of England, French-speaking Christians, they were originally, as their name indicates, "north-men," that is, Scandinavian. Rollo (c. 845–c. 930), the first duke of Normandy, was probably of Norwegian descent; in the early 900s, he sailed down the Seine and set about ravaging and pillaging in the approved Viking fashion. Roughly a decade later, the French king Charles the Simple (r. 898–922) made an agreement with him: if Rollo ceased his attacks, he and his men would be granted lands in northern France. William the Conqueror was Rollo's direct descendant. In one sense, then, the Norman Conquest is the last of the great Viking invasions of England that had begun in the late eighth century.

In the meantime, England had even had Scandinavian rulers: Sweyn Forkbeard, a Dane, ruled in 1013–14, and his descendants held the English throne from 1016 until 1042. Edward the Confessor (r. 1042–66), whose death without an heir in 1066 provoked the succession controversy between Harold Godwinsson and William of Normandy that ended in the Norman Conquest, was the half-brother of the last of the Danish kings of England,

---

1 Geoffrey's *Historia* is discussed in more detail below; see p. 20, n. 4. See also Appendix D1.

Harthacnut (r. 1040–42).[1] There were, in addition, Viking kings or co-kings of the kingdom of Dublin, in Ireland, almost continuously from the mid-ninth century until 1171. Thus, despite being an island, Britain was tightly linked, politically and culturally, to a network of other countries. The transnational aristocratic culture that encompassed the various French kingdoms, the British Isles, Scandinavia, and beyond is conveyed, for example, in the lai *Milun*, where the knightly protagonist, originally from south Wales, "was well known in Ireland and in Norway and in Gotland [an island now part of Sweden]; in England and in Scotland" (ll. 15–17; p. 251); at another point, he attends a tournament where there are "Normans and Bretons ... and the Flemish and the French"—though, in that case, "hardly any English" (ll. 388–90; p. 271). Marie's *Lais*, and their later transmission, reflect the interactions of Scandinavian, Celtic, English, and French cultures.

"Dame Marie"

While the literary and administrative output of the Norman and Angevin rulers of England, and particularly the "phenomenal upsurge of historical writing" in this period, gives us a reasonably clear sense of the broader historical context of the Anglo-French court in the late twelfth century, we have much less information as to the precise identity of the author of the *Lais*.[2] The four works signed "Marie," as noted above, offer suggestive (even if not definitive) grounds for taking them as the work of a single poet, but this gets us hardly any closer to knowing who that poet might have been. We do, though, have a few pieces of evidence that begin to fill in the blanks.

One particularly valuable testimony to the existence and reputation of a woman named Marie who composed lais comes from

---

1 Their mother was Emma (c. 985–1052), also called Ælfgifu, who was married first to the Anglo-Saxon ruler Æthelred (r. 978–1013, 1014–16, the father of Edward the Confessor) and then to the Danish king Cnut; the latter ruled England (r. 1016–35) as well as Denmark (r. 1018–35) and Norway (r. 1028–35) and was the father of Harthacnut, who reigned over Denmark 1035–42 and, as noted, over England as well in 1040–42. Emma was the daughter of Richard I, the Duke of Normandy (r. 942–96), a reminder that England's fortunes were bound up with Normandy's well before the Norman Conquest.
2 The quoted phrase is from Hollister 1.

a hostile witness. In his *Vie seint Edmund le rei* *(Life of St. Edmund the King)*, Denis Piramus, a monk of the Benedictine abbey of Bury St. Edmunds, repents of his own earlier secular compositions and objects to the "fables and lies ... [and] dream[s]" purveyed by the author of the continental French romance *Partenopeu de Blois*. He goes on to critique "Dame Marie autresi, / Ki en ryme fist et basti / E compensa les vers dé lays / Ke ne sunt pas de tut verais, / E si en est ele mult loee, / E la ryme partut amee" (Lady Marie also, who made and arranged in rhyme and composed the verses of lais that are not at all true, and yet she is greatly praised for it, and the rhyme is loved everywhere, ll. 29–30, 35–40; see Appendix C6, pp. 396, 397). He also reports at some length the enthusiastic reception of the lais by noble readers—"counts, barons, and knights" as well as ladies (ll. 41–48). The *Vie seint Edmund*, once thought to be from around 1170, has more recently been dated to the early 1190s.[1] Given its testimony to the extensive popularity of the *Lais*, however, it seems reasonable to suppose that it may postdate them by some years.[2]

While Piramus's reference does not, of course, enable us to link any particular lai to Marie, it does confirm that she was a well-known poet in her own time and author of more than one such work. It also accords her a certain social status, though without much specificity; "dame" could be a title given to a noblewoman or to a nun, especially a high-ranking one. These two groups had substantial overlap—many aristocratic women became nuns by their own or their family's wishes—and it is not surprising that a woman capable of translating and composing poetry would have come from a noble background, given the much higher levels of education among aristocratic women than those lower on the social scale.

Piramus's comment also strengthens the case for locating Marie principally in England. Marie's specification that she is "of France" may well refer to the Île-de-France, rather than the whole of what we know as modern France, and could thus have been meant to distinguish her from (for example) someone from Normandy or Anjou. It seems more likely, though, to have been intended to emphasize her *francophonie* to an audience based

---

1 Short, "Denis Piramus" 319–40; see also Piramus 7–9.

2 Piramus says of the aristocratic readers of the lais, "si en ayment mult l'escrit / E lire le funt, si unt delit, / E si les funt sovent retreire" (they love the writing greatly and have it read, and take pleasure in it, and so they often have them [the tales] retold, ll. 43–45; see Appendix C6, p. 397).

outside of modern France. While the cultural and literary contact between various French-speaking realms and the British Isles in this period was extensive, as noted above, Piramus's remark seems to suggest a certain proximity: he does not name, for example, the (continental) author of *Partenopeu de Blois*, and the extensive enthusiasm for Marie's lais that he notes may imply a particularly England-based celebrity.[1]

The Prologue to the *Lais* further asserts their connection to court culture; they are dedicated to a "noble king," usually assumed—due to the probability that Marie was writing in England—to have been Henry II Plantagenet, or sometimes his son Henry the Young King (r. 1170–83).[2] In any case, it seems clear that the *Lais* were directed to and warmly received by an Anglo-French courtly audience but very possibly composed by someone not originally from England; and their combination of French, English, and British/Breton locales reflects the intersecting and sometimes tense investments of noble readers in northern France, England, Wales, and Ireland in the wake of the Norman Conquest.[3] The Norman and Angevin rulers of England were interested not only in the political subjugation of the peoples and lands of the British Isles but also in the cultural appropriation of their traditions, and Marie's incorporation of Brythonic Celtic narratives, loan-words, and legendary figures into her tales, alongside occasional English loan-words and many settings in the British Isles, echoes works such as Geoffrey of Monmouth's *Historia regum Britanniae* that aimed to give the Anglo-French aristocracy a sense of, and a certain claim on, the existing traditions of their new realm.[4] The transnational phe-

---

1 Russell points out, however, that there is no particular reason to associate Piramus himself with the royal court, although he is known to have visited it in 1182; he may well be referring to one (or more) of the "small baronial courts in England that were also active patrons of vernacular writers" when he discusses the popularity of *Partenopeu* and the lais of Dame Marie (Piramus 5).

2 The *Fables*, slightly less exaltedly, are dedicated to a "Count William," for whom there are many possible candidates, and Marie credits an unnamed "prosdom" (worthy man, l. 9; Appendix C2, p. 391) with encouraging her to translate the *Espurgatoire*.

3 See Kinoshita; Bartlett 18–19, 68–102.

4 See Faletra. The *History* was composed around 1138 for the Norman nobleman Robert of Gloucester (c. 1090–1147), the illegitimate son of Henry I; it provided an allegedly historical account of the ancient kings of the island stretching back to Brutus, a descendant of Aeneas, the founder of Rome. Geoffrey's *History* both

nomenon of the "francophone court" and its cultural influence throughout Europe, that is, rested to a significant degree on the transmission of Brythonic Celtic material, as Marie's lais among others remind us; the romance poets of the French-speaking world borrowed and adapted the *matière* of a subjugated culture to shape their own culturally powerful courtly norms.[1]

If the author of the *Lais* can be placed with reasonable certainty in the French-speaking England of the later twelfth century, her precise individual identity nevertheless remains shadowy despite her investment in self-naming and the scholarly detective work that has striven to link her with specific historical women. Given the social position implied by her level of education and her references to powerful patrons, the figures suggested have been women with strong aristocratic ties in England or northern France, or both. While early efforts to link Marie to the French royal house have now been discarded, the popularity of the name "Marie," in a period when the explosion of late-medieval devotion to the Virgin Mary was well underway, yields a number of possible candidates. These have included Marie, countess of Boulogne, daughter of Stephen of Blois and briefly abbess of Romsey (1136–82); Mary, abbess of Barking and sister of Thomas Becket (c. 1130–after 1173); the historically shadowy Marie de Meulan or de Beaumont, supposedly the Norman-born wife of a baron with lands in both northern France and England (born, if at all, c. 1140s); and Mary, abbess of Shaftesbury and half-sister of Henry II (d. 1216).[2]

---

offered the first coherent and extensive account of King Arthur as a (pseudo-)historical figure and claimed, like Marie's *Lais*, to be a translation from a Brythonic source—in Geoffrey's case a "British book" that may or may not have ever existed as a single object but that presumably represented Geoffrey's knowledge of written and oral Brythonic Celtic traditions. The *History* was translated into French verse by the Jerseyman Wace (c. 1100–after 1171) around 1154 and dedicated to Eleanor of Aquitaine; Wace's version (known as *Brut*, after Brutus) expands on the account of court behavior and pushes the narrative more in the direction of the emerging genre of romance. Brief excerpts from Geoffrey's and Wace's work are included in Appendices C5, D1, and E1.

1 On French influence in Germany, see Bumke 61–102; on the fran-cophone court's cultural imperialism, see Rikhardsdottir.

2 On Marie de Boulogne, see Knapton; on Mary, abbess of Barking, see Rossi, *Marie de France* 177–92; on Marie de Meulan, see Pont-farcy, "Si Marie"; and on Mary, abbess of Shaftesbury, see Bullock-Davies. Bloch 3–4 provides a brief overview of these and other candidates, with references to the case made for each.

(While it might seem unlikely that an abbess would write a collection of twelve love stories, many of them involving adultery, the interplay between secular and sacred literature in the Middle Ages, the willingness to read worldly literature for its instructional value, and the mutual borrowing between romance and saints' lives make this no reason automatically to exclude a given figure.) Considerable effort and ingenuity have been expended in the pursuit of these various possibilities, but it is worth noting that often the effort to pin down an identification requires hypothesizing a figure whose historical existence remains unsubstantiated (Marie de Meulan) or taking as figurative Marie's own declaration "si sui de France" and identifying her with a native-born Englishwoman, albeit of Norman parents (Mary, abbess of Barking).[1]

Unless further information about any of these figures or about the *Lais* themselves comes to light, the attempt to tie the "Marie" of *Guigemar*, the other lais of which Denis Piramus speaks, or any of the other works under that name to a specific historical person must remain speculative. While the possibility of situating the author(s) Marie more precisely is alluring, it is worth remembering that biographical detail does not necessarily contribute greatly to our understanding of a literary work. In what follows, I accept the traditional treatment of these twelve lais as the work of one person who gathered them deliberately into a collection and provided that collection with a Prologue, and I suppose that person to be the same one who composed the *Fables*, *Espurgatoire*, and *Vie seinte Audree*. My emphasis, however, will be on the internal correspondences and resonances in the *Lais* that make this a plausible claim. Whoever their original composer(s) was or were, these texts seemed to a thirteenth-century scribe-compiler worth presenting as a collection headed by a Prologue that serves to encompass them in a single overall project of instruction, and I consider them as such.

The Stories and Genres of the *Lais*

While each of the lais has its own distinctive qualities and difficulties, they are also a coherent group in many ways, beginning with their consistent inclusion of a love relationship in an aristo-

---

1 On the lack of historical evidence for a twelfth-century Marie de Meulan, see Rossi, "Brevi note"; on the idea of "si sui de France" as an authorial "posture" rather than an accurate autobiographical detail, see Rossi, *Marie de France* 15.

cratic setting. That quality in itself is enough to link them to the important emerging genre of romance. The development of French as a literary language in the twelfth century manifested itself in many genres, but romance was one of the most lasting and culturally influential. The very word "romance" comes from *roman* or *romanz*, one name for the vernacular language we know as French; it became so closely associated with narratives of love and adventure that the genre eventually took the name of the language.

Perhaps not surprisingly, this new kind of story that began to appear in the twelfth century, emphasizing courtly behavior, female characters, and love relationships alongside the already traditional chivalric prowess and dynastic concerns of epic, was closely associated with the rise of female literacy and patronage.[1] The lais, while they claim a different genre—one associated particularly with song and performance—can be considered "romance fictions" that, while shorter than the typical romance, "use the same kinds of materials and operate in the same context for medieval writers and their public."[2] And while the *Lais* show considerable internal variety in characters, setting, and message, they adhere to a foundational norm of romance in their use of an intimate, dyadic relationship as a basis or context for exploring other social institutions and problems.

Within that larger context, there are nevertheless certain recurrent situations or themes that draw the lais together, as a brief account of the narratives can begin to show. Several important recurring elements are introduced in the first story in the collection, the lai of *Guigemar*. The titular hero, who does not care for love, wounds a talking, androgynous deer—a hind with a stag's antlers, accompanied by a fawn—who then puts him under a destiny of suffering for love until he finds someone who will suffer equally for him; this turns out to be the imprisoned wife of a jealous old man, whom Guigemar reaches by way of a magical, self-directing ship. She rescues him and they fall in love. They are discovered and separated, only to be reunited in the end—against the wishes of yet a third man who finds the lady after she, fol-

---

1 Krueger, "Questions of Gender"; Short, "Patrons and Polyglots."
2 Bruckner, *Shaping Romance* 1; see also 157–63. On the mysterious etymology of "lai"—which has been variously attributed Germanic, Brythonic, and Latin roots—and some of its resonances as a word, see Bloch 29–32. The term seems to be used primarily to refer to narratives performed with musical accompaniment, though like many medieval genre terms it has fuzzy boundaries.

lowing Guigemar, is brought by the ship to his lands. The reunion is enabled by a knotted shirt (for Guigemar) and a belt (for his lady) that can be undone only by the true beloved. Thus we have an animal whose qualities seem to overlap with or borrow from those of humans; the presence of mysterious, otherworldly forces; the figure of the *mal mariée*, the unhappily married woman who finds a deserved and deserving true love outside marriage; and the object, or here objects, that represent the lovers' privacy, their secret knowledge of one another. All of these aspects of *Guigemar* recur repeatedly across the twelve lais.[1]

Immediately after presenting such characteristic narrative elements, however, Marie offers a very different story in which *none* of these is present: in *Equitan*, a selfish king conceives a passion for the wife of his loyal and hard-working seneschal, and the two begin an affair. When they eventually conspire to get rid of the unwanted husband, their plan backfires, bringing about their own destruction. If *Guigemar* suggests, that is, that love must sometimes make its own rules, and that the larger world will collude with the lovers, *Equitan* makes it clear that not every adulterous affair can claim such numinous power and justification. As a result, a reader who takes the *Lais* in their Harley 978 order is alerted from the beginning that each lai must be read on its own terms and assessed independently with the help of the reader's judgment.

The lais that follow can be grouped in various ways; below is a very brief account, according to the order in Harley 978, with some attention to how each lai includes or omits the elements noted above (confining marriage, significant animals and/or objects, otherworldly or magical features) and to its place in a sequence. *Le Fresne*, the third of the lais in Harley 978, introduces one important theme scarcely touched on in *Guigemar* or *Equitan*, that of familial relationships. A baby abandoned by her mother at an abbey grows into a beautiful young woman (Le Fresne, "ash-tree," named for the tree where she was found). Prevented from marrying her beloved because of her unknown ancestry, she is eventually rediscovered due to her own generosity in allowing her lover, Gurun, to become betrothed to another—who is, unbeknownst to her, her own twin sister—and

---

1 Kinoshita and McCracken similarly explore, though with regard to somewhat different elements, "the way the multiepisodic *Guigemar* juxtaposes and recombines plots developed separately in other tales" (191).

even decorating their marriage bed with the cloth left with her as an infant. Her mother recognizes the cloth and the family is reunited. Thus the meaningful object so frequently seen in Marie's lais is present here, but as a sign between mother and daughter rather than between lovers, and apart from Fresne's almost miraculous selflessness the story has no magical element.

Bisclavret, on the other hand, centers on a version of the human-animal conjunction that we first saw in the talking hind of *Guigemar*: the central character, a *bisclavret* or werewolf, is trapped in wolf form by his terrified wife, who hides his clothing, preventing his re-transformation. He is eventually restored thanks to the affection of the king, whose court he has (re)joined as a pet, when his vengeful attack on his wife is understood not as random violence but as a meaningful act and the story comes to light. The tale partly echoes the reversed *mal-mariée* elements of *Equitan*: here the good husband is, at least according to one reading, the *mal marié* in relation to his unappreciative wife. The tale is one instance of a widespread cultural interest in lycanthropy; two other Old French lais, *Melion* (included in Appendix A1) and *Biclarel*, tell versions of the same story.

If the masculine court and its chivalric bonds are salvific in *Bisclavret*, they are quite the reverse in *Lanval*. Here the hero, a young, foreign king's son unjustly neglected by King Arthur, whose court he has joined, wanders into the countryside and is more or less collected by a beautiful, wealthy, and powerful otherworldly lady who declares herself his beloved, on one condition: he must tell no one of their affair. Not surprisingly, after a period of bliss, he breaks this promise (under provocation from the queen, who solicits his affections) and loses his beloved, only to be tried by the court for having insulted the king's wife. The lengthy legal deliberations that follow end when his beloved takes pity and comes in person to demonstrate that she is, in fact, incomparably more beautiful than the queen, thus justifying his harsh words. Lanval jumps onto the back of her horse as she rides off to Avalon and is never seen again. *Lanval* was one of the most widely disseminated of Marie's lais in the Middle Ages—it survives in four French manuscripts, more than any other apart from *Yonec*—and there are two versions in Middle English, *Sir Landevale* and *Sir Launfal*, both from the fourteenth century.

Lanval is one of the most emphatically "legendary" of the lais, in its invocation both of King Arthur and of the Celtic otherworld; the tale that follows, *Deus Amanz* (*The Two Lovers*), returns to a much more everyday setting, giving a particularly precise topographical location for its action. Near Pîtres, in Normandy, is a great mountain; the king of this region, unwilling to give his daughter in marriage, insists that any suitor must carry her to its top without stopping. The girl's young beloved, carrying a potion that will give him strength, attempts the feat but collapses and dies due to his unwillingness to take the potion; she dies of grief and they are buried together on the mountain, which flowers abundantly after the unused potion spills across it.

This sad ending is the tale's main link to the one that follows it, *Yonec*, which in other ways strongly recalls both *Guigemar* (in its use of the *mal-mariée* theme) and *Lanval* (through the presence of a powerful fairy lover). Here, the neglected wife of an elderly husband sends up a prayer for true love, only to have an enormous goshawk fly through her window and transform into a handsome knight. The discovery of the rapturous affair that ensues leads to the fatal wounding of the knight, but before he dies, he gives the lady a ring of forgetfulness and his sword and tells her to tell their story to the son with whom (he reveals) she is pregnant. Having used the ring to ensure that her son grows to adulthood without any suspicion from his stepfather, she chooses an opportune moment to relay the tale, and then dies of grief on the tomb of her beloved; her son, Yonec, avenges his father. This tale, whose link to Celtic analogues is particularly strongly traceable, exists, like *Lanval*, in four different manuscripts, suggesting that lais with an otherworldly element may have been particularly entrancing to medieval audiences.[1]

Yonec, with its Celtic debts, is followed by *Laüstic*, a tale that has often drawn comparison to the classical story of Philomela, the raped and silenced maiden transformed into a nightingale.[2] *Laüstic* presents a muted version of the *mal-mariée* narrative by depicting a woman in love with her neighbor, though able to interact with him almost exclusively at a distance. When she tells her suspicious husband that she stands by the window at night out of a desire to hear the nightingale sing, her husband traps and kills the bird and throws the body at her; she wraps it in an embroidered cloth and sends it to her lover, who creates a jeweled

---

1 On *Yonec*'s Celtic elements and analogues, see Boyd.
2 The most famous version of the story can be found in Ovid's *Meta-morphoses* (8 CE), which were widely known in the Middle Ages. There is an Old French poem from the late twelfth century, *Philomela*, that also tells her tale; it is sometimes attributed to Marie's contemporary, the continental poet Chrétien de Troyes.

casket for it and carries it with him forever. This brief and oblique tale showcases Marie's interest in powerfully significant objects that elicit a desire to interpret while resisting any definitive "solution" to their meaning.

Laüstic's emblematic bird (which itself recalls the murdered hawk-knight of *Yonec*) is echoed in the next lai, *Milun*, where two young lovers who cannot marry have their child raised by the lady's sister and sustain their love over the course of twenty years by exchanging messages carried by a trained swan. When the child is grown, he becomes, like his father, an outstanding knight, and the two are finally reunited when they meet in combat at a tournament and the father recognizes the son by means of the ring he was given as an infant (an aspect of the tale that harks back to *Le Fresne*). The whole family is reunited and the son sees to the marriage of his parents.

From the tournament-focused world of the end of *Milun* we turn to another in *Le Chaitivel, ou Quatre Dols (The Wretched One, or The Four Sorrows)*, where a lady cannot choose among her four young, noble, valiant suitors. Desperate to win her favor, they compete in a tournament where three are killed and the last badly wounded. Tending to the survivor and mourning the dead, the lady laments her losses, saying that she will make a lai called *Quatre Dols* (Four Sorrows). The knight retorts that it should be called *Le Chaitivel* (The Wretched One), since the others cannot suffer any more while he remains close to his beloved but cannot enjoy her favors. The lady agrees and the lai is duly named *Le Chaitivel*, though Marie records that many still call it *Quatre Dols*.

Both the soldiering theme of *Chaitivel* and its emphasis on alternative titles will be picked up in *Guildelüec et Guilliadun* (or *Eliduc*), the last of the lais, but first we have the shortest and possibly most enigmatic, an episode from the Tristan and Yseult story called *Chevrefoil (Honeysuckle)*. It briefly recounts the sorrows of the doomed lovers, separated by the jealousy of King Mark of Cornwall, who is Tristan's uncle and Yseult's husband. As the tale begins, Tristan is in exile but awaiting the passage of the queen, who is traveling a route he knows well. Beside the road he leaves a sign for her made from a hazel tree, with an inscription that includes his name and whose exact message, highly ambiguous to the reader, somehow conveys that the lovers are like the symbiotic hazel tree and honeysuckle: if separated, they will die. Though mysterious to us, the message is immediately legible to the queen, who sees it, dismounts, goes to "rest" in the forest and is reunited there—briefly—with Tristan, who subsequently makes a lai in remembrance of these events, becoming, like the lady in *Chaitivel*, both a participant in the story and the original creator of the lai that commemorates it.

Guildelüec et Guilliadun (or *Eliduc*), the longest and last of the lais, also showcases the concern with naming that is so characteristic of Marie in her prologues as well as within the *Lais* themselves. Later readers, beginning with the one who wrote titles into the margins of Harley 978, have tended to call this lai by the name of its male protagonist, Eliduc, but Marie makes it very clear that while this was the lai's original name, "now the name is changed" (ore est li nuns remuez, l. 24; p. 300) to reflect the fact that it is truly the women's story, "because it happened to the ladies" (Kar des dames est avenu, l. 25). This only emerges slowly in the course of the story itself, however, which begins as the tale of the knight Eliduc, happily married and cherished by his lord, the king of Brittany, until he undeservingly falls out of favor at court and crosses the sea to seek a place in "Logres" (deriving from the Old Welsh name for England). He defends one of the kings of Logres from his enemies and becomes his cherished retainer. Eliduc's fame reaches the ears of the king's only daughter, Guilliadun, who falls in love with him, knowing nothing of his marriage; he eventually comes to reciprocate her love despite his guilt over the wife he has left behind, though they do not consummate their affair.

Eliduc then receives word that his former lord is in need of his help, and he returns to Brittany, promising to come back for the maiden, which he duly does after rescuing his original lord. He spirits her away from her father's castle by night and they set sail back to Brittany, but on the journey she learns of his marriage and falls in a deathlike faint. Once they have landed, Eliduc carries her to a chapel in the forest near his house and returns to his wife, but he is sad and distracted and repeatedly goes to visit the body of his beloved. His wife, Guildelüec, eventually has him followed and visits the chapel herself; she finds the maiden and realizes what has happened. Seeing a weasel revive a wounded companion with a red flower, she uses the same flower to wake Guilliadun. Guildelüec decides to become a nun, enabling Eliduc to marry his new beloved. Eliduc builds his former wife an abbey and he and Guilliadun marry and live happily; ultimately he builds a second church where he can become a monk while Guilliadun enters the abbey with Guildelüec. While the religious ending of *Guildelüec et Guilliadun* is unusual in the *Lais*, its resolution of a love triangle with two women and one man (an unusual configuration) by way of a woman's extraordinary generosity is reminiscent of *Le Fresne*, and its depiction of chivalric culture and court politics resonates with several other lais; it also offers, in the affectionate weasels with their magic flower, another instance of the significant animals who populate so many of the lais.

As this suggests, while there is no obvious principle of organization that accounts for the order of the lais, one can see connections between each pair as they progress. Matilda Bruckner has pointed out, though, that the very pervasiveness of such links means that one could arrange them in other orders as long as the framing tales, *Guigemar* and *Guildelüec et Guilliadun*, remained in place.[1] At the same time, it is noteworthy that in its present form the collection has a consistent pattern of lengths: its two longest pieces, *Guigemar* at 884 lines and *Guildelüec et Guilliadun* at 1184, frame an alternation between lais of approximately 300 lines or fewer (*Equitan, Bisclavret, Deus Amanz, Laüstic, Chaitivel, Chevrefoil*) and lais of more than 500 lines (*Le Fresne, Lanval, Yonec, Milun*). The one break in the pattern—necessitated by the even number of lais—comes with the two short lais that precede *Guildelüec et Guilliadun*, namely *Chaitivel* and *Chevrefoil*; the latter, at 118 lines, is almost exactly one-tenth the length of *Guildelüec*, the last in the collection, and their conjunction draws attention to the different effects one can achieve in narratives of different lengths.[2]

While the lais have, as noted above, many points of contact with Old French romances from England and the Continent, and to a large degree participate in their worldview, they do diverge from the norms of romance in certain respects. An attentiveness to female characters and viewpoints, and the privacy often associated with them, is much in evidence, as it is in romance, but the effort to balance this realm with that of public, chivalric identity is much less consistently present. While figures such as Guige-

---

1 *Shaping Romance* 162. Bruckner also argues for the importance of the title *Guildelüec et Guilliadun*, 182–84. The echo between the two "framing" titles in the Harley 978 ordering is another argument in favor of retaining Marie's preferred names, if we suppose that this ordering was her intention (or even that of the scribe).

2 Even the longer lais, of course, are shorter than most chivalric romances (those of Chrétien de Troyes, for instance, are 6,000–7,000 lines long apart from *Perceval*, which although unfinished is over 9,000 lines long). On Marie's interest in short narrative, see Badel.

mar, Gurun in *Le Fresne*, the young man in *Deus Amanz*, and even Equitan function as examples (sometimes negative) of how one might negotiate the demands of courtly masculinity, the investigation of their struggles is, as a rule, treated far more briefly and instrumentally than the journeys of, for example, Chrétien de Troyes's heroes Erec or Yvain. The exception to this rule is Eliduc, who appears in the longest and last of the *Lais*, the only one not translated into Old Norse, and the only one with a significant religious element—in other words, in a lai that sets itself apart from the others in some key respects. Even in this instance, though, the account of the chivalric male is strongly shaped by his inclusion in a story that, as Marie's chosen title indicates, is ultimately that of two women who resolve the internal contradictions that the knight himself is unable to manage.

This relative lack of interest in the demands of courtly masculinity is echoed in the *Lais'* general avoidance of national mythology or long-term dynastic investment. Stories such as *Lanval* or *Chevrefoil* that are linked to famous narratives involving legendary kings inevitably touch on such issues; *Lanval* even makes specific reference to them when it notes that Arthur is off fighting the Picts and Scots who threaten his empire from the north, a detail that hints at the larger historical narratives favored by writers such as Geoffrey of Monmouth. But for the most part the *Lais*, in keeping with their intense attention to the privacy of lovers and (to a lesser degree) the bonds within families, turn aside from this larger stage. There are certainly potential lessons for rulers in these texts, but despite such locational clues as Guigemar's name (a traditional one among the viscounts of Léon, in northwestern Brittany) or the setting of *Deus Amanz* in Pîtres, no effort is made to shape the *Lais* into an origin story or an account of triumphant return to and rule over any particular realm; even the dramatic reinstatement of Yonec as his father's heir is meaningful in relation to the past events of the story he inhabits rather than any broader history or future. Rather than being episodic narratives that sustain an account of idealized and divinely sanctioned rulership, they provide a series of quite different angles on interpersonal relationships that do not add up to a justification for a particular nation or people.

The *Lais'* tendency to use only intermittently or in passing features that are much more central to romance can also be seen with regard to travel. In romances, protagonists may go into exile, seek adventure, flee overbearing parents, pursue malefactors, or be cast adrift in rudderless boats, only to end up where they started and, very often, assume the throne. What they do *not* do is stay in one place. Marie's *Lais* certainly include narratives of extensive travel—*Guigemar, Yonec, Milun,* and *Guildelüec et Guilliadun* all involve substantial journeys that recall the quests for adventure, love, and identity familiar from romance—and make characters' movements between places a significant part of the story that reflects other kinds of transitions and transformations.[1] In some cases, though, the action is much less peripatetic. In *Equitan* and *Laüstic,* for instance, the events are so tightly confined in space as to become claustrophobic, and indeed both tales end with a climactic enclosure. *Bisclavret* and *Lanval,* until their endings, imagine only local journeys, setting their action in a small ambit that nonetheless allows for extraordinary events and transformations—which, however, are not designed to prepare the central figures for rulership. *Chevrefoil* seems almost to play with romance expectations in this regard: taking one brief interlude from the long and episodic tale of Tristan and Yseult, it acknowledges the lovers' many travels—indeed, Yseult is on a journey in the lai itself—while offering us a view of them briefly encapsulated, almost suspended, in a moment of rest and peace that somehow transcends their wanderings.

The ostentatious brevity of both the events recounted in *Chevrefoil* and the lai itself also draws our attention to Marie's use of time. Here, too, the *Lais* stray from the norms of romances proper, which—in part simply because they are longer—tend to cover a considerable span of time. Some of Marie's lais, such as *Milun* or *Yonec,* recount events over a period of many years; in both of those cases, the time is measured by the life of a child who grows to manhood. In others, like *Guigemar* or *Guildelüec et Guilliadun,* the action covers several years. But while in romances series of similar events (most often, adversaries overcome, one after another, but also multiple journeys, court visits, etc.) tend to provide a sense of process and progress, the *Lais* are more likely to focus on moments of intensity or transformation: a hunting accident, a declaration of love, a decisive ambush, a shape-shifting, a sprung trap, a tragic parting or unexpected reunion. There is connective tissue between these moments, but like the resonant objects that recur throughout the lais, they remain in memory less as sequence than as instant; many of them could effectively

---

1 Kinoshita and McCracken discuss the ways in which "[m]ovement generates meaning" in the *Lais* (113–30).

be encapsulated in a series of stained-glass windows, or indeed in a single one.[1]

Finally, Marie has a distinctive interest in landscape, which reflects a sense—deriving from her sources—that there is something inherently marvelous in the world where her stories are set, a world that, as noted above, can sometimes have a loose relationship to geography. As a wise man in *Bisclavret* puts it, "Meinte merveille avum veü / Que en Bretaigne est avenu" (We have seen many a wonder come to pass in Brittany, ll. 259–60; p. 159).[2] In the *Lais*, landscape serves not as a passive background but as an expression of meaning or a shaper of stories: the mountain of *Deus Amanz*, the improbable harbor where Guigemar encounters his magic ship, the marsh in which Eliduc stages an ambush all serve as proving grounds for the heroes, telling us something about them and making the tales they inhabit distinctive as surely as their actions do. The forest, too, often a relatively undifferentiated space of adventure in romance, here takes on very different roles depending on who uses it. For Tristan and the queen it offers a place of rest as well as a means of communication; it separates the past and the future of the abandoned infant Fresne; in *Bisclavret* it is a refuge where the title character can safely be a werewolf—until it turns into an arena in which he can be hunted. (*Bisclavret*, like *Equitan* or *Guigemar*, reminds us that for Marie hunting is an activity that impinges on humans as well as animals, putting both in play in a way that echoes other romances—such as *Erec and Enide*, where the hunt for the white stag enables Enide's arrival at court—and anticipates the intensive use of this motif in *Sir Gawain and the Green Knight*.)

While the *Lais* have much in common with romance, then, considering them in the context of this other genre can reveal some of their distinctive qualities, while also drawing our attention to the considerable internal variety of Marie's collection. But despite their central focus on a love relationship—and usually on moments of crisis or decision-making (for better or worse) in that relationship—romance is by no means the only other genre the

---

1 Emilie Mercier's animated short film *Bisclavret* (2011) makes intermittent use of this correspondence to shape its visual presentation of the narrative; excerpts can be seen on YouTube.

2 Given the lack of any specific place names in *Bisclavret*, this particular "Bretaigne" is perhaps best understood as referring to an imaginary Brittonic world, though due to Marie's references to traceably Breton words it is usually understood as Brittany, and I have translated it as such in the lai itself.

Lais evoke.[1] *Equitan*, with its destructive adulterous relationship and didactic conclusion, is often compared to fabliaux, the bawdy short narratives that tend to feature adulterous affairs and the motif, as here, of the trickster tricked; the concluding moral, however, might also point us toward the related genre of the exemplum, a brief illustrative story often used in preaching. The lovely, selfless, and under-appreciated heroine of *Le Fresne* has drawn comparison to figures such as Cinderella or patient Griselda, marking her story's similarity to folktales; *Guildelüec et Guilliadun*, whose plot also turns on extraordinary generosity, has a folk-tale aspect in the form of the weasels who enable the plot's resolution. Other extraordinary beasts, particularly the werewolf of *Bisclavret*, recall the natural histories and bestiaries popular in the late twelfth century and beyond. *Chaitivel ou Quatre Dols* involves a version of the *demande d'amour*, in which the relative misery of two lovers is assessed, though here the question is resolved within the lai rather than being posed to the audience—unless we understand its two possible titles as an ongoing invitation to take sides. And *Laüstic*, as noted above, famously recalls Ovid's tale of Philomela, from the *Metamorphoses*, in the emphasis each puts on the conjunction of voice and textuality, making this brief narrative of a confined love affair open onto a far larger story of the creation and transformations of the world.

Yonec, in addition to having suggestive links to Irish legend, finally turns the mirror back on itself, when the neglected wife recalls, and thus brings to life, stories that sound very much like the ones we are reading:

Mut ai sovent oï cunter	I have often heard tell
Que l'em suleit jadis trover	that once one used to find
Aventures en cest païs	adventures in this country
Ki rechatouent les pensis:	that gave hope to the sorrowful:
Chevalers trovoent puceles	knights would find maidens
A lur talent gentes e beles,	to their liking, noble and beautiful,
E dames truvoent amanz	and ladies would find lovers
Beaus e curteis e vaillanz,	who were handsome and courtly and valiant,
Si que blame[es] n'en esteient,	so that they were not blamed for it,
Ne nul fors eus nes veeient.	nor could anyone else see them.

(ll. 91–100; pp. 214, 215)

---

1 On the importance of such generic interaction in the formation of romance, see Gaunt; Rector.

This passage nicely reinforces the gender rebalancing that we see in the *Lais* as a whole and that, as noted above, partly distinguishes them from romance: the lady in *Yonec* recalls not only "knights [who] would find maidens" but "ladies [who] would find lovers," as this lady herself is about to do. While there are many "wooing women" in romance, their stories tend to begin as the stories of the men they pursue; even in Chrétien de Troyes's *Erec and Enide*, whose traditional title rightly reflects the protagonists' joint importance, the resourceful, intelligent, and active Enide enters the story only as an accidental "finding" of Erec's. In the *Lais* the initiating journey, action, or (as here) desire is often the lady's.

Indeed, it is striking how important female agency is in moving these narratives forward. If "the knight sets forth" is one of the guiding tropes of romance, as Erich Auerbach argued many years ago, it is far less prevalent in the *Lais*; we begin with such a story, in *Guigemar*, but even here the knight sets forth largely against his will, constrained by his violent encounter with a speaking, androgynous deer, and before he reaches his beloved we get her own origin story, emphasizing her independent existence before his arrival. Throughout the *Lais*, while many of the women start off enclosed, often unhappily, by marriage, they are far from passive. Sometimes their activity is cast in a negative light: the initiatives taken by the seneschal's wife in *Equitan* and the wife of the werewolf in *Bisclavret* have disastrous consequences. In other instances, however, women's action is essential to the resolution of the story: the enclosure of the nightingale in *Laüstic* and the pursuit of the wounded hawk-lover in *Yonec* enable the ladies who undertake them to bring their tales to a conclusion, even if not a happy one.

In many instances, too, women turn to other women for help that allows for the story's continuance. Guigemar's lady, with help from her maid, rescues him and cures his wound, the first step in their love affair; the ladies of *Milun* and *Deus Amanz* call on, respectively, a sister and an aunt for help in sustaining their love relationships; in *Le Fresne* the multiple bonds between mother, foster-daughter, daughter, and sisters partly repair the opening catastrophe (a catastrophe created by speaking ill of other women) and enable the happy ending. Here again, it seems hardly coincidental that the collection ends with a story where a woman's attentiveness and generosity to another woman undoes the knot of a love triangle; over the course of the *Lais* we move from the struggle between two men for possession of a woman that concludes *Guigemar* to the cooperation between two women that releases a man from his conflicting bonds at the close of *Guildelüec et Guilliadun*. In one stroke, Marie suggests that the rivalrous desire driving the male-female-male triangles that dominate medieval romance is a choice rather than a structural necessity; a female-male-female triangle turns out to have (as also in *Le Fresne*) a very different shape.[1]

The *Lais* and Learning

If Marie challenges, as well as deploys, certain forms and expectations of the world of romance, she also demonstrates to the full that that world can offer ethically and intellectually substantial narratives, not the "fables et mensonges" (fables and lies) of which romances are so often accused. This demonstration is evident in the course of the *Lais* themselves, but it is most emphatically highlighted by the Prologue of the collection, which both lays claim to culturally authoritative contexts (biblical, classical, scholastic) and implies the need to read the ensuing stories as an instructive group—without, however, laying out any explicit program for how to do so.[2] It combines the effects of control and receptiveness, authority and flexibility, that are evident throughout the *Lais*: readers are, to use Marie's famous phrase, encouraged to "supply the rest through their understanding" (de lur sen le surplus mettre, l. 16; p. 48) of what they read, but without any insistence about what the result should be.

Simply by writing a Prologue, Marie claims a particular role for herself: the inclusion of a Prologue effectively turns the compilation into a coherent work and links Marie to the innumerable other medieval authors, across many genres, who felt the need to offer some framing or entry into their texts.[3] In Marie's case, that

---

1   Most obviously, it actually retains its shape *as* a triangle (through the ongoing mutual affection of the three characters) rather than excluding one member to become a (new) dyad, as in tales of the *mal mariée*.

2   On the Prologue's intellectual claims, see for example Spitzer and Nichols.

3   As Bruckner observes, "Although the reader of ms. S's twenty-four *lais* might see some of the same effects we can follow in Marie's collection, there is no *auctoritas*, no named author, asking us to do so and guaranteeing through the density or 'obscurity' of written textuality the significance of a continuous reading that links   (*continued*)

framing engages, in a brief space, with several weighty topics: the role, duties, and efforts of a poet; the relationship between past authors and present readers (or, implicitly, present authors and future readers); and the value of study. She particularly invokes two important topoi: the duty of those with God-given gifts to share them, and the ability of later readers to interpret fruitfully the sometimes obscure writings of earlier authors. The first of these evokes the biblical parables of the sower and of the talents; the second makes explicit reference to a famous phrase from the first-century CE Roman grammarian Priscian—"quanto iuniores, tanto perspicaciores" (the more recent the readers, the more perceptive)—which by Marie's time had become a commonplace of introductory education.[1] Together, these topoi set her Prologue, "one of the earliest powerful assertions of vernacular authorship," in the context of the two most authoritative discourses of her time: biblical teaching and the classical inheritance.[2]

Both of these themes, it is important to note, emphasize the role and responsibilities of a recipient—first in the opening insistence that "[o]ne whom God has given knowledge and good eloquence in speaking should not keep quiet nor hide on this account, but rather should willingly show herself [or himself]" (Prologue, ll. 1–4, p. 49), and second by pointing out that those who read works of the past must labor to understand them and make proper use of them. At the same time, though, both recipients become givers: the person gifted in eloquence (like Marie herself) by creating a text that is explicitly given to the king in the course of the Prologue, and the reader of earlier texts (again, Marie herself, as well as her own readers) by interpreting them and passing on knowledge to others. The Prologue, then, insists on mutuality, generosity, and the transmission of knowledge, which are also central values in the lais themselves, but does so in an intellectual key that is not necessarily what one might immedi-

---

individual *lais* in intertextual dialogue within the collection as a whole" (*Shaping Romance* 161). On the tradition of the scholastic prologue, see the classic work by Minnis; Hamesse's *Les Prologues médiévaux*, though dedicated primarily to Latin prologues, is also of interest. Wogan-Browne, Fenster, and Russell offer numerous examples of prologues in Anglo-French and discuss their varied aims.

1 On the cultural contexts for Marie's use of this text from Priscian, see Donovan and Silvestre.

2 The quoted phrase is that of Taylor (102), who offers a brief, helpful discussion of the Prologue (101–08).

ately expect at the head of a collection of love stories. Its placement there makes it clear that Marie sees her *Lais* not as a frivolous pastime for either herself or her readers, but instead as a product and producer of intellectual and ethical work. She herself has, she famously claims, often worked late into the night to create these lais (ll. 41–42; p. 50), and she says that that "heavy task" and the study it requires has defended her from vice (ll. 23–25) just as, implicitly, the labor of properly understanding the *Lais* will defend her readers.

In this Marie is in step with her times and her romance context; if writers of religious works liked to denigrate the truthvalue and moral worth of romances—which, of course, competed all too successfully for their potential readers' attention—writers of romances do not hesitate to assert the value of their writings. The particular emphases of Marie's Prologue, however, can usefully be highlighted by a comparison of the version in Harley 978 with that in the Old Norse collection, which includes added material at the beginning and downplays certain aspects of the original. The opening of the Old Norse version praises those who "lived in olden days" for their skill, cleverness, valor, manners, and nobility, and indicates that their deeds were recorded "as an everlasting reminder, as entertainment, and as a source of great learning for posterity" (see Appendix C7, p. 398): the initial emphasis falls on the characters within the lais, here imagined as historical figures, rather than on the task of the poet, and adds to Marie's focus on memory and instruction an acknowledgement of the stories' entertainment value.

The Old Norse Prologue goes on to say that the collection offers each reader the opportunity to "amend and illumine his life with the knowledge of past events" in order that he may "prepare and improve himself for the kingdom of God by means of fitting behavior and good deeds and a holy life's end" (p. 398). Such a religiously oriented aim is present only very faintly and by implication in Marie's Prologue, which invokes God only at its beginning, and there to discuss the role of the composer rather than that of the reader.[1] Her suggestion that the labor of study helps defend a person from vice is compatible with what the Norse translator says, but he goes much further in this direction. The centrally intellectual and ethical, rather than religious or entertaining, value of the *Lais* is thus what Marie puts at the forefront.

---

1 Potkay suggests that Marie replaces the "fruit" of the biblical Parable of the Sower with "flowers" because retaining "fruit ... would have emphasized the moral dimension of her writing" (368).

The Norse translator also omits the allusions to staying up late to work on the lais and to the daring it requires to present them to the noble king, two touches that, in Marie's Prologue, increase the sense of the writer's personal presence and investment. And he diminishes the focus on remembrance that is so characteristic of the works whose author calls herself Marie; her assertions that "they made them [the lais] for remembrance" and "I do not wish to leave them aside or forget them" (Prologue ll. 35, 40; p. 51) do not appear in the Old Norse. The Prologue to the Old Norse collection is thus valuable not only in its own right but also for indicating that the Old French Prologue circulated along with (most of) Marie's lais in contexts other than that of Harley 978, and for demonstrating, by way of the points where it diverges from the original, what is particularly characteristic of Marie's Prologue. Like Denis Piramus's comments, moreover, though in a less hostile vein, it gives a sense of the distinctive ways in which vernacular authors of the twelfth and thirteenth centuries might view and present the same material.

If the opening Prologue establishes an important frame for an actively interpretive reading of the *Lais*, one that requires the reader's judgment and labor, the individual narratives bear this out. For the most part they avoid narratorial comment of a kind that would direct the reader's sympathies; while they may contain hints or suggestions about the lesson we might take from them, the variety of interpretations they have elicited demonstrates the room Marie leaves for readers to "supply the rest through their understanding" when reading old texts. Even where loaded language appears, as it does for example in *Equitan*, *Le Fresne*, or *Bisclavret*, the internal variety of the collection and the repeated insistence on the possibility of what Howard Bloch calls a "rival reality" offer ample opportunity to read against the grain.[1] By presenting multiple narratives that refuse to yield up a single coherent way of evaluating love affairs, the *Lais* encourage independent and resistant readings.

Medieval references to, copying and adaptations of, borrowings from, and translations of Marie's lais demonstrate that her early readers took up the invitation to apply their own intelligence to her texts in various ways. While there can be no question that the appeal of the *Lais* has much to do with the emotional force of the love stories they relate, their longevity also reflects the

---

1 Bloch 22. Examples of such "resistant reading" include Leicester or Guynn.

complexity and nuance with which they refract the literary, intellectual, and cultural traditions of their time and place, including a fascination with various pasts—biblical, classical, "bretun." Given Marie's own commitment to the remembrance and reception of these stories, translating them for new audiences who can take their places in the chain of *translatio studii* seems like a particularly appropriate task.

The Life and Times of Marie de France: A Brief Chronology

Given our lack of information about who precisely Marie was, the chronology below offers dates relevant for the cultural context of her works and their sources or influences. Dates for Marie's own works should be understood as speculative.

c. 1138   Geoffrey of Monmouth's *Historia regum Britanniae*

c. 1140s?   Possible birth of Marie

1151   Henry Plantagenet marries Eleanor of Aquitaine

1154   Henry Plantagenet becomes King Henry II of England

c. 1155   Wace's *Brut*, a French verse translation of Geoffrey's *Historia*

c. 1160   *Roman d'Eneas*

c. 1160s–70s   Marie's *Lais*

1170s–80s   Romances of Chrétien de Troyes

c. 1180s   Marie's *Fables*

c. 1185   *Tractatus de Purgatorio Sancti Patricii*, the source for Marie's *Espurgatoire seint Patriz*

1189   Death of King Henry II; accession of King Richard I

c. 1190   Marie's *Espurgatoire seint Patriz*

early 1190s   Denis Piramus makes reference to "dame Marie" and her lais in his *Vie seint Edmund le rei*

c. 1200   Marie's *Vie seinte Audree*

1204	Death of King Richard I; accession of King John
early 13th c.	Earliest manuscripts of the *Fables*
1217	Hákon Hákonarson becomes King of Norway
mid-13th c.	Translation of Marie's *Lais* into Old Norse
2nd half of 13th c.	Copying of the sections of London, British Library, Harley MS 978, containing Marie's *Fables* and *Lais*
late 13th c.	Unique manuscript of *Espurgatoire seint Patriz* copied (Paris, Bibliothèque nationale de France, fr. 25407)
early 14th c.	Unique manuscript of *Vie seinte Audree* copied (London, British Library, Additional MS 70513)

A Note on the Text

There are good existing translations of Marie de France's *Lais* into modern English, and good editions of the Old French text. My reason for undertaking yet another edition and translation of this work is the lack of a facing-page Old French and modern English version, and the fact that it is now easier than it has ever been to see, in digital form, the only manuscript that preserves all twelve lais. This is London, British Library, Harley MS 978, and it can be viewed in its entirety on the British Library's website, at http://www.bl.uk/manuscripts/Viewer.aspx?ref=harley_ms_978 _f118r.

The aim of this book is therefore to make both the Old French text and, by way of that text, Harley 978 more accessible to those unfamiliar with the language. To this end I have stayed as close as I could to the text of the *Lais* as they appear in Harley 978; I make changes to the Old French only where grammar or sense seems to me to require it, and where I have done so I put the changed material in brackets or, in the case of omissions with no substitution, mark the change with ⁺, and place the original reading in a list in Appendix F; in each text the first instance of such a change is footnoted as a reminder. I have not emended the text for the sake of meter, and I have retained unusual spellings if they are attested in the Anglo-Norman Dictionary (http://www.anglo-norman.net/).

In a few instances I have given readings from other manuscripts in the notes, or incorporated them into the text if needed for the sense. In addition to the Old Norse translation discussed in the Introduction, five manuscripts besides Harley 978 include one or more of the lais in Old French, though in these other manuscripts the lais are interspersed among other texts, and in some cases the lai appears in an incomplete form. Paris, Bibliothèque nationale de France (BnF), nouv. acq. fr. 1104 (known as manuscript S), from the late thirteenth century, is the most extensive and includes nine of Marie's lais: *Guigemar, Lanval, Yonec, Chevrefoil, Deus Amanz, Bisclavret, Milun, Le Fresne,* and *Equitan.*[1] Also important is the late-thirteenth-century manuscript BnF, fr. 2168 (*Yonec, Guigemar, Lanval*; known as manuscript P), and variant readings used here come from either S or P. Individual lais appear

---

1 This manuscript, in which the lais appear in this order but interspersed with other lais not by Marie, is discussed in Pickens.

in BnF, fr. 24432 (manuscript Q, containing *Yonec*) and London, British Library, Cotton Vespasian B.XIV (manuscript C, containing *Lanval*). In some cases scholars think that these versions may well be closer to the original composition than the version in Harley 978: all medieval scribes made some changes to the text they copied (whether on purpose or by accident), and I do not suggest that the Harley MS is "correct" in all cases. But staying as close as I could to its text gives a sense of how one medieval reader made sense of the work and offers more direct access to the text in that manuscript.

Similarly, I have tried to provide a translation that follows the original Old French as closely as possible, attending carefully to verb tenses and trying to convey the "expressive syntax, deliberate ambiguity, and purposeful repetition of words"[1] of the poems without doing excessive violence to modern English idiom or creating confusion for the reader. Inevitably, at times, I have found a conflict between these aims, and others may well feel that I have veered too far in one direction or the other at various points. It is my hope, however, that for the most part I have made it possible for a reader to work back and forth among the texts and the manuscript and to get a sense of the beauty and deceptive transparency of Marie's language.

One important feature of Marie's texts that is particularly difficult to convey is the charged quality of certain words. Again, the aim of this edition and translation is to make patterns of words in French easier to access for the reader beginning from English, but one particular word, *aventure*, and the related verb *avenir* defy straightforward translation and deserve special mention.[2] *Aventure* is a ubiquitous word in Old French romance tradition. It derives from the Latin *adventurus*, a future participle of the verb "to happen," and it indicates not so much "adventure" in the modern sense of "a novel or exciting experience" as a set of meanings that range from simply "event" or "what happened" to encompass marvels, dangers, or unexpected encounters and situations. In romance, especially chivalric romance, *aventure* is most likely to confront a knight or other protagonist if he or she is in the right state of preparation to encounter it, and the word can suggest the uncontrollable but also the inevitable. At times translating it as "adventure" is an overstatement and I have simply translated it as "what happened"; but here too the force of "happen"—something that *befalls*, perhaps by chance but with a

---

1 Alter xv.
2 On the significance of *aventure*, see also Bloch 26–29.

sense of obscure purpose—should be felt. Similarly, the verb *avenir* does primarily mean "to happen," and I have usually translated it as such, but its etymological relationship to *aventure* should be noted, and the charge that it conveys felt. In some cases, but not all, I have highlighted the appearance of *aventure* in the footnotes; these also aim to offer basic information on terms, places, or practices that may be unfamiliar.

Changes I have made to the lais as they appear in Harley 978 include, in addition to the emendations for sense and grammar mentioned above, the modernization of capitals and word division; the addition of punctuation (which is generally, as in this case, much scantier in medieval manuscripts than in modern printed texts); the substitution of v for u and j for i where these would be expected in modern French; and the silent expansion of abbreviations. The hand of the Harley scribe is very clear and easy to read with a bit of practice; a little time spent looking at it should enable any reader to compare my edited text with the manuscript, in order both to read the latter in its original situation and to see in detail the changes I have made to produce this edited text. Like many Old French verse texts, the *Lais*, as they appear in Harley 978, are copied in two parallel columns. A note at the start of each lai indicates which folios it occupies in the manuscript, indicating the folio (leaf) number, front or back of that leaf (recto or verso, r or v) and the column (a or b), so that, for instance, f. 140rb means the front of leaf 140, second column. The start of a new folio or column is indicated in brackets. It should also be noted that in Harley 978 the texts follow one another with no indication of a break except for the large blue-and-red initial that begins each lai, though a later reader has added a title for each lai in the upper margin. In accordance with modern presentation, and to make the book easier to navigate, I have presented each lai as a separate text, but it is worth remembering that they were much less divided in their original format.

THE *LAIS* OF MARIE DE FRANCE

Prologue

*Ki Deus ad duné [e]science†
E de parler bone eloquence,
Ne s'en deit taisir ne celer,
Ainz se deit volunters mustrer.
5 Quant uns granz biens est mult oïz,
Dunc a primes est il fluriz,
E quant loez est de plusurs,
Dunc ad espandues ses flurs.
Custume fu as anciens,
10 Ceo tesmoine Preciens,
Es liveres ke jadis feseient
Assez oscurement diseient
Pur ceus ki a venir esteient
E ki aprendre les deveient,
15 Ki puessent gloser la lettre
E de lur sen le surplus mettre.
Li philesophe le saveient,
E par eus memes entendeient,
Cum plus trespasserunt¹ le tens,
20 E plus serreient sutil de sens
E plus se savereient garder
De ceo ki ert a trespasser.
Ki de vice se volt defendre
Estudier deit e entendre
25 E grevos overe comencier;
Par [ceo] se puet plus esloignier
E de grant dolur deliverer.
Pur ceo comenc[ai] a penser
De aukune bone estoire faire
30 E de latin en romaunz traire;

---

* These lines appear on ff. 118ra–b of Harley 978. They have no title
  in the manuscript.
† Here and throughout, square brackets in the text indicate an emen-
  dation to the text as it appears in Harley 978; the original reading
  can be found, keyed to the line number, in Appendix F.
1 Many editors emend this to "trespassereit," taking the subject to be
  "le tens": "the more time passed." Given the many complexities of
  this notoriously difficult passage, however, which among other
  things uses the verb *trespasser* in what seem to be two quite different
  senses and whose grammatical subject is shifty, I have preferred to
  retain the Harley 978 reading.

Prologue

One whom God has given knowledge
and good eloquence in speaking
should not keep quiet nor hide on this account
but rather should willingly show herself.
When a great good is widely heard,   5
then it is first in flower,
and when it is praised by many,
then it has spread forth its flowers.
It was the custom of the ancients,
as Priscian bears witness,   10
in the books that they once used to make
to speak quite obscurely
for those who were to come
and who would have to learn them,
who would be able to interpret the letter   15
and supply the rest through their understanding.[1]
The philosophers knew this,
and understood by their own experience
how, the more people passed through time,
the more subtle their intelligence would be,   20
and the more they would know how to guard themselves
from that which was to be passed over.
Whoever wishes to protect himself from wrongdoing
should study and understand
and begin a heavy task;   25
through this he can further distance himself
and deliver himself from great sorrow.
Therefore I began to think
of making some good story
and translating from Latin to French.   30

---

1 To "interpret" or "gloss" (*gloser*) a book is to add material that helps
to explain or interpret it—such as footnotes, for example, though
medieval glosses were more often written in the side margins. Marie
is referring here not merely to interpretation in general but to a spe-
cific literary practice that was widespread in the Middle Ages.
Priscian was a Latin grammarian of the early sixth century whose
Institutiones grammaticae was an influential textbook in the Middle
Ages.

Mais ne me fust guaires de pris:
Itant se sunt altres entremis.
Des lais pensai k'oï aveie.
Ne dutai pas, bien le saveie,
35 Ke pur remambrance les firent
Des aventures k'il oïrent,
Cil ki primes les comencierent
E ki avant les enveierent.
Plusurs en ai oï conter,
40 Ne[s] voil laisser ne oblier.
Rimez en ai e fait ditié,
Soventes fiez en ai veillié.
En le honur de vus, nobles reis,
Ki tant estes pruz e curteis,
45 A ki tute joie se encline
E en ki quoer tuz biens racine,
M'entremis des lais assembler
Par rime faire e reconter.
En mun quoer pensoe e diseie,
50 Sire, ke[s] vos presentereie.
Si vos les plaist a receveir,
Mult me ferez grant joie aveir;
A tuz jurz mais en serrai lié.
Ne me tenez a surquidié,
55 Si vos os faire icest present.
Ore oez le comencement.

But it would hardly be worth it to me:
so many others have undertaken it.
I thought of lais that I had heard.
I did not doubt, I knew well
that they made them for remembrance   35
concerning adventures that they heard,
those who first began them
and who sent them forth.
I have heard many of them told;
I do not wish to leave them aside or forget them.   40
I have made rhymes from them and written poems;
many times I have stayed up to do it.
In your honor, noble king,[1]
who are so valiant and courteous,
to whom all joy bows   45
and in whose heart every good thing takes root,
I undertake to bring together some lais
by making rhymes and retelling them.
In my heart I thought and said to myself,
sire, that I would present them to you.   50
If it pleases you to receive them,
you will give me great joy;
I will be happy forevermore.
Do not consider me arrogant
if I dare to make you this present.   55
Now hear the beginning.

---

1   The identity of the "nobles reis" is not certain, but since Marie was
    writing in England in the second half of the twelfth century, the
    likeliest candidate is Henry II Plantagenet (r. 1154–89). Since his
    son, Henry the Young King (r. 1170–83), was crowned during his
    father's lifetime, it is also possible that he is the addressee.

Guigemar

*Ki de bone mateire traite,
Mult li peise si bien n'est faite.
Oez, seignurs, ke dit Marie,
Ki en sun tens pas ne s'oblie.
5 Celui deivent la gent loer
Ki en bien fait de sei parler.
Mais quant il i ad en un païs
Humme u femme de grant pris,   [f. 118ᵛ]
Cil ki de sun bien unt envie
10 Sovent en dient vileinie.
Sun pris li volent abeisser;
Pur ceo comencent le mestier
Del malveis chien coart felun,
Ki mort la gent par traïsun.
15 Nel voil mie pur ceo leissier;
Si gangleur u losengier
Le me volent a mal turner,
Ceo est lur dreit de mesparler!
Les contes ke jo sai verrais,
20 Dunt li bretun unt fait les lais,
Vos conterai assez briefment.
El chief de cest comencement,
Sulunc la lettre e l'escriture,
Vos mosterai un[e]† aventure
25 Ki en Bretaigne la menur

---

* This lai appears on ff. 118ʳᵇ–125ʳᵇ of British Library MS Harley 978.

† Here and throughout, square brackets in the text indicate an emendation to the text as it appears in Harley 978; the original reading can be found, keyed to the line number, in Appendix F.

Guigemar

If someone is dealing with good material,
it weighs on her greatly if it is not done well.
Listen, lords, to what Marie says,
who does not forget her duty in her time.[1]
People should praise a person   5
who causes herself to be well spoken of.[2]
But when there is in a country
a man or woman of great worth,
those who envy their goodness
often say vile things about them.   10
They wish to diminish their worth;
thus they take up the role
of the wicked, cowardly, felonous dog
who bites people out of wickedness.
I certainly won't leave off on this account;   15
if jabberers or slanderers
want to turn it against me,
it's their right to speak ill!
The stories I know to be true,
from which the Bretons made the lais,   20
I will tell you quite briefly.
At the end of this beginning,
according to the letter and the writing,
I will show you an adventure[3]
that happened in Brittany[4]   25

---

1 "Pas ne s'oblie" literally means "does not forget herself" or "is not
   forgotten" but can also mean, idiomatically, "does not forget/fail in
   her duty." There is no way to be certain which meaning Marie
   intended here. See l. 539, below.
2 "Li" (l. 2) and "Celui ... Ki ... sei" (ll. 5–6) give no indication of
   the gender of the person spoken of. Since it later becomes clear that
   Marie is thinking of her own situation, I translate them as feminine.
3 *Aventure*, and the related verb *avenir*, are significant words in many
   of Marie's lais and in other works of medieval romance. While *aven-
   ture* can mean something like "adventure" in our sense it often also
   means "chance," "happenstance," or even just "what happened."
   See Note on the Text, pp. 44–45. There are a number of instances
   of both *aventure* and *avenir* in *Guigemar*.
4 Brittany constitutes the northwest corner of France and was, like
   the British Isles, settled by Brythonic Celts in the late centuries
   BCE. As is the case here, it is sometimes called "Bretun le menur,"
   "Britain the lesser," to distinguish it from "Britain the   (*continued*)

Avint al tens ancienur.[1]

En cel tens tint Hoilas la tere,
Sovent en peis, sovent en guere.
Li reis aveit un sun barun
30   Ki esteit sire de Liun:
Oridials esteit apelez.
De sun seignur fu mult privez;
Chivaliers ert pruz e vaillan[z].
De sa moillier out deus enfanz,
35   Un fiz e une fille bele.
Noguent ot nun la damaisele,
Guigeimar noment le dancel;
El reaulme n'en out plus bel.   [col. b]
A merveille l'amot sa mere
40   E mult esteit bien de sun pere.
Quant il le pout partir de sei,
Sil enveat servir un rei.
Li vadlet fu sages e pruz;
Mult se faseit amer de tuz.
45   Quant fu venu termes e tens
K'il aveit eage e sens,

---

1 Two lines are left blank in manuscript at the end of this prologue
   (ll. 1–26). There is no other indication of a new section (such as a
   paraph mark or larger initial). A later hand has written "Guygemar"
   in the upper left margin of this folio (f. 118va), rather than the pre-
   vious one (f. 118rb), suggesting that this early reader regarded the
   lai proper as beginning after the prologue; the same hand titles each
   subsequent lai in the upper margin of the folio and column where it
   begins.

in olden times.

In that time Hoel[1] held the land,
often in peace, often in war.
The king had one of his men
who was lord of Léon:[2]   30
he was called Oridials.
He was very close to his lord;
he was a bold and valiant knight.
By his wife he had two children,
a son and a beautiful daughter.   35
The girl's name was Noguent,
they named the boy Guigemar;[3]
there was no one handsomer in the kingdom.
His mother loved him enormously
and he pleased his father very much.   40
When the father could bear to be parted from him,
he sent him to serve a king.[4]
The boy was wise and bold;
he made himself well-loved by all.
When the time and the moment had come   45
that he had age and sense,

---

greater," the larger of the two British Isles; however, it must be said
that in Marie's works "Bretaigne" can be a kind of imaginary "Brit-
tonic" space, rather than designating a specific locale in northern
France or western England. Similarly, "bretun" (see l. 20), though
translated here and elsewhere as "Breton(s)," may well be a capa-
cious designation that could apply to peoples living in the British
Isles as well as Brittany.

1 This is a likely but not certain translation of the French "Hoilas."
   Hoel is the Duke of Brittany in many of the stories of King Arthur;
   see for example the story of the Giant of Mont St. Michel
   recounted in Geoffrey of Monmouth's *History of the Kings of
   Britain*.
2 Liun or Léon, now known as St.-Pol-de-Léon, is in the department
   of Finistère in France, on the northern coast.
3 Alfred Ewert points out that this was a traditional name among the
   lords of Léon (166, note to l. 37).
4 It was a standard practice to foster out noble children, sending
   them to other noble households to be raised.

Li reis le adube richement,
Armes li dun[e] a sun talent.
Guigemar se part de la curt;
50 Mult i dona ainz k'il s'en turt.
En Flaundres vait pur sun pris quere:
La out tuz jurz estrif e guerre.
En Lorreine ne en Burguine,
Ne en Angoue ne en Gascuine,
55 A cel tens ne pout hom truver
Si bon chevalier ne sun per.
De tant i out mespris Nature
Ke unc de nul[e] amur n'out cure.
Suz ciel n'out dame ne pucele
60 Ki tant par fust noble ne bele,
Se il de amer la requeïst,
Ke volentiers nel retenist.
Plusurs le requistrent suvent,
Mais il n'aveit de ceo talent.
65 Nuls ne se pout aparceveir
K'il volsist amur aveir:
Pur ceo le tienent a peri
E li estrange e si ami.
En la flur de sun meillur pris
70 S'en vait li ber en sun païs   [f. 119ʳ]
Veer sun pere e sun seignur,
Sa bone mere e sa sorur,
Ki mult l'aveient desiré.
Ensemble od eus ad sujurné,
75 Ceo m'est avis, un meis entier.
Talent li prist d'aler chacier:
La nuit somunt ses chevaliers,
Ses veneurs e ses berniers;
E al matin vait en la forest,
80 Kar cel deduit forment li plest.
A un grant cerf sunt aruté,

the king dubs him richly,[1]
he gives him all the arms he desires.
Guigemar leaves the court;
he gave many gifts there before he went.   50
He goes to seek glory in Flanders:
there was always war and strife there.[2]
Neither in Lorraine nor in Burgundy,
not in Anjou nor in Gascony
could one find at that time   55
so good a knight, or one who was his peer.
Only in this did Nature make a mistake with him:[3]
that he never had any interest in love.
There was no lady or maiden under heaven,
no matter how noble or beautiful,   60
who, if he had asked for her love,
would not willingly have accepted him.
Many asked him often,
but he had no desire for that.
No one could perceive   65
that he wished to have love:
on account of this both strangers and his friends
considered him lost.
In the flower of his greatest glory
the young man goes into his country   70
to see his father and his lord,
his good mother and his sister,
who had missed him greatly.
He stayed with them, I believe,
for an entire month.   75
He was seized by a desire to go hunting:
in the night he summons his knights,
his hunters and dog handlers,
and in the morning he goes to the forest,
for that pastime pleased him very much.   80
They set out after a large stag

---

1 "Dubbing" is the ceremony in which a young man is made a knight
   and invested with sword and armor.
2 Flanders, now largely part of modern Belgium, was an independent
   area ruled by the counts of Flanders in this period; they were often
   at war with the kings of France, partly because of their wealth.
3 Or "He had to this extent undervalued Nature." The French leaves
   it unclear whether it is Guigemar or Nature who has "mespris," that
   is, erred.

E li chien furent descuplé.
Li veneur curent devaunt;
Li damaisels se vait targaunt.
85 Sun arc li porte un vallez,
Sun ansac e sun berserez.
Traire voleit, si mes eust,
Ainz ke d'iluec se remeust.
En l'espeise d'un grant buissun
90 Vit une bise od un foün;
Tute fu blaunche cele beste,
Perches de cerf out en la teste.
Sur le bai del brachet sailli.
Il tent sun arc, si trait a li,
95 En l'esclot la feri devaunt;
Ele chaï demeintenaunt.
La seete resor[t] ariere:
Guigemar fiert en tel maniere,
En la quisse deske al cheval,
100 Ke tut l'estuet descendre aval.
Ariere chiet sur l'erbe drue
Delez la bise ke out ferue.   [col. b]
La bise, ke nafree esteit,
Anguissuse esteit, si se plaineit;
105 Aprés parla en itel guise:
"Oï, lase, jo sui ocise!
E tu, vassal, ki m'as nafree,
Tel seit la tue destinee:
Jamais n'aies tu medcine!
110 Ne par herbe ne par racine
Ne par mire ne par pociun
N'avras tu jamés garisun

and the hounds were released.
The hunters run ahead;
the youth goes dawdling along.
A servant carries his bow, 85
his hunting sword and his quiver.[1]
He wanted to shoot, if he were in range,
before he left that place.
In a thicket made by a large bush
he saw a hind with a fawn: 90
the beast was all white;
it had stag's antlers on its head.
At the bark of his hound it leapt.[2]
He takes his bow and shoots at her,
he wounded her in the forehead;[3] 95
she fell at once.
The arrow bounces back:
it wounds Guigemar in such a way,
through the thigh right down to his horse,
that he must dismount at once. 100
He falls back on the thick grass
beside the hind that he had hurt.
The hind, who was badly wounded,
was distraught, and lamented;
then she spoke in this way: 105
"Alas, wretched me, I am killed!
And you, vassal, who wounded me,
let this be your destiny:
you will never have a remedy!
Neither from herb nor root, 110
neither from doctor nor potion
will you ever find healing

---

1   *Berserez* usually means "hound" and may do so here, but it can also
    mean "quiver," and this seems a likelier object to carry than a
    hunting dog.
2   The strangeness of the hind's color and of her having a stag's
    antlers makes it clear from the beginning that she is a supernatural
    creature. White deer appear as significant figures in other medieval
    tales, including Chrétien de Troyes's *Erec et Enide*, where the story
    begins with the hunt of the white hart.
3   A more common meaning for *esclot* is "hoof," but Rychner points to
    other cases where it clearly means "forehead," and this seems more
    probable here (241, note to l. 95).

De la plaie ke as en la qu[i]sse,
Deske cele te guarisse
115 Ki suffera pur tue amur
Issi grant peine e tel dolur
Ke unkes femme taunt ne suffri;
E tu refras taunt pur li,
Dunt tut cil s'esmerveillerunt
120 Ki aiment e amé averunt
U ki pois amerunt aprés.
Va t'en de ci; lais m'aver pes!"
Guigemar fu forment blescié;
De ceo k'il out est esmaiez.
125 Començat sei a purpenser
En quele tere purrat aler
Pur sa plaie faire guari[r],
Kar ne se volt laissier murir.
Il set assez e bien le dit
130 Ke unke femme nule ne vit
A ki il turnast s'amur
Ne ki le guaresist de dolur.
Sun vallet apelat avaunt:
"Amis," fait il, "va tost poignaunt!
135 Fai mes compaignuns returner,   [f. 119ᵛ]
Kar jo voldrai od eus parler."
Cil point avaunt, e il remaint;
Mult anguissusement se pleint.
De sa chemise estreitement
140 Sa plaie bende fermement.
Puis est muntez, d'iluec s'en part;
Ke esloignez se[i]t, mult li est tart:
Ne volt ke nul des suens i vienge,
Ki le desturbast ne ki le retienge.
145 Le travers del bois est alez
Un [vert] chemin ki l'ad menez
Fors a la launde, en la plaigne;
Vit la faleise e la muntaigne.
De une ewe ke desuz cureit
150 Braz fu de mer, hafne i aveit.[1]
El hafne out une sule nef,

---

1 I adopt Jean Rychner's punctuation, the period after "muntaigne";
he discusses the tricky syntax and meaning of this passage at length
(242, note to ll. 145–50).

from the wound you have in your thigh,
until she shall heal you
who will suffer, for love of you,   115
such great pain and sorrow
that no woman ever suffered so much;
and you will do as much for her,
so that all those who love or ever have loved
or who ever will love afterward   120
will be amazed.
Go from here; let me have peace!"
Guigemar was badly hurt;
he is frightened by what he hears.
He began to ponder   125
to what land he will be able to go
to have his wound healed,
for he does not want to let himself die.
He knows well enough and says indeed
that he has never seen any woman   130
to whom he could give his love
nor who could cure him of his sorrow.
He called his boy forward:
"Friend," he says, "go quickly, ride!
Have my companions return,   135
for I would like to speak with them."
The boy rides off, and he remains;
he laments in great distress.
With his shirt he tightly
and firmly binds his wound.   140
Then he mounted, he leaves that place;
he cannot wait to get far from there:
he did not want any of his men to come
who might trouble him or hold him back.
He went across the woods   145
on a green path that led him
out to the open land, onto the plain;
he saw the cliff and the mountain.
A stream that ran beneath
was an arm of the sea, there was a harbor there.   150
In the harbor there was a single ship,

Dunt Guigemar choisi le tref;
Mult esteit bien apparillee.
Defors e dedenz fu peiee:
155 Nuls hum n'i pout trover jointure.
N'i out cheville ne closture
Ki ne fust tute d'ebenus;
Suz ciel n'at o[r] ki vaille plus.
La veile fu tute de seie,
160 Mult est bele ki la depleie.
Li chivaliers fu mult pensis:
En la cuntree n'el païs
N'out unkes mes oï parler
Ke nefs i pussent ariver.
165 Avaunt alat, si descendi jus;
A graunt anguisse munta sus.   [col. b]
Dedenz quida hummes truver
Ki la nef deussent garder;
N'i aveit nul, ne nul ne vit.
170 En mi la nef trovat un lit
Dunt li pecun e li limun
Furent al overe Salemun,
Tailliez a or, tut a triffure,
De ciprés e de blanc ivoure;
175 D'un drap de seie a or teissu
Est la coilte ki desus fu.
Les altres dras ne sai preisier,
Mes tant vos dirrai del oreillier:
Ki sus eust sun chief tenu
180 Jamais le peil n'avreit chanu;
Le covertur tut sabelin
Vols fu du purpre alexandrin.
Deus chandelabres de fin or—
Le pire valeit un tresor—
185 El chief de la nef furent mis;
Desus out deus cirges espris.

whose mast Guigemar saw;
it was very well outfitted.
It was caulked outside and in:
no man could find a seam there.   155
There was no peg or spike
that was not made completely of ebony;
under heaven there is no gold worth more.
The sail was entirely of silk,
very beautiful when unfurled.   160
The knight was very thoughtful:
he had never heard it said
in the region or the country
that ships could land there.[1]
He went forward, and clambered down;   165
in great anguish he climbed aboard.
Inside he thought he would find men
who were supposed to guard the ship;
there was none, and he saw no one.
In the midst of the ship he found a bed   170
whose foot and posts
were of Solomon's work,[2]
made of gold all finely shaped,
of cypress and white ivory;
the quilt that was on it   175
was made of a silk cloth woven with gold.
I cannot tell the value of the other bedclothes,
but I will just tell you about the pillow:
whoever put his head on it
would never have white hair;   180
the cover, all of sable,
was enveloped in Alexandrian silk.
Two candelabra of fine gold—
the lesser was worth a treasury—
were placed at the front of the ship;   185
in them were two burning candles.

---

1 Like the white deer, the rich and mysterious ship that steers itself is
   a feature of many romances. Similar boats appear in, for example,
   the twelfth-century romance *Partenopeu de Blois* and the widespread
   stories of a wrongly accused queen set adrift by her husband, father,
   or another antagonist, of which Chaucer's *Man of Law's Tale* (the
   story of Custance) is a famous example.
2 "Al overe Salemun" and similar phrases refer to decoration with
   gold inlay or chased gold.

De ceo s'esteit il esmerveilliez.
Il s'est sur le lit apuiez;
Reposé s'est, a sa plaie dolt.
190 Puis est levez, aler s'en volt.
Il ne pout mie returner:
La nef est ja en halte mer,
Od lui s'en vat deliverement;
Bon oret eurent e suef vent.[1]
195 N'i ad mais nient de sun repaire;
Mult est dolent, ne seit ke faire.
N'est merveille se il s'esmaie,
Kar grant dolur out en sa plaie;   [f. 120ʳ]
Suffrir li estut l'aventure.
200 A Deu prie k'en prenge cure,
K'a sun poeir l'ameint a port
E si le defende de la mort.
El lit se colcha, si s'en dort.
Hui ad trespassé le plus fort:
205 Ainz le vespré ariverat
La ou sa guarisun avrat,
Desuz une antive cité,
Ki esteit chief de cel regné.
Li sires ki la mainteneit
210 Mult fu velz humme e femme aveit,
Une dame de haut parage,
Franche, curteise, bele e sage.
Gelus esteit a desmesure,
Kar ceo purportoit sa nature.
215 Ke tut li veil seient gelus—
Mult hiet chascun ke il seit cous—
Tels [est] de eage le trespas.
Il n[e] la guardat mie a gas.
En un vergier suz le dongun,
220 La out un clos tut envirun;
De vert marbre fu li muralz,
Mult par esteit espés e halz;
N'i out fors une sule entree,
Cele fu noit e jur guardee.
225 Del altre part fu clos de mer;

---

1 This line is echoed in two other lais. See *Milun*, "Bon oré orent e suef vent" (l. 508), and *Guildelüec et Guilliadun*, "Bon vent eurent e bon oré" (l. 813).

He was astonished at this.
He leaned on the bed;
he rested, he suffered from his wound.
Then he got up, he wished to leave. 190
He could not go back:
the ship is already on the high sea,
it carries him along quickly;
they had a good breeze and a gentle wind.
There is no longer any chance of his returning; 195
he is very sad, he does not know what to do.
No wonder if he is dismayed,
for his wound hurt very much;
he must undergo the adventure.
He prays to God that he take care of him, 200
that he bring him to port through his power
and protect him from death.
He lay down on the bed; he goes to sleep.
Today he has passed through the worst of it:
before evening he will arrive 205
at the place where he will be cured,
below an ancient city
that was the capital of that realm.
The lord who kept it
was a very old man and had a wife, 210
a lady of high lineage,
noble, courteous, beautiful and wise.
He was insanely jealous,
for that was what his nature inclined him to.
That all old men should be jealous— 215
every one would hate to be a cuckold—
that is the failing of old age.
He took seriously the task of guarding her.
In an orchard below the keep
there was an enclosure all around; 220
the wall was of green marble,
very thick and high;
there was only a single entrance,
which was guarded night and day.
On the other side it was enclosed by the sea; 225

Nuls ne pout eissir ne entrer,
Si ceo ne fust od un batel,
Se busuin eust al chastel.
Li sire out fait dedenz le mur,
230   Pur mettre i sa femme a seür,   [col. b]
Chaumbre; suz ciel n'out plus bele.
Al entree fu la chapele.
La chaumbre ert peinte tut entur;
Venus, [la] deuesse d'amur,
235   Fu tresbien [mise] en la peinture,
Les traiz mustrez e la nature
Cument hom deit amur tenir
E lëalment e bien servir.
Le livre Ovide, ou il enseine
240   Coment chascun s'amur estreine,
En un fu ardant l[e] gettout
E tuz iceus escumengout
Ki ja mais cel livre lirreient
Ne sun enseignement nient fereient.
245   La fu la dame enclose e mise.
Une pucele a sun servise
Li aveit sis sires bailliez,
Ki mult ert franche e enseigniez,
Sa niece, fille sa sorur.
250   Entre les deus out grant amur.
Od li esteit quant il errout,
De ci la k'il reparout;
Hume ne femme n'i venist,
Ne fors de cel murail ne issist.
255   Uns vielz prestres blancs e floriz
Guardout la clef de cel postiz.
Les plus bas membres out perduz:
Autrement ne fust il pas creüz.
Le servise Deu li diseit
260   E a sun mangier la serveit.
Cel jur meisme ainz relevee
Fu la dame el vergier alee;   [f. 120ᵛ]
Dormie aveit aprés mangier,
Si s'est alee esbanier,

no one could leave or come in
unless it were by boat,
if they needed to come to the castle.
The lord had made, inside the wall,
a chamber in which to secure his wife;   230
there was none more beautiful under heaven.
At the entrance was the chapel.
The chamber was painted all around;
Venus, the goddess of love,
was beautifully depicted in the painting,   235
and the qualities and nature
of how a man should behave in love
and serve loyally and well were shown.
The book of Ovid, where he teaches
how everyone should control his love,[1]   240
Venus threw in a burning fire,
and excommunicated all those
who would ever read that book
or follow its teaching in any way.
The lady was enclosed and kept there.   245
Her lord had given her
a girl to serve her
who was very noble and well brought up,
his niece, the daughter of his sister.
There was great love between the two of them.   250
She was with her whenever he went out
until he returned;
no man nor woman came there,
nor did the lady go outside the wall.
An old priest, white of hair and beard,   255
kept the key of the gate.
He had lost his lower parts:
otherwise he would not have been trusted.[2]
He would say divine service
and serve her at dinner.   260
That very day, before afternoon,
the lady went into the orchard;
she had slept after her meal
and then went to amuse herself,

---

1 The reference is probably to Ovid's *Remedia amoris*, where he tells
   how love should be avoided and rejected.
2 That is, the priest is trusted in the lady's company only because he
   is a eunuch.

265 Ensemble od li la meschine.
   Gardent aval vers la marine;
   La neif virent al flot muntant,
   Que el hafne veneit siglant;
   Ne veient rien que la cunduie.
270 La dame voleit turner en fuie:
   Si ele ad poür n'est merveille;
   Tute en fu sa face vermeille.
   Mes la meschine, qui fu sage
   E plus hardie de curage,
275 La recunforte e aseure.
   Cele part vunt grant aleure.
   Sun mantel ost[e] la pucele;
   Entre en la neif, que mult fu bele.
   Ne trovat nule rien vivant
280 For sul le chevaler dormant.
   Pale le vit, mort le quida;
   Arestu[t] [sei], si esgarda.
   Ariere vait la dameisele:
   Hastivement la dame apele,
285 Tute la verité li dit,
   Mut pleint le mort que ele vit.
   Respunt la dame: "[I] alums!
   S'il est mort, nus l'enfuirums;
   Nostre prestre nus aidera.
290 Si vif le truis, il parlera."
   Ensemble vunt, ne targent mes,
   La dame avant e ele aprés.
   Quant ele est en la neif entree,
   Devant le lit est arestee;   [col. b]
295 Le chevaler ad esgardé,
   Mut pleint sun cors e sa beuté;
   Pur li esteit triste e dolente,
   E dit que mar fu sa juvente.
   Desuz le piz li met sa mai[n];
300 Chaut le senti e le quor sei[n],
   Que suz les costez li bateit.
   Le chevaler, qui se dormeit,
   S'est esveillez, si l'ad vue.
   Mut en fu lez, si la salue:
305 Bien seit k'il est venu a rive.
   La dame, plurante e pensive,
   Li respundi mut bonement,

the girl along with her. 265
They look down toward the sea;
on the rising tide they saw the ship,
which came sailing into the harbor;
they can't see anything guiding it.
The lady wanted to turn and flee: 270
no wonder if she is afraid;
her face was quite red from it.
But the girl, who was wise
and of a bolder disposition,
comforts and reassures her. 275
They go there in great haste.
The girl takes off her mantle;
she enters the ship, which was very beautiful.
She found no living thing there
except the sleeping knight. 280
She saw him pale, she thought him dead;
she stopped and looked at him.
The damsel goes back:
quickly she calls the lady,
she tells her the whole truth, 285
she greatly laments the dead man she saw.
The lady replies, "Let's go there!
If he is dead, we will bury him;
our priest will help us.
If I find him alive, he will speak." 290
They go together, they do not delay,
the lady ahead and the maiden after.
When the lady entered the ship,
she stopped in front of the bed.
She looked at the knight, 295
she laments greatly for his body and his beauty;
she was sad and sorrowful for him,
and says that his youth was ill-fated.
She puts her hand on his chest;
she felt that he was warm and his heart strong, 300
beating under his ribs.
The knight, who was sleeping,
woke up and saw her.
He was very happy about it, and greeted her:
he knows well that he has come to shore. 305
The lady, weeping and fearful,
responded to him very readily;

Demande li cumfaitement
Il est venuz e de queile tere,
310 S'il est eisselez pur guere.
"Dame," fet il, "ceo n'i ad mie.
Mes si vus plest que jeo vus die
La verité vus cunterai;
Nent ne vus celerai.
315 De Bretaine la menur fui.
En bois alai chacier jeo ui;
Une blanche bise feri,
E la saete resorti.
En la quisse m'ad si nafré,
320 Jamés ne quid estre sané.
La bise se pleint e parlat,
Mut me maudist e jurat
Que ja n'eus[se] guarisun
Si par une meschine nun;
325 Ne sai u ele seit trovee.
Quant jeo oï la destinee,   [f. 121^r]
Hastivement del bois eissi;
En un hafne cest[e] nef^{+1} vi.
Dedenz entrai, si fis folie;
330 Od mei s'en est la neif ravie.
Ne sai u jeo sui arivez,
Coment ad nun ceste citez.
Bele dame, pur Deu vus pri,
Cunseillez mei, vostre merci!
335 Kar jeo ne sai queil part aler,
Ne la neif ne puis governer."
El li respunt: "Bel sire chiers,
Cunseil vus dirai volenters.
Ceste cité est mun seignur
340 E la cuntré tut entur;
Riches hum est de haut parage,
Mes mut par est de grant eage;
Anguissusement est gelus.
Par cele fei ke jeo dei [vu]s,
345 Dedenz cest clos m'ad enseree.
N'i ad fors une sule entree;
Un viels prestre la porte garde.

---

1 Here and throughout, a superscript cross indicates a place where I
have omitted a word or words from Harley 978 without making a
substitution (and where therefore there are no brackets).

she asks him how exactly
he has come, and from what land,
if he has been exiled due to war.   310
"Lady," he says, "it is not that.
But if it pleases you that I tell you,
I will recount to you the truth;
I will hide nothing from you.
I was from Brittany.   315
I went hunting in the woods one day;
I wounded a white hind
and the arrow bounced back.
It hurt me so in the thigh
I think I will never be healed.   320
The hind lamented and spoke:
she cursed me greatly and swore
that I would never be healed
except by a young woman;
I do not know where she may be found.   325
When I heard my destiny,
I quickly left the woods;
in a harbor I saw this ship.
I went inside, I did a foolish thing;
the ship took off with me in it.   330
I do not know where I have arrived,
what the name of this city is.
Beautiful lady, I beg you in God's name,
advise me, by your mercy!
For I do not know where to go,   335
nor can I steer the ship."
She replies, "Dear handsome sir,
I will willingly advise you.
This city, and the region all around,
belongs to my lord;   340
he is a rich man of noble family,
but he is very aged;
he is painfully jealous.
By the faith I owe you,
he has shut me up in this enclosure.   345
There is only one entrance;
an old priest guards the door.

Ceo doins[e] Deus que mal feu l'arde!
Ici sui nuit e jur enclose;
350 Ja nule fiez n'en ierc si ose
Que jo en ise s'il nel comande,
Si mis sires ne me demande.
Ci ai une chambre e une chapele,
Ensemble od mei ceste pucele.
355 Si vus plest a demurer
Tant que pussez errer,
Volenters vus sojurnerum
E de queor vus servirum." [col. b]
Quant il ad la parole oïe,
360 Ducement la dame mercie:
Od li sujurnerat, ceo dit.
En estant [s']est drecié [d]el lit.
Celes li aïent a peine;
La dame en sa chambre le meine.
365 Desur le lit a la meschine,
Triers un dossal que pur cortine
Fu en la chambre apareillez,
La est li dameisels cuchez.
E bacins de or aporterent,
370 Sa plaie e sa quisse laverent,
De un bel drap de cheisil blanc
Li osterent entur le sanc;
Pus l'unt estreitement bendé.
Mut le tienent en grant chierté.
375 Quant lur manger al vespré vient,
La pucele tant en retient
Dunt li chevaler out asez;
Bien est peuz e abevrez.
Mes amur l'ot feru al vif;
380 Ja ert sis quors en grant estrif,
Kar·la dame l'ad si nafré,
Tut ad sun païs ublié.
De sa plaie nul mal ne sent;
Mut suspira anguisusement.
385 La meschine kil deit servir
Prie que le laist dormir.
Cele s'en part, si l'ad laissié,
Puis k'il li ad duné cungé;
Devant sa dame en est alee,
390 Que aukes esteit reschaufee [f. 121ᵛ]

May God grant that an evil fire burn him!
Here I am enclosed night and day;
never shall I be so bold 350
as to go out if he does not order it,
if my lord does not ask me.
Here I have a chamber and a chapel,
and this maiden to be with me.
If it pleases you to stay 355
until you are able to travel,
we will willingly care for you
and gladly serve you."
When he heard her speech,
he sweetly thanked the lady: 360
he will stay with her, he says.
Standing, he got up from the bed.
The women help him with difficulty;
the lady leads him into her chamber.
On the girl's bed, 365
behind a cloth that was arranged
as a curtain in the chamber,
the young man lay down.
And they brought golden bowls,
they washed his wound and his thigh; 370
with a fine cloth of white linen
they wiped away the blood that was there;
then they bandaged it tightly.
They take very good care of him.
When their dinner comes in the evening, 375
the maiden keeps some back
so that the knight had enough;
he was well supplied with food and drink.
But love had stabbed him to the quick;
his heart was in great turmoil, 380
for the lady has so wounded him
that he has quite forgotten his country.
He feels no pain from his wound;
he sighed most grievously.
He asks the girl who is there to serve him 385
to let him sleep.
She goes away, she left him,
since he has sent her away;
she went off to see her lady
who was somewhat warmed 390

Del feu dunt Guigemar se sent
Que sun queor alume e esprent.
Li chevaler fu remis suls;
Pensif esteit e anguissus.
395 Ne seit uncore que ceo deit,
Mes nepurquant bien s'aparceit
Si par la dame n'est gariz,
De la mort est seurs e fiz.
"Allas," fet il, "quei ferai?
400 Irai a li, si li dirai
Que ele eit merci e pité
De cest cheitif descunseillé.
Si ele refuse ma priere
E tant seit orgoilluse e fiere,
405 Dunc m'estuet a doel murir
E de cest mal tuz jurs languir."
Lors suspirat; en poi de tens
Li est venu novel purpens,
E dit que suffrir li estoet,
410 Kar si fait k'il mes ne poet.
Tute la nuit ad si veillé
E suspiré e travaillé;
En sun queor alot recordant
Les paroles e le semblant,
415 Les oilz vairs e la bele buche,
Dunt la dolur al quor li tuche.
Entre ses denz merci li crie;
Pur poi nel apelet sa amie.
Si il seust quei ele senteit
420 E cum l'amur l[a] destreineit,
Mut en fust liez, mun escient;
Un poi de rasuagement   [col. b]
Li tolist auques la dolur
Dunt il ot pal[e] la colur.
425 Si il ad mal pur li amer,
Ele ne s'en peot nient loer.
Par matin,[+] einz l'ajurnee,
Esteit la dame sus levee;
Veillé aveit, de ceo se pleint;
430 Ceo fet amur que la destreint.
La meschine, que od li fu,
Ad le semblant aparceu
De sa dame, que ele amout

by the fire that Guigemar feels
lighting and kindling his heart.
The knight was left alone;
he was pensive and distressed.
He no longer knows what he should do,   395
but nevertheless he can see well
that if he is not cured by the lady,
he is sure and certain of death.
"Alas," he says, "what shall I do?
I will go to her, I will tell her   400
that she must have mercy and take pity
on this poor helpless wretch.
If she refuses my plea
and is proud and arrogant,
then I will have to die of sorrow   405
and waste away of this illness forever."
Then he sighed; in a little while
a new thought came to him,
and he says to himself that he must endure,
for things are such that he has no choice.   410
He lay awake like this all night
and sighed and suffered;
He went along remembering in his heart
the words and the appearance,
the bright eyes and the lovely mouth   415
through which pain has touched him to the heart.
With gritted teeth he begs her for mercy;
he can barely keep from calling her his beloved.
If he knew what she was feeling
and how love was afflicting her,   420
he would be very happy, I believe;
a little consolation
would take away a bit of the pain
from which his complexion grows pale.
If he is suffering from love of her,   425
she can't be glad of it at all.
In the morning, before daybreak,
the lady had got up;
she had lain awake, she laments about this;
love, which afflicts her, is the cause.   430
The girl, who was with her,
perceived by the appearance
of her lady that she loved

Le chevaler que sojurnout
435 En la chambre pur guarisun;
Mes ele ne seit si il eime u nun.
La dame est entree el muster,
E cele vait al chevaler;
Asise se est devant le lit
440 E il l'apele, si li dit:
"Amie, u est ma dame alee?
Pur quei est el si tost levee?"
Atant se tut, si suspira.
La meschine l'areisuna:
445 "Sire," fet ele, "vus amez;
Gardez que trop ne vus celez!
Amer poez en iteu guise
Que bien ert vostre amur assise.
Ki ma dame vodreit amer
450 Mut devreit bien de li penser;
Cest'amur sereit covenable,
Si vus amdui feussez estable.
Vus estes bels e ele est bele."
Il respundi a la pucele: [f. 122ʳ]
455 "Jeo sui de tel amur espris,
Bien me purrat venir a pis,
Si jeo n'ai sucurs e aïe.
Cunseillez me, ma duce amie!
Que ferai jeo de cest'amur?"
460 La meschine par grant duçur
Le chevaler ad conforté
E de sa aïe aseuré
De tuz les riens que ele pout fere;
Mut ert curteise e deboneire.
465 Quant la dame ad la messe oïe,
Ariere vait, pas ne se ublie;
Saver voleit quei cil feseit,
Si il veilleit u dormeit,
Pur ki amur sis quors ne fine.
470 Avant l'apelat la meschine,
Al chevaler la feit venir:
Bien li purrat tut a leisir
Mustrer e dire sun curage,
Tur[t] li a pru u a damage.
475 Il la salue e ele lui;

the knight who was staying
in the chamber to be cured;   435
but she does not know if he loves her or not.
The lady went into the church
and the girl goes to the knight;
she sat down in front of the bed
and he calls her, saying to her,   440
"Friend, where has my lady gone?
Why did she get up so early?"
With that he fell silent and sighed.
The girl addressed him:
"Sir," she said, "you are in love;   445
Take care not to conceal yourself too well!
You may love in such a way
that your love will be well placed.
One who wished to love my lady
should indeed think very highly of her;[1]   450
this love would be fitting
if both of you were constant.
You are handsome and she is beautiful."
He replied to the maiden,
"I am inflamed by such a love   455
that it may well go badly for me
if I do not have help and assistance.
Advise me, my sweet friend!
What shall I do about this love?"
The girl comforted the knight   460
with great sweetness
and assured him of her help
in everything that she could do;
she was very courteous and kind.
When the lady has heard mass,   465
she goes back, she does not forget her task.
She wanted to know what he was doing,
if he were awake or sleeping,
he for whose love her heart cannot be still.
The girl called her forth,   470
she has her go to the knight:
quite at her leisure she will be able
to show him and tell him her feelings,
whether it turn out well or badly.
He greets her and she him;   475

---

1 This could also mean "should certainly think about her."

En grant effrei erent amdui.
Sil ne l'osot nient requere;
Pur ceo qu'il ert d'estrange tere,
Aveit poür, [s'il] li mustra[s]t,
480 Que ele l'en haïst e s'esloina[s]t.
Mes ki ne mustre s'[enf]erté
A peine en peot aver santé:
Amur est plai[e] denz cors,
E si ne piert nient defors.
485 Ceo est un mal que lunges tient,
Pur ceo que de nature vient;   [col. b]
Plusurs le tienent a gabeis,
Si cum li vilain curteis,
Ki [j]olivent par tut le mund,
490 Puis se avantent de ceo que funt.
N'est pas amur, einz est folie
E mauveisté e lecherie.
Ki un en peot leal trover,
Mut le deit servir e amer,
495 Estre a sun comandement.
Guigemar e[im]oit durement:
U il averat hastif sucurs,
U li esteot vivre a reburs.
Amur li dune hardement:
500 Il li descovre sun talent.
"Dame," fet il, "jeo meorc pur vus;
Mis quors en est mut anguissus.
Si ne me volez guarir,
Dunc m'estuet en fin murir.
505 Jo vus requeor de druerie;
Bele, ne me escundiez mie!"
Quant ele l'at bien entendu,
Avenaument ad respundu;
Tut en riant li dit: "Amis,
510 Cest cunseil sereit trop hastis,
De otrier vus ceste priere:
Jeo ne sui mie acustumere."
"Dame," fet il, "pur Deu, merci!
Ne vus ennoit si jol vus di!

both of them were very anxious.
He did not dare ask her for anything;
because he was from a foreign land
he was afraid, if he were to reveal himself to her,
that she would hate him for it and withdraw from him.   480
But one who will not show his sickness
can scarcely regain health;
love is a wound within the body,
and does not appear at all outside.
It is an illness that lasts a long time,   485
because it comes from nature;
many take it as a joke,
just like those vile courtly people[1]
who amuse themselves with everyone
and then boast about what they've done.   490
That is not love; rather, it's folly
and wickedness and lechery.
One who can find someone loyal
should serve and love that person well
and be at his command.   495
Guigemar loved fiercely:
either he will soon get help,
or he must live in misery.
Love gives him courage:
he reveals his desire to her.   500
"Lady," he says, "I am dying for you;
my heart is wretched because of it.
If you do not wish to cure me,
then in the end I must die.
I ask you for your love;   505
beautiful one, do not refuse me!"
When she heard him out,
she replied becomingly:
laughing, she says, "Friend,
it would be too hasty a decision   510
to grant you this request:
I am not at all used to this."
"Lady," he said, "mercy, by God!
Do not be angry if I say this to you!

---

1   "Vilain curteis" is a deliberate oxymoron; *vilain* means a base or
    wicked person and is generally the opposite of *curteis*, "courtly,"
    since a truly courtly person was supposed to be noble, kind, and
    virtuous.

515 [Fem]me [jo]live del mestier
Se deit lungeme[nt] faire preier
Pur sei cherier, que cil ne quit
Que ele eit us[é] cel deduit; [f. 122ᵛ]
Mes la dame de bon purpens
520 Ki en sei eit valur ne sens,
S'ele treve hume de sa manere,
Ne se ferat vers li trop fiere.
Ainz l'amerat, si en averat joie;
Ainz ke nul le sachet u oie,
525 Averunt il mut de lur pruz fait.
Bele dame, finum cest plait!"
La dame entent que veirs li dit,
E li otreie sanz nul respit
L'amur de li, e il la baise.
530 Desore est Guigemar a aise.
Ensemble gisent e parolent
E sovent baisent e acolent;
Bien lur covienge del surplus,
De ceo que li autre unt en us!
535 Ceo m'est avis, an e demi
F[u] Guigemar ensemble od li;
Mut fu delituse la vie.
Mes fortune, [ki ne] se oblie,
Sa [roe] turne en poi de hure,
540 L'un met desuz, l'autre desure.
Issi est de ceus [a]venu,
Kar tost furent aparceü.
Al tens d'esté par un matin
Just la dame lez le meschin;
545 La buche li baise e le vis,
Puis si li dit: "Beus duz amis,
Mis quors me dit que jeo vus perc:
Seü serum e descovert.

A woman who makes a practice of being fickle[1]   515
should make someone pursue her for a long time
to increase her value, so that he does not think
that she has been used to this pleasure;
but the lady of good intentions
who has worth and sense,   520
if she finds a man who suits her,
will not be too proud toward him.
Rather she will love him, and it will bring her joy;
before anyone knows or hears of it
they will have done something much to their benefit.   525
Beautiful lady, let us finish this debate!"
The lady understands that he is telling her the truth,
and without any delay she grants him
her love, and he kisses her.
Now Guigemar is at ease.   530
They lie together and talk
and often kiss and embrace;
most fitting for them is the rest,
which others have experienced!
For a year and a half, so I understand,   535
Guigemar was with her;
life was most delightful.
But Fortune, who does not forget her task,
spins her wheel in a moment;
she puts one down, another up.[2]   540
So it happened with them,
for soon they were noticed.
One morning in the summertime
the lady lay beside the youth;
she kisses his mouth and his face,   545
then says to him thus: "Beautiful sweet friend,
my heart tells me that I will lose you:
we will be found out and discovered.

---

1 The expression "femme del mestier" could refer to a prostitute, and
   Guigemar may be suggesting that some women make a business, in
   effect, of being pursued.
2 This is a reference to the very common idea of Fortune as a
   goddess (often blindfolded) whose wheel controls human status and
   happiness: when she turns the wheel, those who were wealthy,
   lucky, or in power fall and those who were poor or struggling are
   lifted up. Most commonly, as here, it is the fall rather than the rise
   that is emphasized.

Si vus murrez, jeo voil murir;
550 E si vus en poez partir, [col. b]
Vus recoverez autre amur,
E jeo remeindrai en dolur."
"Dame," fet il, "nel dites mes!
Ja n'eie jeo joie ne pes,
555 Quant vers nul'autre averai retur;
N'aiez de ceo nule poür."
"Amis, de ceo me aseurez!+
Vostre chemise me livrez:
El pan desuz ferai un plait;
560 Cungé vus doins, u ke ceo seit,
De amer cele kil desferat
E ki despleer le saverat."
[Il] li baile, si l'aseure.
Le plet i fet en teu mesure:
565 Nule femme nel desfereit,
Si force u cutel n'i meteit.
La chemise li dune e rent;
Il la receit par tel covenent
Que ele le face seur de li
570 Par une ceinture autresi,
Dunt a sa char nue se ceint,
Par mi le flanc aukes estreint.
Ki la bucle purrat ovrir
Sanz depescer e sanz partir,
575 Il li prie que celui aint.
Il la baise, ataunt remaint.
Cel jur furent aparceü,
Descovert, trové e veü
D'un chamberlenc mal veisié
580 Que si sires li out enveié.
A la dame voleit parler;
Ne pout dedenz la chambre entrer. [f. 123ʳ]
Par une fenestre les vit;
Veit a sun seignur, si lui dit.
585 Quant li sires l'ad entendu,
Unques mes tant dolent ne fu.
De ses priveiz demanda treis,
A la chambre vait demaneis;
Il en ad fet l'us depescer,
590 Dedenz trovat le chevaler.
Pur la grant ire qu'il a

If you die, I want to die;
and if you can get away,   550
you will find another love,
and I will remain in sorrow."
"Lady," he says, "don't say that!
May I never have joy nor peace
if I resort to another woman;   555
have no fear of that."
"Beloved, assure me of this!
Give me your shirt:
at the bottom of it I will make a knot;
I give you leave, wherever it may be,   560
to love her who will undo it
and who will know how to untie it."
He gives it to her, and reassures her.
She makes the knot in it in this way:
no woman could undo it   565
unless she used force, or a knife.
She gives him the shirt and returns it;
he takes it with this agreement:
that she will make him sure of her
in the same fashion, by a belt   570
that she girds around her naked body
and wraps quite tightly around her waist.
He asks her to love that man
who can open the buckle
without breaking it or cutting it off.   575
He kisses her, and there it rests.
That day they were perceived,
discovered, found and seen
by a wickedly cunning chamberlain
whom her lord had sent to her.   580
He wanted to speak to the lady;
he could not get into the chamber.
He saw them through a window;
he goes to his lord and tells him.
When the lord heard it,   585
he had never been so upset.
He sent for three of his closest companions,
he goes to the chamber at once;
he had its door broken down,
inside he found the knight.   590
Because of his great anger

A ocire le cumaunda.
Guigemar est en piez levez,
Ne s'est de nient effreez.
595 Une grosse perche de sap,
U suleient pendre li drap,
Prist en ses mains e sis atent.
Il en ferat aukun dolent:
Ainz ke il de eus seit aprimez,
600 Les averat il tut maimez.
Le sire l'ad mut esgardé,
Enquis li ad e demandé
Ke il esteit e dunt fu nez
E coment est la einz entrez.
605 Cil li cunte cum il i vient
E cum la dame le retient;
T[ute] li dist la destinee
De la bise ke fu nafree,
E de la neif e de sa plaie;
610 Ore est del tut en sa manaie.
Il li respunt que pas nel creit
E si issi fust cum il diseit,
Si il peust la neif trover,
Il le metreit giers en la mer: [col. b]
615 Si il guaresist, ceo li pesast,
E bel li fust si il neiast.
Quant il l'ad bien aseuré,
El hafne sunt ensemble alé.
La barge trevent, enz l'unt mis;
620 Od lui s'en vet en sun païs.
La neif eire, pas ne demure.
Li chevaler suspire e plure,
La dame regretout sovent
E prie deu omnipotent
625 Qu'il li dunast hastive mort
E que jamés ne vienge a port,
S'il ne repeot aver s'amie,
K'il desirat plus que sa vie.
Tant [a]d cele dolur tenue
630 Que la neif est a port venue
U ele fu primes trovee:
Asez iert pres de sa cuntree.
Al plus tost k'il pout s'en issi.

he ordered him killed.
Guigemar got to his feet;
he was not frightened at all.
He takes in his hands a large pole made of fir,   595
from which they used to hang clothes,
and waits for them.
He is going to make someone sorry:
before they get to him,
he will have maimed them all.   600
The lord looked at him carefully;
he questioned him and asked
who he was and where he was born
and how he got in there.
Guigemar tells him how he came there   605
and how the lady kept him;
he tells him the whole prophecy
of the hind that was hurt,
and of the ship, and his wound;
now he is entirely in his power.   610
The lord replies that he does not believe it,
and if it were as he said,
if he could find the ship,
then he would put him out to sea:
if he survived, that would be too bad,   615
and if he drowned he would be delighted.
When he has made this assurance,
they all went to the harbor.
They find the boat, they put him in it;
it goes off with him to his country.   620
The ship travels fast, it does not delay.
The knight sighs and weeps,
he often lamented the lady
and prays to almighty God
to give him a swift death   625
and never let him come to port
if he cannot have his beloved again,
whom he wants more than his life.
He kept up this sorrow so long
that the ship came to port   630
where it was first found:
he was quite close to his homeland.
As soon as he could he got out.

Un damisel qu'il ot nurri
635 Errot aprés un chevaler;
En sa mein menot un destrer.
Il le conut, si⁺ l'apelat,
E li vallez se reguardat:
Sun seignur veit, a pié descent,
640 Le cheval li met en present;
Od li s'en veit. Joius en sunt
Tut si ami ki trové l'unt.
Mut fu preisez en sun païs,
Mes tuz jurs ert maz e pensis.
645 Femme voleient qu'il preisist,
Mes il del tut les escundist: [f. 123ᵛ]
Ja ne prendra femme a nul jur,
Ne pur aveir ne pur amur,
Si ele ne peust despleier
650 Sa chemise sanz depescer.
Par Breitaine veit la novele;
Il n'i ad dame ne pucele
Ki n'i alast pur asaier:
Unques ne la purent despleier.
655 De la dame vus voil mustrer,
Que Guigemar pot tant amer.
Par le cunseil d'un sun barun
Ses sires l'ad mis[e] en prisun
En une tur de marbre bis.
660 Le jur ad mal, e la nuit pis:
Nul humme el mund ne purreit dire
Sa grant peine ne le martire
Ne l'anguisse ne la dolur
Que la dame suffri en la tur.
665 Deus anz i fu, e plus, ceo quit;
Unc n'oït joie ne deduit.
Sovent regrete sun ami:
"Guigemar, sire, mar vus vi!
Meuz voil hastivement murir
670 Que lungement cest mal suffrir.
Amis, si jeo puis eschaper,
La u vus fustes mis en mer

A boy whom he had raised[1]
was following a knight;   635
he led a warhorse with his hand.
Guigemar recognized him and called to him
and the boy looked around:
he sees his lord, dismounts,
and gives him the horse at once;   640
Guigemar sets off with him. All his friends
are happy that they have found him.
He was greatly cherished in his land,
but he was always downcast and pensive.
They wanted him to take a wife,   645
but he completely refused them:
he will never take a wife, ever,
not for money nor for love,
if she cannot untie his shirt
without tearing it.   650
The news goes out across Brittany;[2]
there is no lady or maiden
who did not go there to try:
they could never untie it.
I want to tell you about the lady   655
whom Guigemar loved so much.
On the advice of one of his men
her lord put her in prison,
in a tower of grey marble.
Her days were bad and her nights worse;   660
no man in the world could tell
of her great pain nor the suffering,
the anguish and sorrow,
that the lady suffered in the tower.
She was there for two years and more, I believe;   665
she never had any joy or pleasure.
She often laments her beloved:
"Guigemar, my lord, woe that I saw you!
I would rather die swiftly
than suffer this unhappiness for long.   670
Beloved, if I can escape,
there where you were put to sea

---

1 That is, a boy who had been sent to his household to grow up, just
   as Guigemar himself was at the beginning of the story.
2 On the location of "Breitaine," see note to l. 25, above.

Me [neie]rai." Dunc lieve sus;
Tut esbaïe vient al hus,
675 Ne treve cleif ne serure;
Fors s'en eissi par aventure.
Unques nul ne la turba.
Al hafne vient, la neif trova: [col. b]
Atachie fu al rochier
680 U ele se voleit neier.
Quant el la vit, enz est entree;
Mes de une chose s'est purpensee:
Que ilec fu sis amis neez.
Ne pout ester sur ses pez.
685 Se desqu'al [b]ort peust venir,
El se laissast defors chaïr:
Asez seofre travail e peine.
La neif s'en vet, que tost l'enmeine.
En Bretaine est venu al port
690 Suz un chastel vaillant e fort.
Li sires a ki le chastel fu
Aveit a nun Meriadu.
Il guerr[ei]ot un sun veisin;
Pur ceo fu levé par matin,
695 Sa gent voleit fors enveier
Pur sun enemi damager.
A une fenestre s'estot⁺
E vit la neif u ele arivot.
Il descendi par un degré,
700 Sun chamberlein ad apelé,
Hastivement a la neif vunt.
Par l'eschele muntent amunt;
Dedenz unt une dame trovee
Ke de beuté resemble fee.
705 Il la saisist par le mantel,
Od lui l'enmeine en sun chastel.
Mut fu liez de la troveüre,
Kar bele esteit a demesure;
Ki que l'ust mis[e] en la barge,
710 Bien seit que ele esteit de grant parage.   [f. 124ʳ]
A li turnat tel amur,
Unques a femme n'ot greinur.
Il out une serur pucele
En sa chambre, que mut fu bele;
715 La dame li ad comandee.

I will drown myself." Then she gets up;
greatly upset, she comes to the door,
she finds no key nor lock; 675
as it happens, she goes out.
No one stopped her at all.
She comes to the harbor, she found the ship:
it was moored to the rock
where she wanted to drown herself. 680
When she saw it, she went inside,
but a thought comes to her:
that her beloved drowned there.
She could not stay on her feet.
If she could get to the side, 685
she would let herself fall out:
she is suffering that much trouble and pain.
Off goes the ship, which soon carries her away.
In Brittany she came to port
below a strong and worthy castle. 690
The lord who owned the castle
was called Meriaduc.
He was making war on a neighbor of his;
for this reason he got up in the morning:
he wanted to send his people out 695
to harm his enemy.
He stood at a window
and saw the ship as it arrived.
He went down the stairs,
called his chamberlain, 700
and they quickly go to the ship.
They climb up the ladder;
inside they found a lady
who is like a fairy in her beauty.
He seized her by the mantle 705
and brings her with him into his castle.
He was very pleased with his find,
for she was extremely beautiful;
whoever had put her in the boat,
it is clear that she has come of high lineage. 710
He felt such love for her,
he never had more for any woman.
He had a young sister
in his room, who was very beautiful;
he entrusted the lady to her. 715

Bien fu servie e honuree;
Richement la veste è aturne,
Mes tuz jurs ert pensive e murne.
Il veit sovent a li parler,
720 Kar de bone quor la peot amer.
Il la requert; ele n'ad cure,
Ainz li mustre de la ceinture:
Jamés humme ne li amera,
Si celi nun ki l'[u]ver[r]a
725 Sanz depescer. Quant il l'entent,
Si li respunt par maltalent:
"Autresi ad en cest païs
Un chevaler de mut grant pris:
De femme prendre en iteu guise
730 Se defent par une chemise
Dunt li destre pan est pleiez;
Il ne peot estre de[slie]z,
Que force u cutel n'i met[r]eit.
Vus feïstes, jeo quit, cel pleit."
735 Quant el l'oï, si suspira;
Par un petit ne se pasma.
Il la receit entre ses braz,
De sun bliaut tre[n]che les laz:
La ceinture voleit ovrir,
740 Mes [n'en] poeit a chief venir.
Puis n'ot el païs chevaler
Que il ne feïst essaier.   · [col. b]
Issi remist bien lungement
De ci que a un turneiement,
745 Que Meriadus afia
Cuntre celui que il guerreia.
Chevalers manda e retient;
Bien seit que Guigemar i vient.
Il li manda par guerdun,
750 Si cum ami e cumpainun,
Que a cel busuin ne li failist,
En s'aïe a lui venist.
Alez i est mut richement;
Chevalers ameine plus de cent.
755 Meriadus dedenz sa tur ·
Le herbergat a grant honur.

She was well served and honored;
he dresses her and adorns her richly,
but she was always pensive and sad.
He often goes to talk to her,
for he loves her with a true heart. 720
He asks for her love; she does not care,[1]
but rather shows him the belt:
no man will ever be her lover
but the one who will open it
without breaking it. When he hears this 725
he replies angrily,
"There is a knight of great worth in this country
who is just the same:
he protects himself from ever taking a wife
by means of a shirt 730
whose right side is knotted;
it cannot be untied
unless one were to use force or a knife.
You made that knot, I think."
When she heard this, she sighed; 735
she barely managed not to faint.
He takes her in his arms,
he cuts the laces of her tunic:
he wanted to open the belt,
but he could not achieve it. 740
Then there was no knight in the country
whom he did not make try it.
So it remained for a long time
until there was a tournament,
which Meriaduc proclaimed 745
against the man he was making war on.
He sent for and retained knights;
he knows well that Guigemar will come there.
He sent to ask him, in return for a reward,
as a friend and companion, 750
not to fail him in this need
but to come to his aid.
Guigemar went there very richly;
he brings more than a hundred knights.
Meriaduc lodged him most honorably 755
in his tower.

---

1 That is, she is not worried; but also, she does not care for (love)
 him.

Encuntre lui sa serur mande,
Par deus chevalers li commande
Que se aturne e vienge avant,
760 La dame meint qu'il eime tant.
Cele ad fait sun commandement.
Vestues furent richement,
Main a main vienent en la sale;
La dame fu pensive e pale.
765 Ele oï Guigemar nomer,
Ne pout desur ses pez ester:
Si cele ne l'eust tenue,
Ele fust a tere chaüe.
Li chevalers cuntre eus leva;
770 La dame vit e esgarda
E sun semblant e sa manere;
Un petit se traist ariere.
"Est ceo," fet il, "ma duce amie,
M'esperaunce, mun quor, ma vie,   [f. 124ᵛ]
775 Ma bele dame ke me ama?
Dun[t] vient ele? Ki l'amena?
—Ore ai pensé grant folie:
Bien sai que ceo n'est ele mie;
Femmes se resemblent asez.
780 Pur nient changent mis pensez.
Mes pur cele que ele resemble,
Pur ki mi quors suspire e tremble,
A li parlerai volenters."
Dunc vet avant li chevalers;
785 Il la baisat, lez lui l'asist;
Unques nul autre mot ne dist,
Fors tant que seer la rovat.
Meriadus le esguardat;
Mut li pesat de cel semblant.
790 Guigemar apele en riant:
"Sire," fet il, "si vus pleseit,
Ceste pucele essaiereit
Vostre chemise a despleier,
Si ele peot riens espleiter."
795 Il li respunt, "E jeo l'otrei."
Un chamberlenc apele a sei,
Que la chemise ot a garder;
Il li comande [a] aporter.
A la pucele fu baillie,

He sends his sister to meet him;
through two knights he orders her
to prepare herself and come forward,
bringing the lady whom he loves so much.   760
She did what he told her.
They were richly dressed;
hand in hand they come into the hall.
The lady was pensive and pale.
She heard Guigemar's name,   765
she could not stand on her feet:
if the maiden had not held her up,
she would have fallen to the ground.
The knight got up to meet them;
he saw the lady and looked at her   770
and her appearance and her manner;
he drew back just a little.
"Is this," he says, "my sweet beloved,
my hope, my heart, my life,
my beautiful lady who loved me?   775
Where has she come from? Who brought her?
—Now, I have had a foolish thought:
I know well that that is not her at all;
women look so much alike.
My thoughts are changing for no reason.   780
But for the sake of her whom she resembles,
for whom my heart sighs and trembles,
I will gladly speak to her."
Then the knight goes forward;
he kissed her, he sat beside her;   785
he never said another word,
except to ask her to be seated.
Meriaduc regarded him;
he did not at all like the way things were looking.
He calls out laughingly to Guigemar: 790
"Sir," he says, "if it pleased you,
this maiden could try
to untie your shirt,
to see if she could succeed at all."
He replied, "I grant it."   795
He calls a chamberlain to him
who had the keeping of the shirt;
he orders him to bring it.
It was given to the maiden,

800   Mes ne l'ad [mie] despleïe.
       La dame conut bien le pleit;
       Mut est sis quors en grant destreit,
       Kar volenters essaiast,
       S'ele peust u ele osast.
805   Bien se aparceit Meriadus;
       Dolent en fu, il ne pot plus.   [col. b]
       "Dame," fait il, "kar assaiez
       Si desfere le puriez!"
       Quant ele ot le comandement,
810   Le pan de la chemise prent;
       Legerement le despleiat.
       Li chevaler s'esmerveillat;
       Bien la conut, mes nequedent
       Nel poeit creire fermement.
815   A li parlat en teu mesure:
       "Amie, duce creature,
       Estes vus ceo? dites mei veir!
       Lessez mei vostre cors veeir,
       La ceinture dunt jeo vus ceins!"
820   A ses costez li met ses meins,
       Si ad trovee la ceinture.
       "Bele," fet il, "queile aventure
       Que jo vus ai issi trovee!
       Ki vus ad ci amenee?"
825   Ele li cunte la dolur,
       Les peines granz e la tristur
       [De la prisun u ele fu,
       E coment li est avenu,]¹
       Coment ele eschapa;
830   Neer se volt, la neif trova,
       Dedeinz entr[a], a cel port vient,
       E li chevalers la retient.
       Gardee l'ad a grant honur,
       Mes tuz jurs la requist de amur.
835   Ore est sa joie revenue:
       "Amis, menez en vostre drue!"
       Guigemar s'est en piez levez.
       "Seignurs," fet il, "ore escutez!   [f. 125ʳ]

---

1   In Harley 978, the lines "De la prisun u ele fu / E coment li est
    avenu" appear after "Neer se volt, la neif trova" (l. 830), but since
    this does not make very much sense as a sequence of events, editors
    usually move them to where I place them here.

but she did not untie it. 800
The lady knew the knot well;
her heart was in great distress,
for she would gladly try,
if she could, or dared.
Meriaduc saw this clearly; 805
he was as sad as could be about it.
"Lady," he says, "just try
to see if you can undo it!"
When she heard this command,
she takes the side of the shirt; 810
she untied it easily.
The knight was astonished;
he recognized her, but nevertheless
he could not fully believe it.
He spoke to her in this way: 815
"Beloved, sweet creature,
is that you? tell me the truth!
Let me see your body,
the belt I girded on you!"
He puts his hands on her sides 820
and found the belt.
"Beauty," he says, "what a chance
that I have found you like this!
Who brought you here?"
She told him the sorrow, 825
the great pains and sadness
of the prison where she was,
and what happened to her,
how she escaped;
she wanted to drown herself, she found the ship, 830
went inside, came to this port,
and the knight kept her.
He looked after her with great honor,
but constantly asked for her love.
Now her joy has returned: 835
"Beloved, lead your love away!"
Guigemar got to his feet.
"Lords," he says, "listen now!

Une m'amie ai cun[e]ue
840 Que jeo quidoue aver perdue.
Meriaduc requer e pri
Rende la mei, sue merci!
Ses hummes liges devendrai;
Deus anz u treis li servirai
845 Od cent chevalers u od plus."
Dunc respundi Meriadus:
"Guigemar," fet il, "beus amis,
Jeo ne sui mie si suspris
Ne si destrei[z] pur nule guere
850 Que de ceo me deiez requere.
Jeo la trovai, si la tendrai
E cuntre vus la defendrai."[1]
Quant il l'oï, hastivement
Comanda a munter sa gent.
855 D'ileoc se part, celui defie;
Mut li peise qu'il lait s'amie.
En la vile n'out chevaler
Que fust alé pur turneier
Ke Guigemar ne meint od sei.
860 Chescun li afie sa fei:
Od lui irunt queil part k'il aut.
Mut est huniz que ore li faut.
La nuit sunt al chastel venu
[K]i guerei[ot] Meriadu.
865 Li sires les ad herbergez,
Que mut en fu joius e lez
De Guigemar e de s'aïe:
Bien seit que la guere est finie.
El demain par matin leverent,
870 Par les ostelz se cunreierent.   [col. b]
De la vile eissent a grant bruit;
Guigemar primes les cunduit.
Al chastel vienent, si l'asaillent;
Mes fort esteit, a[u] pre[nd]re faillent.
875 Guigemar ad la vile assise;
N'en turnerat, si sera prise.
Tanz li crurent amis e genz
Que tuz les affamat dedenz.

---

1 As Leicester notes, *tenir* is the word one uses of holding land, and
   Meriaduc's attitude here is distinctly territorial.

I have recognized as my beloved
one whom I thought to have lost. 840
I request and ask of Meriaduc
that he restore her to me, by his mercy!
I will become his liege man;
I will serve him for two or three years
with a hundred knights or more." 845
Then Meriaduc replied:
"Guigemar," he says, "handsome friend,
I am not so harassed
nor so afflicted by any war
that you should request this of me. 850
I found her, I will keep her,
and I will defend her against you."
When Guigemar heard this, quickly
he ordered his people to mount.
He leaves that place, he defies him; 855
it troubles him greatly that he must leave his beloved.
In the town there was no knight
who had gone there to tourney
that Guigemar did not take with him.
Each one pledged him his faith: 860
they will go with him wherever he may go.
The one who fails him now will have great shame.
At night they arrived at the castle
of the man who was making war on Meriaduc.
The lord lodged them, 865
being very pleased and glad
about Guigemar and his help:
he knows well that the war is over.
The next day they got up in the morning;
near their lodgings they prepared for battle. 870
They leave the town with a great racket;
Guigemar leads them at their head.
They come to the castle, they attack it;
but it was strong, they cannot capture it.
Guigemar has besieged the town; 875
he will not give up until it is taken.
So many friends and people flocked to him
that he starved out all those inside.

Le chastel ad destruit e pris
880 E le seignur dedenz ocis.
A grant joie s'amie enmeine;
Ore ad trespassé sa peine.
De cest cunte ke oï avez
Fu *Guigemar* le lai trovez,
885 Que hum fait en harpe e en rote:
Bone est a oïr la note.

He destroyed and captured the castle
and killed the lord within.   880
With great joy he leads out his beloved;
now he has passed through his suffering.
From this story that you have heard
the lai of *Guigemar* was composed,
which is played on harp and rote: 885
it is pleasant to hear the tune.

Equitan

*Mut unt esté noble barun
Cil de Bretaine, li bretun.
Jadis suleient par pruesce,
Par curteisie e par noblesce
5 [D]es† aventures que oieent,
Ki a plusur gent aveneient,
Fere les lais pur remembrance,
Que [hum] nes meïst en ubliance.
[Un en] firent, ceo oi cunter,
10 Ki n[e] fet mie a ublier,
D'Equitan que mut fu curteis,
Sire d[e] Nauns, jostis e reis.
Equitan fu mut de grant pris
E mut amez en sun païs.
15 Deduit amout e druerie:
Pur ceo amot chevalerie.   [f. 125^v]
Cil met[ent] lur vie en nu[n] cure
Que d'amur n'unt sen e mesure;
Tels est la mesure de amer
20 Que nul n'i deit reisun garder.
Equitan ot un seneschal,
Bon chevaler, pruz e leal;
Tute sa tere li gardoit
E meinteneit e justisoit.
25 Ja, se pur ostier ne fust,

---

*   This lai appears on ff. 125rb–127vb of Harley 978. A later hand has
    written "Equitan" in the upper margin of the folio.

†   Here and throughout, square brackets in the text indicate an emen-
    dation to the text as it appears in Harley 978; the original reading
    can be found, keyed to the line number, in Appendix F.

Equitan

They were very noble men,
those of Brittany, the Bretons.[1]
In times past, out of worthiness,
out of courtliness and nobility,
they used to make lais in remembrance   5
of the adventures that they heard
that used to happen to many people,
so that they would not be forgotten.
They made one, I have heard tell,
that it does not do to forget,   10
of Equitan, who was very courtly,
the lord of Nantes,[2] judge and king.
Equitan was of very great renown
and much loved in his country.
He loved pleasure and love-play: 15
for this reason he loved chivalry.
They do not care for their lives
who do not have sense and moderation in love;
such is the measure[3] of love
that no one in that state keeps his reason.   20
Equitan had a seneschal,[4]
a good knight, brave and loyal;
he took care of all his land for him
and protected it and administered justice.
Never, unless it were to wage war,   25

---

1 On the meanings of *bretun* and *Bretaine*, see Introduction (pp.
   16–17) and the note to *Guigemar*, l. 25.
2 The manuscript has "Sire des Nauns"; often, as here, this is
   emended to "Sire de Nauns" and "Nauns" is identified with the city
   of Nantes, formerly in Brittany, which would be in keeping with
   Marie's localization of many of the lais in northwestern France or
   the British Isles. Others have suggested that it is a corruption of
   "Sire des nains," king of the dwarves, or that "Nauns" should be
   understood as a term for the inhabitants of Nantes.
3 The meaning of "mesure" shifts slightly in these two lines: while in
   the first it clearly has its standard sense of "moderation," in the
   second it could mean "misfortune," "nature," or even "dwelling-
   place." I have translated it as "measure" both in the sense of taking
   the measure of something (i.e., assessing its nature) and in the sense
   that love's idea of moderation involves losing your reason.
4 A seneschal serves as a steward of his lord's holdings; this particular
   seneschal's role is detailed in the lines that follow.

Pur nul busuin ki li creüst
Li reis ne laissast sun chacier,
Sun deduire, sun riveier.
Femme espuse ot li seneschals,
30 Dunt puis vient el païs grant mal.
La dame ert bele durement
E de mut bon affeitement,
Gent cors out e bele faiture.
En li former [uvr]at nature;
35 Les oilz out veirs e bel le vis,
Bele buche, neis ben asis.
El reaume n'out sa per.
Li reis l'oï sovent loer.
Soventefez la salua,
40 De ses aveirs li enveia;
Sanz veue la coveita,
E cum ainz pot a li parla.
Priveement esbanier
En la cuntree ala chacier
45 La u li seneschal maneit.
El chastel u la dame esteit
Herberjat li reis la nuit,
Quant repeirout de sun deduit.   [col. b]
Asez poeit a li parler
50 Sun curage e sun bien mustrer.
Mut la trova curteise e sage,
Bele de cors e de visage,
De bel semblant e enveisie.
Amurs l'ad mis a sa maisnie:
55 Une sete ad vers li traite,
Que mut grant plaie li ad faite,
El quor li ad lancie e mise.
N'i ad mestier sens ne cointise;
Pur la dame l'ad si suspris,
60 Tut en est murnes e pensis.
Ore l'i estut del tut entendre,
Ne se purrat nient defendre;
La nuit ne dort ne respose,
Mes sei memes blasme e chose.
65 "Allas," fet il, "queil destinee
M'amenat en ceste cuntree?
Pur ceste dame que ai veüe
M'est un'anguisse al quor ferue

for any need that impinged on him
did the king leave off his hunting,
his pleasure, his hawking by the river.
The seneschal had taken a wife,
from which great evil later came to the country.   30
The lady was most beautiful
and of very good breeding;
she had a lovely body and beautiful form.
Nature worked hard to make her:
she had bright eyes and a beautiful face,   35
a lovely mouth, a well-set nose.
The kingdom did not hold her equal.
The king often heard her praised.
Many times he sent her greetings,
he sent her gifts;   40
he coveted her without seeing her,
and as soon as he could he spoke to her.
To amuse himself on his own
he went hunting in the region
where the seneschal lived.   45
In the castle where the lady was
the king stayed the night,
when he returned from his pleasures.
He was able to talk to her enough
to show her his feelings and his worth.   50
He found her very courteous and wise,
lovely in form and face,
attractive and amusing.
Love brought him into his retinue:
he shot an arrow at him   55
that gave him a dreadful wound;
it struck him right in the heart.
Neither intelligence nor wit is of any use;
love, through the lady, has so captured him
that he is quite mournful and downcast.   60
Now he must completely submit,
he will not be able to protect himself at all;
that night he does not sleep nor rest,
but reproaches and scolds himself.
"Alas," he says, "what destiny   65
led me into this region?
On account of this lady whom I have seen
anguish has wounded me to the heart

Que tut le cors me fet trembler.
70 Jeo quit que mei l'estuet amer;
E si jo l'aim, jeo ferai mal:
Ceo est la femme al seneschal.
Garder li dei amur e fei,
Si cume jeo voil k'il face a mei.
75 Si par nul engin le saveit,
Bien sai que mut l'enpesereit.
Mes nepurquant pis iert asez
Que pur li seie afol[e]z.
Si bele dame, tant mar fust
80 Si ele n'amast u dru ust!   [f. 126ʳ]
Que devendreit sa curteisie,
Si ele n'amast de druerie?
Suz ciel n'ad humme, si ele amast,
Ki d'amur n'en amendast.
85 Li seneschal, si l'ot cunter,
Ne l'en deit mie trop peser;
Sul ne la peot il nient tenir:[1]
Certes jeo voil od li partir."
Quant ceo ot dit, si suspira;
90 Enprés se jut e si pensa.
Aprés parlat e dist: "De quei
Sui en estrif e en effrei?
Uncore ne sai ne n'ai seu
Si ele fereit de mei sun dreu;
95 Mes jeo saverai hastivement.
Si ele sentist ceo ke jeo sent,
Jeo perdrei ceste dolur.
E Deus! Tant ad de ci que al jur!
Jeo ne puis ja repos aveir:
100 Mut ad ke jeo cuchai eirseir."
Li reis veilla tant que jur fu;
A grant peine ad atendu.
Il est levez, si vet chacier;
Mes tost se mist el repeirer
105 E dit que mut est deshaitiez.
El chambre vet, si s'est cuchiez.
Dolent en est li senescaus;
Il ne seit pas queils est li maus

---

1 The word *tenir* is also used of holding land; compare *Guigemar* l.
   852.

so that it makes my whole body tremble.
I think that I must love her; 70
and if I love her, I will do wrong:
she is the seneschal's wife.
I should maintain love and faith toward him,
just as I want him to do toward me.
If by any means he found out, 75
I know well that it would upset him greatly.
But nevertheless it would be even worse
if I were to go mad on her account.
What a shame if so beautiful a lady
did not love or have a lover! 80
What would become of her courtliness,
if she did not have a love affair?
There is no man under heaven she could love
who would not be improved by her love.
The seneschal, if he hears tell of it, 85
should not be too upset about it;
he can't by any means hold her alone:
indeed, I wish to share her with him."
When he had said this, he sighed;
then he lay and thought. 90
Afterward he spoke and said, "What
am I worked up and worried about?
I still don't know, nor have I found out,
whether she would take me as her lover;
but I will know soon. 95
If she felt what I feel,
I would be rid of this sorrow.
And God! It is such a long time until day!
I cannot get any more rest:
it is a long time since I lay down last night." 100
The king lay awake until it was day;
he waited with great difficulty.
He got up, he goes hunting;
but soon he made his return
and says that he is very ill. 105
He goes to his room and gets into bed.
The seneschal is sad about this;
he does not know what illness it is

De quei li reis sent les friçuns:
110 Sa femme en est dreit[e] acheisuns.
Pur sei deduire e cunforter
La fist venir a li parler. [col. b]
Sun curage li descovri,
Saver li fet qu'il meort pur li;
115 Del tut li peot faire confort
E bien li peot doner a mort.
"Si[re]," la dame li ad dit,
"De ceo m'estuet aveir respit:
A ceste primere feiee
120 Ne s[u]i jeo mie cunseillee.
Vus estes rei de grant noblesce;
Ne sui mie de teu richesce
Que [a] mei deiez arester
De druerie ne [de vus] amer.
125 S'aviez fait vostre talent,
Jeo sai de veir, ne dut nent,
Tost me averez entrelaissie[e],
Jeo sereie mut empeiree.
Se si fust que vus amasse
130 E vostre requeste otreiasse,
Ne sereit pas uel partie
Entre nus deus la druerie.
Pur ceo que estes rei puissaunz
E mi sire est de vus tenaunz,
135 Quidereiez, a mun espeir,
Le danger de l'amur aveir.
Amur n'est pruz se n'est egals.
Meuz vaut un povre hum leals,
Si en sei ad sen e valur,
140 Greinur joie est de s'amur
Qu'il n'est de prince u de rei
Quant il n'ad lëauté en sei.
S'aukun am[e] plus ha[u]tement
Que [a] sa richesce n'en apent, [f. 126ᵛ]
145 Cil se dut[e] de tute rien.
Li riches humme requid[e] bien
Que nuls ne li toille s'amie
Qu'il volt amer par seignurie."
Equitan li respunt aprés:
150 "Dame, merci! Nel dites mes!
Cil ne sunt mie del tut curteis;

that is giving the king such fevers:
his wife is the true cause of it. 110
To please and comfort him
the king had her come to talk with him.
He revealed his wishes to her,
he lets her know that he is dying for her;
she can give him full relief 115
or indeed she can give him over to death.
"Sire," the lady said to him,
"I must have some time to consider:
right at this moment
I am not at all prepared. 120
You are a most noble king;
I am not by any means so wealthy
that you should fix on me
for love games or for loving you.
Once you had had your desire, 125
I know truly, I doubt not at all,
that soon you will have abandoned me;
I would be ruined.
If it were the case that I loved you
and granted your request, 130
the love affair would not be
equally shared between us two.
Since you are a powerful king
and my husband holds his lands from you,
you would expect, I imagine, 135
to have dominion in love.
Love is not worthy if it is not equal.
A loyal poor man is worth more,
if he has intelligence and good qualities,
and there is greater joy in his love 140
than in that of a prince or king
when he does not have any loyalty.
If someone loves more exaltedly
than is appropriate to his wealth,
he will be afraid of everything. 145
The rich man for his part feels certain
that no one will take from him his beloved,
whom he wishes to love through lordship."
Equitan then replies,
"Lady, mercy! Say no more! 150
Such people are not at all courtly;

Ainz est bargainc de burgeis,
Que pur aveir ne pur grant fieu
Mettent lur peine en malveis liu.
155 Suz ciel n'ad dame, s'ele est sage,
Curteise e franche de curage,
Pur quei d'amer se tienge chiere,
Que ele ne seit mie novelere,
Si ele n'ust fors sul sun mantel,
160 Que uns riches princes de chastel
Ne se deust pur li pener
E lealment e bien amer.
Cil ki de amur sunt nov[e]lier
E ki se aturnent de trichier,
165 Il sunt gabé e deceu;
E de plusurs l'avum nus veu.
N'est pas merveille se cil pert
Ki par s'overeine le desert.
Ma chiere dame, a vus m'[o]trei!
170 Ne me tenez mie pur rei,
Mes pur vostre hum e vostre ami!
Seurement vus jur e di
Que jeo ferai vostre pleisir.
Ne me laissez pur vus murir!
175 Vus seiez dame e jeo servant,
Vus orguilluse e jeo preiant!"   [col. b]
Tant ad li reis parlé od li
E tant li ad crié merci,
Que de s'amur l'aseura,
180 E ele sun cors li otria.
Par lur anels s'entresaisirent,
Lur fiaunce s'entreplevirent.
Bien les tiendrent, mut s'entramerent;
Puis [en] mururent e finerent.
185 Lung tens durrat lur druerie,
Que ne fu pas de gent oïe.
As termes de lur assembler,
Quant ensemble durent parler,
Li reis feseit dire a sa gent

rather, it's a townsman's bargain
when for goods or for a great fief
they set their efforts in the wrong place.
There is no lady under heaven, if she is wise,   155
courtly, and noble in heart—
provided she values herself enough in love
not to be fickle—
for whom, if she had nothing but her mantle,
a rich prince of a castle   160
should not suffer
and love her loyally and well.
Those who are fickle in love
and who set themselves up to deceive,
they are mocked and tricked;   165
we have seen many cases of it.
It is no wonder if someone loses out
who deserves it for his deeds.
My dear lady, I offer myself to you!
Do not consider me as a king,   170
but as your vassal and your lover!
I firmly swear and say to you
that I will do your pleasure.
Do not let me die for you!
You will be the lady and I the servant,   175
you the proud one and I the supplicant!"
The king talked so much with her
and begged so many times for mercy,
that he assured her of his love,[1]
and she granted him her body.   180
They exchanged rings with one another,
They pledged one another their troth.
They pleased one another and loved each other very much;
then in the end they died of it.
Their affair lasted a long time,   185
without anyone hearing of it.
At the times set for their assignations,
when they were going to talk together,
the king had his people told

---

1   This could also mean, "she assured him of her love." Since the
emphasis of the preceding passage is on her suspicion of his
motives, I have read it to mean that he pleaded with her for so long
that he made her feel secure in what he said, but certainly either
meaning is possible.

190 Que seignez iert priveement.
    Les us des chambres furent clos;
    Ne troveissez humme si os,
    Si li rei pur lui n'enveiast,
    Ja une feiz dedenz entrast.
195 Li seneschal la curt teneit,
    Les plaiz e les clamurs oieit.
    Li reis l'ama mut lungement,
    Que d'autre femme n'ot talent:
    Il ne voleit nule espuser,
200 Ja n'en rovast oïr parler.
    La gent le tindrent mut a mal,
    Tant que la femme al seneschal
    L'oï suvent; mut li pesa,
    E de lui perdre se duta.
205 Quant ele pout a lui parler
    E ele li duit joie mener,
    Baisier, estreindre e acoler
    E ensemble od lui juer,   [f. 127ʳ]
    Forment plur[a] e grant deol fist.
210 Li reis demanda e enquist
    Que deveit e que ceo fu.
    La dame li ad respundu:
    "Sire, jo plur pur nostre amur,
    Que mei revert a grant dolur:
215 Femme prendrez, fille a un rei,
    Si vus partirez de mei;
    Sovent l'oi dire e bien le sai.
    E jeo, lasse! que devendrai?
    Pur vus m'estuet aver la mort;
220 Car jeo ne sai autre cunfort."
    Li reis li dit par grant amur:
    "Bele amie, n'eiez poür!
    Certes, ja femme ne prendrai
    Ne pur autre vus larrai.
225 Sacez de veir e si creez:
    Si vostre sire fust finez,
    Reine e dame vus fereie;
    Ja pur [nul] humme nel lerreie."
    La dame l'en ad mercié

that he would be bled in private.[1]
The doors of the chamber were closed;
you would not find any man so bold—
unless the king sent for him—
that he would ever enter within.
The seneschal would oversee the court,   195
hearing pleas and claims.
The king loved the lady for a very long time,
for he did not want any other woman:
he did not wish to marry anyone,
he did not even want to hear it spoken of.   200
The people took this very badly,
so much so that the seneschal's wife
often heard about it; it weighed on her,
and she feared losing him.
When she was able to talk to him   205
and she should have been expressing her joy,
kissing, holding and embracing
and amusing herself with him,
she wept bitterly and showed great sorrow.
The king asked and inquired   210
what it meant and what the matter was.
The lady answered him:
"Sire, I weep for our love,
which turns to great sorrow for me:
you will take a wife, a king's daughter,   215
and you will leave me;
I often hear it said and I know it well.
And I—alas! what will become of me?
On your account I must have my death,
for I know no other solace."   220
The king said to her very lovingly,
"Beautiful beloved, do not be afraid!
I shall certainly never take a wife
nor leave you for another.
Know this for the truth and believe it: 225
if your lord were dead,
I would make you queen and lady;
no one could prevent me."
The lady thanked him for this

---

1 It was believed that bloodletting—taking some blood from the
   patient's body—was conducive to good health.

230 E dit que mut li sot bon gre,
　　E si de ceo l'aseurast,
　　Que pur autre ne la lessast,
　　Hastivement purchacereit
　　A sun seignur que mort sereit;
235 Legier sereit a purchacier,
　　Pur ceo k'il li vousist aidier.
　　Il li respunt que si ferat:
　　Ja cele rien ne li dirrat
　　Que il ne face a sun poeir,
240 Turt a folie u a saveir.　　　　　　　　　　[col. b]
　　"Sire," fet ele, "si vus plest,
　　Venez chacer en la forest,
　　En la cuntree u jeo sujur.
　　Dedenz le chastel mun seignur
245 Sujurnez; si serez seignez,
　　E al terz jur si vus baignez.
　　Mis sires od vus se baignera
　　E od vus se dignera;
　　Dites li bien, nel lessez mie,
250 Que il vus tienge cumpainie!
　　E jeo ferai les bains temprer
　　E les deus cuves aporter,
　　Sun bain si chaut e si buillant,
　　Suz ciel n'en ad humme vivant
255 Ne fust escaudez e malmis
　　Einz que dedenz [se] fust asis.
　　Quant mort serat e escaudez,
　　Vos hummes e les soens mandez;
　　Si lur mustrez cumfaitement
260 Est mort al bain sudeinement."
　　Li reis li ad tut granté
　　Qu'il en ferat sa volenté.
　　Ne demurat mie treis meis
　　Que el païs vet chacier li reis.
265 Seiner se fet cuntre sun mal,
　　Ensemble od li sun senescal.
　　Al terz jur dist k'il baignereit;
　　Li senescal mut le voleit.
　　"Vus baignerez," dist il, "od mei."
270 Li senescal dit: "Jo l'otrei."
　　La dame fet les bains temprer
　　E les deus cuves aporter;　　　　　　　　　[f. 127ᵛ]

and said that she was very grateful to him,   230
and if he assured her of this,
that he would not leave her for another,
she would quickly arrange
for her husband's death;
it would be easy to arrange,   235
provided he were willing to help her.
He replies that he will do so:
never will she tell him anything
that he will not do to the best of his ability,
whether it be foolishness or wisdom.   240
"Lord," she says, "if you please,
come to hunt in the forest,
in the area where I live.
Stay in the castle of my lord;
have yourself bled,   245
and on the third day have a bath.
My lord will bathe with you
and dine with you;
be sure to tell him, do not forget,
that he must keep you company!   250
And I will have the baths heated
and the two tubs brought,
his bath so hot and so boiling
there is no living man under heaven
who would not be scalded and destroyed   255
as soon as he sat in it.
When he is dead and scalded,
send for your men and his;
show them just how
he died suddenly in the bath."   260
The king fully granted her
that he will do as she wishes.
Not even three months passed
before the king goes to hunt in the country.
He has himself bled to fend off illness,   265
his seneschal along with him.
On the third day he said that he would bathe;
the seneschal was very willing.
"You will bathe," he said, "with me."
The seneschal says: "I will."   270
The lady has the baths heated
and the two tubs brought;

Devant le lit tut a devise
Ad chescune de[s] cuves mise.
275 L'ewe buillante feit aporter,
U li senescal deust entrer.
Li produm esteit sus levez:
Pur deduire fu fors alez.
La dame vient parler al rei
280 E il la mist dejuste sei.
Sur le lit al seignur cucherent
E deduistrent e enveiserent;
Ileoc unt ensemble geü.
Pur la cuve que devant f[u],
285 L'us firent tenir e garder;
Une meschine i deust ester.
Li senescal hastif revint,
A l'hus buta, cele la tint;
Icil le fiert par tel haïr,
290 Par force li estut ovrir.
Le rei e sa femme ad trovez
U il gisent entreacolez.
Li reis garda, sil vit venir:
Pensa sa vileinie covrir.
295 Dedenz la cuve saut joinz pez,
E il fu nuz e despuillez;
Unques garde ne s'en dona.
Ileoc murut [e] escauda;
Sur li est le mal revertiz,
300 E [c]il est sauf e gariz.
Le senescal ad bien veu
Coment del rei est avenu.
Sa femme prent demeintenant,
El bain la met le chief avant.   [col. b]
305 Issi mururent ambdui,
Li reis avant, e ele od lui.
Ki bien vodreit reisun entendre,
Ici purreit ensample prendre:
Tel purcace le mal d'autrui
310 Dunt le mals revert sur lui.
Issi avient cum dit vus ai.
Li bretun en firent un lai,
D'Equitan, cum il fina
E la dame que tant l'ama.

in front of the bed, just as planned,
she put each of the tubs.
She has the boiling water brought   275
for the seneschal to get into.
The good man got up:
he went out to enjoy himself.
The lady comes to speak to the king
and he pulled her down beside him.   280
They were lying on the lord's bed
and enjoying themselves and playing;
they lay there together.
Because of the tub that was in front,
they had the door held and guarded;   285
a girl was supposed to stand there.
The seneschal came back quickly,
he knocked at the door, she held it;
he strikes it with such fierceness,
he made it open by force.   290
He found the king and his wife
where they lay embracing one another.
The king looked and saw him coming:
he wanted to disguise his wickedness.
He jumped feet first into the tub,   295
and he was naked and unclothed;
he never paused to take care.
There he died and was scalded;
the evil turned back on him,
and the other is safe and sound.   300
The seneschal saw well
what happened to the king.
He takes his wife at once
and puts her head first into the bath.
Thus they both died,   305
the king first, and she with him.
Whoever might wish to listen to reason
could learn by example here:
one who pursues another's harm
may find the wrong rebounds on him.   310
So it happened as I have told you.
The Bretons made a lai about it,
about Equitan, how he died,
and the lady who loved him so much.

Le Fresne

*Le lai del freisne vus dirai
Sulunc le cunte que jeo sai.
En Bretaine jadis aveient
Dui chevaler, veisin esteient;
5 Riches hummes furent e manant
E chevalers pruz e vaillant.
Prochein furent, de une cuntree;
Chescun femme aveit espusee.
L'une des dames enceinta;
10 Al terme que ele delivera,
A cele feiz ot deus enfanz.
Sis sires est liez e joianz;
Pur la joie qu'il en a
A sun bon veisin le manda
15 Que sa femme ad deus fiz eüz:
De tanz enfanz esteit creüz.
L'un li tramettra a lever,
De sun nun le face nomer.
Li riches humme sist al manger;
20 Atant es vus le messager.
Devant le deis se agenoila,
Tut sun message li cunta.   [f. 128ʳ]
Li sires en ad Deu mercié;
Un bel cheval li ad doné.
25 La femme al chevaler surist—
K[i]† dejuste li al manger sist—
Kar ele ert feinte e orguilluse
E mesdisante e enviuse.
Ele parlat mut folement

---

*   This lai appears on ff. 127ᵛᵇ–131ᵛᵃ of Harley 978. In the upper
margin a later hand has written "Fresne."
†   Here and throughout, square brackets in the text indicate an emen-
dation to the text as it appears in Harley 978; the original reading
can be found, keyed to the line number, in Appendix F.

Le Fresne (The Ash Tree)

I will tell you the lai of the ash tree[1]
according to the story that I know.
In Brittany once there were
two knights, who were neighbors;
they were rich and powerful men   5
and bold and valiant knights.
They were neighbors, from the same region;
each one had married a wife.
One of the ladies became pregnant;
at the time when she delivered,   10
she had two babies at once.
Her husband is happy and joyful;
because of his joy about this
he sent word to his good neighbor
that his wife has had two sons: 15
by so much had he increased in children.
He will send him one to raise at the font;
he should have it given his name.[2]
The rich man sat at dinner;
behold, here is the messenger!   20
He kneeled before the dais,
he told him his whole message.
The lord thanked God for it;
he gave him a good horse.
The knight's wife smiled,   25
who was sitting right beside him at dinner,
for she was false and proud
and backbiting and envious.
She spoke most foolishly

---

1 As in the lai that follows, *Bisclavret*, the names in this lai can be dif-
   ficult to translate because they are both proper names and common
   nouns. "Le fresne" means "ash tree" in Old French, but is also the
   name of the central female character; rather than calling her Ash or
   Ash Tree, I have chosen, as most translators do, to keep the French
   name, as in *Bisclavret*. Unlike "Bisclavret," however, the names here
   consistently retain a definite article ("le Fresne," "la Codre").
   Although the Harley scribe usually spells the title word "freisne,"
   later convention is to use the spelling "fresne," and I have done so
   here.
2 The verb *lever* here has the specific sense "to hold [a baby] over the
   baptismal font," that is, to become its godparent.

30 E dist, oant tute sa gent:
    "Si m'eit Deus, jo m'esmerveil
    U cest produm prist cest conseil
    Que il ad mandé a mun seinur
    Sa hunte e sa deshonur,
35 Que sa femme ad eu deus fiz.
    E il e ele en sunt huniz.
    Nus savum bien qu'il i afiert:
    Unques ne fu ne ja nen iert
    Ne n'avendrat cel[e] aventure
40 Que a une sule porteure
    Que une femme deus fiz eit,
    Si deus hummes ne li unt feit."
    Si sires l'aveit mut esgardee,
    Mut durement l'en ad blamee.
45 "Dame," fet il, "lessez ester!
    Ne devez mie issi parler!
    Verité est que ceste dame
    Ad mut esté de bone fame."
    La gent que en la meisun erent
50 Cele parole recorderent.
    Asez fu dite e conue;
    Par tute Bretaine fu seüe.
    Mut en fu la dame haïe,
    Pois en dut estre maubailie.   [col. b]
55 Tutes les femmes ki l'oïrent,
    Povres e riches, l'en haïrent.
    Cil que le message ot porté
    A sun seignur ad tut cunté.
    Quant il l'oï dire e retraire,
60 Dolent en fu, ne sot quei faire;
    La prodefemme en haï
    E durement la mescreï,
    E mut la teneit en destreit
    Sanz ceo que ele nel deserveit.
65 La dame que si mesparla
    En l'an memes enceinta.
    De deus enfanz est enceintie:
    Ore est sa veisine vengie.
    Desque a sun terme les porta;
70 Deus filles ot. Mut li pesa,
    Mut durement en est dolente;
    A sei memes se desmente:

and said, in the hearing of all her people, 30
"So help me God, I do wonder
where this good man got the advice
to send my lord word
of his shame and his dishonor,
that his wife has had two sons. 35
Both he and she are shamed by it.
We know well what this means:
it never was, nor ever will be,
nor will it chance to happen
that in one single pregnancy 40
a woman should have two sons,
unless two men have done this to her."
Her husband gave her a hard look,
he reproached her very harshly for this.
"Madam," he says, "let it be! 45
You should not speak that way at all!
The truth is that this lady
has always had a good reputation."
The people who were in the house
kept in mind what was said. 50
It was much talked of and discussed;
it was known throughout all Brittany.
The lady was greatly hated for it;
later she must pay the price.
All the women who heard this, 55
poor and rich, hated her for it.
The man who had carried the message
told his lord everything.
When he heard it said and recounted,
he was upset, he did not know what to do; 60
he hated his worthy wife on this account
and greatly mistrusted her,
and kept her closely confined
without her deserving it.
The lady who spoke so wrongly 65
became pregnant in the same year.
She was pregnant with two children:
now her neighbor is avenged.
She carried them to term;
she had two daughters. It distressed her greatly, 70
she is terribly upset about it;
she lamented to herself:

"Lasse!" fet ele, "quei ferai?
Jamés pris ne honur n'avrai!
75 Hunie sui, c'est veritez.
Mis sire e tut si parentez,
Certes, jamés ne me crerrunt,
Desque ceste aventure saverunt;
Kar jeo memes me jugai:
80 De tutes femmes mesparlai.
Dunc dis jeo que unc ne fu
Ne nus ne l'avium veü
Que femme deus enfanz eust,
Si deus humes ne coneust.
85 M'en ai deus: ceo m'est avis,
Sur mei est turné le pis.
Ki sur autri mesdit e ment
Ne seit mie qu'a l'oil li pent;
De tel hum peot l'um parler
90 Que meuz de li fet a loer.
Pur mei defendre de hunir,
Un des enfanz m'estuet murdrir:
Meuz le voil vers Deu amender
Que mei hunir e vergunder."
95 Ces que en la chambre esteient
La cunfort[ou]ent e diseient
Que eles nel suffreient pas:
De humme ocire n'est pas gas.
La dame aveit une meschine
100 Que mut esteit de franche orine;
Lung tens l'ot gardee e nurie
E mut amee e mut cherie.
Cele oï sa dame plurer,
Durement pleindre e doluser;
105 Anguissusement li pesa.
Ele vient, si la cunforta.
"Dame," fet ele, "ne vaut rien.
Lessez cest dol, si ferez bien!
L'un des enfanz me baillez ça:
110 Jeo vus en deliverai ja,
Si que honie ne serez

[f. 128ᵛ]

"Wretch!," she said, "what shall I do?
I will never have respect or honor!
I am shamed, that's the truth.   75
My husband and all his family
surely will never believe me,
once they know what has happened;
for I condemned myself:
I spoke ill of all women.   80
I said then that it never happened
nor have we ever seen
that a woman should have two children
if she had not known two men.
I have had two: it seems to me   85
the worst of it rebounds on me.
Someone who slanders or lies about another
does not at all realize what is in his own eye;[1]
one may speak of a person
who is more to be praised than he.   90
To protect myself from shame,
I must kill one of the children:
I would rather make amends toward God
than shame and humiliate myself."
Those who were in the chamber   95
comforted her and said
that they would not allow it:
killing a person is not to be taken lightly.
The lady had a handmaiden
who was of very noble birth;   100
she had cared for and raised her for a long time
and greatly loved and cherished her.
This maiden heard her lady crying,
lamenting and sighing terribly;
it caused her great anguish.   105
She came and comforted her.
"Lady," she said, "this does not help.
You will do well to leave off this sorrow!
Give me one of the babies:
I will make you free of it right now,   110
so that you will not be shamed,

---

1   The reference seems to be to the Bible: "Why do you see the speck
    that is in your brother's eye, and not see the beam in your own?"
    (Matt. 7:3). That is, why do you see others' tiny faults and not your
    own larger ones?

Ne ke jamés ne la verrez.
A un mustier la geterai,
Tut sein e sauf l[a] porterai.
115 Aucun produme la trovera;
Si Deu plest, nurir la fra."
La dame oï quei cele dist;
Grant joie en out, si li promist,   [col. b]
Si cel service li feseit,
120 Bon guerdun de li avereit.
En un chi[ef] de mut bon chesil
Envolupent l'enfant gentil
E desus une paile roé—
Ses sires li ot aporté
125 De Costentinoble, u il fu;
Unc si bon n'[o]rent veü.
A une pice de sun laz
Un gros anel li lie al braz.
De fin or i aveit un[e] unce;
130 En ches[t]un out une jagunce;
La verge entur esteit lettree.
La u la meschine ert trovee,
Bien sachent tuit vereiement
Que ele est nee de bone gent.
135 La dameisele prist l'enfant,
De la chambre s'en ist atant.
La nuit, quant tut fu aseri,
Fors de la vile s'en eissi;
En un grant chemin est entré,
140 Ki en la forest l'ad mené.
Par mie le bois sa veie tint
Od tut l'enfant; utre en vint;
Unques del grant chemin ne eissi.
Bien loinz sur destre aveit oï

nor will you ever see her again.
I will leave her at a church,
I will carry her[1] quite safe and sound.
Some worthy man will find her;   115
if God pleases, he will raise her."
The lady heard what the maiden said;
she rejoiced greatly at it, and promised her
that if she did her this service,
she would have a good reward.   120
In a cloth of very fine linen
they wrap up the noble child
and put over it a patterned[2] silk cloth—
her husband had brought it to her
from Constantinople, where he had been;   125
they had never seen such a good one.
With a length of her dress-lace
she ties a heavy ring to the baby's arm.
There was an ounce of pure gold in it;
in the setting there was a jacinth;[3]   130
the border around it was inscribed.
Wherever the girl was found,
they would know in all truth
that she was born of a good family.
The maiden took the infant   135
and went out of the chamber at once.
That night, when it was quite dark,
she left the town;
she got onto a broad road
that led her into the forest.   140
She made her way right through the woods
along with the baby; she came out the other side;
she never left the broad path.
Far off to the right she had heard

---

1 The manuscript here reads "le" (it) rather than "la" (she), but since
  elsewhere in this passage the baby is consistently called "she," I
  have emended to "la."

2 "Roé" literally means "wheeled," and here probably refers to a cloth
  embroidered with a pattern of wheels or roundels.

3 A jacinth is a red stone, now usually called red zircon. The manu-
  script here reads "chescun turn" rather than "chestun" (setting),
  which could mean that the ring had jacinths on every side (literally,
  at every turn), but this would make it difficult to understand where
  the inscribed border is meant to be.

145 Chiens abaier e coks chanter:
      Iloc purrat vile trover.
      Cele part vet a grant espleit
      U la noise des chiens oieit.
      En une vile riche e bele
150 Est entree la dameisele.   [f. 129ʳ]
      En la vile out une abeïe,
      Durement riche e garnie;
      Mun escient noniens i ot
      E abbeesse kis guardot.
155 La meschine vit le muster,
      Les turs e les murs e le clocher:
      Hastivement est la venue,
      Devant l'us est areste[u]e.
      L'enfant mist jus que ele aporta;
160 Mut humblement se agenuila.
      Ele comence sa oreisun:
      "Deus," fait ele, "par tun seint nun,
      Si ceo te vient a pleisir,
      Cest enfant garde de perir."
165 Quant la priere out finee,
      Ariere se est regardee.
      Un freisne vit lé e branchu
      E mut espés e bien ramu;
      E quatre fois esteit ramé;
170 Pur umbre fere i fu planté.
      Entre ses braz ad pris l'enfant,
      De si que al freisne vient corant.
      Desuz le mist, puis le lessa;
      A Deu le veir le comanda.
175 La dameisele ariere vait,
      Sa dame cunte quei ele ad fait.
      En l'abbeïe ot un porter:
      Overir suleit l'us del muster
      Defors par unt la gent veneient
180 Que le servise Deu oïr voleient.
      Icel[e] nuit par tens leva,
      Chandeille e lampes aluma,   [col. b]
      Les seins sona e l'us ovri.
      Sur le freisne les dras choisi;
185 Quidat ke aukun les ust pris
      En larecin e ileoc mis.
      D'autre chose n'ot il regard.

dogs barking and cocks crowing: 145
there she will be able to find a town.
She goes very quickly
to where she heard the noise of dogs.
The maiden entered
a rich and beautiful town.   150
In the town was an abbey,
very wealthy and well supplied;
as I understand there were nuns there
and an abbess who watched over them.
The maiden saw the church,   · 155
the towers and the walls and the bell-tower:
quickly she went there,
she stopped before the door.
She set down the baby that she carried;
she knelt very humbly.   160
She begins her prayer:
"God," she says, "by your holy name,
if it should please you,
guard this child from death."
When she had finished the prayer,   165
she looked behind her.
She saw a large ash tree with many branches,
very leafy and well grown,
that had branched off four times;
it had been planted there to give shade.   170
She took the baby in her arms,
she came running up to the ash tree.
She put her in it, then left her;
she commended her to the true God.
The damsel goes back,   175
she tells her lady what she has done.
In the abbey was a porter:
he used to open the outer door of the church
through which the people would come
who wanted to hear divine service.   180
That night he got up early,
he lit the tapers and lamps,
rang the bells and opened the door.
He saw the cloths on the ash tree;
he thought that someone had taken them   185
by theft and put them there.
He did not notice anything else.

Plus tost qu'il pot vint cele part,
Taste, si ad l'enfant trové.
190 Il en ad Deu mut mercié,
E puis l'ad pris, si nel laist;
A sun ostel ariere vait.
Une fille ot que vedue esteit;
Si sires fu mort. Enfant aveit
195 Petit en berz e aleitant.
Li produm l'apelat avant.
"Fille," fet il, "levez, levez!
Fu e chaundele alumez!
Un enfaunt ai ci aporté,
200 La fors el freisne l'ai trové.
De vostre leit le alaitez,
Eschaufez le e sil baignez!"
Cele ad fet sun comandement:
Le feu alum'e l'enfant prent,
205 Eschaufé l'ad e bien baigné;
Pus l'ad de sun leit aleité.
Entur sun braz treve l'anel;
Le palie virent riche e bel.
Bien surent cil tut a scient
210 Que ele est nee de haute gent.
El demain aprés le servise,
Quant l'abbesse eist de l'eglise,
Li portiers vet a li parler;
L'aventure li veut cunter   [f. 129ᵛ]
215 De l'enfant, cum il le trovat.
L'abbeesse le comaundat
Que devaunt li seit aporté
Tut issi cum il fu trové.
A sa meisun vet li portiers;
220 L'enfant aporte volenters,
Si l'ad a la dame mustré.
E ele l'ad forment esgardé
E dit que nurir le fera
E pur sa niece la tendra.
225 Al porter ad bien defendu

As soon as he could he went over there,
felt around, and found the baby.
He greatly thanked God for this, 190
and then he took it, he did not leave it behind;
he goes back to his house.
He had a daughter who was a widow;
her husband was dead. She had a little baby,
in a cradle and still nursing. 195
The good man called her to come.
"Daughter," he says, "get up, get up!
Light the fire and a candle!
I have brought a baby here;
I found it out there in the ash tree. 200
Nurse it with your milk,
warm it up and bathe it!"
She did as he told her:
she lights the fire and takes the baby,
she warmed it up and bathed it well; 205
then she nursed it with her milk.
She finds the ring tied to the baby's arm;
they saw the rich and beautiful cloth.
They knew for certain
that she was born of a noble family. 210
The next day, after the service,
when the abbess leaves the church,
the porter goes to talk to her;
he wants to tell her the story[1]
of the baby, how he found it. 215
The abbess commanded him
that it be brought before her
just exactly as it had been found.
The porter goes to his house;
willingly he brings the baby 220
and showed it to the lady.
She looked at it intently
and says that she will have it brought up
and will treat her as her niece.
She strictly forbade the porter 225

---

1 This lai is particularly apt to use *aventure* to mean both "the adven-
ture, what happened" and "the story of what happened," a duality
that appears throughout the lais and that they themselves represent.
See the discussion of *aventure* in the Note on the Text (pp. 44–45)
and ll. 347, 492, 496, 515 below, as well as ll. 39 and 78 above.

Que il ne die cument il fu.
Ele memes l'ad levee.
Pur ceo que al freisne fu trovee,
L[e] Freisne li mistrent a nun,
230 E Le Freisne l'apelet hum.
La dame la tient pur sa niece.
Issi fu celee grant piece:
Dedenz le clos de l'abbeïe
Fu la dameisele nurie.
235 Quant [ele] vient en tel eé
Que nature furme beuté,
En Bretaine ne fu si bele
Ne tant curteise dameisele:
Franche esteit e de bone escole
240 En semblant e en parole;
Nul ne la vist que ne l'amast
E a merveille la preisast.
A Dol aveit un bon seignur;
Unc puis ne einz n'i ot meillur.
245 Ici vus numerai sun nun:
El païs l'apelent Gurun.   [col. b]
De la pucele oï parler,
Si la cumença a amer.
A un turneiement ala.
250 Par l'abbeie se returna,
La dameisele ad demandee;
L'abeesse li ad mustree.
Mut la vit bele e enseignee,
Sage, curteise e afeitee.
255 Si il n'ad l'amur de li,

to say how things happened.
She herself raised her at the font.
Because she was found in the ash tree,
they gave her the name Le Fresne,[1]
and Le Fresne is what people called her.[2]   230
The lady treats her as her niece.
In this way she was hidden for a long time:
within the abbey close[3]
the damsel was brought up.
When she came to the age   235
at which nature gives beauty,
in Brittany there was no maiden so beautiful
nor so courteous.
She was gracious and well taught
in manner and in speech;   240
no one saw her who did not love her
and hold her in the highest esteem.[4]
At Dol there was a good lord;[5]
never before nor since was there a better.
Here I will tell you his name: 245
in that country they call him Gurun.
He heard the maiden spoken of and
began to love her.
He went to a tournament.
He returned by way of the abbey   250
and asked for the damsel;
the abbess showed her to him.
He saw that she was lovely and well brought up,
wise, courteous, and well-bred.
If he does not obtain her love,   255

---

1 On the form of this name, see p. 117, note 1.

2 *Fresne* is a masculine noun and is treated as such in the text, except
when the title is given at the very end, but here the scribe has
written "La" and then expuncted the –a without adding a correc-
tion, suggesting some uncertainty about which definite article to
use. See note to l. 335.

3 That is, within the private, enclosed parts of the monastery, rather
than any public areas, making it clear that Le Fresne has no interac-
tion with the outside world.

4 The French text says that they valued her "a merveille," "wonder-
fully"; compare ll. 357, 381.

5 The city of Dol, now called Dol-de-Bretagne, is on the northwest
coast of France.

Mut se tendrat a maubailli.
Esguarez est, ne seit coment,
Kar si il repeirout sovent
L'abeesse se aparcevereit;
260 Jamés des oilz ne la vereit.
De une chose se purpensa:
L'abeie crestre vodera.
De sa tere tant i dura
Dunt a tuz jurs l'amendera;
265 Kar il vout aveir retur
E le repaire e le se[j]ur.
Pur aver lur fraternité
La ad grantment del soen doné;
Mes il ad autre acheisun
270 Que de receivre le pardun.
Soventefeiz i repeira,
A la dameisele parla;
Tant li pria, tant li premist
Que ele otria ceo ke il quist.
275 Quant a seur fu de s'amur,
Si la mist a reisun un jur.
"Bele," fet il, "ore est issi
Ke de mei avez fet ami: [f. 130ʳ]
Venez vus ent del tut od mei!
280 Saver poez, jol qui e crei,
Si vostre aunte s'aparceveit,
Mut durement li pesereit;
Si entur li feussez enceintez,
Durement sereit curuciez.
285 Si mun cunseil crere volez,
Ensemble od mei vus en vendrez.
Certes, jamés ne vus faudrai,

he will consider himself very unfortunate.
He is at a loss, he does not know what to do,
for if he went there often
the abbess would notice it;
he would never get a glimpse of her.   260
He thought of something:
the abbey will want to grow.
He will give them so much of his land
that it will benefit him forever;[1]
for he wants the right to return,   265
and to be welcome and able to stay.
To be part of their brotherhood
he gave generously of his goods;
but he had another reason
than the receiving of pardon.[2]   270
Many times he went back there,
he spoke to the damsel;
he begged her so much, promised her so much,
that she granted what he asked.
When he was certain of her love,   275
he spoke to her one day.
"Beautiful one," he says, "now it is the case
that you have made me your beloved,
come away with me entirely!
You must know, I trust and believe,   280
that if your aunt were to find out,
it would grieve her terribly;
if you became pregnant under her care,
she would be extremely angry.
If you want to take my advice,   285
you will come along with me.
Truly, I will never fail you;

---

1 I take "abbey" as the subject of "will want (to grow)," but it could
   also be Gurun who wishes this, in which case the meaning would
   be, "he wants to expand the abbey; he will give them so much of his
   land that it will improve the abbey forever." In any case, the ambi-
   guity reinforces the mutual benefits of this arrangement (see next
   note).
2 Laypeople could become part of the "family" of an abbey or
   monastery, participating in a limited way in its religious life and
   gaining spiritual credit, usually (as here) in return for offering some
   kind of financial support. The "receiving of pardon" here refers to
   the forgiveness of sins.

Ke richement vus cunseillerai."
Cele que durement l'amot
290 Bien otriat ceo que li plot:
Ensemble od lui en est alee;
A sun chastel l'ad menee.
Sun pali porte e sun anel;
De ceo li pout estre mut bel.
295 L'abeesse li ot rendu,
E dist coment est avenu.
Quant primes li fu enveiee:
Suz le freisne fu cuchee;
Le palie e l'anel li bailla
300 Cil que primes li enveia.
Plus de aveir ne receut od li;
Come sa niece la nuri.
La meschine ben les gardat;
En un cofre les afermat.
305 Le cofre fist od sei porter,
Nel volt lesser ne ublier.
Li chevaler ki l'amena
Mut la cheri e mut l'ama,
E tut si humme e si servant.
310 N'i out un sul, petit ne grant,
Pur sa franchise ne l'amast
E ne cherist e honurast.
Lungement ot od lui esté,   [col. b]
Tant que li chevaler fiufé
315 A mut grant mal li aturnerent:
Soventefeiz a lui parlerent
Que une gentile femme espusast
E de cele se deliverast:
Lié sereit s'il eust heir,
320 Que aprés lui puist aveir
Sa tere e sun heritage.
Trop i avreit grant damage,
Si il laissast pur sa suinant
Que de espuse n'eust enfant.
325 Jamés pur seinur nel tenderunt,
Ne volenters nel servirunt,
Si il ne fait lur volenté.
Le chevalers ad granté
Que en lur cunseil femme prendra;
330 Ore esgardent u ceo sera.

I will provide for you richly."
She, who loved him dearly,
willingly granted what pleased him: 290
she went away along with him;
he took her to his castle.
She takes her silk cloth and her ring;
that may turn out very well for her.
The abbess had given them back to her 295
and told her how things happened
when she was first sent to her:
she was sleeping in the ash tree;
the person who first sent her away
gave her the cloth and the ring. 300
She did not receive anything else with her;
she brought her up as her niece.
The girl took good care of them;
she closed them up in a coffer.
She had the coffer brought with her, 305
she did not want to leave it or forget it.
The knight who took her away
loved her and cherished her greatly,
as did all his people and his servants.
There was not a single one, small or great, 310
who did not love her for her graciousness
and cherish and honor her.
She had been with him for a long time,
so long that the knights who held their lands from him
reproached him strongly: 315
they told him many times
that he should marry a noblewoman
and get rid of this one:
he would be happy if he had an heir
who could hold his land 320
and his heritage after him.
It would be a great loss to him
if, because of his mistress, he failed
to have a child by a wife.
They will never have him as their lord 325
nor willingly serve him,
if he does not do what they want.
The knight agreed
to take a wife according to their counsel;
now they should consider where that will be. 330

"Sire," funt il, "ci pres de nus
Ad un produm parlé od nus;
Une fille ad, que est suen heir:
Mut poez tere od li aveir.
335 La Codre ad nun la damesele;
En cest païs ne ad si bele.
Pur Le Freisne, que vus larrez,
En eschange Le Codre avez.
En la codre ad noiz e deduiz;
340 Freisne ne porte unke fruiz.
La pucele purchacerums;
Si Deu plest, si la vus durums."
Cel mariage unt purchacié
E de tutes parz otrié.
345 Allas! cum est [mes]avenu
Que li [prudume] ne unt seü
L'aventure des dameiseles,
Que esteient serur[s] gemeles!   [f. 130ᵛ]
Le Freisne, cele, fu celee;
350 Sis amis ad l'autre espusee.
Quant ele sot ke il la prist,
Unc peiur semblant ne fist:
Sun seignur sert mut bonement
E honure tute sa gent.
355 L[i] chevaler de la meisun
E li vadlet e li garçun
Merveillus dol en menerent
De ceo ke perdre la deveient.
Al jur des noces qu'il unt pris,
360 Sis sires i maunde ses amis,
E l'erceveke i esteit,
Cil de Dol, que de lui teneit.

"Lord," they say, "here, close to us,
a worthy man has spoken with us;
he has one daughter, who is his heir:
you could have a lot of land with her.
La Codre is the damsel's name;[1]   335
in this country there is none so beautiful.
For Le Fresne, whom you will leave,
you have Le Codre in exchange.
The hazel tree has nuts and delights;
the ash tree never bears fruit.   340
We will obtain the maiden;
if it pleases God, we will give her to you."
They arranged the marriage
and got everyone's consent.
Alas! how unfortunate   345
that the worthy men did not know
the story of the damsels,
that they were twin sisters![2]
Le Fresne, for her part, was hidden away;
her beloved became engaged to the other.   350
When Le Fresne knew that he had accepted her,
she never looked any the worse.
she serves her lord most kindly
and honors all his people.
The knights of the house   355
and the young men and the serving boys
were extremely upset about this,
because they were going to lose her.
On the day that they had chosen for the wedding,
her lord sends for his friends,   360
and the archbishop of Dol was there,
who held his see from him.[3]

---

1   Like her sister, La Codre has the name of a tree, and the implica-
    tions are spelled out in the next few lines. Again, as with Le Fresne,
    rather than calling her Hazel I have chosen to keep the French
    name. While *fresne* is a masculine noun and *codre* is feminine, the
    scribe is not consistent in the pronouns he uses (see note to ll.
    229–30), and I have carried over the variation into the translation.
2   The word I have translated here as "story" is, again, *aventure*; see
    note to l. 214.
3   That is, Gurun is the feudal overlord of the archbishop, who holds
    his "see" (area of jurisdiction) from him. There was considerable
    debate about the precise roles of the Church in relation   *(continued)*

S'espuse li unt amenee.
Sa mere est od li alee;
365 De la meschine aveit poür,
Vers ki sis sires ot tel amur,
Que a sa fille mal tenist
Vers sun seignur, si ele poïst.
De sa meisun la getera,
370 A sun gendre cunseilera
Que a un produm la marit;
Si s'en deliverat, ceo quit.
Les noces tindrent richement;
Mut i out esbaniement.
375 La dameisele es chambres fu;
Unques de quanke ele ad veü
Ne fist semblant que li pesast
Ne tant que ele se curuçast;
Ent[ur] la dame bonement
380 Serveit mut afeitément.
A grant merveile le teneient
Cil e celes ki la veient.
Sa mere l'ad mut esgardee,   [col. b]
En sun qor preisie e amee.
385 Pensat e dist, si ele le seüst,
La maniere ke ele fust,
Ja pur sa fille ne perdist,
Ne sun seignur ne li tolist.
La noit, al lit aparailler
390 U l'espuse deveit cucher,
La damisele i est alee.
De sun mauntel est desfublee.
Les chamberleins i apela,
La maniere lur enseigna
395 Cument si sires le voleit,
Kar meintefeiz veu l'aveit.
Quant le lit fu apresté,
Un covertur unt sus jeté;
Li dras esteit d'un viel bofu.

They brought his bride to him.
Her mother went with her;
she was afraid of the girl   365
whom the lord loved so much,
that she would make trouble for her daughter
with her lord, if she could.
She will throw her out of his house,
she will advise her son-in-law   370
that he marry her to a good man;
thus he will be free of her, she thinks.
They celebrated the wedding lavishly;
there was great enjoyment.
The damsel was in the private chambers   375
never did she make any sign
that anything she had seen troubled her
nor that she was at all angry;
she served the lady kindly
and very courteously.   380
The men and women who saw her
considered it a great marvel.
Her mother looked at her carefully,
and valued and loved her in her heart.
She thought and said to herself that if she had known   385
the sort of person Le Fresne was,
Le Fresne would not have suffered loss for her daughter's sake
nor would she have taken her lord away from her.
That night, the damsel went
to prepare the bed   390
where the bride would lie.
She took off her mantle.
She called the chamberlains there
and showed them the way
that her lord wished it to be,   395
for she had seen it many times.
When the bed was made ready,
they threw a coverlet over it;
the material was an old woven silk.

---

to earthly lords and the granting or "investiture" of jurisdiction; by
the time Marie was writing, the official position was that the earthly
lord invested the archbishop with the temporal aspects of his power
(primarily land), while the Church granted him the spiritual power
of his office, but it is not clear here whether Gurun may also have
invested the archbishop with his spiritual role.

400 La dameisele l'ad veü;
    N'ert mie bons, ceo li sembla;
    En sun curage li pesa.
    Un cofre overi, sun pali prist,
    Sur le lit sun seignur le mist.
405 Pur lui honurer le feseit;
    Kar l'erceveke i esteit
    Pur eus beneistre e enseiner;
    Kar ceo afereit a sun mestier.
    Quant la chambre fu deliveree,
410 La dame ad sa fille amenee,
    E ele la volt fere cuchier.
    Si la cumande a despoilier.
    La palie esgarde sur le lit,
    Que unke mes si bon ne vit
415 Fors sul celui que ele dona
    Od sa fille ke ele cela.
    Idunc li remembra de li,
    Tut li curages li fremi;   [f. 131ʳ]
    Le chamberlenc apele a sei.
420 "Di mei," fait ele, "par ta fei,
    U fu cest bon pali trovez?"
    "Dame," fait il, "vus le saverez:
    La dameisele l'aporta;
    Sur le covertur le geta
425 Kar ne li sembla mie bons.
    Jeo qui que le pali est soens."
    La dame l'aveit apelee,
    Ele est devant li alee;
    De sun mauntel se desfubla
430 E la mere l'areisuna:
    "Bele amie, nel me celez!
    U fu cist bons palies trovez?
    Dunt vus vient il? kil vus dona?
    Kar me dites kil vus bailla!"
435 La meschine li respundi:
    "Dame, m'aunte, ke me nuri,
    L'abeesse, kil me bailla,
    A garder le me comanda;
    Cest e un anel me baillerent
440 Cil ki a nurir me enveierent."
    "Bele, pois jeo veer l'anel?"
    "Oïl, dame, ceo m'est bel."

The damsel saw it: 400
it was not right, it seemed to her;
it weighed on her heart.
She opened a chest, took out her cloth,
put it on the bed of her lord.
She did it to honor him; 405
for the archbishop was there
to bless them and make the sign of the cross,
for that was appropriate to his role.
When the chamber was ready,
the lady led her daughter there, 410
and wanted to put her to bed.
She tells her to get undressed.
She looks at the silk cloth on the bed;
she never saw such a good one
except the one that she gave 415
with her daughter whom she hid.
Then she remembered her,
her whole heart trembled;
she calls the chamberlain to her.
"Tell me," she said, "by your faith, 420
where did you find this lovely silk cloth?"
"Lady," he said, "you shall know:
the damsel brought it;
she threw it over the coverlet
because the latter did not seem good to her. 425
I believe that the cloth is hers."
The lady called her,
she came before her;
she took off her mantle
and the mother questioned her: 430
"Dear friend, do not hide it from me:
where did you find this lovely cloth?
Where did you get it? Who gave it to you?
You must tell me who gave it to you!"
The girl replied, 435
"Lady, my aunt who brought me up,
the abbess, who gave it to me,
told me to take care of it;
this and a ring were given to me
by those who sent me away to be raised." 440
"Dear one, can I see the ring?"
"Certainly, my lady, I would be delighted."

L'anel li ad dunc aporté,
E ele l'ad mut esgardé;
445 Ele l'ad tresbien reconeü
E le pali ke ele ad veü.
Ne dute mes, bien seit e creit
Que ele memes sa fille esteit;
Oiant tuz, dist, ne ceil[e] mie:
450 "Tu es ma fille, bele amie!"
De la pité ke ele en a
Ariere cheit, si se pauma.
E quant del paumeisun leva,   [col. b]
Pur sun seignur tost enveia,
455 E il vient tut effreez.
Quant il est en chambre entrez,
La dame li cheï as piez,
Estreitement l'ad baisiez,
Pardun li quert de sun mesfait.
460 Il ne feseit nient del plait.
"Dame," fet il, "quei dites vus?
Il n'ad si bien nun entre nus.
Quanke vus plest seit parduné!
Dites mei vostre volunté."
465 "Sire, quant parduné l'avez,
Jel vus dirai; si m'escutez!
Jadis par ma grant vileinie
De ma veisine dis folie;
De ses deus enfanz mesparlai.
470 Vers mei memes errai:
Verité est que jeo enceintai,
Deus filles oi, l'une celai;
A un muster la fis geter
E nostre pali od li porter
475 E l'anel que vus me donastes
Quant vus primes od mei parlastes.
Ne vus peot mie estre celé:
Le drap e l'anel ai trové.
Nostre fille ai ici conue,
480 Que par ma folie oi perdue;
E ja est ceo la dameisele
Que tant est pruz e sage e bele,
Ke li chevaler ad amee
Ki sa serur ad espusee."
485 Li sires dit, "De ceo sui jeo liez;

Then she brought her the ring,
and she looked at it carefully;
she recognized it very well,   445
and the cloth that she saw.
She no longer doubts, she knows and believes
that this very girl was her daughter;
in everyone's hearing she says, not hiding it at all,
"You are my daughter, lovely friend!"   450
From the pity that she feels at this
she fell down in a faint.
And when she recovered from her faint,
she quickly sent for her lord;
and he came, very worried.   455
When he entered the chamber,
the lady fell at his feet,
kissed him earnestly,
asks his pardon for her misdeed.
He could not understand her plea.   460
"Lady," he says, "what are you saying?
There is nothing but good between us.
You are pardoned as much as you please!
Tell me whatever you like."
"Lord, since you have pardoned it,   465
I will tell you; hear me well!
Once upon a time, in my great wickedness,
I spoke ill of my neighbor;
I slandered her concerning her two infants.
I did wrong against myself: 470
The truth is that I became pregnant,
I had two daughters, I hid one;
I had her left at a church
and had our silk cloth taken with her
and the ring that you gave me   475
when you first spoke with me.
It cannot be hidden from you:
I have found the cloth and the ring.
I have recognized our daughter here,
whom I had lost through my folly;   480
and indeed it is the damsel
who is so worthy and wise and beautiful,
whom the knight loved
who has married her sister."
The lord says, "I am delighted with this;   485

Unc mes ne fu[i] si haitiez.
Quant nostre fille avum trovee,
Grant joie nus ad Deu donee,   [f. 131ᵛ]
Ainz que li pechez fust dublez.
490 Fille," fet il, "avant venez!"
La meschine mut s'esjoï
De l'aventure ke ele oï.
Sun pere ne volt plus atendre:
Il memes vet pur sun gendre,
495 E l'erceveke i amena;
Cele aventure li cunta.
Li chevaler, quant il le sot,
Unc si grant joie nen ot.
L'erceveke ad cunseilié
500 Que issi seit la noit laissié;
El demain les departira,
Lui e cele qu'[il] espusa.
Issi l'unt fet e granté.
El demain furent desevré;
505 Aprés ad s'amie espusee,
E li peres li ad donee,
Que mut ot vers li bon curage;
Par mie li part sun heritage.
Il e la mere as noces furent
510 Od lur fille, si cum il durent.
Quant en lur païs s'en alerent,
La Coudre lur fille menerent;
Mut richement en lur cuntree
Fu puis la meschine donee.
515 Quant l'aventure fu seue,
Coment ele esteit avenue,
Le *Lai de la Freisne* en unt trové:
Pur la dame l'unt si numé.

I have never been so happy.
Since we have found our daughter,
God has given us great joy,
rather than doubling the sin.
Daughter," he says, "come forward!"   490
The girl rejoiced greatly
at the story she heard.[1]
Her father does not want to wait any more:
he goes himself for his son-in-law,
and brought the archbishop there;   495
he told him this story.
The knight, when he knew of it,
had never felt such great joy.
The archbishop advised
that things should be left as they are for the night;   500
the next day he will separate
the knight and the woman he married.
They agreed to do this.
The next day they were separated;
afterward he married his beloved,   505
and the father gave her to him,
who felt very warmly toward her;
he divides his possessions in half for her.
He and the mother were at the wedding
with their daughter, just as they should be.[2]   510
When they went to their lands,
they took their daughter La Codre;
afterward the girl was bestowed
very richly in their country.
When the story was known,   515
how this had happened,
they composed the *Lay of Le Fresne* about it:
for the lady they named it so.

---

1 Here and in the following lines, the word *aventure* is again used to
   mean both "what happened" and "the story of what happened."
2 Or "for as long as they [the wedding celebrations] lasted."

Bisclavret

*Quant de lais faire m'entremet,
Ne voil ublier Bisclaveret.
Bisclaveret ad nun en bretan,
Garwaf l'apelent li Norman.

5 Jadis le poeit hume oïr,   [col. b]
E sovent suleit avenir,
Humes plusurs garual devindrent
E es boscages meisun tindrent.
Garualf, c'est beste salvage:
10 Tant cum il est en cele rage,
Hummes devure, grant mal fait.
Es granz foré[s]† converse e vait.
Cest afere les ore ester;
Del bisclaveret voil cunter.
15 En Bretaine maneit un ber,
Merveille l'ai oï loer;
Beaus chevalers e bons esteit
E noblement se cunteneit.
De sun seinur esteit privez
20 E de tuz ses veisins amez.
Femme ot espuse mut vailant
E que mut feseit beu semblant.
Il amot li e ele lui,

This lai appears on ff. 131^(va)–133^(vb) of Harley 978. A later hand has
added the title "Bisclavret" in the upper left margin.

† Here and throughout, square brackets in the text indicate an emen-
dation to the text as it appears in Harley 978; the original reading
can be found, keyed to the line number, in Appendix F.

Werewolf

Since I have undertaken to compose lais,
I don't want to forget *Bisclavret*.
Bisclavret is the name in Breton;[1]
the Normans call it *Garwaf*.
There was a time when one would hear,   5
and it often used to happen,
that many people became werewolves
and kept house in the woods.[2]
The werewolf is a wild beast:
when it is in that frenzy,   10
it devours people and does great harm.
It lives in and roams the great forests.
Now I let this matter be;
I want to tell of the *bisclavret*.
In Brittany there lived a worthy man   15
whom I have heard marvelously praised;
he was a handsome, good knight
and conducted himself nobly.
He was a dear friend of his lord
and beloved by all his neighbors.   20
He had a very worthy wife
who seemed lovely
He loved her and she him,

---

1 Here as elsewhere, "bretan" may be understood to mean "Breton"
   but also, in a broader sense, "Brittonic"; see Introduction (pp.
   16–17). The word *bisclavret*, however, has been plausibly traced to
   Breton cognates meaning "speaking wolf."
2 When referring to werewolves generally in her opening lines, Marie
   uses the name she has identified as Norman: *garualf/garwaf*. After
   this, in talking about her protagonist, she uses the Breton (or Bry-
   thonic) word *bisclavret*. This translation signals the change in terms
   at line 14, where she switches to "bisclavret," but thereafter I trans-
   late *bisclavret* as "werewolf" when it is used with a definite article or
   seems to be a generic term, and as "Bisclavret" (a name) when it
   specifically designates the protagonist himself—which is usually at
   key moments in the story. The difficulties raised by this common
   and proper noun are somewhat similar to those noted in the previ-
   ous lai, *Le Fresne*, but here the noun is also a loan word from
   another language (whereas *fre[i]sne* and *codre* are French words).
   The scribe of Harley 978 consistently spells the word *bisclaveret*,
   with two 'e's, but the modern convention is to spell it *B/bisclavret*,
   and I have done so here (as with *freisne/fresne*).

Mes d'une chose ert grant ennui:
25 Que en la semeine le deperdeit
Treis jurs entiers, que ele ne saveit
U deveneit ne u alout,
Ne nul des soens nient ne sout.
Une feiz esteit repeirez
30 A sa meisun joius e liez.
Demandé li ad e enquis:
"Sire," fait ele, "beau duz amis,
Une chose vus demandasse
Mut volenters, si jeo osasse;
35 Mes jeo creim tant vostre curuz,
Que nule rien tant ne redut."
Quant il l'oï, si⁺ l'acola,
Vers li la traist, si la beisa.
"Dame," fait il, "demandez!
40 Ja cele chose ne me direz,   [f. 132ʳ]
Si jo la sai, ne la vus die."
"Par fei," fet ele, "ore sui garie!
Sire, jeo sui en tel effrei
Les jurs quant vus partez de mei;
45 El lever en ai mut grant dolur
E de vus perdre tel poür,
Si jeo n'en ai hastif cunfort,
Bien tost en puis aver la mort.
Kar me dites u vus alez,
50 U vus estes, u vus conversez!
Mun escient que vus amez,
E si si est, vus meserrez."
"Dame," fet il, "pur Deu, merci!
Mal m'en vendra si jol vus di,
55 Kar de m'amur vus partirai
E mei memes en perdirai."
Quant la dame l'ad entendu,
Ne l'ad neent en gab tenu.
Suventefeiz li demanda;
60 Tant le blandi e losenga
Que s'aventure li cunta;

but she was greatly troubled by one thing:
each week she lost him 25
for three whole days, when she did not know
what became of him nor where he went,
nor did any of his people know at all.
One day he had returned
to his house joyful and happy. 30
She questioned him and inquired:
"Lord," she says, "fair sweet beloved,
I would very much like to ask you
one thing, if I dared;
but I am so afraid of your anger 35
that there is nothing I fear more."
When he heard this, he embraced her,
drew her toward him and kissed her.
"Lady," he said, "just ask!
You will never say anything to me that, 40
if I know it, I will not tell you."
"By my faith," she said, "now I am restored!
Lord, I am so anxious
on those days when you leave me;
when I arise I am so sad about it 45
and have such fear of losing you
that if I do not get reassurance shortly,
very soon I may die of it.
So do tell me where you go,
where you are, where you live! 50
It is my belief you are in love,
and if it is so, you do wrong."
"Lady," he said, "mercy, by God!
Trouble will come to me if I tell you,
for I will divide you from my love 55
and destroy myself in doing so."
When the lady heard him,
she considered it no joke.
Many times she asked him;
she cajoled and flattered him so much 60
that he told her what happened to him;[1]

---

1 Or, "he told her his adventure." Here, as in many of the lais, the
   important word *aventure* has a range of meanings that can be diffi-
   cult to convey in English; see Note on the Text (pp. 44–45) and also
   ll. 99, 269, 315 below, where the word sometimes works alongside
   the related verb *avenir*, "to happen, to come to pass."

Nule chose ne li cela.
"Dame, jeo devienc bisclaveret:
En cele grant forest me met,
65 Al plus espés de la gaudine,
Si vif de preie e de ravine."
Quant il li aveit tut cunté,
Enquis li ad e demaundé
Si il se despuille u vet vestu.
70 "Dame," fet il, "jeo vois tut nu."
"Di mei, pur Deu, u sunt voz dras."
"Dame, ceo ne dirai jeo pas;
Kar si jeo les eusse perduz
E de ceo feusse aparceüz
75 Bisclaveret sereie a tuz jurs;   [col. b]
Jamés n'avereie mes sucurs,
De si k'il me fussent rendu.
Pur ceo ne voil k'il seit seü."
"Sire," la dame li respunt,
80 "Jeo vus eim plus que tut le mund:
Nel me devez nient celer,
Ne de nule rien duter;
Ne semblereit pas amisté.
Quei ai jeo forfait? pur queil peché
85 Me dutez vus de nule rien?
Dites mei, si ferez bien!"
Tant l'anguissa, tant le suzprist,
Ne pout el faire, si li dist.
"Dame," fet il, "delee cel bois,
90 Lez le chemin par unt jeo vois,
Une vielz chapele i esteit,
Ke meintefeiz grant bien me feit:
La est la piere cruose e lee
Suz un bussun, dedenz cavee;
95 Mes dras i met suz le buissun
Tant que jeo revi[e]nc a meisun."
La dame oï cele merveille;
De poür fu tute vermeille.
De l'aventure se esfrea,
100 E maint endreit se purpensa,
Cum ele s'en puist partir;
Ne voleit mes lez lui gisir.
Un chevaler de la cuntree,
Que lungement l'aveit amee

he hid nothing from her.
"Lady, I become a werewolf:
I go into that great forest,
to the deepest part of the woods,   65
and live on prey and plunder."
When he had told her everything,
she inquired and asked him
whether he undresses or goes clothed.
"Lady," he says, "I go quite naked."   70
"Tell me, by God, where your clothes are."
"Lady, that I will not tell;
for if I should lose them
and were discovered due to this,
I would be a werewolf always;   75
there would never again be hope for me,
until they were returned to me.
For this reason I don't want it known."
"Sir," the lady replies to him,
"I love you more than all the world: 80
you should hide nothing from me,
nor mistrust me in any way;
that would not seem like friendship.
What have I done wrong? For what misdeed
do you mistrust me in any way?   85
You will do well to tell me!"
She so tormented and pestered him
that he could not do otherwise, and so he told her.
"Lady," he says, "near this wood,
beside the path by which I travel,   90
there stands an old chapel,
which many times has been a great help to me:
there the stone is hollow and wide,
carved-out inside, below a bush;
I put my clothes under the bush   95
until I return home."
The lady heard this marvel;
she turned quite red with fear.
She was terrified by this adventure,
and she thought hard about it,   100
how she could get away from this;
she did not want to lie beside him any more.
A knight of that region,
who had loved her a long time

105 E mut preie[e] e mut requisè
E mut duné en sun servise—
Ele ne l'aveit unkes amé
Ne de s'amur aseuré—
Celui manda par sun message,
110 Si li descoveri sun curage.   [f. 132ᵛ]
"Amis," fet ele, "seez leéz!
Ceo dunt vus estes travaillez
Vus otri jeo sanz nul respit:
Ja n'i averez nul cuntredit.
115 M'amur e mun cors vus otrei:
Vostre drue fetes de mei!"
Cil l'en mercie bonement
E la fiance de li prent;
E ele le met par serement.
120 Puis li cunta cumfaitement
Ses sires ala e k'il devint;
Tute la veie ke il tint
Vers la forest l[i] enseigna;
Pur sa despuille l'enveia.
125 Issi fu Bisclaveret trahiz
E par sa femme maubailiz.
Pur ceo que hum le·perdeit sovent,
Quidouent tuz communalment
Que dunc s'en fust del tut alez.
130 Asez fu quis e demandez,
Mes n'en porent mie trover;
Si lur estuit lesser ester.
La dame ad cil dunc espusee,
Que lungement aveit amee.
135 Issi remist un an entier,
Tant que li reis ala chacier;
A la forest ala tut dreit,
La u li bisclaveret esteit.
Quant li chiens furent descuplé,
140 Le bisclaveret unt encuntré.
A lui cururent tute jur
E li chien e li veneür,
Tant que pur poi ne l'eurent pris
E tut deciré e maumis,
145 De si qu'il ad le rei choisi: [col. b]

and greatly implored and courted her 105
and greatly devoted himself to her service—
she had never loved him
or promised him her love—
she sent for this man by messenger
and revealed her feelings to him. 110
"Friend," she says, "rejoice!
That for which you have labored
I grant you without delay:
you will find no resistance.
I grant you my love and my body; 115
take me as your lover!"
He thanks her warmly
and accepts her promise,
and she binds him by an oath.
Then she told him exactly how 120
her lord went away and what he became;
she taught him the whole path
he took to the forest;
she sent him for the discarded clothes.
Thus Bisclavret was betrayed 125
and brought to ruin by his wife.
Since they often lost track of him,
everyone generally believed
that this time he had gone away for good.
He was widely sought and asked after, 130
but they could not find him at all;
so they had to let it be.
The lady then was married to the one
who had loved her for a long time.
Things remained this way for a whole year, 135
until the king went hunting;
he went straight to the forest
where the werewolf was.
When the hounds were unleashed,
they found the werewolf. 140
All day long they pursued it,
both the hounds and the hunters,
so that they very nearly caught it
and completely tore it to shreds and destroyed it,
until it saw the king: 145

Vers lui curut quere merci.
Il l'aveit pris par sun estrié,
La jambe li baise e le pié.
Li reis le vit, grant poür ad;
150 Ses cumpainuns tuz apelad.
"Seignurs," fet il, "avant venez!
Ceste merveille esgardez,
Cum ceste beste se humilie!
Ele ad sen de hume, merci crie.
155 Chacez mei tuz ces chiens arere,
Si gardez que hum ne la fiere!
Ceste beste ad entente e sen.
Espleitez vus! Alum nus en!
A la beste durrai ma pes,
160 Kar jeo ne chacerai hui mes."
Li reis s'en est turné atant.
Le bisclaveret li vet siwant;
Mut se tint pres, n'en vout partir,
Il n'ad cure de lui guerpir.
165 Li reis l'enmeine en sun chastel;
Mut en fu liez, mut li est bel,
Kar unke mes tel n'ot veü.
A grant merveille l'ot tenu
E mut le tient a grant chierté.
170 A tuz les suens ad comaundé
Que sur s'amur le gardent bien
E li ne mesfacent de rien,
Ne par nul de eus ne seit feruz;
Bien seit abevreiz e peüz.
175 Cil le garderent volenters.
Tuz jurs entre les chevalers
E pres del rei se alout cuchier.
N'i ad celui que ne l'ad chier;
Tant esteit franc e deboneire,
180 Unc ne volt a rien mesfeire.

[f. 133^r]

it ran to him to ask mercy.[1]
It had taken him by the stirrup,
it kisses his leg and his foot.
The king sees it and is very much afraid;
he called all his companions.   150
"Lords," he says, "come here!
Look at this wonder,
how this beast humbles itself!
It has human understanding, it begs mercy.
Get all these dogs away from me,   155
make sure that no one strikes it!
This beast has intelligence and understanding.
Hurry up! Let's go!
I will extend my peace to the beast,
for I will hunt no more today."   160
The king turned back at once.
The werewolf goes along following him;
it stayed very close, it did not wish to leave,
it does not care to part from him.
The king takes it into his castle;   165
he was very happy about it, it was delightful to him,
for he had never seen such a thing.
He considered it a great wonder
and held it very dear.
He commanded all his people   170
to take good care of it for love of him
and not ill-treat it in any way,
nor should any of them strike it;
it should be given plenty to drink and eat.
They willingly took care of it.   175
Every day it went to bed
among the knights and close to the king.
There is no one who does not hold it dear;
it was so noble and kind,
it never wished to do wrong in any way.   180

---

1 Although the noun *bisclavret* is masculine, I refer to the werewolf in English as "it" when it is in wolf form; the human protagonist Bisclavret, who is of course the same "person," is "he." This both helps to distinguish the wolf from the king and other masculine characters and also conveys his dual nature. Only at the end, when the wise counselor seems to realize that the werewolf is indeed also the man Bisclavret, is the werewolf called "he" in the translation (ll. 283–92).

U ke li reis deust errcr,
Il n'out cure de deseverer;
Ensemble od li tuz jurs alout.
Bien s'aparceit que il l'amout.
185 Oez aprés cument avint.
A une curt ke li rei tint
Tuz les baruns aveit mandez,
Ceus ki furent de lui chacez,
Pur aider sa feste a tenir
190 E lui plus beal faire servir.
Li chevaler i est alez,
Richement e bien aturnez,
Ki la femme Bisclaveret ot.
Il ne saveit ne ne quidot
195 Que il le deust trover si pres.
Si tost cum il vint al paleis
E le bisclaveret le aparceut,
De plain esleis vers li curut;
As denz le prist, vers li le trait.
200 Ja li eust mut grant leid fait
Ne fust li reis ki l'apela,
De une verge le manaça.
Deus feiz le vout mordre al jur.
Mut s'esmerveillent li plusur,
205 Kar unkes tel semblant ne fist
Vers nul hume k'il veïst.
Ceo dient tut par la meisun
Ke il nel fet mie sanz reisun:
Mesfait li ad, coment que seit,
210 Kar volenters se vengereit.
A cele feiz remist issi,
Tant que la feste departi
E li barun unt pris cungé;
A lur meisun sunt repeiré.
215 Alez s'en est li chevaliers,   [col. b]
Mien escient, tut as premers,
Que le bisclaveret asailli;

Wherever the king had to go,
it did not care to be apart from him;
it always went along with him.
He could see well that it loved him.
Listen to what happened afterwards. 185
One time when the king held court
he had sent for all his men,
those who were his vassals,[1]
to help him celebrate
and to serve him as pleasingly as possible. 190
The knight who had Bisclavret's wife
went along there,
well and richly dressed.
He did not know nor expect
that he would find Bisclavret so close. 195
As soon as he came to the palace
and the werewolf saw him,
it ran toward him at full speed;
it grabbed him with its teeth and drags him toward it.
It would have done him great injury 200
were it not for the king, who called to it
and threatened it with a staff.
Twice that day it tried to bite the knight.
Most people are astonished,
for it had never acted like this 205
toward anyone it saw.
Everyone in the household says
that surely it is not doing this without a reason:
the knight must somehow have done it wrong
for now it would willingly avenge itself. 210
Things went along this way
until the festivities broke up
and the noblemen took their leave;
they went back to their houses.
The knight the werewolf had attacked 215
went away, I believe,
among the first;

---

1 Literally, "those who were enfeoffed/endowed by him"—that is, to
  whom the king had granted land in return for their loyalty and
  service to him. The homophones *chacer/chaser* (both of which could
  be spelled with either an *s* or a *c* in Anglo-French), meaning "to
  hunt" and "to endow with land," are an intriguing pair in this lai,
  where hunting is so important to the plot.

N'est merveille s'il le haï.
Ne fu puis gueres lungement,
220 Ceo m'est avis, si cum jeo entent,
Que a la forest ala li reis,
Que tant fu sages e curteis,
U li bisclaveret fu trovez;
E il i est od li alez.
225 La nuit quant il s'en repeira,
En la cuntree herberga.
La femme le bisclaveret le sot.
Avenantment se appareilot;
Al demain vait al rei parler,
230 Riche present li fait porter.
Quant Bisclaveret la veit venir,
Nul hume nel poeit retenir;
Vers li curut cum enragiez.
Oiez cum il est bien vengiez:
235 Le neis li esracha del vis!
Quei li pust il faire pis?
De tutes parz l'unt manacié;
Ja l'eussent tut depescié,
Quant un sages humme dist al rei:
240 "Sire," fet il, "entent a mei![1]
Ceste beste ad esté od vus;
N'i ad ore celui de nus
Que ne l'eit veu lungement
E pres de li alé sovent.
245 Unke mes humme ne tucha
Ne felunie ne mustra,
Fors a la dame que ici vei.
Par cele fei ke jeo vus dei,
Aukun curuz ad il vers li,
250 E vers sun seignur autresi.   [f. 133ᵛ]
Ceo est la femme al chevaler
Que taunt par suliez aveir chier,
Que lung tens ad esté perduz;
Ne s[e]umes u est devenuz.
255 Kar metez la dame en destreit,

---

1 In his speeches to the king, the wise man mostly uses the polite
second-person form "vus," but he occasionally switches to the infor-
mal second person, as in this line ("entent" is an informal second-
person command) or l. 289 ("En tes chambres le fai mener": both
"tes" and "fai" are informal).

it's no wonder if it hated him.[1]
It was not long after,
it seems to me, as I understand it, 220
that the king, who was so wise and courteous,
went to the forest
where the werewolf had been found,
and it went with him.
That night, when the king came back from there, 225
he took lodging in the area.
The wife of the werewolf found this out.
She dressed herself becomingly;
the next day she goes to talk to the king,
she has a rich present brought to him. 230
When Bisclavret sees her coming,
no one could hold him back;
he ran toward her as though he were mad.
Hear how well he avenged himself:
he tore the nose from her face! 235
What worse could he have done to her?
They threatened him from all sides;
they would surely have torn him all to pieces,
when a wise man said to the king.
"Sire," he says, "listen to me! 240
This beast has been living with you;
there is now not one of us
who has not watched it for a long time
and often gone near it.
It has never touched anyone 245
nor shown any wickedness,
except to the lady I see here.
By the faith I owe you,
it has some cause for anger against her,
and also against her husband. 250
This is the wife of the knight
whom you used to hold so dear,
who has been missing for a long time;
we never knew where he ended up.
Put the lady under duress about this, 255

---

1 This could also mean "it's no wonder if he hated it," that is, if the
   knight hated the werewolf.

Si aucune chose vus direit,
Pur quei ceste beste la heit;
Fetes li dire s'el le seit!
Meinte merveille avum veü
260 Que en Bretaigne est avenu."
Li reis ad sun cunseil creü:
Le chevaler ad retenu;
De l'autre part ad la dame prise
E en mut grant destresce mise.
265 Tant par destresce e par poür
Tut li cunta de sun seignur:
Coment ele l'aveit trahi
E sa despoille li toli,
L'aventure qu'il li cunta,
270 E quei devint e u ala.
Puis que ses dras li ot toluz,
Ne fud en sun païs veüz.
Tresbien quidat e bien creeit
Que la beste Bisclaveret seit.
275 Le reis demande la despoille;
U bel li seit u pas nel voille,
Ariere la fet aporter.
Al bisclaveret la fist doner.
Quant il les urent devant li mise,
280 Ne se prist garde en nule guise.
Li produme le rei apela,
Cil ki primes le cunseilla:
"Sire, ne fetes mie bien:
Cist nel fereit pur nule rien,
285 Que devant vus ses dras reveste   [col. b]
Ne muet la semblance de beste.
Ne savez mie que ceo munte:
Mut durement en ad grant hunte.
En tes chambres le fai mener
290 E la despoille od li porter;
Une grant piece l'i laissums.
S'il devient hume, bien le verums."
Li reis memes le mena
E tuz les hus sur lui ferma.
295 Al chief de piece i est alez,

to see if she will tell you anything
about why this beast hates her;
make her tell it if she knows!
We have seen many a wonder
come to pass in Brittany."[1]   260
The king had faith in his counsel:
he arrested the knight;
moreover he took the lady
and put her to severe torture.
On account of such torture and out of fear   265
she told him all about her lord:
how she had betrayed him
and taken his clothes away,
the adventure that he told her,
and what he became and where he went.   270
Since she had taken away his clothes,
he had not been seen in his country.
She fully believed and supposed
that the beast must be Bisclavret.
The king asks for the discarded clothes;   275
whether she likes it or not,
she has them brought back.
He had them given to the werewolf.
When they had put them in front of it,
it did not take any notice at all.   280
The wise man, the one
who had first advised the king, addressed him:
"Sire, you are not doing this properly:
he wouldn't, for anything,
put his clothing back on in front of you   285
nor change his animal appearance.
You have no idea how important this is:
he feels terrible shame about it.
Have him led into your rooms
and take the clothing with him;   290
we'll leave him there for a good while.
We shall see if he becomes a man."
The king himself led the wolf in
and closed all the doors on him.
After a while he went there,   295

---

1 On the meaning of "Bretaigne" here, see Introduction (pp. 16–17,
   32 n. 2).

Deuz baruns ad od li menez;
En la chambre entrent tut trei.
Sur le demeine lit al rei
Trova il dormant le chevaler.
300 Li reis le curut enbracier;
Plus de cent feiz l'acole e baise.
Si tost cum il pot aver aise,
Tute sa tere li rendi;
Plus li duna ke jeo ne di.
305 La femme ad del païs ostee
E chacie de la cuntree.
Cil s'en alat ensemble od li
Pur ki sun seignur ot trahi.
Enfanz en ad asés eüz.
310 Puis unt esté bien cunuz
Del semblant e del visage:
Plusurs femmes del lignage,
Ceo est verité, senz nes sunt ne[es]
E [si vivei]ent esnasees.
315 L'aventure ke avez oïe
Veraie fu, n'en dutez mie.
De Bisclaveret fu fet li lais
Pur remembrance a tutdis mais.

taking two men with him;
all three of them enter the chamber.
On the king's own bed
he found the knight sleeping.
The king ran to embrace him;   300
more than a hundred times he hugs and kisses him.
As soon as he could get an opportunity,
he returned all his land to him;
he gave him more than I can say.
He banished the wife from the country   305
and drove her out of the region.
The man for whom she had betrayed her lord
went along with her.
She had a number of children by him.
They were quite recognizable   310
in appearance and face:
many women of that line,
in truth, were born without noses
and lived like that, noseless.
The adventure you have heard   315
was true, have no doubt.
The lai was made about *Bisclavret*[1]
to be remembered forevermore.

---

1   Here "Bisclavret" could be either the character's name or the lai's
    title (or both): "the lai was made about Bisclavret" or "the lai *Bis-
    clavret* was made."

Lanval

*L'aventure d'un autre lai,
Cum ele avient, vus cunterai.
Fait fu d'un mut gentil vassal;
En bretans l'apelent Lanval.
5 A Kardoel surjurnot li reis
Artur, li pruz e li curteis,
Pur les Escoz e pur les Pis,
Que destrui[ei]ent† le païs;
En la tere de Loengre entroent
10 E mut suvent la damagoent.
A la Pentecuste en esté
I aveit li reis sujurné.
Asez i duna riches duns
E as cuntes e as baruns.
15 A ceus de la table runde—
N'ot tant de teus en tut le munde—
Femmes e tere departi
Par tut, fors un ki l'ot servi:
Ceo fu Lanval, ne l'en sovient,
20 Ne nul de[s] soens bien ne li tient.
Pur sa valur, pur sa largesce,
Pur sa beauté, pur sa pruesce
L'envioent tut li plusur;
Tel li mustra semblant d'amur,
25 Si al chevaler mesavenist,
Ja une feiz ne l'en pleinsist.
Fiz a rei fu de haut parage,
Mes luin ert de sun heritage.
De la meisné le rei fu.

---

* This lai appears on ff. 133ᵛᵇ–138ᵛᵃ of Harley 978 and is given the
   title "Lanval" in the upper margin by a later hand.
† Here and throughout, square brackets in the text indicate an emen-
   dation to the text as it appears in Harley 978; the original reading
   can be found, keyed to the line number, in Appendix F.

Lanval

I shall tell you the adventure
of another lay, just as it happened.
It was made about a very noble vassal;
in Breton they call him Lanval.[1]
King Arthur, the valiant and courteous,   5
was staying at Carlisle[2]
on account of the Scots and Picts
who were ravaging the country:
they came into the land of England[3]
and repeatedly caused destruction to it.   10
At Pentecost,[4] in the summer,
the king had been staying there.
He gave many rich gifts
both to counts and to barons.
To the members of the Round Table—   15
there was no such gathering in all the world—
he shared out wives and land
among all except one who had served him:
that was Lanval, whom he does not remember,
nor do any of his men favor him.   20
For his valor, his generosity,
his beauty, his prowess,
a great many people envied him;
many a one pretended to love him
who wouldn't have complained for a moment   25
if something bad had befallen the knight.
He was a king's son, of high lineage,
but he was far from his heritage.
He was part of the king's household.

---

1 On the meaning of "bretans," see Introduction (pp. 16–17).
2 Carlisle is in the far north of England, very close to the western end
  of Hadrian's Wall.
3 Old French "Loengre" or "Logres" is derived from the Brythonic
  Celtic name for England (Old Welsh Lloegyr, modern Welsh
  Lloegr); it is often used in Arthurian literature (and in *Milun* l. 17).
  Geoffrey of Monmouth, in his *History of the Kings of Britain*, calls it
  Loegria.
4 The feast of Pentecost takes place seven weeks after Easter, in mid-
  to late May or early June (in the western Christian Church). Eccle-
  siastical feast days were a standard way of marking time in medieval
  culture.

30 Tut sun aveir ad despendu,
　 Kar li reis rien ne li dona
　 Ne Lanval rien ne li demanda.
　 Ore est Lanval mut entrepris,
　 Mut est dolent e mut pensis.
35 Seignurs, ne vus esmerveillez:
　 Hume estrange descunseillez
　 Mut est dolent en autre tere,　　　　　　　　　[col. b]
　 Quant il ne seit u sucurs quere.
　 Le chevaler dunt jeo vus di,
40 Que tant aveit le rei servi,
　 Un jur munta sur sun destrer,
　 Si s'est alez esbaneer.
　 Fors de la vile est eissuz,
　 Tut sul est en un pre venuz;
45 Sur une ewe curaunt descent—
　 Mes sis cheval tremble forment.
　 Il le descengle, si s'en vait;
　 En mi le pre vuiltrer le lait.
　 Le pan de sun mantel plia
50 Desuz sun chief puis le cucha.
　 Mut est pensis pur sa mesaise;
　 Il ne veit chose ke li plaise.
　 La u il gist en teu maniere,
　 Garda aval lez la riviere,
55 Vit venir deus dameiseles;
　 Unc n'en ot veu[es] plus beles.
　 Vestues ierent richement,
　 Lacie[es] mut estreitement
　 En deus blians de purpre bis;
60 Mut par aveient bel le vis.
　 L'eisnee portout un[s] bacins,
　 Doré furent, bien faiz e fins
　 (Le veir vus en dirai sanz faile);
　 L'autre portout une tuaile.
65 Eles s'en sunt alees dreit
　 La u li chevaler giseit.
　 Lanval, que mut fu enseigniez,
　 Cuntre eles s'en levad en piez.
　 Celes l'unt primes salué,

He has spent all his wealth,   30
for the king gave him nothing
nor did Lanval ask him for anything.
Now Lanval is very unhappy,
very sorrowful and anxious.
Lords, do not wonder: 35
a foreign man without support
is very sorrowful in another land
when he does not know where to seek help.
The knight of whom I'm telling you,
who had served the king so well,   40
got on his horse one day
and went off to enjoy himself.
He went out of the town;
all alone, he came to a meadow;
he dismounts beside running water   45
but his horse trembles greatly.[1]
He unsaddles it and it goes off;
he lets it roll around in the middle of the meadow.
He folded the end of his mantle
and lay down with it under his head.   50
He is very worried by his difficult situation,
he sees nothing that pleases him.
As he lay there like this
he looked down toward the river bank,
he saw two maidens coming;   55
he had never seen any more beautiful.
They were richly dressed
and very tightly laced
in two tunics of dark purple;
they had exceedingly lovely faces.   60
The elder carried basins
of gold, fine and well made
(I shall tell you the truth of it without fail);
the other carried a towel.
They went right along   65
to where the knight was lying.
Lanval, who was very well bred,
got to his feet to meet them.
They greeted him first

---

1 The Celtic otherworld is often reached by crossing a stream or
   other body of water; the implication may be that the horse can
   sense its proximity here.

70 Lur message li unt cunté:
　"Sire Lanval, ma dameisele,
　Que tant est pruz e sage e bele,　　　　　　　　[f. 134ᵛ]
　Ele nus envei[e] pur vus;
　Kar i venez ensemble od nus!
75 Sauvement vus i cundurums:
　Veez, pres est li paveilluns!"
　Li chevalers od eles vait;
　De sun cheval ne tient nul plait,
　Que devant li peist al pre.
80 Treske al tref l'unt amené,
　Que mut fu beaus e bien asis.
　La reine Semiramis,[1]
　Quant ele ot unkes plus aveir
　E plus pussaunce e plus saveir,
85 Ne l'emperere Octovien
　N'esligasent le destre pan.
　Un aigle d'or ot desus mis;
　De cel ne sai dire le pris,
　Ne des cordes ne des peissuns
90 Que del tref tienent les giruns;
　Suz ciel n'ad rei ki[s] esligast
　Pur nul aver k'il i donast.
　Dedenz cel tref fu la pucele:
　Flur de lis, rose nuvele,
95 Quant ele pert al tens d'esté,
　Trespassot ele de beauté.
　Ele jut sur un lit mut bel—
　Li drap valeient un chastel—
　En sa chemise senglement.
100 Mut ot le cors bien fait e gent.
　Un cher mantel de blanc hermine,
　Covert de purpre alexandrine,
　Ot pur le chaut sur li geté.
　Tut ot descovert le costé,
105 Le vis, le col e la peitrine;
　Plus ert blanche que flur d'espine.
　Le chevaler avant ala　　　　　　　　　　　　　[col. b]

1　Semiramis was an Assyrian queen of the ninth century BCE who
　was widely known in classical and medieval legend as a powerful
　warrior and ruler.

and told him their message: 70
"Sir Lanval, my lady,
who is most noble, wise and beautiful,
sends us for you;
now come along with us!
We will take you there safely: 75
look, the pavilion is right close by!"
The knight goes with them;
he takes no heed of his horse,
who is off grazing in the meadow.
They led him up to the tent, 80
which was very beautiful and well situated.
Not Queen Semiramis,
when she had her greatest wealth
and greatest power and greatest wisdom,
nor the emperor Octavian[1] 85
could have bought the right flap.
A golden eagle was set on top;
I can't tell its value,
nor of the cords nor of the stakes
that held the sides of the tent; 90
no king under heaven could buy them
for any wealth he might offer.
Inside the tent was the maiden:
she surpassed in beauty
the lily and the new rose 95
when they appear in summertime.
She lay on a very beautiful bed—
the sheets were worth a castle—
in nothing but her shift.
Her body was very elegant and comely. 100
She had thrown on for warmth
a costly mantle of white ermine,
lined with alexandrine silk.
Her side was entirely uncovered,
her face, her neck and her breast; 105
she was whiter than hawthorn blossom.
The knight went forward

---

1 The historical Gaius Octavius, later Augustus, ruled Rome as
emperor from 27–14 BCE. The thirteenth-century Old French
romance *Octavian,* which presents itself as being about the emperor
but has no relation to his actual biography, may derive from older
vernacular traditions known to Marie.

E la pucele l'apela;
Il s'est devant le lit asis.
110 "Lanval," fet ele, "beus amis,
Pur vus vienc jeo fors de ma tere;
De luinz vus sui venu[e] quere.
Se vus estes pruz e curteis,
Emperere ne quens ne reis
115 N'ot unkes tant joie ne bien;
Kar jo vus aim sur tute rien."
Il l'esgarda, si la vit bele;
Amurs le puint de l'estencele
Que sun quor alume e esprent.
120 Il li respunt avenantment:
"Bele," fet il, "si vus pleiseit
E cele joie me aveneit
Que vus me vousissez amer,
Ja n[e] s[av]riez rien comander
125 Que jeo ne face a mien poeir,
Turt a folie u a saveir.
Jeo frai voz comandemenz;
Pur vus guerpirai tutes genz.
Jamés ne queor de vus partir:
130 Ceo est la rien que plus desir."
Quant la meschine l'oï parler,
Celui que tant la peot amer,
S'amur e sun cors li otreie.
Ore est Lanval en dreite veie!
135 Un dun li ad duné aprés:
Ja cele rien ne vudra mes
Que il nen ait a sun talent.
Doinst e despende largement,
Ele li troverat asez.
140 Mut est Lanval bien herbergez:
Cum plus despendra richement,
Plus averat or e argent.   [f. 135ʳ]
"Ami," fet ele, "or vus chasti,
Si vus comant e si vus pri,
145 Ne vus descovrez a nul humme!
De ceo vus dirai ja la summe:
A tuz jurs m'avriez perdue,
Se ceste amur esteit seüe;
Jamés ne me purriez veeir
150 Ne de mun cors seisine aveir."

and the maiden called to him;
He sat beside the bed.
"Lanval," she said, "handsome friend, 110
for you I have come out of my own land;
I have come from afar to look for you.
If you are valiant and courteous,
no emperor, count, or king
ever had such joy or good fortune; 115
for I love you more than anything."
He looked at her, and saw she was beautiful;
love stings him with a spark
that lights and inflames his heart.
He replies to her becomingly: 120
"Beautiful one," he says, "if it pleased you
and if such joy should come to me
that you should wish to love me,
you could command nothing
that I would not do to the best of my power, 125
be it folly or wisdom.
I will do what you command;
for you I will give up everyone.
I never wish to part from you:
this is the thing I most desire." 130
When the girl heard him speak,
the one who can love her so well,
she grants him her love and her body.
Now Lanval is on the right path!
She gave him still one more gift: 135
he will never again want for anything
but that he will have as much of it as he likes.
Let him give and spend generously:
she will provide him with enough.
Lanval is very well lodged: 140
the more richly he spends,
the more gold and silver he will have.
"Friend," she says, "now I warn you,
I command and beg you,
do not reveal your secret to anyone! 145
I will tell you the whole truth:
you would lose me forever
if this love were known;
you could never see me again
or have possession of my body." 150

Il li respunt que bien tendra
Ceo que ele li comaundera.
Delez li s'est al lit cuchiez:
Ore est Lanval bien herbergez!¹
155 Ensemble od li la relevee
Demurat tresque a l[a] vespree,
E plus i fust, se il poïst
E s'amie lui cunsentist.
"Amis," fet ele, "levez sus!
160 Vus n'i poez demurer plus.
Alez vus en, jeo remeindrai;
Mes un[e] chose vus dirai:
Quant vus vodrez od mei parler,
Ja ne saverez cel liu penser
165 U nuls puist aver sa amie
Sanz repreoce, sanz vileinie,
Que jeo ne vus seie en present
A fere tut vostre talent;
Nul humme fors vus ne me verra
170 Ne ma parole nen orra."
Quant il l'oï, mut en fu liez;
Il la baisa, puis s'est dresciez.
Celes que al tref l'amenerent
De riches dras le cunreerent;
175 Quant il fu vestu de nuvel,
Suz ciel nen ot plus bel dancel.
N'esteit mie fous ne vileins.   [col. b]
L'ewe li donent a ses meins
E la tuaille a suer;
180 Puis li portent a manger.
Od s'amie prist le super:
Ne feseit mie a refuser.
Mut fu servi curteisement,
E il a grant joie le prent.
185 Un entremés i ot plener,
Que mut pleiseit al chevalier:
Kar s'amie baisout sovent
E acolot estreitement.
Quant del manger furent levé,
190 Sun cheval li unt [a]mené.
Bien li unt la sele mise;
Mut ad trové riche servise.

---

1 Because this repeats line 140, above, editors sometimes change it.

He replies that he will certainly hold to
what she commands.
He lay down beside her on the bed:
now Lanval is well lodged!
All afternoon he stayed with her   155
until the evening,
and he would have stayed longer, if he could
and his beloved had allowed him.
"Friend," she says, "get up!
You can't stay here any longer.   160
You go on, I will stay;
but one thing I will tell you:
when you want to talk with me,
there is no place you can think of
where one could have his beloved   165
without reproach or base behavior,
that I will not be with you at once
to do all your will;
no man but you will see me
or hear my words."   170
When he heard this, he was delighted by it;
he kissed her, then got up.
The maidens who brought him to the tent
covered him with rich clothes;
when he was newly dressed,   175
there was no handsomer young man under heaven.
He was not at all foolish or base.
They give him water for his hands
and the towel to dry them;
then they bring him to the table.   180
He took supper with his beloved:
it would not do to refuse.
He was served very courteously,
and he accepts it with great joy.
There was an excellent extra dish   185
that greatly pleased the knight—
for he often kissed his lady
and embraced her closely.
When they had got up from eating,
they brought him his horse.   190
They have put its saddle on well;
it has had excellent care.

Il prent cungé; si est muntez,
Vers la cité s'en est alez.
195 Suvent esgarde ariere sei.
Mut est Lanval en grant esfrei;
De s'aventure vait pensaunt
E en sun curage [d]otaunt.
Esbaïz est, ne seit que creir,
200 Il ne la quide mie a veir.
Il est a sun ostel venuz;
Ses humme[s] treve bien vestuz.
Icele nuit bon ostel tient;
Mes nul ne sot dunt ceo li vient.
205 N'ot en la vile chevalier
Ki de surjur ait grant mestier,
Que il ne face a lui venir
E richement e bien servir.
Lanval donout les riches duns,
210 Lanval aquitout les prisuns,
Lanval vesteit les jugleürs,
Lanval feseit les granz honurs: [f. 135ᵛ]
N'i ot estrange ne privé
A ki Lanval nen ust doné.
215 Mut ot Lanval joie e deduit:
U seit par jur u seit par nuit,
S'amie peot veer sovent,
Tut est a sun comandement.
Ceo m'est avis, memes l'an,
220 Aprés la feste seint Johan,
D[e si] qu'a trente chevalier
Si erent alé esbanier
En un vergier desuz la tur
U la reine ert a surjur.
225 Ensemble od eus [esteit] Walwains
E sis cusins, li beaus Ywains.

He takes his leave; he mounted,
he went toward the city.
Often he looks behind him.   195
Lanval is greatly troubled;
he goes along thinking about his adventure
and worrying to himself.
He is amazed, he doesn't know what to think,
he does not expect that he will see her.[1]   200
He came to his lodging;
he finds his men handsomely dressed.
That night he keeps a rich table,
but no one knew where this came from.
There was no knight in the town   205
who greatly needed sustenance
whom Lanval does not have brought to him
and well and richly served.
Lanval gave rich gifts,
Lanval ransomed prisoners,   210
Lanval clothed minstrels,
Lanval did great honor:
there was no stranger or dear friend
to whom Lanval would not give.
Lanval had great joy and pleasure: 215
he can see his beloved often,
whether by day or by night;
she is entirely at his command.
That same year, as I understand,
after the feast of St. John,[2]   220
about thirty knights
had gone out to enjoy themselves
in an orchard below the tower
where the queen was staying.
Gawain was with them   225
and his cousin, the handsome Yvain.[3]

---

1 This line could also mean "he cannot believe it/she is true," convey-
ing his uncertainty about the reality of his experience (and perhaps
the lady) as well as his uncertainty about whether she will appear to
him again..
2 Given the outdoor setting, this is presumably the feast day of John
the Baptist, 24 June, rather than John the Evangelist, 27 December.
3 Gawain, King Arthur's nephew, is a central figure in Arthurian
romance, often noted for his courtesy. Yvain is the hero of a
romance by Chrétien de Troyes, *Le chevalier au lion* (*The Knight
with the Lion*), in which he is Gawain's close friend, not his cousin.

E dist Walwains, li francs, li pruz,
Que tant se fist amer de tuz:

230 "Par Deu, seignurs, nus feimes mal
De nostre cumpainun Lanval,
Que tant est larges e curteis,
E sis peres est riches reis,
Que od nus ne l'avum [a]mené."

235 Atant se sunt ariere turné;
A sun ostel rev[u]nt ariere,
Lanval ameinent par preere.
A une fenestre entaillie
S'esteit la reine apuïe;

240 Treis dames ot ensemble od li.
La maisné [le rei] choisi;
Lanval choisi e esgarda.
Une des dames apela;
Par li manda ses dameiseles,

245 Les plus quointes, les plus beles:
Od li s'irrunt esbainier
La u cil erent al vergier.
Trente en menat od li e plus;   [col. b]
Par les degrez descendent jus.

250 Les chevalers encuntre vunt,
Que pur eles grant joie unt.
Il les unt prises par les mains;
Cil parle[menz] [n']ert pas vilains.
Lanval s'en vait a une part,

255 Mut luin des autres. Ceo li est tart
Que s'amie puist tenir,
Baiser, acoler e sentir;
L'autrui joie prise petit,
Si il n'ad le suen delit.

260 Quant la reine sul le veit,
Al chevaler en va tut dreit;
Lunc lui s'asist, si l'apela,
Tut sun curage li mustra:
"Lanval, mut vus ai honuré

265 E mut cheri e mut amé.
Tute m'amur poez aveir;
Kar me dites vostre voleir!
Ma druerie vus otrei;
Mut devez estre lié de mei."

270 "Dame," fet il, "lessez m'ester!

And Gawain, the noble, the worthy,
who made himself so beloved by everyone, said,
"By God, my lords, we did wrong
 by our companion Lanval,   230
who is so generous and courteous
and whose father is a rich king.
when we did not bring him with us."
They turned back at once;
they go back to his lodging   235
and persuade Lanval to accompany them.
The queen was leaning
on a window ledge;
she had three ladies along with her.
She looked at the king's household;   240
she looked at Lanval and admired him.
She called one of her ladies;
she had her send for her maidens,
the most elegant and lovely:
they will go with her to enjoy themselves   245
there where the men were in the orchard.
She took more than thirty of them with her;
they go down by the stairs
The knights, who are delighted to see them,
go to meet them.   250
They took the ladies by the hand;
the conversation was not unrefined.
Lanval goes off by himself,
quite far from the others. It seems to him too long
until he might have his beloved,   255
kiss, embrace, and touch her;
the joy of others he values little
if he does not have what pleases him.
When the queen sees him alone,
she goes straight to the knight;   260
she sat by him and addressed him,
she revealed to him all her feelings:
"Lanval, I have honored you greatly
and loved you and held you very dear.
You can have all my love;   265
so tell me your desire!
I grant you my love;
you should be delighted with me."
"Lady," he says, "let me be!

Jeo n'ai cure de vus amer.
Lungement ai servi le rei;
Ne li voil pas mentir ma fei.
Ja pur vus ne pur vostre amur
275 Ne mesfrai a mun seignur."
La reine s'en curuça;
Irie fu, si mesparla.
"Lanval," fet ele, "bien le quit,
Vuz n'amez gueres cel delit.
280 Asez le m'ad humme dit sovent
Que des femmez n'avez talent.
Vallez avez bien afeitiez;
Ensemble od eus vus deduiez.   [f. 136ʳ]
Vileins cüarz, mauveis failliz,
285 Mut est mi sires maubailliz
Que pres de lui vus ad suffert;
Mun escient que Deus en pert!"
Quant il l'oï, mut fu dolent;
Del respundre ne fu pas lent.
290 Teu chose dist par maltalent
Dunt il se repenti sovent.
"Dame," dist il, "de cel mestier
Ne me sai jeo nient aidier;
Mes jo aim, si sui amis
295 Cele ke deit aver le pris
Sur tutes celes que jeo sai.
E une chose vus dirai,
Bien le sachez a descovert:
Une de celes ke la sert,
300 Tute la plus povre meschine,
Vaut meuz de vus, dame reine,
De cors, de vis e de beauté,
D'enseignement e de bunté."
La reine s'en par[t] atant,
305 En sa chambre en vait plurant.
Mut fu dolente e curuciee
De ceo k'il [l']out avilee.
En sun lit malade cucha;
Jamés, ceo dit, ne levera,
310 Si li reis ne l'en feseit dreit

I have no interest in loving you.   270
For a long time I have served the king;
I don't want to betray my faith to him.
Never for you nor for your love
shall I wrong my lord."
The queen grew furious at this;   275
in her anger, she spoke wrongly.
"Lanval," she says, "it's quite clear to me
you have no interest in that pleasure.
People have often told me
that you have no desire for women.   280
You have shapely young men
and take your pleasure with them.
Base coward, infamous wretch,
my lord is greatly harmed
by having allowed you near him;   285
I believe that he will lose God by it!"[1]
When he heard this, he was very distressed;
he was not slow to respond.
Out of anger he said something
that he would often regret.   290
"Lady," he said, "I know nothing
about that line of work;
but I love and am the beloved of
one who should be valued more highly
than all the women I know.   295
And I'll tell you one thing,
know it well and openly:
any one of the girls who serve her,
even the very poorest maid,
is worth more than you, lady queen,   300
in body, face, and beauty,
in manners and goodness."
The queen leaves at once;
she goes into her chamber, crying.
She was very upset and angry   305
about the way he had insulted her.
She took to her bed, sick;
never, she says, will she get up
if the king did not do the right thing

---

1 The queen implies that since Lanval's (supposed) desire for young
   men is a sin, the king's (supposed) toleration of it makes him sinful
   as well—he is tainted by association.

De ceo dunt ele se pleinereit.
Li reis fu del bois repeiriez;
Mut out le jur esté haitiez.
As chambres la reine entra.
315 Quant el le vit, si se clamma;
As piez li chiet, merci crie,
E dit que Lanval l'ad hunie.
De druerie la requist;   [col. b]
Pur ceo que ele l'en escundist,
320 Mut [la] laidi e avila.
De tele amie se vanta,
Que tant iert cuinte e noble e fiëre
Que meuz valut sa chamberere,
La plus povre que [la] serveit,
325 Que la reine ne feseit.
Li reis s'en curuçat forment;
Juré en ad sun serment:
S'il ne s'en peot en curt defendre,
Il le ferat arder u pendre.
330 Fors de la chambre eissi li reis,
De ses baruns apelat treis;
Il les enveit pur Lanval,
Que asez ad dolur e mal.
A sun [o]stel fu revenuz;
335 Il s'est bien aparceüz
Qu'il aveit perdue s'amie:
Descovert ot la druerie.
En une chambre fu tut suls,
Pensis esteit e anguissus;
340 S'amie apele mut sovent,
Mes ceo ne li valut neent.
Il se pleigneit e suspirot,
D'ures en autres se pasmot;
Puis li crie cent feiz merci
345 Que ele par[ol]t a sun ami.
Sun quor e sa buche maudit;
Ceo est merveille k'il ne s'ocit.
Il ne seit tant crier ne braire
Ne debatre ne sei detraire
350 Que ele en veulle merci aveir
Sul tant que la puisse veeir.
Oi las, cument se cuntendra?
Cil ke li reis ci enveia,   [f. 136ᵛ]

about the complaint she would make to him. 310
The king returned from the woods;
he had had a very pleasant day.
He went into the queen's rooms.
When she saw him, she made her appeal;
she falls at his feet and asks for mercy 315
and says that Lanval has shamed her.
He asked her to be his lover;
because she refused him this,
he insulted her and said ugly things.
He boasted of such a beloved, 320
one who was so elegant, noble, and proud,
that her chambermaid,
the poorest girl who served her,
was worth more than the queen.
The king got extremely angry; 325
he swore his oath on this:
if Lanval cannot defend himself in court,
he will have him burnt or hanged.
The king went out of the chamber
and called three of his men; 330
he sends them for Lanval,
who has sorrow and trouble enough.
He had gone back to his lodging;
he fully realized
that he had lost his beloved: 335
he had revealed their love affair.
He was all alone in a chamber,
he was anxious and distraught;
he calls on his beloved over and over,
but it did him no good at all. 340
He lamented and sighed,
he fainted repeatedly;
then a hundred times he begs her to have mercy
and speak to her beloved.
He curses his heart and his mouth; 345
it's a wonder he does not kill himself.
He cannot cry out or wail
or reproach or torment himself
enough to make her want to have mercy on him,
even enough that he might see her. 350
Alas, what will he do?
Those the king sent there

Il sunt venu, si li unt dit
355 Que a la curt voise sanz respit.
Li reis l'aveit par eus mandé;
La reine l'out encusé.
Lanval i vet od sun grant doel;
Il l'eussent ocis [sun] veoil.
360 Il est devant le rei venu;
Mut fu dolent, taisanz e mu,
De grant dolur mustre semblant.
Li reis li dit par maltalant,
"Vassal, vus me avez mut mesfait!
365 Trop començastes vilein plait
De mei hunir e aviler
E la reine lendengier.
Vanté vus estes de folie:
Trop par est noble vostre amie,
370 Quant plus est bele sa meschine
E plus vaillante que la reine."
Lanval defent la deshonur
E la hunte de sun seignur
De mot en mot, si cum il dist,
375 Que la reine ne requist;
Mes de ceo dunt il ot parlé
Reconut il la verité,
De l'amur dunt il se vanta:
Dolent en est, perdue l'a.
380 De ceo lur dit qu'il en ferat
Quanque la curt esgarderat.
Li reis fu mut vers li irez;
Tuz ses hummes ad enveiez
Pur dire dreit quei il en deit faire,
385 [Que] [hum] ne li puis[se] a mal retraire.
Cil unt sun commandement fait,
U eus seit bel, u eus seit lait.
Comunement i sunt alé   [col. b]
E unt jugé e esgardé
390 Que Lanval deit aveir un jur;
Mes plegges truisse a sun seignur
Qu'il atendra sun jugement
E revendra en sun present:
Si serat la curt esforcie[e],
395 Kar n'i ot dunc fors la maisné.
Al rei revienent li barun,

180   LANVAL

arrived, and said to him
that he must go to the court without delay.
The king had sent the order through them;   355
the queen had accused him.
Lanval goes there in his great sorrow;
they could have killed him for all he cared.
He came before the king;
he was very sad, silent and unspeaking,   360
he has the appearance of great sorrow.
The king says to him angrily,
"Vassal, you have done me a great wrong!
You began a very churlish argument
when you shamed and reviled me   365
and insulted the queen.
You boasted foolishly:
your beloved is far too exalted
when her maid is more beautiful
and worthy than the queen."   370
Lanval denies the dishonor
and shame of his lord
word by word, just as he said it,
in that he had not requested the queen's love;
but he acknowledged the truth   375
of what he had said
concerning the love about which he boasted:
he is distressed, for he has lost it.
Concerning this he says that he will do
whatever the court decides.   380
The king was quite furious with him;
he sent for all his men
to say rightly what he should do about this,
so that no one can blame him for it.
They did what he ordered,   385
whether they liked it or not.
They all went off together
and judged and decided
that Lanval should have his day in court;
but he must provide guarantees for his lord   390
that he will await his judgment
and return to his presence:
a larger court will be gathered,
for now there was no one there but the household.
The nobles return to the king   395

Si li mustrent la reisun.
Li reis ad pledges demandé.
Lanval fu sul e esgaré;
400 N'i aveit parent ne ami.
Walwain i vait, ki l'a plevi,
E tuit si cumpainun aprés.
Li reis lur dit: "E jol vus les
Sur quanke vus tenez de mei,
405 Teres e fieus, chescun par sei."
Quant plevi fu, dunc n'ot el;
Alez s'en est a sun ostel.
Li chevaler l'unt conveé;
Mut l'unt blasmé e chastié
410 K'il ne face si grant dolur,
E maudient si fol[e] amur.
Chescun jur l'aloent veer,
Pur ceo k'il voleient saveir
U il beust, u il mangast;
415 Mut dotouent k'il s'afolast.
Al jur que cil orent numé
Li barun furent asemblé.
Li reis e la reine i fu,
E li plegge unt Lanval rendu.
420 Mut furent tuz pur li dolent:
Jeo quid k'il en i ot teus cent
Ki feissent tut lur poeir
Pur lui sanz pleit delivre aveir;   [f. 137ʳ]
Il iert retté a mut grant tort.
425 Li reis demande le recort
Sulunc le cleim e les respuns;
Ore est trestut sur les baruns.
Il sunt al jugement alé;
Mut sunt pensifs e esgaré
430 Del franc humme d'autre païs
Que entre eus ert si entrepris.
Encumbrer le veulent plusur
Pur la volenté sun seignur.
Ceo dist li quoens de Cornwaille:
435 "Ja endreit nu[s] n'i avera faille;

and tell him their judgment.
The king demanded guarantees.
Lanval was alone and forsaken;
he had no relative or friend there.
Gawain goes there, who pledged himself,   400
and all his companions after him.
The king says to them: "I commend him to you
on the basis of whatever you hold of me,
lands and fiefs, each one for himself."[1]
Once the pledge was made, there was nothing more to do;   405
Lanval went off to his lodging.
The knights went along with him;
they greatly rebuked and chastised him
for showing such sorrow,
and they curse such mad love.   410
Every day they would go to see him,
because they wanted to know
whether he was drinking, or if he was eating;
they were greatly afraid that he would go mad.
On the day that they had named   415
the nobles gathered.
The king and queen were there,
and the guarantors brought Lanval.
Everyone was very sad for him:
I believe that there were some hundred there   420
who would have done anything in their power
to free him without a trial;
he was very wrongly accused.
The king asks for the record
of the claim and the rebuttals;   425
now it is entirely up to the nobles.
They went to sit in judgment;
they are very anxious and distressed
over the noble man from another country
who was in such trouble among them.   430
Many want to find him guilty
according to their lord's wishes.
The count of Cornwall said,
"We must not fall short,

---

1 In serving as pledges or sureties for Lanval, Gawain and the other
   knights are, in effect, providing bail: Lanval is released on the
   understanding that they will bring him back safe and sound in time
   for the trial, or give up the lands they hold from the king.

Kar ki que en plurt e ki que en chant,
Le dreit estuet aler avant.
Li reis parla vers sun vassal,
Que jeo vus oi numer Lanval;
440 De felunie le retta
E d'un mesfait l'acheisuna.
Nuls ne l'apele fors le rei;
Par cele fei ke jeo vus dei,
Ki bien en veut dire le veir,
445 Ja n'i deust respuns aveir—
Si pur ceo nun, que a sun seignur
Deit [hum] par tut faire honur,
E ma dame s'en curuça
D'un[e] amur dunt il se vanta.
450 Un serement l'engagera,
E li reis le nus pardura.
E s'il peot aver sun guarant
E s'amie venist avant
E ceo fust veir k'il en deïst,
455 Dunt la reine se marist,
De ceo avera il bien merci,
Quant pur vilté nel dist de li.
E s'il ne peot garant aveir,   [col. b]
Ceo li devum faire saveir:
460 Tut sun servise per[t] del rei,
E sil deit cungeer de sei."
Al chevaler unt enveé,
Si li unt dit e nuntié
Que s'amie face venir
465 Pur lui tencer e garentir.
Il lur dit qu'il ne poeit:
Ja p[a]r li sucurs nen avereit.
Cil s'en rev[un]t as jugeürs,
Ki n'i atendent nul sucurs.
470 Li reis les hastot durement
Pur la reine kis atent.
Quant il deveient departir,
Deus puceles virent venir
Sur deus beaus palefreiz amblanz.
475 Mut par esteient avenanz;
De cendal purpre sunt vestues

for whoever may weep or sing,[1]   435
the law must take precedence.
The king has spoken against his vassal,
whom I hear you call Lanval;
he charged him with a crime
and accused him of wrongdoing.   440
No one accuses him but the king;
by the faith I owe you,
if one wants to tell the truth about this,
there would not even be a case—
except for this, that a man should do honor   445
to his lord in all matters,
and my lady became angry
concerning a love of which he boasted.
He will be bound by oath
and the king will turn him over to us.   450
And if he can have his guarantor—
if his lady should come forward
and it was true what he said about her,
which made the queen angry—
then he will certainly receive mercy,   455
since he did not say it out of baseness.
And if he cannot produce proof,
we must make him understand this:
he will lose all his service to the king
and must take his leave of him."   460
They sent to the knight
and they told him and announced
that he should have his beloved come
to defend and bear witness for him.
He told them that he could not: 465
he would never get help from her.
They go back to the judges,
who expect no help from that quarter.
The king urged them fiercely
for the sake of the queen who is waiting.   470
Just as they were about to give their verdict,
they saw two maidens coming
on two beautiful brisk palfreys.
They were extremely lovely;
they were dressed in nothing but purple taffeta   475

---

1   This is a proverbial expression: "whoever may or may not like it."

Tut senglement a lur char nues.
Cil les esgardouent volenters.
Walwain, od lui treis chevalers,
480 Vait a Lanval, si li cunta;
Les deus puceles li mustra.
Mut fu haitié, forment li prie
Qu'il li deist si ceo ert [s]'amie.
Il lur ad dit ne seit ki sunt
485 Ne dunt vienent ne u eles vunt.
Celes sunt alees avant
Tut a cheval; par tel semblant
Descendirent devant le deis,
La u seeit Artur li reis.
490 Eles furent de grant beuté,
Si unt curteisement parlé:
"Reis, fai tes chambres delivrer
E de palies encurtiner,   [f. 137ᵛ]
U ma dame puïst descendre
495 Si ensemble od vus veut ostel prendre."¹
Il lur otria mut volenters,
Si appela deus chevalers:
As chambres les menerent sus.
A cele feiz ne distrent plus.
500 Li reis demande a ses baruns
Le jugement e les respuns
E dit que mut l'unt curucié
De ceo que tant l'unt delaié.
"Sire," funt il, "nus departimes
505 Pur les dames que nus veïmes,
Ni av[um] nul esgart fait.
Ore recumencerum le plait."
Dunc assemblerent tut pensif;
Asez i ot noise e estrif.
510 Quant il ierent en cel esfrei,
Deus puceles de gent cunrei—
Vestues de deus palies freis,
Chevauchent deus muls espanneis—
Virent venir la rue aval.
515 Grant joie en eurent li vassal;

---

1 These maidens and those who come later address the king with the
informal "tu" ("fai tes chambres delivrer"); this contrasts with the
formal "vus" at the end of the sentence, but the latter could be
intended as a plural "you," meaning the court collectively.

down to their bare skin.
Everyone was gazing at them eagerly.
Gawain, and three knights with him,
goes to Lanval and told him;
he showed him the two maidens.   480
He was very happy, and begs him
to say whether this was his beloved.
Lanval tells them that he does not know who they are
nor where they come from nor where they are going.
The maidens went along   485
on their horses; in this fashion
they dismounted in front of the dais
where King Arthur was sitting.
They were very beautiful
and spoke courteously: 490
"King, have your chambers made ready
and hung with silks
where my lady can dismount
if she wants to take lodging with you."
He very willingly granted this to them,   495
and called two knights:
they led them up to the chambers.
At that time they said no more.
The king asks his nobles
for the verdict and the rebuttals   500
and says that they have made him very angry
by delaying for so long.
"Sire," they say, "we broke off our discussion
on account of the ladies that we saw,
nor have we made a decision.   505
Now we will resume the trial."
Then they gathered, quite concerned;
there was a great deal of noise and debate.
While they were in this disarray,
they saw two maidens of noble bearing,   510
dressed in two light silk dresses,
riding two Spanish mules,
coming down the road.
The vassals were delighted by this;

Entre eus dient que ore est gariz
Lanval, li pruz e li hardiz.
Yweins i est a lui alez,
Ses cumpainuns i ad menez.
520 "Sire," fet il, "rehaitiez vus!
Pur amur Deu, parlez od nus!
Ici vienent deus dameiseles
Mut acemees e mut beles:
Ceo est vostre amie vereiment!"
525 Lanval respunt hastivement
E dit qu'il pas nes avuot
Ne il nes cunut ne nes amot.
Atant furent celes venues;   [col. b]
Devant le rei sunt descendues.
530 Mut les loerent li plusur
De cors, de vis e de colur;
N'i ad cele meuz ne vausist
Que unkes la reine ne fist.
L'aisnee fu curteise e sage;
535 Avenantment dist sun message:
"Reis, kar nus fai chambres baillier
A oés ma dame herbergier;
Ele vient ici a tei parler."
Il les cumande amener
540 Od les autres que ainceis v[i]ndrent;
Unkes des muls nul plai ne tindrent.
Quant il fu d'eles deliverez,
Puis ad tuz ses baruns mandez
Que le jugement seit renduz:
545 Trop ad le jur esté tenuz.
La reine s'en curuceit,
Que si lunges les atendeit.
Ja departissent a itant,
Quant par la vile vient errant
550 Tut a cheval une pucele:
En tut le secle n'ot plus bele.
Un blanc palefrei chevachot,
Que bel e suef la portot.
Mut ot bien fet e col e teste:
555 Suz ciel nen ot plus bele beste.
Riche atur ot al palefrei:
Suz ciel nen ad quens ne rei
Ki tut peust eslegier

they say to each other that now Lanval,   515
the bold and strong, is saved.
Yvain went to him,
taking his companions with him.
"Sir," he says, "rejoice!
For the love of God, speak to us!   520
Here come two maidens,
very elegant and beautiful:
surely it is your beloved!"
Lanval responds hastily
and says that he did not recognize them   525
nor did he know them or love them.
Just then the maidens arrived;
they dismounted before the king.
Many people greatly praised
their bodies, faces and coloring;   530
both of them were certainly worth
more than the queen ever was.
The elder was courteous and wise;
she spoke her message becomingly:
"King, provide rooms for us   535
in order to receive my lady;
she is coming here to speak to you."
He orders that they be taken
to the others who arrived earlier;
they did not need to worry about the mules.   540
When he had sent them off,
he ordered all his nobles
that the verdict be given:
too much of the day had been taken up.
The queen was getting angry   545
that she was kept waiting so long by them.
They were about to take a decision,
when through the town
a maiden comes riding on a horse:
in all the world there was none more beautiful.   550
She rode a white palfrey,
which carried her well and gently.
It had a well-shaped neck and head:
there was no handsomer animal under heaven.
The palfrey was richly harnessed: 555
no count or king under heaven
could have afforded the whole thing

Sanz tere vendre u engagier.
560 Ele iert vestue en itel guise:
De chainsil blanc e de chemise
Que tuz les costez li pareient,
Que de deus parz laciez esteient.   [f. 138ʳ]
Le cors ot gent, basse la hanche,
565 Le col plus blanc que neif sur branche;
Les oilz ot vairs e blanc le vis,
Bele buche, neis bien asis,
Les surcilz bruns e bel le frunt
E le chef cresp e aukes blunt;
570 Fil d'or ne gette tel luur
Cum s[i] chev[e]l cuntre le jur.
Sis manteus fu de purpre bis;
Les pans en ot entur li mis.
Un espervier sur sun poin tient,
575 E un leverer aprés [li] vient.
Il n'ot al burc petit ne grant
Ne li veillard ne li enfant
Que ne l'alassent esgarder.
Si cum il la veent errer,
580 De sa beauté n'iert mie gas.
Ele veneit meins que le pas.
Li jugeur, que la veeient,
A merveille le teneient;
Il n'ot un sul ki l'esgardast
585 De dreite joie ne s'eschaufast.
Cil ki le chevaler amoent
A lui veneient, si li cuntouent
De la pucele ki veneit,
Si Deu plest, que le delivereit:
590 "Sire cumpain, ci en vient une,
Mes el n'est pas fave ne brune;
Ceo'st la plus bele del mund,
De tutes celes ke i sunt."
Lanval l'oï, sun chief dresça;
595 Bien la cunut, si suspira.
Li sanc li est munté al vis;
De parler fu aukes hastifs.
"Par fei," fet il, "ceo est m'amie!   [col. b]
Or m'en est gueres ki m'ocie,

without selling or mortgaging land.
She was dressed in this manner:
in a white cloak and shift   560
which let both her sides be seen,
as they were laced on either side.
She had a lovely body, a long waist,
a neck whiter than snow on a branch;
she had sparkling eyes and white skin,   565
a beautiful mouth, a well-formed nose,
dark eyebrows and a lovely forehead
and curling golden hair;
no golden thread casts such a gleam
as did her hair against the sun.   570
Her mantle was dark purple;
she had wrapped its ends around her.
She holds a sparrowhawk on her fist,
and a greyhound runs behind her.[1]
There was no one in the town, great or small,   575
not the old men nor the children,
who did not go to look at her.
As they saw her pass,
there was no joking about her beauty.
She came along quite slowly.   580
The judges, who saw her,
considered it a wonder;
there was not one who looked at her
who did not grow warm with true joy.
Those who loved the knight   585
came to him, and told him
of the maiden who was coming,
who, if it pleased God, would set him free:
"Sir, companion, here comes one
who is not tawny nor dark;   590
she's the loveliest in the world
of all the women there are."
Lanval heard this, he lifted his head;
he knew her well, and sighed.
The blood rose to his face;   595
he was very quick to speak.
"In faith," he said, "it is my beloved!
Now I care little who may kill me,

---

1 The sparrowhawk and the greyhound are both typically courtly
 animals and thus markers of high status.

600 Si ele n'ad merci de mei;
　　Kar gariz sui, quant jeo la vei."
　　La dame entra al palais;
　　Unc si bele n'i vient mais.
　　Devant le rei est descendue
605 Si que de tuz iert bien ve[u]e.
　　Sun mantel ad laissié cheir,
　　Que meuz la puissent veer.
　　Li reis, que mut fu enseigniez,
　　Il s'est encuntre l[i] dresciez,
610 E tuit li autre l'enurerent,
　　De li servir se presenterent.
　　Quant il l'orent bien esgardee
　　E sa beauté forment loee,
　　Ele parla en teu mesure,
615 Kar de demurer nen ot cure:
　　"Reis, jeo ai amé un tuen vassal:
　　Veez le ici, ceo est Lanval!
　　Acheisuné fu en ta curt.
　　Ne vuil mie que a mal li turt
620 De ceo qu'il dist; ceo sachez tu
　　Que la reine ad tort eü:
　　Unc nul jur ne la requist.
　　De la vantance ke il fist,
　　Si par me peot estre aquitez,
625 Par voz baruns seit deliverez!"
　　Ceo qu'il jugerunt par dreit
　　Li reis otrie ke issi seit.
　　N'i ad un sul que n'ait jugié
　　Que Lanval ad tut desrainié.
630 Deliverez est par lur esgart,
　　E la pucele s'en depart.
　　Ne la peot li reis retenir;
　　Asez gent ot a li servir.　　　　　　　　　　[f. 138ᵛ]
　　Fors de la sale aveient mis
635 Un grant perrun de marbre bis,
　　U li pesant humme muntoent,
　　Que de la curt le rei venoent:
　　Lanval esteit munté desus.
　　Quant la pucele ist fors a l'us,
640 Sur le palefrei, detriers li,
　　De plain eslais Lanval sailli.

if she does not have mercy on me;
for I am cured when I see her."   600
The lady entered the palace;
never had one so beautiful come there.
She dismounted before the king
so that she could easily be seen by all.
She let her mantle fall   605
so that they could see her better.
The king, who was very well-bred,
got up to meet her,
and all the others honored her
and offered themselves to serve her.   610
When they had looked at her well
and greatly praised her beauty,
she spoke in this way,
for she did not wish to stay:
"King, I have fallen in love with one of your vassals: 615
you see him here, it is Lanval!
He was accused in your court.
I do not wish it to be held against him,
concerning what he said; you should know
that the queen was wrong: 620
he never asked for her love.
And concerning the boast he made,
if he can be acquitted by me,
let your nobles set him free!"
Whatever they judge by law,   625
the king grants that it shall be so.
There is not one who does not judge
that Lanval has completely won his case.
He is freed by their decision,
and the maiden takes her leave.   630
The king could not keep her;
she had enough people to serve her.
Outside the hall they had put
a great block of dark marble,
where heavy men would mount   635
who were coming from the king's court:
Lanval had climbed up on it.
When the maiden went out the gate,
with one leap Lanval
jumped on the palfrey, behind her.   640

Od li s'en vait en Avalun,
Ceo nus recuntent li bretun,
En un isle que mut est beaus;
645 La fu ravi li dameiseaus.
Nul humme n'en oï plus parler,
Ne jeo n'en sai avant cunter.

With her he goes to Avalon,
so the Britons tell us,[1]
to a very beautiful island;
the young man was carried off there.
No one ever heard another word of him,   645
and I can tell no more.

---

1 Avalon is mentioned in Geoffrey of Monmouth's *History of the Kings of Britain* as the origin of Arthur's sword Excalibur and as the place he goes to recover from his mortal wounds; it is generally regarded as an otherworldly place. Its broad association with Brythonic Celtic traditions (from Wales, Cornwall, and Brittany) and the setting of this lai in Britain leads me to translate "bretun" here as "Britons" rather than the usual "Bretons." See Introduction, pp. 16–17.

Deus Amanz

*Jadis avint en Normendie
Une aventure mut oïe
De deus [enf]anz† que s'entramerent;
Par amur ambedeus finerent.
5   Un lai en firent li bretun:
De *Deus Amanz* recuilt le nun.
Verité est ke en Neustrie,
Que nus apelum Normendie,
Ad un haut munt merveilles grant:
10   La sus gisent li dui enfant.
Pres de cel munt a une part
Par grant cunseil e par esgart
Une cité fist faire uns reis
Que esteit sire de Pistreis;
15   Des Pistreins la fist numer
E Pistre la fist apeler.
Tuz jurs ad puis duré li nuns;
Uncore i ad vile e maisuns.
Nus savum bien de la contree,
20   Li vals de Pistre est nomee.
Li reis ot une fille bele,   [col. b]
Mut curteise dameisele.

---

*   This lai appears on ff. 138va–140rb of Harley 978. In the upper
margin the later hand has titled it "Deus amaunz."

†   Here and throughout, square brackets in the text indicate an emen-
dation to the text as it appears in Harley 978; the original reading
can be found, keyed to the line number, in Appendix F.

The Two Lovers

Once there happened in Normandy
an adventure widely retold
concerning two children who loved one another;
both of them died for love.
The Bretons made a lai of it:[1]   5
it got the name *The Two Lovers*.
It is true that in Neustria,
which we call Normandy,[2]
there is a high mountain, marvelously large:
the two children lie upon it.   10
Near this mountain, on one side,
by great counsel and with care
a king who was lord of Pistreis
had a city made;
he had it named for the Pistrians   15
and had it called Pistre.[3]
The name then lasted forever after;
there is still a town and houses.
We know the region well;
it is called the valley of Pistre.   20
The king had a beautiful daughter,
a very courteous maiden.[4]

---

1 As is the case elsewhere, "bretun" may refer specifically to Bretons,
  but could also be a more general reference to a "Brittonic" tradition.
2 As Marie says, in her time the name "Neustrie" was applied to the
  area we now call Normandy, in northwest France. However, the
  name Neustria originally referred to a larger region—the western
  part of the Frankish kingdoms—in the sixth to eighth centuries; it
  bordered on the Breton areas, now Brittany, that form the north-
  westernmost part of modern France.
3 Pîtres still exists; it is a small town in Upper Normandy.
4 In BnF nouv. acq. fr. 1104, known as manuscript S, and in the Old
  Norse translation, after this line follow eight lines that do not appear
  in MS Harley 978 but that make the story more comprehensible.
  They read, "Filz ne fille fors lui n'avoit; / Forment l'amoit e chieris-
  soit. / De riches hommes fu requise, / Qui volentiers l'eussent prise; /
  Mes li rois ne la volt donner, / Car ne s'em pooit consirer. / Li rois
  n'avoit autre retor; / Pres de li estoit nuit et jor": "He had no other
  son or daughter apart from her; / he loved and cherished her greatly.
  / She was wooed by rich men / who would willingly have taken her, /
  but the king did not want to give her up, / because he could not do
  without her. / The king had no one else to turn to; / she was close to
  him night and day." I modify the French text from Ewert 178.

Cunfortez fu par la meschine,
Puis que perdue ot la reine.
25 Plusurs a mal li aturnerent,
Li suen meisné le blamerent.
Quant il oï que hum en parla,
Mut fu dolent, mut li pesa;
Cumença sei a purpenser
30 Cument s'en purrat deliverer
Que nul sa fille ne quesist.
Luinz e pres manda e dist,
Ki sa fille vodreit aveir,
Une chose seust de veir:
35 Sortit esteit e destiné,
Desur le munt fors la cité
Entre ses braz la portereit,
Si que ne se reposereit.
Quant la nuvele est seüe
40 E par tut la cuntree espandue,
Asez plusurs s'i as[ai]erent
Que nule rien n'i espleiterent,
Teus que tant s'esforçouent
Que en mi le munt la portoent;
45 Ne poeient avant aler,
Iloec l'esteut laissier ester.
Lung tens remist cele a doner,
Que nul ne la volt demander.
Al païs ot un damisel,
50 Fiz a un cunte, gent e bel;
De bien faire pur aveir pris
Sur tuz autres s'est entremis.
En la curt le rei conversot,
Asez sovent i surjurnot;
55 La fille al rei ama,
E meintefeiz l'areisuna   [f. 139ʳ]
Que ele s'amur li otriast
E par druerie l'amast.
Pur ceo ke pruz [fu] e curteis
60 E que mut le presot li reis,
[Li otria sa druerie,
E cil humblement l'en mercie.]

He was comforted by the girl,
since he had lost the queen.
Many people held it against him,   25
his own household blamed him for it.
When he heard that people were talking about this,
he was very sad, it weighed on him greatly;
he began to give careful thought
to how he can free himself   30
from having anyone ask for his daughter.
Far and near he sent out and said
that anyone who would like to have his daughter
must know one thing for certain:
it was set down and destined that   35
up the mountain outside the city
he must carry her in his arms
without resting.
When the news was known
and spread throughout the whole country,   40
a great many tried it
who could by no means achieve it,
some who pushed themselves so hard
that they carried her halfway up the mountain;
they could go no further,   45
they had to give up there.
For a long time she was still to be given away,
for no one wanted to ask for her.
In that country there was a youth,
the son of a count, noble and handsome;   50
he undertook to do well
so as to have renown above all others.
He lived in the king's court,
quite often he stayed there;
he loved the king's daughter,   55
and many times he asked her
to grant him her love
and accept him as her beloved.
Because he was worthy and courteous
and the king valued him greatly,   60
she granted him her love,
and he humbly thanked her for it.[1]

---

1   These two lines, which complete the idea begun in the previous
    two, do not appear in Harley 978; I supply them here as they
    appear in manuscript S, from Ewert 76, ll. 61–62.

Ensemble parlerent sovent
E s'entreamerent lëaument
65 E celereient a lur poeir,
Que hum nes puist aparceveir.
La suffrance mut lur greva;
Mes li vallez se purpensa
Que meuz en volt les maus suffrir
70 Que trop haster e dunc faillir.
Mut fu pur li amer destreiz.
Puis avient si que a une feiz
Que a s'amie vient li damiseus,
Que tant est sages, pruz e beus;
75 Sa pleinte li mustrat e dist:
Anguissusement li requist
Que s'en alast ensemble od lui,
Ne poeit mes suffrir l'enui.
Si a sun pere la demandot,
80 Il saveit bien que tant l'amot
Que pas ne li vodreit doner
Si il ne la puist porter
Entre ses braz en sum le munt.
La damisele li respunt:
85 "Amis," fait ele, "jeo sai bien,
Ne me porteriez pur rien:
N'estes mie si vertuus.
Si jo m'en vois ensemble od vus,
Mis peres avereit e doel e ire,
90 Ne vivereit mie sanz martire.
Certes, tant l'eim e si l'ai chier,
Jeo nel vodreie curucier.
Autre cunseil vus estuet prendre,   [col. b]
Kar cest ne voil jeo pas entendre.
95 En Salerne ai une parente,
Riche femme, mut ad grant rente;
Plus de trente anz i ad esté.
L'art de phisike ad tant usé
Que mut est saives de mescines:
100 Tant cunust herbes e racines,
Si vus a li volez aler
E mes lettres od vus porter

They often spoke together
and loved one another loyally
and hid it as best they could, 65
so that no one would notice them.
The suffering weighed on them greatly;
but the youth decided
that he would rather suffer these pains from it
than hurry too much and so fail. 70
He was greatly distressed by his love for her.
Then it so happens that one time the young man,
who is so wise, worthy, and handsome,
comes to his beloved;
he presented and told her his lament: 75
he begged her desperately
to go away along with him,
he could not bear the strain any longer.
If he asked her father for her,
he knew well that he loved her so much 80
that he would not want to give her up
if the youth could not carry her
in his arms to the top of the mountain.
The maiden replies to him:
"Friend," she says, "I know well 85
you could not carry me by any means.
you are not strong enough.
If I go away with you,
my father would be sad and angry,
he would live only with great torment. 90
Truly, I love him so much and he is so dear to me
I would not wish to anger him.
You must follow another plan,
for I do not want to hear about this one.
In Salerno I have a relative, 95
a rich woman, she has great wealth;
she has been there more than thirty years.[1]
She has practiced the art of medicine so long
that she is very expert in cures:
she knows so much about herbs and roots, 100
if you want to go to her
and take my letters with you

---

1 Salerno, on the western coast of southern Italy, was well known as a
   center of medical expertise by the eleventh century.

E mustrer li vostre aventure,
Ele en prendra cunseil e cure;
105 Teus lettuaires vus durat
E teus beivres vus baillerat
Que tut vus recunforterunt
E bone vertu vus durrunt.
Quant en cest païs revendrez,
110 A mun pere me requerez;
Il vus en tendrat pur enfant,
Si vus dirat le cuvenant:
Que a nul humme ne me durrat,
Ja cele peine n'i mettrat,
115 Si al munt ne me peust porter
Entre ses braz sanz resposer."
Li vallez oï la novele
E le cunseil a la pucele;
Mut en fu liez, si l'en mercie.
120 Cungé demande a s'amie,
En sa cuntree en est alez.
Hastivement s'est aturnez
De riche[s] dras e de d[eni]ers,
De palefreiz e de sumers.
125 De ses hummes les plus privez
Ad li danzeus od sei menez.
A Salerne vait surjurner,
A l'aunte s'amie vet parler;   [f. 139ᵛ]
De sa part li dunat un brief.
130 Quant el l'ot lit de chief en chief,
Ensemble od li l'a retenu
Tant que sun estre ad t[u]t seü.
Par mescines l'ad esforcié,
Un tel beivre li ad chargié,
135 Ja ne serat tant travaillez
Ne si ateint ne si chargiez,
Ne li resfreschist tut le cors,
Neïs les vaines ne les os,
E qu'il nen ait t[ut]e vertu,

and tell her your situation,[1]
she will give it her thought and care;
she will give you such cordials   105
and will provide you with such draughts
that they will fortify you completely
and will give you good strength.
When you come back to this country,
ask my father for me;   110
he will consider you a child,
and will tell you the agreement:
that he will give me to no man,
no matter how hard he tries,
unless he can carry me up the mountain   115
in his arms without resting."[2]
The youth heard the account
and the advice of the maiden;
he was very happy with it, and thanked her for it.
He asks leave of his beloved   120
and went away to his land.
Quickly he provided himself
with rich clothing and money,
with palfreys and packhorses.
The young man took with him   125
his closest retainers.
He goes to stay in Salerno,
he goes to speak to the aunt of his beloved;
on her behalf he gave her a letter.
When she had read it start to finish,   130
she kept him with her
until she knew his constitution thoroughly.
She strengthened him with medicines,
she entrusted him with such a draught
that he will never be so worn out,   135
so exhausted or overwhelmed,
that it will not entirely refresh his body,
even the veins and bones,
and that he will not have full strength

---

1 The word I have translated as "situation" is the loaded term *aven-
ture*; see the discussion in the Note on the Text, pp. 44–45.
2 Here again there are two lines in manuscript S that do not appear
in Harley 978: "Si li otroie bonement, / Que il ne puet estre
autrement": "Grant him this willingly, for it cannot be otherwise."
Ewert 178.

140 Si tost cum il en avra beü.
　　 Puis le remeine en sun païs;
　　 Le beivre ad en un vessel mis.
　　 Li damiseus, joius e liez,
　　 Quant ariere fu repeiriez,
145 Ne surjurnat pas en la tere.
　　 Al rei alat sa fille quere:
　　 Qu'il li donast, il la prendreit,
　　 En sum le munt la portereit.
　　 Li reis ne l'en escundist mie,
150 Mes mut le tint a grant folie,
　　 Pur ceo qu'il iert de jeofne eage:
　　 Tant produm vaillant e sage
　　 Unt asaié icel afaire
　　 Ki n'en purent a nul chef traire.
155 Terme li ad numé e pris,
　　 Ses humme[s] mande e ses amis
　　 E tuz ceus k'il poeit aveir:
　　 N'en i laissa nul remaneir.
　　 Pur sa fille, pur le vallet
160 Ki en aventure se met
　　 De li porter en sum le munt,
　　 De tutes parz venuz i sunt.
　　 La dameisele s'aturna:　　　　　　　　　　　[col. b]
　　 Mut se destreint e mut jeüna
165 [A sun] manger pur alegier,
　　 Que od sun ami voleit aler.
　　 Al jur quant tuz furent venu,
　　 Li damisels primer i fu;
　　 Sun beivre n'i ublia mie.
170 Devers Seigne en la praerie
　　 En la grant gent tut asemblee
　　 Li reis ad sa fille menee.
　　 N'ot drap vestu fors la chemise;
　　 Entre ses braz l'aveit cil prise.
175 La fiolete od tut sun beivre—
　　 Bien seit que ele nel vout pas deceivre—
　　 En sa mein porter li baille.
　　 Mes jo creim que poi li vaille,

as soon as he has drunk of it.   140
Then he takes it back to his country;
he put the draught in a bottle.
The young man, joyful and happy,
when he had returned back there,
did not stay in the countryside.   145
He went to ask the king for his daughter:
that he should give her to him, he would take her,
he would carry her to the top of the mountain.
The king did not by any means refuse him,
but he considered it a very great folly,   150
since he was of a young age:
so many valiant, wise men
had tried this business
who could not finish it at all.
He gave him a set time,   155
he sends for his retainers and his friends
and everyone he could get:
he did not let anyone stay behind.
For his daughter, for the young man
who risks himself[1]   160
by carrying her to the top of the mountain,
they came from everywhere.
The damsel prepared herself:
she deprived herself greatly and fasted strictly
at her meals to grow lighter,   165
for she wanted to go with her beloved.
On the day when everyone had come,
the youth was the first one there;
he did not by any means forget his draught.
Before the Seine, on the meadow,   170
among the great crowd all gathered there
the king led his daughter.
She had not put on a thing but her shift;
the youth took her in his arms.
He gives her, to carry in her hand,   175
the little vial with all his draught;
he knows well that she does not want to trick him.
But I fear that it will avail him little,

---

1 Here again the word in French is *aventure*; "to put oneself in adven-
   ture" (*se mettre en aventure*) means to endanger oneself, but the term
   connects the young man to many others in the *Lais* who hazard
   themselves in the pursuit of love.

Kar n'ot en lui point de mesure.
180 Od li s'en veit grant aleüre,
Le munt munta de si qu'en mi.
Pur la joie qu'il ot de li
De sun beivre ne li membra.
Ele senti qu'il alaissa.
185 "Amis," fet ele, "kar bevez!
Jeo sai bien que vus lassez:
Si recuverez vostre vertu!"
Li damisel ad respundu:
"Bele, jo sent tut fort mun quer:
190 Ne m'arestereie a nul fuer
Si lungement que jeo beusse,
Pur quei treis pas aler peusse.
Ceste gent nus escri[e]reent,
De lur noise m'esturdireient;
195 Tost me purreient desturber.
Jo ne voil pas ci arester."
Quant les deus parz fu munté sus,
Pur un petit qu'il ne chiet jus.   [f. 140ʳ]
Sovent li prie la meschine:
200 "Ami, bevez vostre mescine!"
Ja ne la volt oïr ne creire;
A grant anguisse od tut l[i] eire.
Sur le munt vint; tant se greva,
Ileoc cheï, puis ne leva:
205 Li quors del ventre s'en parti.
La pucele vit sun ami,
Quida k'il fust en paumeisuns;
Lez lui se met en genuilluns,
Sun beivre li voleit doner;
210 Mes il ne pout od li parler.
Issi murut cum jeo vus di.
Ele le pleint a mut haut cri;
Puis ad geté e espaundu
Li veissel u le beivre fu.
215 Li muns en fu bien arusez,
Mut en ad esté amendez
Tut le païs e la cuntree:
Meinte bone herbe i unt trovee
Ki del beivre orent racine.
220 Ore vus dirai de la meschine:
Puisque sun ami ot perdu,

for there is no moderation in him.
He goes along with her at a great speed, 180
he climbed midway up the mountain.
From the joy he had in her
he did not remember about his draught.
She felt that he grew tired.
"Beloved," she said, "now drink! 185
I know well that you are getting tired:
so recover your strength!"
The youth replied,
"Beautiful one, I feel my heart quite strong:
I would not by any means stop 190
long enough to drink,
for I could go three steps in that time.
These people would cry out to us,
they would stun me with their noise;
they could easily upset me. 195
I do not want to stop here."
When he had gone up two parts of the way,
he could hardly keep from falling down.
The girl begs him often:
"Beloved, drink your medicine!" 200
He did not want to hear or believe her;
with great anguish he goes on with her.
He reached the summit; he exhausted himself so,
there he fell, he rose no more:
the heart left his breast. 205
The maiden saw her beloved,
she thought he was in a faint;
she gets on her knees beside him,
she tried to give him his draught;
but he could not speak to her. 210
So he died just as I tell you.
She laments him with a loud cry;
then she threw and poured out
the vessel that the draught was in.
The mountain was well watered with it, 215
all that area of the country
was greatly bettered by it:
they found many good herbs there
that had their roots in the draught.
Now I will tell you about the girl: 220
when she had lost her beloved,

Unkes si dolente ne fu;
Lez lui se cuche e estent,
Entre ses braz l'estreint e prent,
225 Suvent li baise oilz e buche;
Li dols de li al quor la tuche.
Ilec murut la dameisele,
Que tant ert pruz e sage e bele.
Li reis e cil [kis] atendeient,
230 Quant unt veu qu'il ne veneient,
Vunt aprés eus, sis unt trovez.
Li reis chiet a tere paumez.
Quant pot parler, grant dol demeine,   [col. b]
[E] si firent la gent foreine.
235 Treis jurs les unt tenu sur tere.
Sarcu de marbre firent quere,
Les deus enfanz unt mis dedenz.
Par le cunseil de cele genz
Sur le munt les enfuirent,
240 E puis atant se departirent.
Pur l'aventure des enfaunz
Ad nun li munz des Deus Amanz.
Issi avint cum dit vus ai;
Li bretun en firent un lai.

she had never been so sad;
beside him she lies down and stretches out,
she takes him and clasps him in her arms,
often she kisses his eyes and mouth; 225
sorrow for him touches her heart.
There the damsel died,
who was so worthy and wise and beautiful.
The king and those who were waiting for them,
when they saw that they were not coming, 230
went after them, and found them.
The king falls to the ground in a faint.
When he could speak, he shows great sorrow,
and so did the people from elsewhere.
Three days they kept them above ground. 235
They had a marble tomb brought,
they put the two children inside.
At the advice of these people
they buried them on top of the mountain,
and then went away at once. 240
From the story of the children
the mountain has the name Two Lovers.
So it happened as I have told you;
the Bretons made a lai of it.

Yonec

*Puis que des lais ai comencé,
Ja n'iert par mun travail laissé;
Les aventures que jeo en sai
Tut par rime les cunterai.
5 Enpris ai e en talent
Que d'Iwenec vus die avant,
Dunt il fu nez, e de sun pere
Cum il avint primes a sa mere;
Cil ki engendra Yuuenec
10 Aveit a nun Muldumarec.
En Bretain maneit jadis
Un riches hum viel e antis;
De Carwent fu avouez
E del païs sire clamez.
15 (La cité siet sur Düelas;
Jadis i ot de nes trespas.)
Mut fu tresp[as]sez† en eage.
Pur ceo k'il ot bon heritage,
Femme prist pur enfanz aveir,
20 Que aprés lui fuissent si heir.
De haute gent fu la pucele,
Sage, curteise e forment bele,
Que al riche hume fu donee.
Pur sa beauté l'ad mut amee.   [f. 140ᵛ]
25 De ceo ke ele ert bele e gente,
En li garder mist tute s'entente:
Dedenz sa tur l'ad enserre[e]
En une grant chambre pavee.
Il ot une sue serur,
30 Veille e vedue, sanz seignur;
Ensemble od la dame l'ad mise
Pur li tenir meuz en justise.
Autres femmes i ot, ceo crei,

---

*   This lai appears on ff. 140ʳᵇ–144ʳᵇ of Harley 978. The title given in
     the upper margin by the later hand is "Ywenet."
†   Here and throughout, square brackets in the text indicate an emen-
     dation to the text as it appears in Harley 978; the original reading
     can be found, keyed to the line number, in Appendix F.

Yonec

Since I have begun some lais,
I will never leave off my work;
the adventures[1] that I know of them
I will tell all in rhyme.
I have undertaken and intend 5
to tell you now of Yonec,
of where he was born, and of how his father
first appeared to his mother;
the one who fathered Yonec
was named Muldumarec. 10
In Britain there lived once
a rich and very elderly man;
he was recognized as lord of Caerwent
and acknowledged ruler of the region.
(The city sits on Düelas; 15
Once there was ship traffic there.[2])
He was very far along in age.
Because he had a great deal to leave,
he took a wife so as to have children
who would be his heirs after him 20
The maiden was of noble family,
wise, courteous, and very beautiful,
who had been given to this rich man.
He loved her very much for her beauty.
Because she was beautiful and well-born, 25
he put all his care into guarding her:
he closed her up in his tower
in a great stone-floored chamber.
He had a sister of his,
old and widowed, without a husband; 30
he put her in with the lady
to keep her better under guard.
There were other women, I believe,

---

1 On the word *aventure* and its various meanings, see Note on the
   Text, pp. 44–45; here as in other cases it refers particularly to the
   events that constitute the basis of the lai.
2 Caerwent is in Monmouthshire, England, on the Welsh border; it was
   a substantial settlement beginning in pre-Roman Britain and through
   the early Middle Ages. Düelas, apparently the name of a river, has not
   been identified, though there is a river Daoulas in Brittany (northwest-
   ern France) whose name Marie may borrow here.

En un[e] autre chambre par sei;
35 Mes ja la dame n'i parlast,
Si la vielle ne comandast.
Issi la tient plus de set anz.
Unques entre eus n'eurent enfanz
Ne fors de cele tur ne eissi
40 Ne pur parent ne pur ami.
Quant li sires se ala cuchier,
N'i ot chamberlenc ne huisser
Ki en la chambre osast entrer
Ne devant li cirge alumer.
45 Mut ert la dame en grant tristur;
Od lermes, od suspir e plur
Sa beuté pert en teu mesure
Cume cele que n'en ad cure.
De sei meisme meuz vousist
50 Que mort hastive la preisist.
Ceo fu al meis de avril entrant,
Quant cil oisel meinent lur chant.
Li sires fu matin levez;
De aler en bois s'est aturnez.
55 La vielle ad fet lever sus
E aprés lui fermer les hus.
Cele ad fet sun comandement.
Li sires s'en vet od sa gent;
La vielle portot sun psauter,   [col. b]
60 U ele voleit verseiller.
La dame, [en] plur e [en e]sveil,
Choisi la clarté del soleil.
De la vielle est aparceüe
Que de la chambre esteit eissue.
65 Mut se pleineit e suspirot
E en plurant se dementot:
"Lasse," fait ele, "mar fui nee!
Mut est dure ma destinee.
En ceste tur sui en prisun,
70 Ja n'en istrai si par mort nun.
Cist viel gelus, de quei se crient,
Que en si grant prisun me tient?
Mut par est fous e esbaïz,

in another chamber on their own;
but the lady never spoke to them   35
unless the old woman told her to.
He kept her like that for more than seven years.
They never had any children
nor did she ever leave the tower
for either relative or friend.   40
When the lord went to bed,
there was no chamberlain or doorkeeper
who dared enter the chamber
or light a candle in front of him.
The lady was very sad;   45
with tears, with laments and weeping
she loses her beauty in the manner
of someone who does not care for it.
For her part, she would prefer
that death should take her quickly.   50
This was at the beginning of the month of April,
when the birds put forth their song.
The lord had got up that morning;
he made ready to go to the woods.
He had the old woman get up   55
and close the doors after him.
She did as he told her.
The lord goes off with his people;
the old woman took her psalter
so that she could sing her psalms.[1]   60
The lady, in tears and wakeful,
glimpsed the brightness of the sun.
She noticed that the old woman
had left the room.
She mourned and sighed greatly   65
and, weeping, she lamented:
"Wretched me," she said, "I was born in an evil hour!
My destiny is very harsh.
I am imprisoned in this tower,
I will never leave it except through death.   70
This jealous old man, what is he afraid of,
who keeps me in such a strong prison?
He is completely mad and foolish,

---

1   A psalter is a book containing the biblical Psalms; such books were
    increasingly used as personal prayer books by laypeople starting in
    the late eleventh century.

Il crient tuz jurs estre trahiz.
75 Jeo ne puis al muster venir
Ne le servise Deu oïr.
Si jo puisse od gent parler
E en deduit od eus aler,
Jo li mustrasse beu semblant,
80 Tut n'en eusse jeo talant.
Maleit seient tut mi parent
E li autre communalment
Ki a cest g[e]lu[s] me donerent
E a sun cors me marierent!
85 A forte corde trai e tir:
Il ne purrat jamés murir.
Quant il deust estre baptiziez,
Si fu al flum d'enfern plungiez:
Dur sunt li nerf, dures les veines,
90 Que de vif sanc sunt tutes pleines.
—Mut ai sovent oï cunter
Que l'em suleit jadis trover
Aventures en cest païs
Ki rechatouent les pensis: [f. 141ʳ]
95 Chevalers trovoent puceles
A lur talent gentes e beles,
E dames truvoent amanz
Beaus e curteis e vaillanz,
Si que blame[es] n'en esteient,
100 Ne nul fors eus nes veeient.
Si ceo peot estre e ceo fu,
Si unc a nul est avenu,
Deu, ki de tut ad poesté,
Il en face ma volenté!"
105 Quant ele ot faite pleinte issi,
L'umbre d'un grant oisel choisi
Par mi une estreite fenestre.
Ele ne seit quei ceo pout estre.
En la chambre volant entra;
110 Gez ot as piez, ostur sembla,

he is constantly afraid of being betrayed.
I can't go to church   75
or hear divine service.
If I could talk with people
and go to enjoy myself with them,
I would show him a kind face,
even if I didn't want to.   80
Cursed be all my relatives
and all the others together
who gave me to this jealous man
and married me to his body!
I pull and drag on a strong cord—   85
he will never be able to die.[1]
When he should have been baptized,
he was plunged into the river of hell:
his nerves are hard, his veins are hard,
that are all full of living blood.   90
—I have often heard tell
that once one used to find
adventures in this country
that gave hope to the sorrowful:
knights would find maidens   95
to their liking, noble and beautiful,
and ladies would find lovers
who were handsome and courtly and valiant,
so that they were not blamed for it,
nor could anyone else see them.   100
If this could be and was so,
if this ever happened to anyone,
may God, who has power over all things,
do my will in this regard!"
When she had thus made her lament,   105
she glimpsed the shadow of a great bird
through a narrow window.
She did not know what it could be.
It came flying into the chamber;
it had jesses on its feet. It looked like a goshawk,   110

---

1 This puzzling statement is somewhat clarified by a proverb from
  modern Anjou: "A longue corde tire / Qui d'autrui mort désire"
  ("He who desires the death of another pulls on a long cord"). See
  Ewert 179, n. to l. 85 (drawing on Wilhelm Hertz).

De cinc mues fu u de sis.
Il s'est devant la dame asis.
Quant il i ot un poi esté
E ele l'ot bien esgardé,
115 Chevaler bel e gent devint.
La dame a merveille le tint;
Li sens li remut e fremi,
Grant poür ot, sun chief covri.
Mut fu curteis li chevalers:
120 Il la areisunat primers.
"Dame," fet il, "n'eiez poür!
Gentil oisel ad en ostur;
Si li segrei sunt oscur,
Gardez ke seiez a seür,
125 Si fetes de mei vostre ami!
Pur coe," fet il, "vienc jeo ci.
Jeo vus ai lungement amé
E en mun quor mut desiré;
Unc femme fors vus n'amai   [col. b]
130 Ne jamés autre ne amerai.
Mes ne poeie a vus venir
Ne fors de mun paleis eissir,
Si vus ne me eussez requis.
Or puis bien estre vostre amis!"
135 La dame se raseura;
Sun chief descovri, si parla.
Le chevaler ad respundu
E dit qu'ele en ferat sun dru,
Si en Deu creïst e issi fust
140 Que lur amur estre peüst.
Kar mut esteit de grant beauté:
Unkes nul jur de sun eé
Si beals chevaler ne esgarda,
Ne jamés si bel ne verra.
145 "Dame," dit il, "vus dites bien.
Ne vodreie pur nule rien
Que de mei i ait acheisun,
Mescreaunce u suspesçun.

it was of five or six moltings.[1]
It landed in front of the lady.
When it had stood there for a bit
and she had looked at it carefully,
it turned into a handsome, noble knight. 115
The lady considered this a wonder;
·her mind was upset and troubled,
she was greatly afraid, she covered her head.
The knight was very courteous:
he spoke to her first. 120
"Lady," he says, "do not be afraid!
In the goshawk you have a noble bird;
even if its secrets are obscure,
see that you are safe,
and make me your beloved! 125
For this," he says, "I have come here.
I have loved you for a long time
and desired you greatly in my heart;
I never loved any woman but you
nor will I ever love another. 130
But I could not come to you
nor leave my palace
if you had not asked for me.
Now indeed I can be your beloved!"
The lady was reassured; 135
she uncovered her head and spoke.
She replied to the knight
and said that she would make him her lover,
if he believed in God and things were such
that their love could exist. 140
For he was very beautiful:
never, not once in her life,
had she beheld so handsome a knight,
nor will she ever see one so handsome.
"Lady," he says, "you speak well. 145
I would not wish, on any account,
that there should be any concern about me,
any mistrust or suspicion.

---

1 "Jesses" are leather thongs tied to a raptor's feet and used in train-
ing and flying it; the fact that this goshawk has them indicates that
he is not a (purely) wild bird. Hawks molt once a year, so this bird
is about five or six years old—fully mature but not old, since
goshawks can live ten or eleven years.

Jeo crei mut bien al Creatur,
150 Que nus geta de la tristur
U Adam nus mist, nostre pere,
Par le mors de la pumme amere;
Il est e ert e fu tuz jurs
Vie e lumere as pecheürs.
155 Si vus de ceo ne me creez,
Vostre chapelain demandez;
Dites ke mal vus ad susprise,
Si volez aver le servise
Que Deus ad el mund establi,
160 Dunt li pecheur sunt gari.
Le semblant de vus prendrai,
Le cors Deu receverai,
Ma creance vus dirai tute;
James de ceo ne seez en dute!"   [f. 141ᵛ]
165 Ele li respunt que bien ad dit.
Delez li s'est cuché al lit;
Mes il ne vout a [li] tucher,
De acoler ne de baiser.
Atant la veille est repeirie;
170 La dame trovat esveillie,
Dist li que tens est de lever;
Ses dras li voleit aporter.
La dame dist que ele est malade;
Del chapelain prenge garde,
175 Sil face tost a li venir,
Kar grant poür ad de murir.
La veille dist: "Vus sufferez!
Mis sires est al bois alez;
Nul n'entrera çaenz fors mei."
180 Mut fu la dame en grant esfrei;
Semblant fist que ele se pasma.
Cele le vit, mut s'esmaia.

I truly believe in the Creator,
who cast us out of the sadness 150
into which Adam, our father, placed us
by biting the bitter apple;
he is and will be and was forever
life and light to sinners.
If you do not trust me on this matter, 155
ask for your chaplain;
say that you are suddenly taken ill,
and wish to have the rites
that God established in the world,
by which sinners are healed.[1] 160
I will take on your appearance,
I will receive the body of God,
I will say my whole creed for you;
never be afraid on this account!"[2]
She replies that he has spoken well. 165
He lay down in the bed beside her,
but he did not try to touch her,
to embrace or kiss her.
Just then the old woman came back;
she found the lady awake, 170
told her it was time to get up;
she wanted to bring her her clothes.
The lady says that she is sick;
she should look for the chaplain
and have him come to her quickly 175
for she is greatly afraid she will die.
The old woman said, "Now be patient!
My lord has gone to the woods;
no one will come in here except me."
The lady was very frightened; 180
she made it look like she was fainting.
The old woman saw this and was greatly dismayed.

---

1 These "rites" are the Eucharist or Holy Communion, and here
specifically the last rites (or extreme unction) given to those in
danger of death.
2 In fact the hawk-knight has already partly said his "creed" (profes-
sion of faith) for her in lines 149–54, but he may be referring here
to the Apostles' Creed, the specific creedal formula that all Chris-
tians were supposed to know, which begins "Credo in Deum patrem
omnipotentem, creatorem celi et terrae..." ("I believe in God the
Father almighty, Creator of Heaven and Earth...").

L'us de la chambre ad defermé,
Si ad le prestre demandé;
185 E cil i vint cum plus tost pot,
E corpus domini aportot.
Li chevaler l'ad retenu[1]
E le vin del chalice beü.
Li chapeleins s'en est alez,
190 E la vielle ad les us fermez.
La dame gist lez sun ami:
Unke si bel cuple ne vi.
Quant unt asez ris e jué
E de lur priveté parlé,
195 Li chevaler ad cungé pris;
Raler s'en volt en sun païs.
Ele le prie ducement
Que il la reveie sovent.
"Dame," fet il, "quant vus plerra, [col. b]
200 Ja l'ure ne trespassera.
Mes tele mesure esgardez
Que nus ne seium encumbrez:
Ceste vielle nus traïra;
Nuit e jur nus gaitera.
205 Ele parcevera nostre amur,
Sil cuntera a sun seignur.
Si ceo avi[e]nt cum jeo vus di,
Nus serum issi trahi,
Ne [m'e]n puis mie departir,
210 Que mei n'en estuce murir."
Li chevalers atant s'en veit,
A grant joie s'amie leit.
Al demain lieve tute seine;
Mut fu haitie la semeine.
215 Sun cors teneit a grant chierté,
Tute recovre sa beauté.
Ore li plest plus a surjurner
Que en nul autre deduit aler.
Sun ami volt suvent veer

---

1 Harley 978 has "retenu," which is sometimes emended to "receü,"
"received," a more normal word to use of the taking of the
Eucharist. But *retenir* can mean "to keep (food) down," and
although less elegant, the sense intended may be that he was,
indeed, able to take the Eucharist without any negative effects (such
as might have been expected if he were a demon).

She opened the door of the chamber
and asked for the priest;
and he came as soon as he could,   185
and brought the *corpus Domini*.[1]
The knight took it
and drank the wine from the chalice.
The chaplain went away
and the old woman closed the doors.   190
The lady lay beside her beloved:
I never saw such a beautiful pair.
When they had laughed and played enough
and talked about private matters,
the knight took his leave;   195
he wanted to go back to his land.
She asks him sweetly
to come often and see her again.
"Lady," he says, "when it pleases you,
I will never be late.   200
But preserve such moderation
that we may not be caught:
this old woman will betray us;
night and day she will watch us.
She will perceive our love   205
and tell it to her lord.
If this were to happen as I say to you,
we will be betrayed in such a way
that I could never leave here
without dying of it."   210
With that the knight goes away;
he leaves his beloved very happy.
The next day she gets up quite cured;
she was very happy all that week.
She looked after her body with great care,   215
she entirely recovers her beauty.
Now it pleases her more to stay in
than pursue any other amusement.
She wants to see her beloved often

---

1 "The body of the Lord" (Latin), i.e., the wafer of the Eucharist,
   here administered as part of the last rites given to those on the
   verge of death (as the knight/lady here claims to be).

220   E de lui sun delit aveir.
      Desque sis sires depart,
      E nuit e jur e tost e tart,
      Ele l'ad tut a sun pleisir.
      Ore li duinst Deus lunges joïr!
225   Pur la grant joie u ele fu,
      Que ot suvent pur veer sun dru,
      Esteit tut sis semblanz changez.
      Sis sire esteit mut veizez:
      En sun curage se aparceit
230   Que autrement est k'i[l] ne suleit;
      Mescreance ad vers sa serur.
      Il la met a reisun un jur
      E dit que mut [a] grant merveille
      Que la dame si se appareille;   [f. 142ʳ]
235   Demande li que ceo deveit.
      La vielle dit que el ne saveit
      Kar nul ne pot parler od li,
      Ne ele n'ot dru ne ami
      Fors tant que sule remaneit
240   Plus volenters que ele ne suleit;
      De ceo s'esteit aparceüe.
      Dunc l'ad li sires respundue:
      "Par fei," fet il, "ceo qui jeo bien!
      Ore vus estuet fere une rien:
245   Al matin, quant jeo erc levez
      E vus avrez les hus fermez,
      Fetes semblant de fors eissir,
      Si la lessez sule gisir;
      En un segrei liu vus est[e]z,
250   E si veez e esgardez
      Quei ceo peot estre e dunt ço vient
      Ki en sa grant joie tient."
      De cel cunseil sunt departi.
      Allas! cum ierent malbailli
255   Cil ki l'un veut si agaitier
      Pur eus traïr e enginner!
      Tiers jur aprés, ceo oi cunter,
      Fet li sires semblant de errer.
      A sa femme ad dit e cunté
260   Que li reis [l]'ad par briefs mandé;
      Mes hastivement revendra.
      De la chambre ist e l'us ferma.

and have her enjoyment with him.   220
When her lord goes away,
night and day, early and late,
she has him entirely at her pleasure.
May God grant that her joy last!
From the great joy she felt,   225
that she often had from seeing her lover,
her appearance was entirely changed.
Her husband was very crafty:
he perceived in his heart
that it is not the way it used to be;   230
he feels mistrustful of his sister.
He speaks to her one day
and says that he is greatly astonished
that the lady is so dressed up;
he asks her what this is about.   235
The old woman said that she did not know at all,
because no one could speak with her,
nor did she have a lover or beloved,
except that she stayed alone
more willingly than she used to;   240
this she had noticed.
Then the lord replied:
"By my faith," he says, "I well believe it!
Now you must do something:
in the morning, when I have gotten up   245
and you have closed the doors,
make it look like you are going out,
and let her lie alone;
stand in a secret place,
and look out and watch   250
what it may be and from whence it comes
that keeps her in a state of such great joy."
With this plan they parted.
Alas! how unfortunate are those
whom someone wants to keep watch on like this   255
in order to betray and trick them!
The third day after, as I hear tell,
the lord makes it look as though he were leaving.
He said to his wife and told her
that the king had sent for him by letter;   260
but he will come back quickly.
He left the chamber and shut the door.

Dunc s'esteit la vielle levee,
Triers une cortine est alee;
265 Bien purrat oïr e veer
Ceo que ele cuveite a saver.
La dame jut; pas ne dormi,
Kar mut desire sun ami.
Venuz i est, pas ne demure, [col. b]
270 Ne trespasse terme ne hure.
Ensemble funt joie mut grant,
E par parole e par semblant,
De si ke tens fu de lever;
Kar dunc li estuveit aler.
275 Cele le vit, si l'esgarda,
Coment il vient e il ala;
De ceo ot ele grant poür
Que hume le vit e pus ostur.
Quant li sires fu repeirez,
280 Que gueres n'esteit esluignez,
Cele li ad dit e mustré
Del chevalier la verité,
E il en est forment pensifs.
Des engins faire fu hastifs
285 A ocire le chevalier.
Broches de fer fist furchier
E acerer le chief devant:
Suz ciel n'ad rasur plus trenchant.
Quant il les ot apparaillie[es]
290 E de tutes parz enfurchie[es],
Sur la fenestre les ad mises,
Bien serreies e bien asises,
Par unt le chevaler passot,
Quant a la dame repeirot.
295 Deus! qu'il ne sout la traïsun
Que aparaillot le felun!
Al demain en la matinee
Li sires lieve ainz l'ajurnee
E dit qu'il vot aler chacier.
300 La vielle le vait cunveer,
Pus se recuche pur dormir,
Kar ne poeit le jur choisir.
La dame veille, si atent
Celui que ele eime lealment, [f. 142ᵛ]
305 E dit que ore purreit bien venir

Then the old woman got up,
she went behind a curtain;
she will be well able to hear and see 265
what she longs to know.
The lady lay there; she did not sleep,
for she greatly desires her beloved.
He came to her, he does not delay,
he does not miss his appointed time. 270
They have great joy together,
in words and behavior,
until it was time to get up;
for then he had to go.
The old woman saw him, and looked 275
at how he came and went;
she was greatly frightened by this,
for she saw him as a man and then a hawk.
When the lord had returned—
who had not gone far at all— 280
she told him and showed him
the truth about the knight,
and he was very upset by it.
He hastened to make traps
to kill the knight. 285
He had iron spikes split into points
and their tips sharpened:
no razor under heaven is sharper.
When he had prepared them,
and made them barbed on all sides, 290
he put them, well fixed and well set,
at the window
through which the knight passed
when he came to the lady.
God! he did not know the treason 295
that the wicked one prepared!
The next day, in the morning,
the lord gets up before daybreak
and says that he wants to go hunting.
The old woman sees him off, 300
then she goes back to bed to sleep,
because she could not see the day.
The lady stays awake, and waits
for him whom she loves loyally,
and says that now he could certainly come 305

E estre od li tut a leisir.
Si tost cum ele l'ad demandé,
N'i ad puis gueres demuré:
En la fenestre vient volant,
310 Mes les broches furent devant;
L'une le fiert par mi le cors,
Li sanc vermeil en eissi fors.
Quant il se sot de mort nafré,
Desferré tut enz est entré;
315 Devant la dame al lit descent,
Que tut li drap furent sanglent.
Ele veit le sanc e la plaie,
Mut anguissusement s'esmaie.
Il li ad dit: "Ma duce amie,
320 Pur vostre amur perc jeo la vie.
Bien le vus dis qui en avendreit:
Vostre semblant nus ocireit."
Quant el l'oï, dunc chiet pasmee;
Tute fu morte une loee.
325 Il la cunforte ducement
E dit que dols n'i vaut nent;
De lui est enceinte d'enfant,
Un fiz avera pruz e vaillant:
Icil [la] recunforterat.
330 Yonec numer le frat;
Il vengerat lui e li,
Il oscirat sun enemi.
Il ne peot dunc demurer mes,
Kar sa plaie seignot adés.
335 A grant dolur s'en est partiz;
Ele le siut a mut grant criz.
Par une fenestre s'en ist;
Ceo est merveille k'[el] ne s'ocist,
Kar bien aveit vint piez de haut   [col. b]
340 Iloec u ele prist le saut.
Ele esteit nue en sa chemise.

and be with her quite at leisure.
As soon as she asked for him,
he did not delay at all:
he comes flying to the window,
but the spikes were in front of it;   310
one wounds him through the body,
the red blood spilled forth.
When he knew himself mortally wounded,
pulling himself free he went inside;
he lands before the lady on the bed,   315
so that all the sheets were bloody.
She sees the blood and the wound;
she is terribly distressed.
He says to her: "My sweet beloved,
for your love I lose my life.   320
I told you truly what would come of this:
your appearance would kill us."
When she heard him, she fell in a faint;
for a time[1] she lay as though dead.
He comforts her gently   325
and says that sorrow is no help;
she is pregnant with a child by him,
she will have a worthy and valiant son:
he will bring her comfort.
She should name him Yonec;   330
he will avenge him and her,
he will kill their enemy.
He could not delay any longer then,
for his wound bled so.
With great sorrow he departed;   335
she follows him with great lamenting.
She went out through a window;
it is a wonder she does not kill herself,
for it was a good twenty feet high
from where she jumped.   340
She wore nothing but her shift.[2]

---

1 A "loee" is a league, a measure of distance, but the term is also
used to refer to the length of time it would take to walk a league
(sometimes said to be an hour). Here it probably just means "for a
while."

2 Literally, "she was naked in her shift"; a shift is an under-dress, and
one would not ordinarily go out in public in only this garment.

A la trace del sanc s'est mise,
Que del chevaler curot
Sur le chemin u ele alot.
345 Icel senti[e]r errat e tient,
Desque a une hoge vient.
En cele hoge ot une entree,
De cel sanc fu tute arusee;
Ne pot nent avant aler.
350 Dunc quidot ele bien saver
Que sis amis entré i seit;
Dedenz se met en grant espleit.
El n'i trovat nule clarté.
Tant ad le dreit chemin erré
355 Que fors de la hoge [est] issue
E en un mut bel pre venue;
La trace en siut par mi le pre.
Asez pres ot une cité;
De mur fu close tut entur;
360 N'i ot mesun, sale ne tur,
Que ne parust tute d'argent;
Mut sunt riche li mandement.
Devers le burc sunt li mareis
E les forez e les difeis.
365 De l'autre part vers le dunjun
Curt une ewe tut envirun;
Ileoc arivoent les nefs,
Plus i aveit de treis cent tres.
La porte aval fu desfermee;
370 La dame est en la vile entree,
Tuz jurs aprés le sanc novel
Par mi le burc deske al chastel.
Unkes nul a li ne parla;
Humme ne femme n'i trova.   [f. 143^r]
375 Al paleis vient al paviment,

She followed the trace of blood
that flowed from the knight
on the road where she traveled.
She continued on and held to this path   345
until she came to a hill.
There was an entry into this hill
all wet with the blood;
she could go no farther.
Then she thought she was quite sure   350
that her beloved had gone in there;
she went inside in great haste.
She could see no light there.
She traveled straight along the path
until she came out of the hill   355
and into a beautiful meadow;[1]
she follows the trail through the meadow.
There was a city quite close;
it was enclosed all around by a wall.
There was no house, hall or tower   360
that did not seem entirely made of silver;
the battlements are very grand.
Towards the town are the marshes
and forests and reserves.
On the other side, toward the keep,[2]   365
a stream runs all around;
ships were arriving there,
there were more than three hundred masts.
The gate below was open;
the lady entered the town,   370
always following the fresh blood
through the town to the castle.
No one spoke to her at all;
she found neither man nor woman there.
She comes to the palace, to the tiled hall;   375

---

1 After l. 356 two manuscripts (S and Q) include two more lines:
   "Del sanc trova l'erbe muilliee,/ Dunc s'est ele mut esmaiee" (She
   found the grass wet with the blood, at which she was greatly dis-
   mayed; text from Ewert 91). Since the narrative is clear enough
   without these and they do not appear in Harley 978, I have not
   added them. Compare p. 233, n. 1, below.
2 The keep (donjon) of a medieval castle was a fortified tower, usually
   within an outer wall, that could serve as a refuge if the castle were
   attacked.

Del sanc [le] treve tut sanglent.
En une bele chambre entra;
Un chevaler dormant trova.
Nel cunut pas, si vet avant
380 En un[e] autre chambre plus grant:
Un lit treve e nient plus,
Un chevaler i treve[1] desus.
Ele s'en est utre passee;
En la terz chambre est entree,
385 Le lit sun ami ad trové.
Li pueçon[2] sunt de or esmeré;
Ne sai mie les dras preisier,
Les cirges ne les chandeliers,
Que nuit e jur sunt alumé;
390 Valent tut l'or de une cité.
Si tost cum ele l'ad veu,
Le chevalier ad cuneu.
Avant alat tut esfree,
Par desus lui cheï pasmee.
395 Cil la receit que forment l'aime,
Mal aventurus sovent se claime.
Quant de pasmer fu trespassee,
Il l'ad ducement cunfortee:
"Bele amie, pur Deu, merci!
400 Alez vus en! Fuiez d'ici!
Sempres murai, devant le jur;
Ci einz averat si grant dolur,
Si vus esteiez trovee,
Mut en seriez turmentee:
405 Bien iert entre ma gent seü
Que me unt par vostre amur perdu.
Pur vus sui dolent e pensis."
La dame li ad dit: "Amis,
Meuz voil ensemble od vus murir   [col. b]
410 Que od mun seignur peine suffrir.
Si a lui revois, il me ocira."
Li chevalier l'aseura.

---

1 Because of the repetition of "treve" from the previous line, this is
  sometimes emended to "Un chevaler dormant desus." Since the
  manuscript reading is perfectly coherent, however, even if repeti-
  tious, I have kept it.
2 I take "pueçon" to be a variant spelling of *poçon*, "post," itself a
  variant of *palçon*.

she finds it all covered with blood.
She entered a beautiful chamber;
she found a sleeping knight.
She did not recognize him, so she goes on
into another, larger chamber: 380
she finds a bed and nothing more,
she finds a knight on top of it.
She passed on farther;
she entered the third chamber,
she found the bed of her beloved.   385
The bedposts were of pure gold;
I do not know how to value the sheets,
nor the tapers nor the candelabra,
which were lit night and day;
they are worth all the gold of a city.   390
As soon as she saw him,
she recognized the knight.
She went forward in great distress;
she fell upon him in a faint.
He who loves her dearly holds her;   395
often he calls himself unfortunate.
When she had come out of her faint,
he comforted her sweetly:
"Beautiful beloved, mercy, by God!
Go away! Flee from here!   400
I will die soon, before daybreak;
the people here will have such great sorrow
that if you were found,
you would be greatly punished for it:
it will be well known among my people   405
that they have lost me for your love.
I am distressed and upset for you."
The lady says to him: "Beloved,
I would rather die with you
than suffer pain with my lord.   410
If I go back to him, he will kill me."
The knight reassured her.

Un anelet li ad baillé,
Si li ad dit e enseigné:
415 Ja, tant cum el le gardera,
A sun seignur n'en membera
De nule rien que fete seit,
Ne ne l'en tendrat en destreit.
L'espee li cumande e rent,
420 Puis la cunjure e defent
Que ja nul humme n'e[n] seit saisiz,
Mes bien la gart a oés sun fiz.
Quant il serat creuz e grant
E chevalier pruz e vaillant,
425 A une feste u ele irra,
Sun seignur e lui amerra.
En une abbeie vendrunt;
Par une tumbe k'il verrunt
Orrunt renoveler sa mort
430 E cum il fu ocis a tort.
Ileoc li baillerat s'espeie.
L'aventure li seit cuntee
Cum il fu nez, ki le engendra;
Asez verrunt k'il en fera.
435 Quant tut li ad dit e mustré,
Un chier bliant li ad doné,
Si li cumande a vestir;
Puis l'ad fete de lui partir.
Ele s'en vet, l'anel enporte
440 E l'espee ki la cunforte.
A l'eissue de la cité
N'ot pas demie liwe erré
Quant ele oï les seins suner
E le doel al chastel mener;   [f. 143ᵛ]
445 De la dolur que ele en ad
Quatre feiz se pasmad.
E quant de paumesuns revient,

He gave her a little ring,
and told her and instructed her
that never, so long as she keeps it, 415
will her lord ever remember
anything that was done,
nor will he keep her confined.
He commends and gives to her his sword,
then forbids her and makes her swear 420
that no man will ever take possession of it,
but she will keep it well for his son.
When he is full grown
and a bold and valiant knight,
at a feast she will go to, 425
she will take her lord and him.
They will come to an abbey;
by a tomb that they will see
they will hear his death told again
and how he was wrongly killed. 430
There she will give their son his sword.
Let the story be told to him,
how he was born, who fathered him;
they will see well enough what he will do about it.
When he has said and shown her everything, 435
he gave her a rich gown,
and commands her to put it on;
then he made her leave him.
She goes, she takes with her the ring
and the sword, which comforts her. 440
Upon leaving the city
she had not gone half a league
when she heard the bells ring
and heard lamenting at the castle;[1]
from the sorrow she felt at this 445
she fainted four times.
And when she recovered from her faint,

---

1 Two manuscripts, P and Q, have two lines following this one that
do not appear in Harley 978. They read, "Por lur seignur ki se
mureit. / Ele set bien que morz esteit": "(She heard lamenting at the
castle) for their lord who had died. She knew well that he was
dead"; text from Rychner 116. Although this is more explicit than
Harley 978, the implication that the bells ring for the death of her
beloved seems strong enough that the Harley reading can be left as
it stands. Compare p. 229, n. 1 above.

Vers la hoge sa veie tient;
Dedenz entra, si est passee,
450 Si s'en reveit en sa cuntree.
Ensemblement od sun seignur
Aprés demurat meint jur,
Que de cel fet ne la retta
Ne ne mesdist ne ne garda.
455 Lur fiz fu nez e bien nuriz
E bien gardez e bien cheriz.
Yonec le firent numer;
[Ens el regne n'avoit son per.]¹
Pruz fu e beaus e vaillant
460 E larges e bien despendant.
Quant il fu venuz en eez,
A chevaler l'unt dubez.
A l'an memes que ceo fu,
Oez cum est avenu:
465 A la feste seint Aaron,
C'on selebrot a Karlion
E en plusurs autres citez,
Li sires aveit esté mandez
Qu'il i alast od ses amis
470 A la custume del païs;
Sa femme e sun fiz i amenast
E richement s'aparaillast.
Issi avint, alez i sunt;
Mes il ne seivent u il vunt.
475 Ensemble od eus ot un meschin,
Kis ad mené le dreit chemin,
Tant qu'il viendrent a un chastel;
En tut le mund n'ot plus bel.
Une abbeie i ot dedenz   [col. b]

---

1 At l. 458, Harley 978 has "El nun n'i osa humme trover," "No man
dared find/invent the name." This is not entirely incoherent in itself,
but it does not make very much sense in the context. Two other
manuscripts, S and Q, have "El regne ne pot hum trover / Si bel, si
pruz ne si vaillant," which both Ewert (93) and Rychner (116)
adopt. Manuscript P has "Ens el regne n'avoit son per / Si bel, si
pruz ne si vaillant": "There was none in the realm to equal him, so
handsome, so bold nor so worthy" or "He had no peer in the realm
(etc.)," and I have adopted the first line, since it makes sense with
the following line as it appears in Harley 978; I take the reading
from Rychner 222.

She made her way toward the hill;
she went inside, and went on,
and came back into her country. 450
She remained together with her husband
for a long time after that;
he never reproached her for this deed
nor spoke unkindly to her nor guarded her.
Their son was born and well taken care of, 455
well looked after and cherished.
They had him named Yonec;
there was none in the realm to equal him.
He was bold and handsome and valiant,
and generous and free-spending. 460
When he had come of age,
they made him a knight.
In the very year when that took place,
listen to what happened:
At the feast of St. Aaron,[1] 465
which they celebrated at Caerleon
and in many other cities,
the lord had been sent for
to go with his friends
according to the custom of the land; 470
he took his wife and his son
and dressed himself richly.
So it happened, they went there;
but they do not know where they are going.
There was a young man accompanying them 475
who led them the right way,
until they came to a castle;
there was none more beautiful in all the world.
There was an abbey within it

---

1 St. Aaron was said to have been martyred in Caerleon (which, like
   Caerwent, is in southeast Wales) during the early-fourth-century
   persecution of Christians under the Emperor Diocletian, although
   the earliest mention of him is two centuries later. His feast day in
   Marie's time was 1 July.

480 De mut religiuses genz.
    Li vall[e]z les i [herberja]
    Que a la feste les mena.
    En la chambre que fu l'abbé
    Bien sunt servi e honuré.
485 A demain vunt la messe oïr;
    Puis s'en voleient departir.
    Li abes vet od eus parler,
    Mut les prie de surjurner;
    Si lur mustrat sun dortur,
490 Sun chapitre, sun refeitur,
    E cum il sunt herbergiez.
    Li sires lur ad otriez.
    Le jur quant il unt digné,
    As officines sunt alé.
495 Al chapitre vindrent avant;
    Une tumbe troverent grant
    Covert[e] de une palie roe[e],
    De un chier orfreis par mi bendé.
    Al chief, as piez, e as costez
500 Aveit vint cirges alumez.
    De or fin erent li chandelier,
    E de argent li encensier,
    Dunt il encensouent le jur
    Cele tumbe pur grant honur.
505 Il unt demandé e enquis
    Icels ki erent del païs
    De la tumbe: ki ele esteit,
    E queil humme fu ki la giseit.
    Cil comencerent a plurer
510 E en plurant a recunter
    Que ceo iert le meudre chevalier
    E le plus fort e le plus fier,
    Le plus beaus, le plus amez
    Que jamés seit el secle nez.   [f. 144ʳ]
515 De ceste tere ot esté reis;
    Unc ne fu nul si curteis.
    A Carwent fu entrepris,

of many religious people. 480
The young man who brought them to the feast
had them take lodging there.[1]
In the abbot's chamber
they were well served and honored.
The next day they go to hear mass; 485
then they wanted to leave.
The abbot goes to speak with them,
he asks them many times to stay;
he will show them his dormitory,
his chapterhouse, his refectory, 490
and how the monks are housed.
The lord granted it.
That day, when they had dined,
they went to the different areas.
They came before the chapterhouse; 495
they found a great tomb
covered with silken cloth with circles
of rich golden embroidery from end to end.
At the head, at the feet, and at the sides
there were twenty lit tapers. 500
The candleholders were of pure gold,
the censers of silver,
with which, every day, they would cense
the tomb with great honor.
They asked and inquired 505
of the people who were from that land
about the tomb: whose it was,
and who the man was who lay there.
The people began to weep
and, weeping, to recount 510
that he was the best knight
and the strongest and the boldest,
the most beautiful, the most beloved
who would ever be born in the world.
He had been king of this land; 515
there was never anyone so courtly.
He was attacked at Caerwent,

---

1 Harley 978 has "herla." It seems just possible that the scribe could
have intended this to mean "announced," from a verb *herler*
meaning "to cry out, make a racket," but the possibility is tenuous
enough that I have taken the reading of the other manuscripts,
which agree here on "herberja."

Pur l'amur de une dame ocis.
"Unc puis n'umes seignur;
520 Ainz avum atendu meint jur
Un fiz que en la dame engendra,
Si cum il dist e cumanda."
Quant la dame oï la novele,
A haute voiz sun fiz apele.
525 "Beaus fiz," fet ele, "avez oï
Cum Deus nus ad mené ici!
C'est vostre pere que ici gist,
Que cist villarz a tort ocist.
Ore vus comant e rent s'espee:
530 Jeo l'ai asez lung tens gardee."
Oianz tuz, li ad coneü
Que l'engendrat e sis fiz fu,
Cum il suleit venir a li
E cum si sires le trahi;
535 La verité li ad cuntee.
Sur la tumbe cheï pasmee,
En la paumeisun devia;
Unc puis a humme ne parla.
Quant sis fiz veit que el morte fu,
540 Sun parastre ad le chief tolu;
De l'espeie que fu sun pere
Ad dunc vengié le doel sa mere.
Puis ke si fu dunc avenu
E par la cité fu sceü,
545 A grant honur la dame unt prise
E al sarcu posee e mise.
Lur seignur firent de Yonec
Ainz que il partissent d'ilec.
Cil que ceste aventure oïrent   [col. b]
550 Lunc tens aprés un lai en firent
De la pité de la dolur
Que cil suffrirent pur amur.

killed for the love of a lady.
"Never since have we had a lord;
rather we have waited many days   520
for a son he fathered upon the lady,
as he told and commanded us."
When the lady heard this account,
she calls out clearly to her son.
"Dear son," she said, "you have heard   525
how God led us here!
It is your father who lies here,
whom this old man wrongfully killed.
Now I commend and give to you his sword:
I have kept it for a very long time."   530
In the hearing of everyone, she made known to him
who fathered him and whose son he was,
how his father used to come to her
and how her husband betrayed him;
she told him the truth.   535
She fell fainting upon the tomb,
and in her faint she died;
never again did she speak to anyone.
When her son saw that she was dead,
he cut off the head of his stepfather;   540
with the sword that was his father's
he thus avenged the sorrow of his mother.
When this had happened
and was known throughout the city,
they took the lady with great honor   545
and placed and put her in the tomb.
They made Yonec their lord
before they left that place.
Those who heard this adventure
made a lay of it long afterwards   550
out of pity at the sorrow
that these two suffered for love.

Laüstic

*Une aventure vus dirai
Dunt li bretun firent un lai.
Laüstic ad nun, ceo m'est avis—
Si l'apelent en lur païs;
5   Ceo est "[russinol]"† en franceis
E "nihtegale" en dreit engleis.[1]
[E]n Seint Mallo en la cuntree
Ot une vile renumee.
Deus chevalers ilec maneent
10 E deus for[z] maisuns aveient.
Pur la bunté des deus baruns
Fu de la vile bons li nuns.
Li uns aveit femme espusee
Sage, curteise, mut acemee;
15 A merveille se teneit chiere
Sulunc l'usage e la manere.
Li autres fu un bachelers
Bien conu entre ses pers
De pruesce, de grant valur,
20 E volenters feseit honur:
Mut turneot e despendeit
E bien donot ceo qu'il aveit.
La femme sun veisin ama.
Tant la requist, tant la preia,
25 E tant par ot en lui grant bien
Que ele l'ama sur tute rien,
Tant pur le bien que ele oï,
Tant pur ceo qu'il iert pres de li.

---

*   This lai appears on ff. 144rb–145rb of British Library MS Harley 978. The title given in the upper margin (in a later hand) is "Laustic."

†   Here and throughout, square brackets in the text indicate an emendation to the text as it appears in Harley 978; the original reading can be found, keyed to the line number, in Appendix F.

1   This line is generally emended by editors, since *russinol* is indeed the French word for "nightingale," but it is worth noting that what the Harley 978 scribe actually wrote was "Ceo est reisun en franceis": "That is right/proper in French." This might suggest that he (or his source) took "laüstic" to be an acceptably French term, though in this form the line does not make very much sense in combination with the one that follows.

Laüstic (The Nightingale)

I shall tell you an adventure
of which the Bretons made a lai.
Its name is *Laüstic*, I believe—
so they call it in their country;
that is "rossignol" in French   5
and "nightingale" in proper English.
In the region of St. Malo
there was a well-known town.[1]
Two knights lived there
and had two substantial houses.   10
Because of the goodness of the two men
the town had a good name.
One of them had married a woman
who was wise, courteous, and very gracious;
she had a great deal of self-respect[2]   15
according to custom and usage.
The other was a young knight,
well known among his peers
for prowess and great bravery,
and he willingly behaved with honor: 20
he went tourneying and spent a great deal
and gave out generously what he had.
He loved the wife of his neighbor.
He so often asked her, so often implored her,
and there was such great good in him   25
that she loved him above all things,
partly for the good that she heard of him,
partly because he was near to her.

---

1 St. Malo is on the coast of Brittany in northwest France.
2 A more literal translation would be, "she held herself wondrously
   dear," possibly with a negative implication of unduly high self-
   regard.

Sagement e bien s'entreamerent,
30 Mut se covrirent e esgarderent
Qu'il ne feussent aparceuz
Ne desturbez ne mescreuz;   [f. 144ᵛ]
E eus le poeient bien fere,
Kar pres esteient lur repere.
35 Preceines furent lur maisuns
E lur sales e lur dunguns;
N'i aveit bare ne devise
Fors un haut mur de piere bise.
Des chambres u la dame jut
40 Quant a la fenestre s'estut,
Poeit parler a sun ami
De l'autre part, e il a li,
E lur aveirs entrechangier
E par geter e par lancier.
45 N'unt gueres rien que lur despleise,
Mut esteient amdui a eise—
Fors tant k'il ne poent venir
Del tut ensemble a lur pleisir,
Kar la dame ert estrei[t] gardee
50 Quant cil esteit en la cuntree.
Mes de tant aveient retur,
U fust par nuit u fust par jur,
Que ensemble poeient parler.
Nul nes poeit de ceo garder
55 Que a la fenestre n'i venissent
E iloec s'entreveïssent.
Lungement se sunt entreamé,
Tant que ceo vient a un esté,
Que bruil e pre sunt rever[d]i
60 E li vergier ierent fluri;
Cil oiselet par grant duçur
Mainent lur joie en sum la flur.
Ki amur ad a sun talent,
N'est merveille s'il i entent!

They loved one another wisely and well,
they dissembled and took good care 30
not to be perceived
nor disturbed nor suspected;
and they could easily do this
because they lived close to one another.
Their houses were neighboring, 35
both their halls and their keeps;[1]
there was no obstacle or barrier
except a high wall of grey stone.
From the rooms where the lady slept,
when she stood at the window, 40
she could talk to her beloved
on the other side, and he to her,
and they could exchange things
by tossing or throwing them.
There is hardly anything that displeases them, 45
they were both very much at ease—
except that they cannot be together
entirely at their pleasure,
for the lady was closely guarded
when her husband was at home. 50
But at least they had the consolation,
be it by night or be it by day,
that they could talk to one another.
No one could prevent them
from coming to the window 55
and seeing one another there.
They loved one another for a long time,
until there comes a summer
when the woods and meadow are all green
and the orchards are flowering; 60
the little birds express their joy
with great sweetness among the flowers.
If one has the love he desires,
it is no wonder if he listens to them![2]

---

1 The keep (*donjon*) of a medieval castle was a fortified tower, usually
  within an outer wall, that could serve as a refuge if the castle were
  attacked.
2 It is not entirely clear what "il i entent" refers to here: the one who
  has the love he desires may be listening or attending to the song of
  the birds, or attending to his love. To further complicate matters,
  entendre can mean "to understand" as well as "to listen."

65 Del chevaler vus dirai veir:
Il i entent a sun poeir
E la dame de l'autre part,   [col. b]
E de parler e de regart.
Les nuiz, quant la lune luseit
70 E ses sires cuché esteit,
De juste li sovent levot
E de sun mantel se afublot;
A la fenestre ester veneit
Pur sun ami qu'el i saveit
75 Que autreteu vie demenot:
Le plus de la nuit veillot.
Delit aveient al veer,
Quant plus ne poeient aver.
Tant i estut, tant i leva,
80 Que ses sires s'en curuça
E meintefeiz li demanda
Pur quei levot e u ala.
"Sire," la dame li respunt,
"Il nen ad joie en cest mund
85 Ki nen ot le laüstic chanter.
Pur ceo me vois ici ester.
Tant ducement le oï la nuit
Que mut me semble grant deduit;
Tant me delit[e] e tant le voil
90 Que jeo ne puis dormir de l'oil."
Quant li sires ot que ele dist,
De ire e maltalent en rist.
De une chose se purpensa:
Que le laüstic enginnera.
95 Il n'ot vallet en sa meisun
Ne face engin, reis u la[ç]un;
Puis les mettent par le vergier.
N'i ot codre ne chastainier
U il ne mettent laz u glu,
100 Tant que pri[s] l'unt et retenu.
Quant le laüstic eurent pris,
Al seignur fu rendu tut vis.   [f. 145ʳ]
Mut en fu liez; quant il le tient
As chambres la dame vient.
105 "Dame," fet il, "u estes vus?
Venez avant, parlez a nus!
Jeo ai le laüstic englué

I shall tell you truly about the knight: 65
he attends to it with all his might,
and the lady does so on the other side,
both with words and with looks.
At night, when the moon was shining
and her husband had gone to bed, 70
she often got up from beside him
and put on her mantle;
she would go stand at the window
on account of her beloved, who, she knew,
led a similar life: 75
he was awake most of the night.
They would delight in seeing one another,
when they could have no more.
She stood there so much, she got up so often,
that her husband became angry about it 80
and asked her many times
why she got up and where she went.
"Sir," the lady answers,
"he has no joy in this world
who does not hear the nightingale sing. 85
That is why you see me standing here.
I hear him so sweetly at night
that it seems a great pleasure to me;
it delights me so and I desire it so
that I cannot close my eyes in sleep." 90
When her husband heard what she said,
he laughed out of anger and ill will.
He fixed his thoughts on one thing:
that he will trap the nightingale.
There was no servant in his house 95
who does not make a trap, net or snare;
then they put them in the orchard.
There was no hazel tree or chestnut
where they do not put a snare or birdlime,
until they took and captured it. 100
When they had caught the nightingale,
it was given, still alive, to the lord.
He was very happy with this; as soon as he has it
he comes to the lady's chamber.
"Lady," he says, "where are you? 105
Come here, talk to us!
I have caught the nightingale

Pur quei vus avez tant veillé.
Des ore poez gisir en peis:
110 Il ne vus esveillerat meis."
Quant la dame l'ad entendu,
Dolente e cureçuse fu.
A sun seignur l'ad demandé,
E il l'ocist par engresté:
115 Le col li rumpt a ses deus meins.
De ceo fist il ke trop vileins.
Sur la dame le cors geta,
Se que sun chainse ensanglanta
Un poi desur le piz devant.
120 De la chambre s'en ist a tant.
La dame prent le cors petit;
Durement plure e si maudit
Tuz ceus ki le laüstic traïrent,
E les engins e les laçuns firent,
125 Kar mut li unt toleit grant hait.
"Lasse," fet ele, "mal m'estait!
Ne purrai mes la nuit lever
Ne aler a la fenestre ester,
U jeo suleie mun ami veer.
130 Une chose sai jeo de veir:
Il quidra ke jeo me feigne.
De ceo m'estuet que cunseil preigne.
Le laüstic li trameterai;
L'aventure li manderai."
135 En une piece de samit
A or brusdé e tut escrit
Ad l'oiselet envolupé;   [col. b]
Un sun vatlet ad apelé,
Sun message li ad chargié,
140 A sun ami l'ad enveié.
Cil est al chevalier venuz;
De part sa dame li dist saluz,
Tut sun message li cunta,
E le laüstic li presenta.
145 Quant tut li ad dit e mustré
E il l'aveit bien escuté,
De l'aventure esteit dolenz,
Mes ne fu pas vileins ne lenz.

for which you have so often stayed awake.
From now on you can rest in peace:
he will wake you no more."   110
When the lady heard this,
she was sorrowful and angry.
She asked her lord for it,
and he killed it out of spite:
he breaks its neck with his two hands.   115
In this he behaved most basely.
He threw the body at the lady,
so that her shift was bloodied
a bit above the breast in front.
He left the room at once.   120
The lady takes the little body;
she weeps bitterly and curses
all those who betrayed the nightingale
and made traps and snares,
for they have taken a great happiness from her.   125
"Alas," she said, "it goes ill with me!
I will no longer be able to get up at night
nor go to stand by the window,
where I was accustomed to see my beloved
I know one thing for certain: 130
he will think that I am losing interest.
I must give thought to this matter.
I will convey the nightingale to him;
I will send him the adventure."
In a piece of samite[1]   135
embroidered in gold and inscribed all over
she wrapped the little bird;
she called a servant of hers,
charged him with her message,
sent him to her beloved.   140
He came to the knight;
he greeted him on behalf of his lady,
told him all her message,
and presented the nightingale to him.
When he has told and shown him everything   145
and the knight had listened well,
he was sorrowful over what had happened,
but he was not base or slow.

---

1 A luxury fabric of thick, woven silk.

Un vasselet ad fet forgeer:
150 Unc n'i ot fer ne acer.
Tut fu de or fin od bones pieres,
Mut precïuses e mut cheres;
Covercle i ot tres bien asis.
Le laüstic ad dedenz mis,
155 Puis fist la chasse enseeler.
Tuz jurs l'ad fet od li porter.
Cele aventure fu cuntee,
Ne pot estre lunges celee.
Un lai en firent li bretun:
160 *Le Laüstic* l'apelent hum.

⟩

He has a small casket made:
there was not a bit of iron or steel in it.   150
It was all of fine gold with valuable gems,
most precious and costly;
it had a very well-fitting cover.
He put the nightingale inside,
then had the coffer sealed.   155
He carried it with him always.
This adventure was told;
it could not long be hidden.
The Bretons made a lay of it:
people call it *The Nightingale*.   160

Milun

*Ki divers cunte[s]† vuet traitier,
Diversement deit comencier
E parler si rainablement
K'il seit pleisibles a la gent.
5 Ici comencerai *Milun*
E musterai par brief sermun
Pur quei e coment fu trovez
Li lais ke ci est numez.
Milun fu de Suhtwales nez.
10 Puis le jur k'il fu adubez
Ne trova un sul chevalier
Ki l'abatist de sun destrier.   [f. 145ᵛ]
Mut par esteit bons chevaliers,
Francs, hardiz, curteis e fiers.
15 [Mut] fu conuz en Irlande,
En Norweie e en Guhtlande;
En Loengre e en Albanie
Eurent plusurs de li envie.
Pur sa pruesce iert mut amez
20 E de muz princes honurez.
En sa cuntree ot un barun,
Mes jeo ne sai numer sun nun;
Il aveit une fille bele,
Mut curteise dameisele.
25 Ele ot oï Milun nomer;
Mult le cumençat a amer.
Par sun message li manda
Que, se li pl[e]st, el l'amera.
Milun fu liez de la novele,
30 Si en merciat la dameisele.
Volenters otriat l'amur;
N'e[n] partirat jamés nul jur.

---

* This lai appears on ff. 145ʳᵇ–149ʳᵃ of Harley 978 and is given the
    title "Milun" in the upper margin by a later hand.
† Here and throughout, square brackets in the text indicate an emen-
    dation to the text as it appears in Harley 978; the original reading
    can be found, keyed to the line number, in Appendix F.

Milun

One who wishes to treat varied stories
should begin in various ways
and speak so reasonably
as to be pleasing to people.
Here I will begin *Milun*,   5
and I will show in a few words
why and how the lai that is so named
was composed.
Milun was born in South Wales.
From the day when he was dubbed[1]   10
he found not a single knight
who could knock him from his horse.
He was an excellent knight,
noble, bold, courteous and strong.
He was well known in Ireland,   15
in Norway and in Gotland;
in England and in Scotland
many people had need of him.[2]
For his prowess he was dearly loved
and honored by many princes.   20
In his land there was a worthy man,
but I do not know his name;
he had a beautiful daughter,
a very courteous damsel.
She had heard Milun spoken of;   25
she began to love him dearly.
She sent word to him by a messenger
that, if it pleases him, she will love him.
Milun was delighted at this news
and thanked the damsel for it.   30
Willingly he granted his love;
he will not part from her ever, at any time.

---

1 "Dubbing" is the ceremony in which a young man is made a knight
   and invested with sword and armor.
2 Had need of him as a soldier or mercenary, presumably. Gotland is
   an island off the coast of Sweden; "Loengre" or "Logres" is the
   French version of the Brythonic name for England (Old Welsh
   Lloegyr, modern Welsh Lloegr), often used in Arthurian literature
   (as in *Lanval* l. 9). Geoffrey of Monmouth, in his *History of the
   Kings of Britain*, calls it Loegria and also uses the name "Albania"
   for Scotland (Marie's "Albanie").

Asez li fait curteis respuns.
Al message dona granz duns
35 E grant amistié premet:
"Amis," fet il, "ore entremet
Que a m'amie puisse parler,
E de nostre cunseil celer!
Mun anel de or li porterez
40 E de meie part li direz:
Quant li plerra, si vien pur mei,
E jeo irai ensemble od tei."
Cil prent cungé, si le lait;
A sa dameisele revait.
45 L'anel li dune, si li dist
Que bien ad fet ceo k'il quist.
Mut fu la dameisele lie[e]   [col. b]
De l'amur issi otrie[e].
Delez la chambre, en un vergier
50 U ele alout esbanier,
La justouent lur parlement
Milun e ele bien suvent.
Tant i vint Milun, tant l'ama
Que la dameisele enceinta.
55 Quant aparceit qu'ele est enceinte,
Milun manda, si fist sa pleinte.
Dist li cum est avenu:
Sun pere e sun bien ad perdu,
Quant de tel fet s'est entremise.
60 De li ert fait[e] grant justise:
A gleive serat turmentee
[U] vendue en autre cuntree.
Ceo fu custume as anciens,
Issi teneient en cel tens.
65 Milun respunt qu[e] il fera
Ceo que ele cunseillera.
"Quant l'enfant," fait ele, "ert nez,
A ma serur le porterez,
Que en Norhumbre est mariee,

He makes her a very courteous reply.
He gave great gifts to the messenger
and promises great friendship: 35
"Friend," he says, "now see to it
that I may be able to speak with my beloved,
and keep our plans secret!
You shall take her my golden ring
and say to her on my behalf: 40
when it pleases her, you come for me,
and I will go along with you."
The messenger takes his leave and departs;
he goes back to his damsel.
He gives her the ring and told her   45
that he has done all that he set out to do.
The damsel was very pleased
with the love thus granted her.
Beside her chamber, in an orchard
where she would go to amuse herself,   50
there she and Milun very often
came together to speak.[1]
Milun came there so often, loved her so well,
that the damsel became pregnant.
When she discovered that she was pregnant,   55
she sent for Milun and spoke her lament.
She told him what has happened:[2]
she has lost her father and her good standing
by engaging in such behavior.
She will receive a great punishment: 60
she will be put to the sword
or sold in another country.
This was the custom among the ancients;
so they were doing at that time.
Milun replies that he will do   65
what she advises.
"When the child is born," she says,
"you will take it to my sister,
who is married and lives in Northumbria—

---

1 The verb *juster* means, most broadly, to bring two things together,
   whether in love or combat; it is also the verb for "to joust."
2 Here as elsewhere, the verb *avenir*, "to happen," has an echo of
   aventure; see note to l. 80.

70 Riche dame, pruz e enseignee.
   Si li manderez par escrit
   E par paroles e par dit
   Que c'est l'enfant sa serur,
   Si en ad sufferte meinte dolur.
75 Ore gart k'il seit bien nuriz,
   Queil ke ço seit, u fille u fiz.
   Vostre anel al col li pendrai
   E un brief li enveierai;
   Escrit i ert le nun sun pere
80 E l'aventure de sa mere.
   Quant il serat grant e creüz   [f. 146ʳ]
   E en tel eage venuz
   Que il sache reisun entendre,
   Le brief e l'anel li deit rendre,
85 Si li cumant tant a garder
   Que sun pere puisse trover."
   A sun cunseil se sunt tenu,
   Tant que li termes est venu
   Que la dameisele enfanta.
90 Une vielle ki la garda—
   A ki tut sun estre geï—
   Tant la cela, tant la covri,
   Unc n'e[n] fu aparcevance
   En parole ne en semblance.
95 La meschine ot un fiz mut bel.
   Al col li pendirent l'anel
   E une aumoniere de seie
   E pus le brief que nul nel veie.
   Puis le cuchent en un bercel,
100 Envolupé d'un blanc lincel.
   Desuz la teste a l'enfant
   Mistrent un oreiller vaillant
   E desus lui un covertur,
   Urlé de martre tut entur.

a rich lady, worthy and well brought up.[1]   70
You will send to her in writing,
both in speech and in word,
that this is the child of her sister,
who has suffered many sorrows for it.
Now take care that it is well brought up,   75
whatever it may be, whether daughter or son.
I will hang your ring around its neck
and will send it a letter;
written there will be the name of its father
and what happened to its mother.[2]   80
When it is all grown up
and has come to such an age
that it can understand reason,
she must give it the letter and the ring,
and tell it to attend to them so carefully   85
that it will be able to find its father."
They held to her plan
until the time came
when the damsel gave birth.
An old woman who looked after her—   90
to whom she confessed her whole situation
hid her and disguised her so well
that there was never any sign of it
in word nor in appearance.
The girl had a very fine son.   95
Around his neck they hung the ring
and a silk purse
and then the letter so that no one would see it.
Then they lay him in a cradle,
wrapped in a white linen cloth.   100
Under the baby's head
they put a rich pillow
and over him a coverlet
bordered with marten fur all around.

---

1   The kingdom, later earldom, of Northumbria was in the far north
    of Britain (north of the Humber River), stretching at one point
    roughly from York to Edinburgh; it was ruled, at various times, by a
    combination of Angles, Danes, and Norwegians.
2   The events of the story so far are here explicitly called an "aven-
    ture"; later uses of *avenir* and *aventure* I have similarly translated
    by "happen[ed]." See the discussion in the Note on the Text,
    pp. 44–45.

105 La vielle l'ad Milun baillié;
Cil at [a]tendu el vergier.
Il le cumaunda a teu gent
Ki l'i porterent lëaument.
Par [l]es viles u il errouent
110 Set feiz le jur resposoent;
L'enfant feseient aleitier,
Cucher de nuvel e baignier.
Nurice menoent od eus
Itant furent il lëaus.
115 Tant unt le dreit chemin erré
Que a la dame l'unt comandé
El le receut, si l'en fu bel.   [col. b]
Le brief li baille[nt] e le seel;
Quant ele le sot, ki il esteit,
120 A merveille le cheriseit.
Cil ki l'enfant eurent porté
En lur païs sunt returné.
Milun eissi fors de sa tere
En soudés pur sun pris querre;
125 S'amie remist a meisun.
Sis peres li duna barun,
Un mut riche humme del païs,
Mut esforcible e de grant pris.
Quant ele sot cele aventure,
130 Mut est dolente a desmesure
E suvent regrette Milun:
Mut dute la mesprisun
De ceo que ele ot [eu] enfant;
Il le savera demeintenant.
135 "Lasse," fet ele, "quei ferai?
Avrai seignur! Cum le prendrai?
Ja ne sui jeo mie pucele;
A tuz jurs mes serai ancele!
Jeo ne soi pas que fust issi,
140 Ainz quidoue aveir mun ami.
Entre nus celisum l'afaire,
Ja ne l'oïsse aillurs retraire.

The old woman gave him to Milun;   105
he has been waiting in the orchard.
He commended him to people
who would loyally take him there.
In the towns they went through
they rested seven times a day;   110
they had the baby nursed,
changed, and bathed.
They took a nurse along with them,
so loyal were they.
They went along on the right path   115
until they entrusted him to the lady;
she received him, and was delighted with him.
They deliver the letter and the seal to her;
when she knew who he was,
she doted on him wonderfully.   120
The people who had carried the baby
went back to their country.
Milun left his land
to seek his fortune as a soldier;[1]
his beloved remained at home.   125
Her father gave her a husband,
a very rich man of the country,
powerful and of great worth.
When she knew what was to happen,
she is sorrowful beyond measure   130
and often laments over Milun:
she greatly fears the disgrace
of having had a child;
he will know it right away.
"Wretched me," she says, "what shall I do?   135
I will have a husband! How shall I receive him?
I am no longer a virgin;
I will be a servant forever more!
I did not know that it would be like this;
instead I thought to have my lover.   140
Between us we would have hidden the affair,
I would never hear it retold elsewhere.

---

1 The phrase *en soudée*, used of a knight, refers to working as a paid
   soldier or mercenary. The "pris" Milun seeks has the sense of both
   "value" and "renown": he is looking for both financial and reputa-
   tional rewards.

Meuz me vendreit murir que vivre,
Mes jeo ne sui mie a delivre;
145 Ainz ai asez sur mei gardeins
Veuz e jeofnes, mes chamberleins,
Que tuz jurz heent bone amur
E se delitent en tristur.
Or m'estuverat issi suffrir,
150 Lasse, quant jeo ne puis murir."
Al terme ke ele fu donee,
Sis sires l'ad amenee.   [f. 146ᵛ]
Milun revient en sun païs.
Mut fu dolent e mut pensis,
155 Grant doel fist e demena.
Mes de ceo se recunforta
Que pres esteit de sa cuntree
Cele k'il tant aveit amee.
Milun se prist a purpenser
160 Coment il li purrat mander,
Si qu'il ne seit aparceüz,
Qu'il est el païs venuz.
Ses lettres fist, sis seela.
Un cisne aveit k'il mut ama;[1]
165 Le brief li ad al col lié
E dedenz la plume muscié.
Un suen esquier apela,
Sun message li encharga.
"Va tost," fet il, "change tes dras!
170 Al chastel m'amie en irras;
Mun cisne porteras od tei.
Garde que en prengez cunrei,
U par servant u par meschine,
Que presenté li seit li cisne."
175 Cil ad fet sun comandement.
Atant s'en vet; le cigne prent.
Tut le dreit chemin qu'il sot
Al chastel vient, si cum il pot.
Par mi la vile est trespassez,
180 A la mestre porte est alez.
Le portier apelat a sei.
"Amis," fet [il], "entent a mei!

---

1 The word for "swan," *cisne* or *cigne*, is a homophone for *signe*,
"sign," echoing the bird's role as a messenger between the lovers.

It would be better for me to die than live,
but I am not at all at liberty;
rather I have many keepers around me,   145
old and young, my chamberlains,
who always hate true love
and delight in sadness.
Now I will have to suffer thus,
wretched me, since I cannot die."   150
At the time when she was given away,
her lord led her off.
Milun comes back to his country.
He was very sad and much distressed,
he felt and displayed great sorrow.   155
But he comforted himself with this:
that she whom he had loved so much
was close to his region.
Milun began to consider
how he can send a message to her—   160
in such a way that it will not be noticed—
that he has come to the country.
He wrote his letter and sealed it.
He had a swan that he loved very much;
he tied the letter to its neck   165
and concealed it within its feathers.
He called one of his squires,
he charged him with his message.
"Go quickly," he says, "change your clothes!
You will go to the castle of my beloved;   170
you will take my swan with you.
Take care that you find a way,
whether by a manservant or a maid,
that the swan may be presented to her."
He did as he was told.   175
He goes at once; he takes the swan.
Straight on the right path, which he knew,
he came to the castle, as fast as he could.
He passed through the middle of the town,
he went to the main gate.   180
He called the porter to him.
"Friend," he says, "listen to me!

Jeo sui un hume de tel mester,
De oiseus prendre me sai aider.
185 Une huchie[e][1] desuz Karliun
Pris un cisne od mun laçun.
Pur force e pur meintenement   [col. b]
La dame en voil faire present,
Que jeo ne seie desturbez,
190 E[n] cest païs achaisunez."
Li bachelers li respundi:
"Amis, nul ne parole od li;
Mes nepurec jeo irai saveir:
Se jeo poeie liu veeir
195 Que jeo te puisse mener,
Jeo te fereie a li parler."
A la sale vint li portiers,
N'i trova fors dous chevalers;
Sur une grant table seieent,
200 Od uns granz eschés se deduieent.
Hastivement returne arere.
Celui ameine en teu manere
Que de nul ni fu sceuz,
Desturbez ne aparceuz.
205 A la chambre vient, si apele;
L'us lur ovri une pucele.
Cil sunt devant la dame alé,
Si unt le cigne presenté.
Ele apelat un suen vallet,
210 Puis si li dit: "Ore t'entremet
Que mis cignes seit bien gardez
E ke il eit viande asez!"
"Dame," fet il ki l'aporta,
"Ja nul fors vus nel recevera.
215 E ja est ceo present rëaus;
Veez cum il est bons e beaus!"
Entre ses mains li baille e rent;
Ele le receit mut bonement.
Le col li manie e le chief,
220 Desuz la plume sent le brief.

---

1 Usually the reading from manuscript S, "En un pré desuz Kaer-
   leon," is adopted, but it seems not unreasonable to understand
   "huchie[e]" as meaning "distance où porte la voix" (the distance a
   voice will carry; Godefroy, *Lexique de l'Ancien Français* 280).
   Rychner notes this possibility but considers it too daring.

I am such a poor man
that I support myself by catching birds.
Within shouting distance of Caerleon[1]   185
I caught a swan in my snare.
Out of necessity and in hope of protection
I want to make a present of it to the lady,
so that I am not harassed
or accused in this country."[2]   190
The young man replied:
"Friend, no one speaks with her,
but nevertheless I will go and find out;
if I could find a place
where I could take you,   195
I would have you speak to her."
The porter came to the hall,
he found there only two knights;
they were sitting at a large table,
enjoying themselves at a large chessboard.   200
Quickly he goes back.
He leads the messenger in in such a way
that he was not noticed,
bothered, nor seen by anyone.
He comes to the chamber, and calls;   205
a maiden opened the door to them.
They came before the lady
and presented the swan to her.
She called a servant boy of hers,
then says to him, "Now see to it   210
that my swan is well looked after
and has enough food!"
"Lady," says he who brought it,
"never will anyone but you receive it.
And this is indeed a royal gift;   215
see how good and beautiful it is!"
Into her hands he gives and delivers it;
She receives it very graciously.
She strokes its neck and its head;
she feels the letter beneath its wing.   220

---

1 Caerleon is in south Wales.
2 The implication may be that swans are protected, so catching one
  by accident could get you in trouble, an outcome that the supposed
  poacher is trying to forestall.

Li sanc li remut e fremi:
Bien sot qu'il vient de sun ami.   [f. 147ʳ]
Celui a fet del suen doner,
Si l'en cumande a aler.
225 Quant la chambre fu deliveree,
Une meschine ad apelee.
Le brief aveient deslié;
Ele en ad le sel debrusé.
Al primer chief trovat 'Milun.'
230 De sun ami cunut le nun;
Cent feiz le baise en plurant,
Ainz que ele puist dire avant.
Al chief de piece veit l'escrit,
Ceo k'il ot cumandé e dit,
235 Les granz peines e la dolur
Que Milun seofre nuit e jur.
Ore est del tut en sun pleisir
De lui ocire u de garir.
Si ele seust engin trover
240 Cum il peust a li parler,
Par ses lettres li remandast
E le cisne li renveast.
Primes le face bien garder,
Puis sil laist tant juner
245 Treis jurs qu'il ne seit peüz.
Le brief li seit al col penduz,
Laist l'en aler: il volera
La u il primes conversa.
Quant ele ot tut l'escrit veü
250 E ceo que ele i ot entendu,
Le cigne fet bien surjurner
E forment pestre e abevrer.
Dedenz sa chambre un meis le tint.
Mes ore oez cum l'en avint!
255 Tant quist par art e par engin
Ke ele ot enke e parchemin.
Un brief escrit tel cum li plot,   [col. b]
Od un anel l'enseelot.
Le cigne ot laissié juner;
260 Al col li pent, sil laist aler.
Li oiseus esteit fameillus
E de viande coveitus;
Hastivement est revenuz

Her blood stirred and trembled:
she knew well that it came from her lover.
She had the messenger given gifts
and orders him to go.
When the chamber was empty, 225
she called a maid.
They untied the letter;
she broke its seal.
At the very top she found 'Milun.'
She recognized her lover's name; 230
a hundred times she kisses it, weeping,
before she could speak further.
At the top of the letter she sees the writing,
what he had set down and said,
the great pains and the sorrow 235
that Milun suffers night and day.
Now it is entirely at her pleasure
whether to kill him or heal him.
If she should know how to find a means
by which he could speak to her, 240
she should send it back to him in a letter
and return the swan to him.
First she should have it well looked after,
then let it fast so much
that it is not fed for three days. 245
Let the letter be hung from its neck,
let it go: it will fly
to where it first lived.
When she had seen all the writing
and understood what she hears there, 250
she has the swan well taken care of
and abundantly fed and watered.
She kept it in her chamber for a month.
But hear now what happened!
She sought with such craft and cleverness 255
that she got hold of ink and parchment.
She wrote a letter just as she pleased,
she sealed it up with a ring.
She had let the swan fast;
she hangs the letter from its neck and lets it go. 260
The bird was famished
and wanted food;
swiftly it returned

La dunt il primes fu venuz.
265 A la vile e en la meisun
Descent devant les piez Milun.
Quant il le vit, mut en fu liez;
Par les eles le prent haitiez.
Il apela sun despensier,
270 Si li fet doner a mangier.
Del col li ad le brief osté.
De chief en chief l'ad esgardé,
Les enseignes qu'il i trova,
E des saluz se reheita:
275 "Ne pot sanz li nul bien aveir;
Ore li rem[a]nt tut sun voleir
Par le cigne sifaitement."
Si ferat il hastivement.
Vint anz menerent cele vie
280 Milun entre lui e s'amie.
Del cigne firent messager,
N'i aveient autre enparler;
E sil feseient jeuner
Ainz qu'il le lessassent aler.
285 Cil a ki li oiseus veneit,
Ceo sachez, qu'il le peisseit.
Ensemble viendrent plusurs feiz.
Nul ne pot estre si destreiz
Ne si tenuz estreitement
290 Qu'il ne truisse liu sovent.
La dame que sun fiz nurri
Tant ot esté ensemble od li,   [f. 147ᵛ]
Quant il esteit venuz en eé
A chevalier l'ad adubé.
295 Mut i aveit gent dameisel.
Le brief li rendi e l'anel.
Puis li ad dit ki est sa mere,
E l'aventure de sun pere,
E cum il est bons chevaliers,
300 Tant pruz, si hardi e si fiers,
N'ot en la tere nul meillur
De sun pris ne de sa valur.
Quant la dame li ot mustré
E il l'aveit bien escuté,
305 Del bien sun pere s'esjoï;

to the place from which it had first come.
At the town and in the house   265
it lands before Milun's feet.
When he saw it, he was very happy;
joyfully, he takes it by the wings.
He called his steward
and has it given food.   270
He took the letter from its neck.
He looked at it from top to bottom,
at the signs he found there,
and rejoiced at the greetings:
"She had no happiness without him;   275
now he should send all his wishes back to her
by the swan in just this way."
He will quickly do so.
For twenty years they led this life,
Milun and his beloved.   280
They made a messenger of the swan,
they had no other go between;
and they would have it fast
before they let it go.
The one the swan came to,   285
you may be sure, would feed it.
They came together many times.
No one could be so constrained
or so closely imprisoned
that he would not often find a way.   290
The lady who raised their son
had been with him so long,
when he had come of age
she has him dubbed a knight.
He was a very noble youth.   295
She gave him the letter and the ring.
Then she told him who his mother is,
and what happened to his father,
and how he is a good knight,
so worthy, so bold and so strong   300
there was none better in the land
in either worth or valor.
When the lady had told him
and he had listened well,
he rejoiced in the worth of his father;   305

Liez fu de ceo k'il ot oï.
A sei memes pense e dit:
"Mut se deit humme preiser petit,
Quant il issi fu engendrez
310 E sun pere est si alosez,
S'il ne se met en greinur pris
Fors de la tere e del païs."
Asez aveit sun estuveir.
Il ne demure fors le seir;
315 Al demain ad pris cungié.
La dame l'ad mult chastié
E de bien fere amonesté;
Asez li ad aveir doné.
A Suhtamptune vait passer;
320 Cum il ainz pot, se mist en mer.
A Barbefluet est arivez;
Dreit en Brutaine est alez.
La despendi e turneia;
As riches hummes s'acuinta.
325 Unc ne vint en nul estur
Que l'en nel tenist al meillur.
Les povres chevalers amot;   [col. b]
Ceo que des riches gainot
Lur donout e sis reteneit,
330 E mut largement despendeit.
Unc, sun voil, ne surjurna.
De tutes les teres de la
Porta le pris e la valur;
Mut fu curteis, mut sot honur.
335 De sa bunté e de sun pris
Veit la novele en sun païs:
Que un damisels de la tere,
Ki passa mer pur pris quere,
Puis ad tant fet par sa pruesce,
340 Par sa bunté, par sa largesce,
Que cil ki nel seivent numer

he was glad of that which he had heard.
He thinks and says to himself,
"A man should value himself very little,
when he was born of such a one
and his father is so renowned, 310
if he does not gain even greater renown
outside his land and his country."
He had enough to support himself.
He waits no longer than an evening;
the next day he took his leave. 315
The lady gave him much advice
and admonished him to behave well;
she gave him plenty of money.
He goes to cross at Southampton;
as soon as he could, he put out to sea. 320
He arrived at Barfleur;
he went straight to Brittany.[1]
There he spent money and tourneyed;
he became acquainted with rich men.
He never came to any battle 325
where he was not considered the best.
He loved poor knights;
whatever he won from the rich
he gave to them and made them his retainers,
and he spent very generously. 330
He never willingly stayed in one place.
Of all the lands thereabout
he carried off the prize and the renown;
he was very courtly, he knew all about honor.
The news of his goodness and his renown 335
reaches his country:
that a young man of that land
who crossed the sea to seek renown
then did so much through his prowess,
through his goodness, through his generosity, 340
that those who do not know his name

---

1 Southampton, roughly in the center of the southern coast of
England, was a major embarkation and arrival point for ships cross-
ing the Channel in the Middle Ages, as was Barfleur, which lies
more or less across the Channel from Southampton in what is now
Basse-Normandie.

L'apel[ou]ent par tut Sanz Per.
Milun oï celui loer
E les biens de lui recunter.
345 Mut ert dolent, mut se pleigneit
Del chevaler qui tant valeit:
Pur tant cum il peust errer
Ne turneier ne armes porter,
Ne deust nul del païs nez
350 Estre preisiez ne alosez.
De une chose se purpensa:
Hastivement mer passera,
Si justera al chevalier
Pur li leidier e empeirer.
355 Par ire se vodra cumbatre;
S'il le pout del cheval abatre,
Dunc serat il en fin honiz.
Aprés irra quere sun fiz
Que fors del païs est eissuz,
360 Mes ne saveit u ert devenuz.
A s'amie le fet saveir,   [f. 148ʳ]
Cungé voleit de li aveir.
Tut sun curage li manda,
Brief e seel li envea
365 Par le cigne mun escient:
Ore li remandast sun talent!
Quant ele oï sa volenté,
Mercie l'en, si li sot gre,
Quant pur lur fiz trover e quere
370 Voleit eissir fors de la tere
[E] pur le bien de li mustrer;
Nel voleit mie desturber.
Milun oï le mandement;
Il s'aparaille richement.
375 En Normendie est passez,
Puis est desque Brutaine alez.
Mut s'aquointa a plusurs genz,
Mut cercha les turneiemenz;
Riches osteus teneit sovent
380 E si dunot curteisement.

always called him Peerless.[1]
Milun heard this man praised
and good things said about him.
He was very sad, he lamented greatly   345
about the knight who was so worthy:
as long as he traveled around
or tourneyed or bore arms,
no one else born of that country
would be admired or praised.   350
He formed a plan:
quickly he will cross the sea,
and joust with the knight
to shame him and do him harm.
He wishes to fight him out of anger;   355
if he can knock him from his horse,
then at last he will be shamed.
Afterward he will go to seek his son—
who has left the country,
but he did not know where he had ended up.   360
He lets his beloved know about this,
he wanted to have her leave to go.
He sent her all his thoughts;
he conveyed letter and seal to her
by way of the swan, I believe: 365
now let her respond with her wishes!
When she heard what he wanted,
she thanks him for it, and was grateful
that he wished to leave the country
to seek out and find their son   370
and to show his own worth;
she did not by any means wish to prevent him.
Milun heard her message;
He prepares himself richly.
He crossed over to Normandy,   375
then he went on to Brittany.
He met a great many people,
he searched hard at tournaments;
he often kept rich lodgings
and gave gifts courteously.   380

---

1   This is a pun in Old French that cannot be replicated in English:
    Sanz Per, "peerless, without equal," sounds exactly like *Sanz Père*,
    "fatherless, without a father," a name that fits the young man
    equally well at this point in the story.

Tut un yver, ceo m'est avis,
Conversa Milun al païs.
Plusurs bons chevalers retient,
Desque pres la paske vient,
385 K'il recumencent les turneiz
E les gueres e les dereiz.
Al Munt Seint Michel s'asemblerent;
Normein e Bretun i alerent
E li Flamenc e li Franceis;
390 Mes n'i ot gueres de[s] Engleis.
Milun i est alé primers,
Que mut esteit bons chevalers.
Le bon chevaler demanda.
Asez i ot ki li cunta
395 De queil part il esteit venuz:
A ses armes, a ses escuz
Tut l'eurent a Milun mustré,   [col. b]
E il l'aveit bien esgardé.
Li turneimenz s'asembla:
400 Ki juste quist, tost la trova;
Ki aukes volt les rens cerchier
Tost pout perdre u gaignier
E encuntrer un cumpaignun.
Tant vus voil dire de Milun:
405 Mut le fist bien en cel estur
E mut i fu preisez le jur.
Mes li vallez dunt jeo vus di
Sur tuz les autres ot le cri,
Ne se pot nuls acumpainier
410 De turneer ne de juster.
Milun le vit si cuntenir,
Si bien puindre e si ferir,
Par mi tut ceo k'il l'enviot,
Mut li fu bel e mut li plot.
415 Al renc se met encuntre lui,

One whole winter, so I understand,
Milun lived in that country.
He retains many good knights,
until it gets close to Easter,
when they begin again to have tournaments
and wars and battles.
At Mont Saint-Michel[1] they assembled;
Normans and Bretons went there
and the Flemish and the French;
but there were hardly any English.
Milun, who was a very good knight,[2]
went there first of all.
He asked after the good knight.
There were plenty of people who told him
where he came from:
by his arms, by his shield,
they had pointed him out clearly to Milun,
and he had observed him well.
The tournament was assembled.
anyone who sought a joust soon found it;
anyone who wanted to search the ranks a bit
could soon lose or win
and meet an opponent.
I'll tell you this much about Milun:
it went very well for him in that battle
and that day he was greatly praised there.
But the youth of whom I am telling you
won the day over all the others,
nor could anyone keep up with him
in tourneying nor in jousting.
Milun saw him so carry himself,
pierce and strike so well,
that for all that he envied him,
he was delighted by it and greatly pleased.
He goes up against him on the field;

385

390

395

400

405

410

415

---

1 Mont Saint-Michel is a monastery (dating back to the eighth
   century) that stands on a small island off the northwest coast of
   France; in Marie's time, it could be reached on foot only at low tide
   across the sand. The causeway has since been raised above sea level.
2 Since this rather unspecific description is echoed in the next line,
   editors often substitute the reading of manuscript S, "Ki mut esteit
   hardiz e fiers": "who was very bold and fierce" (see Rychner 138, l.
   390).

Ensemble justerent amdui.
Milun le fiert si durement,
L'anste depiece vereiment,
Mes il ne l'aveit mie abatu.
420 [Cil r]aveit lui feru
Que jus del cheval l'abati.
Desuz la ventaille choisi
La barbe e les chevoz chanuz:
Mut li pesa k'il fu cheüz.
425 Par la reisne le cheval prent,
Devant lui le tient en present.
Puis li ad dit: "Sire, muntez!
Mut sui dolent e trespensez
Que nul humme de vostre eage
430 De[usse] faire tel utrage."
Milun saut sus: mut li fu bel,
Al dei celui cunuit l'anel,   [f. 148ᵛ]
Quant il li rendi sun cheval.
Il areisune le vassal.
435 "Amis," fet il, "a mei entent!
Pur amur Deu omnipotent,
Di mei cument ad nun tun pere!
Cum as tu nun? Ki est ta mere?
Saveir en voil la verité!
440 Mut ai veu, mut ai erré,
Mut ai cerché autres teres
Par turneiemenz e par gueres:
Unc par coup de chevalier
Ne chaï mes de mun destrier!
445 Tu m'as abatu al juster:
A merveille te puis amer!"
Cil li respunt: "Jol vus dirai
De mun pere tant cum jeo en sai.
Jeo quid k'il est de Gales nez
450 E si est Milun apelez.
Fille a un riche humme ama;
Celeement me engendra.
En Norhumbre fu[i] enveez;
La fu[i] nurriz e enseignez.
455 Une meie aunte me nurri.

the two of them jousted together.
Milun strikes him so fiercely
that he completely destroys the shaft of his lance,
but he did not knock him down at all.
He in return had struck Milun   420
so that he knocked him down from his horse.
Below the ventail the young man saw[1]
the white beard and hair:
he was very upset that the other had fallen.
He takes the horse by the reins;   425
he holds it before him, presenting it to him.
Then he says to him, "Sir, mount!
I am most distressed and troubled
that I should have given such an insult
to any man of your age."   430
Milun jumps up: he was delighted,
he recognized the ring on the youth's finger
when he gave him back his horse.
He addressed the young fighter.
"Friend," he says, "listen to me!   435
For the love of God almighty,
tell me the name of your father!
What is your name? Who is your mother?
I want to know the truth of it!
I have seen much, I have traveled much,   440
I have searched many other lands
through tournaments and wars:
never by the blow of any knight
did I ever fall from my horse!
You have knocked me down at jousting: 445
I could love you dearly!"
The other replies: "I will tell you
as much as I know about my father.
I believe that he was born in Wales
and is called Milun.   450
He loved the daughter of a rich man;
he fathered me secretly.
I was sent into Northumbria;
there I was brought up and educated.
An aunt of mine brought me up.   455

---

1 The ventail is the moveable part of a helmet that covers the lower
   part of the face (and thus the beard). Presumably it slips aside as
   Milun falls from his horse.

Tant me garda ensemble od li,
Chevals e armes me dona,
En ceste tere m'envea.
Ci ai lungement conversé.
460 En talent ai e en pensé,
Hastivement mer passerai,
En ma cuntreie m'en irrai.
Saver voil l'estre mun pere,
Cum il se cuntient vers ma mere.
465 Tel anel d'or li musterai
E teus enseignes li dirai,
Ja ne me vodra reneer,   [col. b]
Ainz m'amerat e tendrat chier."
Quant Milun l'ot issi parler,
470 Il ne poeit plus escuter:
Avant sailli hastivement,
Par le pan del hauberc le prent.
"E Deu!" fait il, "cum sui gariz!
Par fei, amis, tu es mi fiz.
475 Pur tei trover e pur tei quere
Eissi uan fors de ma tere."
Quant cil l'oï, a pié descent;
Sun peire baisa ducement.
Bel semblant entre eus feseient
480 E iteus paroles diseient
Que li autres kis esguardouent
De joie e de pité plurouent.
Quant li turneimenz depart,
Milun s'en vet: mut li est tart
485 Que a sun fiz parot a leisir
E qu'il li die sun pleisir.
En un ostel furent la nuit.
Asez eurent joie e deduit;
[De] chevalers eurent plenté.
490 Milun ad a sun fiz cunté
De sa mere, cum il l'ama,
E cum sis peres la duna
Un barun de sa cuntré,
E cument il l'ad puis amee,
495 E ele lui, de bon curage;
E cum del cigne fist message,
Ses lettres lui feseit porter,
Ne se osot en nul[ui] fier.

She looked after me well and kept me with her;
she gave me horses and armor;
she sent me into this land.
I have lived here a long time.
It is my desire and my plan   460
that I will quickly cross the sea;
I will go into my country.
I want to know the situation of my father,
how he behaves to my mother.
I will show him this golden ring   465
and tell him such tokens
that he will never wish to repudiate me
but rather will love and cherish me."
When Milun hears him speak this way,
he could not listen any longer: 470
he jumped forward at once,
he takes him by the skirt of his hauberk.
"By God!" he says, "how I am cured!
In faith, friend, you are my son.
To find you and to seek for you   475
I left my land this year."
When the other heard this, he gets down on foot;
he kissed his father lovingly.
They showed themselves delighted with each other
and said such things   480
that the others who were watching them
wept with joy and sympathy.
When the tournament breaks up,
Milun goes away: he can hardly wait
to speak with his son at leisure   485
and have him tell him what he wishes to do.
They stayed at an inn that night.
They had great joy and pleasure;
there were many knights.
Milun told his son   490
about his mother, how he loved her,
and how her father gave her
a husband from his country,
and how he has loved her ever since,
and she him, with a true heart;   495
and how he made a messenger of the swan,
he had it carry his letter to her,
he did not dare to trust in anyone.

Li fiz respunt, "Par fei, bel pere,
500 Assemblerai vus e ma mere.
Sun seignur que ele ad ocirai
E espuser la vus ferai." [f. 149^r]
Cele parole dunc lesserent
E el demain s'apareillerent.
505 Cungé pernent de lur amis,
Si s'en revunt en lur païs.
Mer passerent hastivement,
Bon oré eurent e suef vent.[1]
Si cum il eirent le chemin,
510 Si encuntrerent un meschin.
De l'amie Milun veneit,
En Bretaigne passer voleit;
Ele l'i aveit enveié.
Ore ad sun travail acurcié:
515 Un brief li baille enseelé.
Par parole li ad cunté
Que s'en venist, ne demurast;
Morz est sis sires, ore s'en hastast!
Quant Milun oï la novele,
520 A merveille li sembla bele.
A sun fiz [l']ad mustré e dit.
N'i ot essuigne ne respit;
Tant eirent que il sunt venu
Al chastel u la dame fu.
525 Mut par fu lie[e] de sun beau fiz
Que tant esteit pruz e gentiz.
Unc ne demanderent parent:
Sanz cunseil de tut[e] autre gent
Lur fiz amdeus les assembla,
530 La mere a sun pere dona.
En grant bien e en duçur
Vesquirent puis, e nuit e jur.
De lur amur e de lur bien
Firent un lai li auncien;
535 E jeo que le ai mis en escrit
Al recunter mut me delit.

---

1 Compare *Guigemar* l. 194, "Bon oret eurent e süef vent," and
Guildelüec et Guilliadun l. 813, "Bon vent eurent e bon oré."

The son replies, "By my faith, dear father,
I will bring you and my mother together.   500
I will kill the husband she has
and have her marry you."
Then they left off this conversation
and the next day prepared themselves.
They take leave of their friends   505
and go back to their country.
They quickly crossed the sea,
they had a good breeze and a gentle wind.
As they were going along on the road,
they met a young man.   510
He was coming from Milun's beloved,
he wanted to cross to Brittany;
she had sent him.
Now he has shortened his labor:
he gives Milun a sealed letter.   515
In words he told him[1]
that he should come along, he should not delay;
her husband is dead, now he should hurry!
When Milun heard the news,
it pleased him wonderfully.   520
He showed and recounted it to his son.
There was no reason for delay or respite;
they kept going until they came
to the castle where the lady was.
She was delighted with her handsome son,   525
who was so worthy and noble.
They never asked any relatives:
without the advice of any other people
their son brought them both together;
he gave his mother to his father.   530
In great joy and in sweetness
they lived afterward, both night and day.
Of their love and their joy
the ancients made a lay;
and I, who have put it in writing,   535
delight greatly in the retelling of it.

---

1 Or, "she told him": the "words" here may be those of the letter,
  but they may also reflect the practice of sending a sealed letter to
  guarantee the bearer, who would speak the actual message.

Le Chaitivel, ou Quatre Dols

*Talent me prist de remembrer   [col. b]
Un lai dunt jo oï parler.
L'aventure vus en dirai
E la cité vus numerai

5   U il fu nez e cum il ot nun.
Le Chaitivel l'apelet hum,
E si [i]† ad plusurs de ceus
Ki l'apelent *Les Quatre Deuls.*
En Bretaine a Nantes maneit

10 Une dame que mut valeit
De beauté e d'enseignement
E de tut bon affeitement.
N'ot en la tere chevalier
Que aukes feist a preisier,

15 Pur ceo que une feiz la veïst,
Que ne l'amast e requeïst.
Ele nes pot mie tuz amer
Ne ele nes vot mie tuer.
Tutes les dames de une tere

20 Vendreit meuz d'amer requere
Que un fol de sun pan tolir;
Kar cil⁺¹ volt an eire ferir.
La dame fait a celui gre
Desuz la bone volunté;

25 Purquant, s'ele nes veolt oïr,
Nes deit de paroles leidir,
Mes enurer e tenir chier,
A gre servir e mercier.

---

*   This lai appears on ff. 149ra–150vb of Harley 978 and the later hand
titles it "Chaitivel" in the upper left margin.

†   Here and throughout, square brackets in the text indicate an emen-
dation to the text as it appears in Harley 978; the original reading
can be found, keyed to the line number, in Appendix F.

1   Here and throughout, a superscript cross indicates a place where I
have omitted a word or words from Harley 978 without making a
substitution (and where therefore there are no brackets); see, again,
Appendix F for the original reading.

The Wretched One, or Four Sorrows

I was taken with a desire to recall
a lay that I heard spoken of.
I will tell you the events[1] of it
and I will name for you the city
where it was born and what its name was.   5
It is called *The Wretched One*,
and yet there are many of those
who call it *The Four Sorrows*.
In Brittany, at Nantes,[2] there lived
a lady who was of great worth   10
in beauty and learning
and in every good behavior.
There was not a knight in the land
who did anything worthy of praise
who would not, if he saw her once,   15
love her and request her love.
She could by no means love them all
nor did she by any means wish to kill them.[3]
It would be better to ask for the love
of all the ladies of a land   20
than to take a fool away from his rag,
for he wants to lash out at once.[4]
The lady will recompense someone
subject to her good will;
however, if she does not want to hear them,   25
she should not speak ill of them,
but honor them and hold them dear,
willingly serve and thank them.

---

1   The word I translate here as "events" is the ubiquitous *aventure*,
    which has a range of meanings in Marie's lais; see Note on the Text,
    pp. 44–45.
2   Nantes is located on the Loire River, in northwestern France.
3   Kill them, that is, by refusing them, since a frequent claim of
    medieval lovers is that they will die if not granted the favor of their
    beloved. See *Guigemar* and *Equitan*, for example.
4   This passage is notoriously confusing and its meaning obscure; the
    general implication seems to be that you will be struck for taking
    away a fool's rag (or his bread, another possible meaning of "pan")
    but not for courting a lady. The following lines more or less bear
    out the idea that a lady will not, or should not, be unkind to those
    who pursue her, whether or not she accepts their love.

La dame dunt jo voil cunter,
30 Que tant fu requise de amer—
Pur sa beauté, pur sa valur,
S'en entremistrent nuit e jur—
En Bretaine ot quatre baruns,
Mes jeo ne sai numer lur nuns.
35 Mes mut erent de grant beauté;
Il n'aveient gueres de eé,   [f. 149^v]
E chevalers pruz e vaillanz,
Larges, curteis e despendanz;
Mut esteient de grant pris
40 E gentiz hummes del païs.
Icil quatres la dame amoent
E de bien fere se penoent:
Pur li e pur s'amur aveir
I meteit chescun sun poeir.
45 Chescun par sei la requereit
E tute sa peine i meteit;
N'i ot celui ki ne quidast
Que meuz d'autre n'i espleitast.
La dame fu de mut grant [s]ens:
50 En respit mist e en purpens
Pur saver e pur demander
Li queils sereit meuz a amer.
Tant furent tuz de grant valur,
Ne pot eslire le meillur.
55 Ne volt les treis perdre pur l'un:
Bel semblant fait a chescun.
Ses drueries lur donout,
Ses messages lur enveiout.
Li uns de l'autre ne saveit,
60 Mes departir nul nes poeit;
Par bel servir e par preier
Quidot chescun meuz espleiter.
A l'assembler des chevaliers
Voleit chescun estre primers
65 De bien fere, si il peust.
Pur ceo que a la dame pleust.

The lady of whom I wish to tell,
who was so often asked for her love—
on account of her beauty and her worth,
they were working at it night and day—
had in Brittany four worthy men,
but I do not know their names.
Yet they were of very great beauty;
they were scarcely of age,
and bold and valiant knights,
generous, courteous and free-spending;
they were of great worth
and noble men of the country.
These four loved the lady
and took pains to do well:
each one did all he could
to get her and her love.
Each one sought her for himself
and put all his effort into it;
there was not one who did not believe
that he would do better than another.
The lady was very sensible:
she took time and careful thought
to know and to ask
which would be best to love.
They were all of such great worth,
she could not choose the best.
She does not wish to lose three for one:
she treats each one kindly.
She gave them her love-tokens,
sent them her messages.
Not one knew of the others,
but none of them could leave;[1]
each one believed he would come out best
through his good service and his pleas.
At the gathering of knights
each one wanted to be first
to do well, if he could,
because it pleased the lady.

30

35

40

45

50

55

60

65

---

1 These lines are sometimes emended to read "Li uns de l'autre *le*
saveit, / Mes departir nul nes poeit": "Each one knew about the
others, but none of them could leave." In the second line, "departir
nul nes poeit" could also mean "no one could distinguish between
them."

Tuz la teneient pur amie,
Tuz portouent sa druerie,
Anel u mance u gumfanun,
70 E chescun escriot sun nun.
Tuz quatre les ama e tient, [col. b]
Tant que aprés une paske vient,
Que devant Nantes la cité
Ot un turneiement crié.
75 Pur aquointer les quatre druz
I sunt d'autre païs venuz
E li Franceis e li Norman
E li Flemenc e li Breban,
Li Buluineis, li Angevin,
80 Cil ki pres furent veisin;
Tuz i sunt volenters alé.
Lunc tens aveient surjurné.
Al vespr[é] del turneiement
S'entreferirent durement:
85 Li quatre dru furent armé
E eisserent de la cité;
Lur chevaliers viendrent aprés,
Mes sur eus quatre fu le fes.
Cil defors les unt coneüz
90 As enseignes e as escuz.
Cuntre enveient chevaliers,
Deus Flamens e deus Henoiers,
Apareillez cum de puindre;
N'i ad celui ne voille juindre.
95 Cil les virent vers eus venir;
N'aveient talent de fuïr.
Lance baissie, tut a espelun,
Choisi chescun sun cumpainun.
Par tel haïr s'entreferirent
100 Que li quatre defors cheïrent.
Il n'eurent cure des destriers,

They all considered her their beloved,
they all carried her love-tokens,
ring or sleeve or pennon,
and each one cried out her name. 70
She loved and kept all four of them
until it came to a time, after one Easter,
that a tournament had been called
before the city of Nantes.
To meet the four lovers 75
there came from other countries
both the French and the Normans
and the Flemish and the Brabants,
the Bolognese, the Angevins,
the ones who were from close by; 80
they all went there eagerly.[1]
They had been staying there a long time.
On the eve of the tournament
they clashed fiercely with one another:
the four lovers were armed 85
and went out from the city;
their knights came after them,
but the burden fell on these four.
Those outside recognized them
by their banners and their shields. 90
They sent knights against them,
two Flemings and two from Hainault,
ready to attack;
there was none who did not wish to join in.
The four saw them come toward them; 95
they had no desire to flee.
Lance lowered, at a full gallop,
each one picked out his opponent.
They struck each other with such violence
that the four outsiders fell. 100
They did not care about the warhorses,

---

1 Both the Flemish and the Brabants come from the area that is now
   Belgium and the Netherlands. In Marie's time these areas were the
   Duchy of Brabant and the County of Flanders. The Bolognese are
   from Bologna, in northern Italy, and the Angevins from the county
   of Anjou, in the lower Loire valley in France (just east of Nantes).
   Anjou was the ancestral homeland of King Henry II of England,
   and he inherited it in 1151.

Ainz les laisserent estraiers;
Sur les abatuz se resturent;
Lur chevalers les succururent.
105 A la rescusse ot grant medlee,
Meint coup i ot feru d'espee.   [f. 150^r]
La dame fu sur une tur;
Bien choisi les suens e les lur.
Ses druz i vit mut bien aidier:
110 Ne seit queil deit plus preisier.
Li turneimenz cumença,
Li reng crurent, mut espessa.
Devant la porte meintefeiz
Fu le jur mellé le turneiz.
115 Si quatre dru bien feseient,
Si ke de tuz le pris aveient,
Tant ke ceo vient a l'avesprer
Qu'il deveient desevrer.
Trop folement s'abaundonerent
120 Luinz de lur gent, sil cumpererent;
Kar li treis furent ocis
E li quart nafrez e malmis
Parmi la quisse e einz al cors
Si que la lance parut defors.
125 A traverse furent [fer]uz
E tuz quatre furent cheüz.
Cil ki a mort les unt nafrez
Lur escuz unt es chans getez:
Mut esteient pur eus dolent,
130 Nel firent pas a escient.
La noise levat e le cri,
Unc tel doel ne fu oï.
Cil de la cité i alerent;
Unc les autres ne duterent.
135 Pur la dolur des chevaliers
I aveit iteus deus milliers
Ki lur ventaille deslacierent,
Chevoiz e barbes detraherent;
Entre eus esteit li doels communs.
140 Sur sun escu fu mis chescuns;
En la cité les unt porté   [col. b]
A la dame kis ot amé.

but let them go unguarded;
they took their stand above the fallen;
their knights came to their aid.
With that reinforcement there was a great battle: 105
many a blow was struck with sword.
The lady was up on a tower;
she clearly saw her men and their knights.
She sees her beloveds perform very well:
she does not know which she should value most.   110
The tournament began,
the ranks grew and became much thicker.
Before the gate, many times
that day, the battle was joined.
Her four lovers were doing well,   115
so that they were the most praised of all,
until night began to fall
when they were supposed to withdraw.
Most foolishly they put themselves in jeopardy
far from their men, and they paid for it;   120
for three of them were killed
and the fourth wounded and injured
through the thigh and into the body
so that the lance stuck out the other side.
They had been struck through   125
and all four had fallen.
Those who mortally wounded them
threw their own shields down on the field;
they were very upset about them:
they did not do it knowingly.   130
The noise rose up and the cry;
never was such sorrow heard.
Those from the city went there;
they never feared the others.
Out of sorrow for the knights   135
there were some two thousand
who unlaced their visors,
tore their hair and beards;
the sorrow was shared among them all.
Each one was placed on his shield;   140
they carried them into the city
to the lady who had loved them.

Desque ele sot cele aventure,
Paumee chiet a tere dure.
145 Quant ele vient de paumeisun,
Chescun regrette par sun nun.
"Lasse," fet ele, "quei ferai?
Jamés haitie ne serai!
Ces quatre chevalers amoue
150 E chescun par sei cuveitoue;
Mut par aveit en eus granz biens;
Il m'amoent sur tute riens.
Pur lur beauté, pur lur pruesce,
Pur lur valur, pur lur largesce
155 Les fis d'amer [a] mei entendre;
Nes voil tuz perdre pur l'un prendre.
Ne sai le queil jeo dei plus pleindre,
Mes ne puis covrir ne feindre.
L'un vei nafré, li treis sunt mort;
160 N'ai rien el mund ki me confort.
Les morz ferai ensevelir,
E si li nafrez po[e]t garir,
Volenters m'entremeterai
E bons mires li baillerai."
165 En ses chambres le fet porter;
Puis fist les autres cunreer.
A grant amur e noblement
Les aturnat e richement.
En une mut riche abeïe
170 Fist grant offrendre e grant partie,
La u il furent enfuï:
Deus lur face bone merci!
Sages mires aveit mandez,
Sis ad al chevalier livrez,
175 Ki en sa chambre jut nafrez,
Tant que a garisun est turnez.   [f. 150ᵛ]
Ele l'alot veer sovent
E cunfortout mut bonement;
Mes les autres treis regretot
180 E grant dolur pur eus menot.

As soon as she heard what had happened[1]
she fell, fainting, to the hard ground.
When she awakes from her faint,   145
she laments each one by name.
"Wretched me," she says, "what shall I do?
Never will I be happy!
I loved these four knights
and desired each for himself;   150
there was such great good in them;
they loved me above all things.
For their beauty, for their prowess,
for their worth, for their generosity
I had them attend to me out of love;   155
I did not wish to lose all to take one.
I do not know which I should lament most,
but I cannot dissemble or pretend.
I see one wounded, three are dead;
there is nothing in the world that comforts me.   160
I will have the dead men buried,
and if the wounded one can heal,
I will willingly do my part
and will give him good doctors."
She has him carried into her chambers;   165
then she had the others made ready.
With great love, nobly
and richly she prepared them.
In a very rich abbey
she made great offerings and donations,   170
where they were buried:
may God have mercy on them!
She had sent for wise doctors,
and brought them to the knight
who lay wounded in her chamber   175
until he should return to health.
She went to see him often
and comforted him kindly;
but she mourned the other three
and showed great sorrow for them.   180

---

1 Literally, "as soon as she knew the adventure ['aventure']." See
   p. 279, n. 1.

Un jur d'esté aprés manger
Parlot la dame al chevaler.
De sun grant doel li remembrot:
Sun chief jus en baissot;
185 Forment comencet a pen[s]er.
E il la prist a regarder;
Bien aparceit que ele pensot.
Avenaument l'areisunot:
"Dame, vus estes en esfrei!
190 Quei pensez vus? Dites le mei!
Lessez vostre dolur ester!
Bien vus devrez conforter."
"Amis," fet ele, "jeo pensoue,
E voz cumpainuns remembroue.
195 Jamés dame de mun parage,
[Ja] tant n'iert bele, pruz ne sage,
Teus quatre ensemble n'amer[a]
N'en un jur si nes perdr[a],
Fors vus tut sul ki nafrez fustes;
200 Grant poür de mort en eüstes.
Pur ceo que tant vus ai amez,
Voil que mis doels seit remembrez:
De vus quatre ferai un lai,
E *Quatre Dols* vus numerai."
205 Li chevalers li respundi
Hastivement, quant il l'oï:
"Dame, fetes le lai novel,
Si l'apelez *Le Chaitivel*!
E jeo vus voil mustrer reisun
210 Qu'il deit issi aver nun: [col. b]
Li autre sunt pieça finé,
E tut le secle unt usé
La grant pein[e] k'il en suffreient
De l'amur qu'il vers vus aveient;
215 Mes jo ki sui eschapé vif,
Tut esgaré e tut cheitif,
Ceo que al secle puis plus amer
Vei sovent venir e aler,
Parler od mei matin e seir
220 Si n'en puis nule joie aveir
Ne de baisier ne d'acoler
Ne d'autre bien fors de parler.
Teus cent maus me fetes suffrir,

One summer day after dinner
the lady was speaking with the knight.
Her great sorrow came to her mind:
at this she hung her head low;
she became very pensive.   185
And he began to look at her;
he could see clearly that she was thinking.
He spoke to her respectfully:
"Lady, you are upset!
What are you thinking? Tell me!   190
Let go of your sorrow!
You should take some comfort."
"Friend," she says, "I was thinking,
and remembering your companions.
Never will a lady of my noble birth,   195
no matter how beautiful, worthy, or wise,
love four such men all together
nor so lose them in one day—
except you alone, who were wounded;
you were in great danger of death from it.   200
Because I have loved you so much,
I want my sorrows to be remembered:
I will make a lay about you four,
and I will call you *Four Sorrows*."
The knight answered her   205
quickly, when he heard this:
"Lady, make the new lay,
but call it *The Wretched One*!
And I want to tell you the reason
that it should be so named: 210
the others are long gone,
and spent their whole lives
in the great pain that they suffered
from the love that they had for you;
but I, who escaped alive,   215
quite lost and wretched,
see that which I most love in the world
often coming and going,
speaking with me morning and evening,
and I cannot have any joy of it,   220
neither kisses nor embraces
nor any other pleasure but talking.
Such are the hundred ills you make me suffer:

Meuz me vaudreit la mort tenir.
225 Pur ceo ert li lais de mei nomez:
Le Chaitivel iert apelez.
Ki *Quatre Dols* le numera
Sun propre nun li changera."
"Par fei," fet ele, "ceo m'est bel:
230 Ore l'apelum *Le Chaitivel*."
Issi fu li lais comenciez
E puis parfaiz e anunciez.
Icil kil porterent avant,
Quatre Dols l'apelent alquant;
235 Chescun des nuns bien i afiert,
Kar la matire le requert.
Le Chaitivel ad nun en us.
Ici finist, n'i ad plus;
Plus n'en oï, ne plus n'en sai,
240 Ne plus ne vus ne cunterai.

it would be better if I were dead.
Therefore let the lay be named for me: 225
it shall be called *The Wretched One*.
Whoever calls it *Four Sorrows*
will be changing its proper name."
"Indeed," she says, "this pleases me:
Now we will call it *The Wretched One*."   230
Thus the lay was begun
and then finished and performed.
Some of those who would tell it abroad
call it *Four Sorrows*;
each of the names suits it well,   235
for the substance calls for it.
It is commonly called *The Wretched One*.
Here it ends, there is no more;
I heard no more, I know no more,
nor will I tell you any more.   240

Chevrefoil

*Asez me plest e bien le voil
Del lai que humme nume *Chevrefoil*
Que la verité vus en cunt,
Pur quei il fu fet e dunt.

5 Plusurs le me unt cunté e dit
E jeo l'ai trové en escrit   [f. 151ʳ]
De Tristram e de la reïne,
De lur amur que tant fu fine,
Dunt il eurent meinte dolur,

10 Puis mururent en un jur.
Li reis Markes esteit curucié,
Vers Tristram sun nevuz irié;
De sa tere le cungea
Pur la reine qu'il ama.

15 En sa cuntree en est alez,
En Suhtwales, u il fu nez.
Un an demurat tut entier;
Ne pot ariere repeirier.
Mes puis se mist en abandun

20 De mort e de destructiun.
Ne vus esmerveilliez neent,
Kar ki eime mut lealment,
Mut est dolenz e trespensez
Quant il nen ad ses volentez.

25 Tristram est dolent e tres pensis:
Pur ceo se met de sun païs.
En Cornwaille vait tut dreit,
La u la reine maneit.
En la forest tut sul se mist;

30 Ne voleit pas que hum le veïst.
En la vespree s'en eisseit,
Quant tens de herberger esteit;
Od païsanz, od povre gent
Perneit la nuit herbergement.

---

*   This lai appears on ff. 150ᵛᵇ–151ᵛᵇ of Harley 978 and is given the
    title "Cheverefoil" in the upper margin by a later hand.

Honeysuckle

It pleases me well and I truly wish
to tell you the truth of the lai
that is called *Chevrefoil*,
why it was made and about what.
Many have told and recounted to me,   5
and I have found it in writing,
about Tristan and the queen
and their love that was so true,
from which they had great sorrow
and afterwards died on the same day.[1]   10
King Mark was angry,
enraged against his nephew Tristan;
he sent him away from his land
on account of the queen, whom he loved.
Tristan went off into his land,   15
into South Wales, where he was born.
He stayed a full year;
he could not go back again.
But then he gave himself up
to death and destruction.   20
Do not be at all astonished by this,
for one who loves most loyally
is most sorrowful and despondent
when he does not have what he wants.
Tristan is sorrowful and very downcast;   25
for this reason he leaves his country.
He goes straight to Cornwall,
where the queen was staying.
He went into the forest quite alone;
he did not want anyone to see him.   30
In the evening he went out,
when it was time to find lodging;
with peasants, with poor people,
he took lodging that night.

---

1 Like *Lanval*, this lai takes up a story and characters that were
  already well known, though their popularity in literature dates from
  the twelfth century, so Marie is still near the beginnings of the
  written tradition. She deftly conveys the key points of the story of
  Tristan and Yseult (or Isolde)—here called simply "the queen"—
  that are relevant to her version of the tale, but many of her readers
  would likely have known more.

35 Les noveles lur enquereit
Del rei, cum il se cunteneit.
Ceo li dient: qu'il unt oï
Que li barun erent bani.
A Tintagel deivent venir;
40 Li reis i veolt sa curt tenir.
A Pentecuste i serunt tuit.   [col. b]
Mut i avera joie e deduit,
E la reine i sera.
Tristram l'oï, mut se haita:
45 Ele ne purrat mie aler
K'il ne la veie trespasser.
Le jur que li rei fu meüz,
E Tristram est al bois venuz.
Sur le chemin qu'il saveit
50 Que la reine passer deveit,
Une codre trencha par mi,
Tute quarreie la fendi.
Quant il ad paré le bastun,
De sun cutel escrit sun nun.
55 [S]e* la reine s'aparceit,
Que mut grant garde en perneit—
Autre feiz li fu avenu
Que si l'aveit aparceü—
De sun ami bien conustra
60 Le bastun quant ele le verra.
Ceo fu la summe de l'escrit
Qu'il li aveit mandé e dit:
Que lunges ot ilec esté
E atendu e surjurné
65 Pur [espier] e pur saver
Coment il la pust veer,
Kar ne pot nent vivre sanz li.
D'euls deus fu il autresi
Cum del chevrefoil esteit
70 Ki a la codre se perneit:
Quant il est si laciez e pris

---

*   Here and throughout, square brackets in the text indicate an emen-
     dation to the text as it appears in Harley 978; the original reading
     can be found, keyed to the line number, in Appendix F.

294   CHEVREFOIL

He asked them for news   35
of the king and how he was behaving.
They tell him this: that they have heard
that the barons were banished.[1]
They are supposed to go to Tintagel;
the king wants to hold court there.   40
At Pentecost[2] they will all be there.
There will be great joy and delight,
and the queen will be there.
Tristan heard this and was very pleased:
there is no way she can travel   45
that he will not see her pass by.
The day that the king had set out,
Tristan came to the wood.
On the road that he knew
the queen must travel,   50
he split a hazel tree along its length
and squared it off.
When he has prepared the staff,
with his knife he writes his name.
If the queen, who was keeping careful watch for it   55
notices it,
it had happened other times
that she had noticed it like this —
she will surely recognize the staff
of her beloved when she sees it.   60
This was the gist of the writing
that he had sent and said:
that he had been there a long time
and waited and sojourned
to find out and to know   65
how he might see her,
for he could by no means live without her.
For the two of them it was just
as it was with the honeysuckle
that clung to the hazel tree: 70
when it is so entwined and attached

---

1 That is, the barons who had made accusations of adultery against
   Tristan and the queen.
2 The feast of Pentecost takes place seven weeks after Easter, in mid
   to late May or early June (in the western Christian Church). Eccle-
   siastical feast days were a standard way of marking time in medieval
   culture.

E tut entur le fust s'est mis,
Ensemble poeient bien durer;
Mes ki puis les volt desevrer,
75 Li codres muert hastivement
E li chevrefoil ensemblement.   [f. 151ᵛ]
"Bele amie, si est de nus:
Ne vus sanz mei, ne mei sanz vus."
La reine vait chevachant;
80 Ele esgardat tut un pendant.
Le bastun vit, bien l'aparceüt,
Tutes les lettres i conut.
Les chevalers que la menoent,
Que ensemble od li erroent,
85 Cumanda tuz [a] arester:
Descendre vot e resposer.
Cil unt fait sun commandement.
Ele s'en vet luinz de sa gent;
Sa meschine apelat a sei,
90 Brenguein, que mut fu de bone fei.
Del chemin un poi s'esluina;
Dedenz le bois celui trova
Que plus l'amot que rien vivant.
Entre eus meinent joie grant.
95 A lui parlat tut a leisir,
E ele li dit sun pleisir;
Puis li mustra cumfaitement
Del rei avrat acordement,
E que mut li aveit pesé
100 De ceo qu'il [l']ot si cungié;
Par encusement l'aveit fait.
Atant s'en part, sun ami lait—
Mes quant ceo vient al desevrer,
Dunc comencent a plurer.
105 Tristram a Wales s'en rala,
Tant que sis uncles le manda.
Pur la joie qu'il ot eue
De s'amie qu'il ot veue
E pur ceo k'il aveit escrit—
110 Si cum la reine l'ot dit,
Pur les paroles remembrer—   [col. b]
Tristram, ki bien saveit harper,
En aveit fet un nuvel lai.

and has grown all around the wood,
together they could endure well;
but if someone then wishes to separate them
the hazel tree dies quickly   75
and the honeysuckle along with it.
"Beautiful beloved, so it is with us:
neither you without me, nor me without you."
The queen goes riding along;
she looked all along the slope.   80
She saw the staff, she noted it well,
she recognized all the letters there.
All the knights who were attending her,
who were traveling with her,
she commanded to stop: 85
she wished to dismount and rest.
They did as she commanded.
She goes off far from her people;
she summoned her maid,
Brangain, who was truly faithful.   90
She went a little way from the road;
in the wood she found him
who loved her more than any living thing.
They share their great joy.
She spoke to him quite at leisure,   95
and told him her pleasure;
then she explained to him just how
he can be reconciled with the king,
and that it had weighed on him greatly
that he had sent Tristan away as he had;   100
he had done it because of the accusation.
With that she departs, leaves her beloved—
but when it comes to the parting,
then they begin to weep.
Tristan went back to Wales   105
until his uncle sent for him.
Because of the joy that he had had
from seeing his beloved,
and because of what he had written—
just as the queen had told him,   110
in order to remember the words—
Tristan, who was a gifted harper,
had made of it a new lai.

Asez brevement le numerai:
115 *Gotelef* l'apelent en engleis,
Chevrefoil le nument en franceis.
Dit vus en ai la verité
Del lai que j'ai ici cunté.

I will name it very briefly:
they call it *Goatleaf* in English;
in French they name it *Chevrefoil*.
I have told you the truth of it,
of the lai I have recounted here.

Guildelüec et Guilliadun, ou Eliduc

*De un mut ancien lai bretun
Le cunte e tute la reisun
Vus dirai, si cum jeo entent
La verité, mun escient.
5 En Britaine ot un chevalier
Pruz e curteis, hardi e fier;
Elidus ot nun, ceo m'est vis.
N'ot si vaillant hume al païs.
Femme ot espuse, noble e sage,
10 De haute gent, de grant parage.
Ensemble furent lungement,
Mut s'entreamerent lëaument;
Mes puis avient par une guere
Que il alat soudees quere:
15 Iloc ama une meschine,
Fille ert a rei e a reïne.
Guilliadun ot nun la pucele,
El rëaume nen ot plus bele.
La femme resteit apelee
20 Guildelüec en sa cuntree.
D'eles deus ad li lai a nun
Guildelüec ha Gualadun.
Elidus fu primes nomez,
Mes ore est li nuns remuez,
25 Kar des dames est avenu.
L'aventure dunt li lais fu,
Si cum avient, vus cunterai;
La verité vus en dirrai.   [f. 152ʳ]
Elidus aveit un seignur,
30 Reis de Brutaine la meinur,
Que mut l'amot e cherisseit,
E il lëaument le serveit.

---

*   This lai appears on ff. 151ᵛᵇ–160ʳᵃ of Harley 978 and is titled
    "Eliduc" in the upper margin by the usual later hand. Like
    Chaitivel, ou Quatre Dols, this lai is given two possible titles by
    Marie; unlike that lai, this one is generally known by the supposedly
    discarded title. I have chosen to follow Marie's suggestion that
    Guildelüec et Guilliadun is its more correct and current title; I use
    her usual spelling of Guilliadun rather than the Breton version she
    gives at l. 22 ("Gualadun").

Guildelüec and Guilliadun, or Eliduc

I will tell you the story and the whole account
of a very old Breton lai
just as I understand the truth of it,
to the best of my knowledge.
In Brittany there was a knight,[1]   5
worthy and courteous, bold and fierce;
Eliduc was his name, as I understand.
There was no man so valiant in the country.
He had married a woman, noble and wise,
of good family, of distinguished descent.   10
They were together a long time,
they loved one another loyally;
but then it happened, on account of a war,
that he went to look for work as a soldier:
there he fell in love with a girl,   15
she was the daughter of a king and a queen.
Guilliadun was the girl's name;
there was none more beautiful in the realm.
The wife for her part was called
Guildelüec in her region.   20
From the two of them the lai is called
Guildelüec and Guilliadun.
It was first named *Eliduc,*
but now the name is changed,
because it happened to the ladies.   25
The adventure about which the lai was made
I will recount for you just as it happened;
I will tell you the truth of it.[2]
Eliduc had a lord,
king of Brittany,   30
who loved and cherished him greatly,
and Eliduc served him loyally.

---

1 On Britaine/Brutaine (la meinur), see note to *Guigemar*, l. 25. While
  "Britaine" can mean either Great Britain or Brittany, it becomes
  clear below that the latter is meant in this case.
2 The word "aventure" and the related verb "avenir" run through this
  lai as they do many others; see the Note on the Text, pp. 44–45.

U que li reis deust errer,
Il aveit la tere a garder;
35 Pur sa pruesce le retint.
Pur tant de meuz mut li avint:
Par les forez poeit chacier;
N'i ot si hardi forestier
Ki cuntredire l[i]* osast
40 Ne ja une feiz en grusçast.
Pur l'envie del bien de lui,
Si cum avient sovent d'autrui,
Esteit a sun seignur medlez,
Empeirez e encusez,
45 Que de la curt le cungea
Sanz ceo qu'il ne l'areisuna.
Eliducs ne saveit pur quei.
Soventefiez requist le rei
Qu'il escundist de lui preïst
50 E que losenge ne creïst:
Mut l'aveit volenters servi.
Mes li rei pas ne li respundi.
Quant il nel volt de rien oïr,
Si l'en covient idunc partir.
55 A sa mesun en est alez,
Si ad tuz ses amis mandez.
Del rei sun seignur lur mustra
E de l'ire que vers lui a;
Mut li servi a sun poeir,
60 Ja ne deust maugré aveir.
Li vileins dit par reprover,
Quant tence a sun charier,
Que amur de seignur n'est pas fieuz,   [col. b]
Sil est sages e vedziez
65 Ki lëauté tient sun seignur,

Whenever the king had to travel,
Eliduc was given the land to guard;
the king retained him for his prowess.   35
From this he gained much advantage:
he could hunt in the forests;
there was no forester so bold
that he would dare to refuse him
nor even grumble about it once.   40
Out of envy for his good fortune,
as often happens to many another,
he was spoken ill of to his lord,
wronged and accused,
so that the king sent him away from the court   45
without even asking him about it.[1]
Eliduc did not know why.
Repeatedly he asked the king
to listen to his defense
and not to believe slander: 50
he had served him very willingly.
But the king did not reply to him.
Since he does not wish to listen to him at all,
Eliduc has to leave there.
He went to his house   55
and sent for all his friends.
He told them about the king his lord
and about his anger toward Eliduc;
he served him to the very best of his ability,
he should not get ill-will for it.   60
The peasant says, as a proverb,
when he squabbles with his plowman,
that the love of a lord is not reliable,[2]
but a man is wise and shrewd
who maintains loyalty to his lord   65

---

1 *Areisuner* can also have a formal, legal sense of "interrogate"; either
   way, the suggestion is that the king did not give Eliduc a chance to
   reply to the charges against him.
2 The word *fieuz* can mean both "loyal, faithful, reliable" and "fief,"
   the land granted by a lord to his vassal in return for the vassal's
   service. Rychner and Ewert point out the implicit message: a lord's
   love, unlike a grant of land, is not a stable thing. Attributing prover-
   bial statements like this to a *vilain* or peasant is typical in medieval
   literature; there is even a proverb collection called the *Proverbes au
   vilain.*

Envers ses bons veisins amur.
Ne volt al païs arester,
Ainz passera, ceo dit, la mer:
Al rëaume de Loengre ira,
70 E une piece se deduira.
Sa femme en la tere larra;
A ses hummes cumandera
Que il la gard[e]nt lëaument
E tuit si ami ensement.
75 A cel cunseil s'est arestez,
Si s'est richement aturnez.
Mut furent dolent si ami
Pur ceo ke de eus se departi.
Dis chevalers od sei mena,
80 E sa femme le cunvea;
Forment demeine grant dolur
Al departir sun seignur;
Mes il l'aseurat de sei
Qu'il li porterat bone fei.
85 De lui se departi atant,
Il tient sun chemin tut avant;
A la mer vient, si est passez,
En Toteneis est arivez.
Plusurs reis [i] ot en la tere,
90 Entre eus eurent estrif e guere.
Vers Excestre en cel païs
Maneit un humme mut poestis,
Vieuz hum e auntien esteit.
Kar heir madle nen aveit,
95 Une fille ot a marier.
Pur ceo k'il ne la volt doner
A sun pe[r], cil le guerriot;
Tute sa tere si gastot.
En un chastel l'aveit enclos;
100 N'aveit el chastel hume si os
Ki cuntre lui osast eissir

[f. 152ᵛ]

and love for his good neighbors.
Eliduc does not wish to stay in the country;
instead, he says, he will cross the sea:
he will go to the realm of England[1]
and will enjoy himself there for a while. 70
He will leave his wife in this land;
he will command his men
to guard her loyally,
and all his friends as well.
He held to this plan 75
and prepared himself richly.
His friends were very sad
because he was leaving them.
He took ten knights with him,
and his wife saw him off; 80
she lamented very greatly
at the departure of her lord,
but he assured her for his part
that he will keep faith with her.
With that he left her, 85
he set forth on his way;
he came to the sea, he crossed over,
he arrived in Totnes.[2]
There were many kings in the land;
there was strife and war between them. 90
Near Exeter in that country
lived a very powerful man
he was an old man, ancient.
Since he had no male heir,
he had to marry off a daughter. 95
Because he did not want to give her
to his neighbor, the latter was making war on him;
he laid waste all his land.
He had trapped him in a castle;
there was not a man in the castle so bold 100
that he dared go forth against him

---

1 "Loengre," derived from Old Welsh Lloegyr or Latin Loegria, is
  often used as a name for England in Old French romance texts.
2 Totnes is in Devon, near the western end of the south coast of
  England. Geoffrey of Monmouth's *History of the Kings of Britain*
  reports that Brutus, the legendary founder of Britain, landed there
  when he first arrived at the island. Exeter, mentioned just below, is
  about twenty miles from Totnes.

Estur ne mellee tenir.
Elidus en oï parler;
Ne voleit mes avant aler
105 Quant iloc ad guere trovee;
Remaner volt en la cuntree.
Li reis ki plus esteit grevez
E damagiez e encumbrez
Vodrat aider a sun poeir
110 E en soudees remaneir.
Ses messages i enveia
E par ses lettres li manda
Que de sun païs iert eissuz
E en s'aïe esteit venuz;
115 Mes li mandast sun pleisir,
E s'il nel voleit retenir,
Cunduit li donast par sa tere
Quant ireit soudees quere.
Quant li reis vit les messagers,
120 Mut les ama e ot chers;
Sun cunestable ad apelez
E hastivement comandez
Que cunduit li appareillast
Ke le barun amenast.
125 Si face osteus appareiller
U il puissent herberger;
Tant lur face livrer e rendre
Cum il vodrunt le meis despendre.
Li cunduit fu appareillez
130 E pur Eliduc enveiez
E a grant honur receüz;
Mut par fu bien al rei venuz.
Sun ostel fu chiés un burgeis   [col. b]
Que mut fu sage e curteis;
135 Sa bele chambre encurtinee
Li ad li ostes delivree.
Eliduc se fist bien servir:
A sun manger feseit venir
Les chevalers meseisez
140 Que al burc erent herbergez.
A tuz ses hummes defendi
Que n'i eust nul si hardi
Que des quarante jurs primers
Preïst livreisun ne deners.

to engage in single combat or in battle.
Eliduc heard tell of this;
he did not want to go on any farther
when he has found war there;   105
he wants to stay in the region.
He will try to help, as best he can,
the king who had been so attacked
and harmed and troubled,
and to stay on as a paid soldier.   110
He sent his messenger there
and conveyed to the king in his letter
that he had set forth from his land
and come to his aid;
but the king should indicate his pleasure,   115
and if he did not wish to retain him,
should give him safe conduct through his land
when Eliduc went to look for work as a soldier.
When the king saw the messengers,
he loved and valued them greatly;   120
he called his constable
and quickly ordered
that he should prepare an escort
that would accompany the nobleman.
He has lodgings made ready   125
where they could stay;
he has them given and provided with as much
as they could wish to spend in a month.
The escort was prepared
and sent for Eliduc   130
and received with great honor;
he was indeed very welcome to the king.
His lodging was at the house of a townsman
who was very wise and courteous;
the host put at his disposal   135
his beautiful tapestried chamber.
Eliduc gained good service for himself:
he had unfortunate knights
who were lodged in the town
come to his feast.   140
He forbade all his men
that anyone should be so bold
as to take gifts or money
for the first forty days.

145 Al terz jur qu'il ot surjurné
Li criz leva en la cité
Que lur enemi sunt venu
E par la cuntree espandu;
Ja vodrunt la vile asaillir
150 E de si ke as portes venir.
Eliduc ad la noise oïe
De la gent ki est esturdie.
Il s'est armé, plus n'i atent,
E si cumpainuns ensement.
155 Quatorze chevalers muntant
Ot en la vile surjurnant;
Plusurs en i aveit nafrez
E des prisuns i ot asez.
Cil virent Eliduc munter;
160 Par les osteus se vunt armer,
Fors de la porte od lui eissirent,
Que sumunse n'i atendirent.
"Sire," funt il, "od vus irum
E ceo que vus ferez, ferum!"
165 Il lur respunt: "Vostre merci!
Avreit i nul de vus ici
Ki maupas u destreit seust,
U l'um encumbrer les peust?   [f. 153ʳ]
Si nus ici les atendums,
170 Peot cel estre, nus justerums;
Mes ceo n'ateint a nul espleit,
Ki autre cunseil en saveit."
Cil li dient: "Sire, par fei,
Pres de cel bois en cel ristei
175 La ad une estreite charriere,
Par unt il repeirent ariere;
Quant il averunt fet lur eschec,
Si returnerunt par ilec.
Desarmez sur lur palefrez
180 S'en revunt soventefez;
Si se mettent en aventure
Cume de murir a dreiture."

On the third day that he had stayed there 145
the cry arose in the city
that their enemies have come
and spread out through the countryside;
now they want to attack the town
and come up as far as the gates. 150
Eliduc heard the noise
of the people, who were dazed.
He armed himself, he waits no longer,
and his companions do the same.
Fourteen mounted knights 155
were staying in the town;
many of them were wounded
and there were a number of prisoners.
They saw Eliduc mount;
they go to the houses to arm themselves, 160
they went out the gate with him,
they did not wait for an order.
"Lord," they say, "we will go with you
and that which you do, we will do!"
He answers them, "Thank you all! 165
Might there be any of you here
who would know of a narrow or difficult path
where one could attack them?
If we wait for them here,
it may be that we will joust; 170
but that does not amount to any sort of exploit,
for one who knew a better plan."
They say to him: "Lord, in faith,
close to this wood, in that field of hemp[1]
there is a narrow cart-track, 175
by which they will make their retreat;
when they have taken their spoils,
they will return that way.
They very often go back by there
unarmed, on their palfreys; 180
thus they put themselves
at risk of almost certain death."[2]

---

1 The word *ristei* is not found elsewhere but may derive from *rista* or
   riste, meaning hemp; this plant can grow high enough to conceal a
   person. Alternative translations are "field of flax" or "thicket of rushes."
2 "Put themselves at risk" here translates "put themselves *en aven-*
   ture," that is, at the mercy of chance or fate, another instance of this
   charged word.

Bien tost les purreit damagier
E eus laidier e empeirier.
185 Elidus lur ad dit, "Amis,
La meie fei vus en plevis:
Ki en tel liu ne va suvent
U il quide perdre a scient,
Ja gueres ne gainera
190 Ne en grant pris ne muntera.
Vus estes tuz hummes le rei,
Si li devez porter grant fei.
Venez od mei la u jeo irai,
Si fetes ceo que jeo ferai!
195 Jo vus asseur lëaument,
Ja n'i avrez encumbrement,
Pur tant cu[m] jo puis aidier.
Si nus poüm rien gainier,
Ceo nus iert turné a grant pris
200 De damagier noz enemis."
Icil unt pris la seurté,
Ci l'unt de si que al bois mené;
Pres del chemin sunt enbuschié,   [col. b]
Tant que cil se sunt repeirié.
205 Elidus lur ad tut demustré
E enseignié e devisé
De queil manere a eus puindrunt
E cum il les escrierunt.
Quant al destreit furent [entrez],
210 Elidus les ad escriez.
Tuz apela ses cumpainuns,
De bien faire les ad sumuns.
Il i fierent durement;
Nes esparnierent nent.
215 Cil esteient tut esbaï,
Tost furent rumpu e departi;
En poi de hure furent vencu.
Lur cunestable unt retenu
E tant des autres chevaliers;
220 Tuit enchargent lur esquiers.
Vint e cinc furent cil de ça,
Trente en pristrent de ceus de la.
Del herneis pristrent a grant espleit;
Merveillus gaain i unt feit.
225 Ariere s'en vunt tut lié:

He could very quickly harm them
and damage and injure them.
Eliduc says to them, "Friends, 185
I pledge you my faith on this:
one who does not often go
into a situation where he truly expects to lose
will scarcely ever win
or achieve great worth. 190
You are all the king's men
and should truly keep faith with him.
Come with me where I will go,
and do what I will do!
I assure you loyally, 195
you will never be harmed
as long as I can help you.
If we can gain anything,
it will redound greatly to our credit
to have harmed our enemies." 200
The men accepted his assurance
and led him up to the wood;
near the path they waited in ambush,
until the others retreated.
Eliduc explained everything to them 205
and instructed them and planned
in what way they will attack them
and how they will challenge them.
When the enemy had come into the narrow path
Eliduc shouted out a challenge to them. 210
He called all his companions,
he urged them to fight well.
They strike fiercely there;
they did not spare them at all.
The enemy were completely overcome, 215
they were quickly broken up and scattered;
in a short time they were defeated.
They held on to the constable
and a number of other knights;
they take command of all their squires. 220
There were twenty-five on Eliduc's side;
they captured thirty of the others.
In great haste they took their gear;
they made enormous gains there.
Back they come, entirely happy: 225

Mut aveient bien espleitié.
Li reis esteit sur une tur,
De ses hummes ad grant poür;
De Eliduc forment se pleigneit,
230 Kar il quidout e cremeit
Qu'il eit mis en abandun
Ses chevaliers par traïsun.
Cil s'en vienent tut aruté,
Tut chargié e tut trussé.
235 Mut furent plus al revenir
Qu'il n'esteient al fors eissir:
Par ceo les descunut li reis,
Si fu en dute e en suspeis.   [f. 153ᵛ]
Les portes cumanda fermer
240 E les genz sur les murs munter
Pur traire a eus e pur lancier;
Mes n'en avrunt nul mester.
Cil eurent enveié avant
Un esquier esperunant,
245 Que l'aventure lur mustra
E del soudeür li cunta,
Cum il ot ceus de la vencuz
E cum il s'esteit cuntenuz;
Unc teu chevalier ne fu.
250 Lur cunestable ad retenu
E vint e noef des autres pris,
E muz nafrez e muz ocis.
Li reis, quant la novele oï,
A merveille s'en esjoï.
255 Jus de la tur est descenduz
E encuntre Eliduc venuz.
De sun bienfait le mercia,
E il les prisuns li livera.
As autres depart le herneis,
260 A sun eos ne retient que treis
Cheval[s] ke li erent loé.
Tut ad departi e duné
La sue part communement,
As prisuns e a l'autre gent.
265 Aprés cel fet que jeo vus di,
Mut l'amat li reis e cheri.
Un an entier l'ad retenu
E ceus ki sunt od lui venu,

they had acquitted themselves very well.
The king was on a tower,
he is very afraid for his men;
he greatly lamented about Eliduc,
for he believed and feared   230
that he has put his knights in danger
by treason.
They come along, all in a troop,
all laden down and carrying things.
They were a great many more upon their return   235
than they were when they set out:
for this reason the king did not recognize them,
and was in doubt and mistrustful.
He ordered that the gates be shut
and people to mount the walls   240
to shoot and throw things at them;
but they will have no need to do so.
Those returning had sent
a squire spurring ahead,
who told them what had happened   245
and reported to them about the soldier,
how he had defeated the outsiders
and how he had behaved;
there was never such a knight.
He has kept their constable   250
and taken twenty-nine of the others,
and wounded and killed many people.
The king, when he heard the news,
rejoiced wonderfully at it.
He came down from the tower   255
and went to meet Eliduc.
He thanked him for his good deeds,
and Eliduc handed over the prisoners to him.
He shares out the spoils among the others;
for his own use he keeps only three   260
horses that were allotted to him.
He divided out and gave out
all his own share generally,
to the prisoners and the other people.
After this deed that I have told you   265
the king loved and cherished him very much.
He retained him for a whole year,
and those who came with him;

La fiance de lui en prist;
270 De sa tere gardein en fist.
Eliduc fu curteis e sage,
Beau chevaler, pruz e large.
La fille le rei l'oï numer   [col. b]
E les biens de lui recunter.
275 Par un suen chamberlenc privé
L'ad requis, prié e mandé
Que a li venist esbanier
E parler e bien acuinter;
Mut durement s'esmerveillot
280 Qu'il a li ne repeirot.
Eliduc respunt qu'il irrat,
Volenters s'i acuinterat.
Il est munté sur sun destrier,
Od lui mena un chevalier;
285 A la pucele veit parler.
Quant en la chambre deust entrer,
Le chamberlenc enveit avant.
Cil s'alat aukes entargant,
De ci que cil revient ariere.
290 Od duz semblant, od simple chere,
Od mut noble cuntenement
Parla mut afeitément
E merciat la dameisele
Guilliadun, que mut fu bele,
295 De ceo que li plot a mander
Que il venist a li parler.
Cele l'aveit par la mein pris,
Desur un lit erent asis;
De plusurs choses unt parlé.
300 Icele l'ad mut esgardé,
Sun vis, sun cors, e sun semblant;
Dit, "en lui n'at mesavenant."
Forment le prise en sun curage.
Amurs i lance sun message,
305 Que la somunt de lui amer;
Palir la fist e suspirer,
Mes nel volt mettre a reisun,
Qu'il ne li turt a mesprisun.   [f. 154ʳ]
Une grant piece i demura;
310 Puis prist cungé, si s'en ala.
Ele li duna mut a enviz,

he accepted his promise of loyalty,
he made him guardian of his land.   290
Eliduc was courteous and wise,
a handsome knight, worthy and generous.
The king's daughter heard him spoken of by name
and heard his good qualities recounted.
By means of a private chamberlain of hers   275
she asked, requested, and sent to him
that he should come to enjoy himself with her
and talk and become well acquainted;
she was greatly surprised
that he did not come to see her.   280
Eliduc replies that he will come,
he will gladly make her acquaintance.
He mounted his warhorse,
he took a knight with him;
he goes to speak with the maiden.   285
When he was about to enter the chamber,
he sends the chamberlain ahead.
He went on waiting for a bit,
until the man came back.
With a gentle appearance, with an open face,   290
with very noble behavior
he spoke most courteously
and thanked the damsel
Guilliadun, who was very beautiful,
for being pleased to send for him   295
to come and talk to her.
She had taken him by the hand,
they were seated on a bed;
they spoke of many things.
She looked at him intently,   300
his face, his body, and his appearance;
she thinks, "in him there is nothing unbecoming."
She prizes him greatly in her heart.
Love sends his messenger there,
who calls upon her to love him;   305
it made her grow pale and sigh,
but she does not wish to talk about it,
lest it should lead her into wrongdoing.
He stayed there a great while;
then he took his leave and went away.   310
She granted it much against her wishes,

Mes nepurquant s'en est partiz;
A sun ostel s'en est alez.
Tut est murnes e trespensez;
315 Pur la bele est en effrei,
La fille sun seignur le rei,
Que tant ducement l'apela;
E de ceo ke ele suspira.
Mut par se tient a entrepris
320 Que tant ad esté al païs,
Que ne l'ad veue sovent.
Quant ceo ot dit, si se repent:
De sa femme li remembra
E cum il li esseüra
325 Que bone fei li portereit
E lëaument se cuntendreit.
La pucele ki l'ot veü
Vodra de lui fere sun dru.
Unc mes tant nul ne preisa;
330 Si ele peot, sil retendra.
Tute la nuit veillat issi,
Ne resposa ne ne dormi.
Al demain est matin levee,
Sun chamberlenc ad apel[é];
335 Tut sun estre li ad mustré.
A une fenestre est alé[e]:
"Par fei," fet ele, "mal m'esteit!
Jo sui cheï[e] en mauvés pleit:
Jeo eim le novel soudeer,
340 Eliduc, li bon chevaler.
Unc anuit nen oi repos
Ne pur dormir les oilz ne clos.
Si par amur me veut amer   [col. b]
E de sun cors asseurer,
345 Jeo ferai trestut sun pleisir,
Si l'en peot grant bien avenir:
De ceste tere serat reis.
Tant par est sages e curteis,
Que, s'il ne m'aime par amur,
350 Murir m'estuet a grant dolur."

but nevertheless he departed;
he went to his lodging.
He is quite downcast and troubled;
he is distressed on account of the beautiful girl,   315
the daughter of his lord the king,
who called him to her so sweetly;
and because she sighed.
He considers himself very unfortunate
to have been in the country so long,   320
and not to have seen her often.
When he had said this to himself, he feels sorry:
he remembered his wife
and how he assured her
that he would keep faith with her   325
and conduct himself loyally.
The girl who had seen him
will wish to make him her lover.
She had never valued anyone so much;
if she can, she will keep him.   330
All night she lay awake like this,
she did not rest or sleep.
The next day she got up in the morning,
she called her chamberlain;
she told him her whole situation.   335
She went to a window:
"In faith," she says, "it goes ill with me![1]
I have fallen into a bad way:
I love the new soldier,
Eliduc, the good knight.   340
At night I can get no rest
nor close my eyes to sleep.
If he wishes to love me truly
and pledge his body to me,
I will do all his pleasure,   345
and great good can come to him from it:
he will be king of this land.
He is so very wise and courteous
that, if he does not love as a lover,
I must die in great sorrow."   350

---

1 Guilliadun's situation—as a princess who has fallen in love with a
  foreign soldier—recalls that of Lavine in the *Roman d'Eneas*, who
  also laments her plight while standing at a window; see Appendix
  B1.

Quant ele ot dit ceo ke li plot,
Li chamberlenc que ele apelot
Li ad duné cunseil leal;
Ne li deit humme turner a mal.
355 "Dame," fet il, "quant vus l'amez,
Enveez i, si li mandez;
Ceinture u laz u anel
Enveiez li, si li ert bel.
Sil le receit bonement
360 E joius seit del mandement,
Seur[e] seez de s'amur!
Il n'ad suz ciel empereür,
Si vus amer le voliez,
Que mut n'en deust estre liez."
365 La dameisele respundi,
Quant le cunseil oï de li:
"Coment savrai par mun present
S'il ad de mei amer talent?
Jeo ne vi unc chevalier
370 Ki se feïst de ceo preier,
Si il amast u il haïst,
Que volenters ne retenist
Cel present ke hum li enveast.
Mut harreie k'il me gabast.
375 Mes nepurquant pur le semblant
Peot l'um conustre li alquant.
Aturnez vus e si alez!"
"Jeo sui," fet il, "tut aturnez."   [f. 154ᵛ]
"Un anel de or li porterez
380 E ma ceinture li durez.
Mil feiz le me saluerez."
Li chamberlenc s'en est turnez.
Ele remeint en teu manere;
Pur poi ne l'apelet arere,
385 E nekedent le lait aler
Si se cumence a dementer:
"Lasse, cum est mis quors suspris
Pur un humme de autre païs!
Ne sai s'il est de haute gent,
390 Si s'en irat hastivement;
Jeo remeindrai cume dolente.
Folement ai mise m'entente.
Unc mes ne parlai fors ier,

When she had said what she wanted to,
the chamberlain whom she called
gave her loyal advice;
no one should take it amiss.
"Lady," he says, "since you love him,   355
send to him, and convey a message;
send him a belt or lace or ring,
and it will please him.
If he receives it warmly
and is happy at its having been sent,   360
you will be sure of his love!
There is no emperor under heaven
who, if you wished to love him,
should not be delighted by it."
The damsel replied,   365
when she heard this counsel from him,
"How will I know, by my present,
if he wishes to love me?
I never saw a knight
who, whether he loved or hated,   370
would have to be begged
before he would willingly keep
a present that someone sent to him.
I would certainly hate for him to mock me.
But nevertheless, one may learn something   375
by his appearance.
Make yourself ready and go ahead!"
"I am," he says, "quite ready."
"You will take him a ring of gold
and give him my belt.   380
You shall greet him a thousand times for me."
The chamberlain went on his way.
She remains as she was;
she very nearly called him back,
and yet she lets him go   385
and begins to lament:
"Wretched me, how my heart is captured
by a man from another country!
I do not know if he is of noble family,
if he will quickly leave;   390
I will stay here, sorrowful.
I have set my heart foolishly.
I never spoke to him but yesterday,

E ore le faz de amer preier.
395 Jeo quid k'il me blamera;
S'il est curteis, gre me savera;
Ore est del tut en aventure.
E si il n'ad de m'amur cure,
Mut me tendrai maubaillie;
400 Jamés n'avrai joie en ma vie."
Tant cum ele se dementa,
Li chamberlenc mut se hasta.
A Eliduc esteit venuz,
A cunseil li ad dit saluz
405 Que la pucele li mandot,
E l'anelet li presentot,
La ceinture li ad donee;
Li chevalier l'ad merciee.
L'anelet d'or mist en sun dei,
410 La ceinture ceint entur sei.
Ne li vadlet plus ne li dist,
Ne il nient ne li requist
Fors tant que de[l] s[u]en li offri.   [col. b]
Cil n'en prist rien, si est parti.
415 A sa dameisele reva,
Dedenz sa chambre la trova;
De part celui la salua
E del present la mercia.
"Diva," fet el, "nel me celer!
420 Veut il mei par amurs amer?"
Il li respunt: "Ceo m'est avis.
Li [chevalier] n'est pas jolis;
Jeo le tienc a curteis e a sage,
Que bien seit celer sun curage.
425 De vostre part le saluai
E voz aveirs li presentai.
De vostre ceinture se ceint,
Par mi les flancs bien s'estreint,
E l'anelet mist en sun dei.
430 Ne li dis plus ne il a mei."
"Nel receut il pur druerie?
Peot cel estre, jeo sui traïe."
Cil li ad dit: "Par fei, ne sai.
Ore oez ceo ke jeo dirai:
435 S'il ne vus vosist mut grant bien,

and now I am asking for his love.
I believe that he will blame me;   395
if he is courtly, he will be grateful to me;
now it is completely up to chance.[1]
And if he does not care for my love,
I will consider myself most unfortunate;
Never in my life will I have joy."   400
While she was lamenting to herself,
the chamberlain hurried along.
He had reached Eliduc,
as directed he gave him the greetings
that the maiden had sent him,   405
and presented the little ring to him,
gave him the belt;
the knight thanked him for it.
He put the golden ring on his finger,
he girds the belt around him.   410
Neither did the youth say any more to him,
nor did he ask him anything
except that he offered him something of his own.
The chamberlain accepted nothing; he departed.
He goes back to his damsel,   415
he found her in her chamber;
he greeted her on behalf of Eliduc
and thanked her for the present.
"Go on," she says, "do not hide it from me!
Will he love me as a lover?"   420
He replies, "So it seems to me.
The knight is not fickle;
I consider him a courtly, wise man
who knows well how to hide his feelings.
I greeted him on your behalf   425
and gave him your gifts.
He girded himself with your belt,
he wound it tightly around his hips,
and he put the ring on his finger.
I said no more to him, nor he to me."   430
"Did he not receive it as a love-token?
If it can be so, I am betrayed."
He said to her, "In faith, I do not know.
Now hear what I will say:
if he did not wish you great good,   435

---

1 The word translated here as "chance" is, again, "aventure."

Il ne vosist del vostre rien."
"Tu paroles," fet ele, "en gas!
Jeo sai bien qu'il ne me heit pas.
Unc ne li forfis de nient,
440 Fors tant que jeo l'aim durement;
E si pur tant me veut haïr,
Dunc est il digne de murir.
Jamés par tei ne par autrui,
De si que jeo paroge a lui,
445 Ne li vodrai rien demander,
K[ar] jeo memes li voil mustrer
Cum l'amur de li me destreint.
Mes jeo ne sai si il remeint."   [f. 155ʳ]
Li chamberlenc ad respundu:
450 "Dame, li reis l'ad retenu
Desque a un an par serement
Qu'il li servirat lëaument.
Asez purrez aver leisir
De mustrer lui vostre pleisir."
455 Quant ele oï qu'il remaneit,
Mut durement s'esjoieit;
Mut esteit lee del sujur.
Ne saveit nent de la dolur
U il esteit, puis que il la vit:
460 Unc n'ot joie ne delit,
Fors tant cum il pensa de li.
Mut se teneit a maubailli,
Kar a sa femme aveit premis
Ainz qu'il turnast de sun païs
465 Que il n'avereit si li nun.
Ore est sis quors en grant prisun.
Sa lëauté voleit garder,
Mes ne s'en peot nent juter
Que il nen eimt la dameisele,
470 Guilliadun, que tant fu bele,
De li veer e de parler
E de baiser e de acoler;
Mes ja ne li querra amur
Ke li turt a deshonur,
475 Tant pur sa femme garder fei,
Tant cum qu'il est od le rei.
En grant peine fu Elidus.
Il est munté, ne targe plus;

he would not want anything of yours."
"You are speaking foolishly!" she says.
"I know well that he does not hate me.
I never did him wrong in anything,
except that I love him so fiercely; 440
and if he wants to hate me for that,
then he is worthy to die.
Never, through you nor through anyone else,
until I may speak to him,
will I wish to ask him for anything, 445
for I want to show him myself
how love of him oppresses me.
But I do not know if he is staying."
The chamberlain replied,
"Lady, the king has retained him 450
for a year, by oath,
to serve him loyally.
You will have enough opportunity
to tell him your wishes."
When she heard that he was staying, 455
she rejoiced greatly;
she was very happy about his stay.
She knew nothing about the sorrow
he was in since he saw her:
he never had joy nor delight 460
except when he thought of her.
He considered himself very unfortunate,
for he had promised his wife
before he left his country
that he would have no one but her. 465
Now his heart is in a terrible trap.
He wanted to maintain his loyalty,
but he can by no means free himself
from loving the damsel,
Guilliadun, who was so beautiful, 470
from seeing and speaking with her,
and kissing and embracing her;
but he will never ask her for love
that would lead to dishonor,
as much to keep faith with his wife 475
as because he is the king's man.
Eliduc was in great distress.
He mounted his horse, he waits no longer;

Ses cumpainuns apele [a] sei.
480 Al chastel vet parler al rei.
La pucele verra s'il peot:
C'est l'acheisun pur quei s'esmeot.
Li reis est del manger levez,   [col. b]
As chambres sa fille est entrez.
485 As eschés cumence a juer
A un chevaler de utre mer;
De l'autre part de l'escheker
Deveit sa fille enseigner.
Elidus est alez avant:
490 Le reis li fist mut bel semblant,
Dejuste lui seer le fist.
Sa fille apele, si li dist:
"Dameisele, a cest chevaler
Vus devriez ben aquinter
495 E fere lui mut grant honur;
Entre cinc cenz nen ad meillur."
Quant la meschine ot escuté
Ceo que sis sires ot cumandé,
Mut en fu lee la pucele.
500 Drescie[e] s'est, celui apele.
Luinz des autres se sunt asis;
Amdui erent de amur espris.
Ele ne l'osot areisuner,
E il dute a li parler,
505 Fors tant ke il la mercia
Del present que ele li enveia:
Unc mes n'ot aveir si chier.
Ele respunt al chevalier
Que de ceo li esteit mut bel,
510 E pur ceo l'enveat l'anel
E la ceinture autresi,
Que de sun cors l'aveit seisi;
Ele l'amat de tel amur,
De lui volt faire sun seignur.
515 E si ele ne peot lui aveir,
Une chose sace de veir:
Jamés n'avera humme vivant.
Ore li redie sun talant!   [f. 155ᵛ]

he calls his companions to him.
He goes to the castle to speak to the king.   480
He will see the girl if he can:
this is the reason he sets out.
The king got up from dinner;
he entered his daughter's chambers.
He begins to play chess   485
with a knight from overseas;
on the other side of the chessboard
the knight was supposed to teach his daughter.
Eliduc stepped forward:
the king looked on him very kindly,   490
he had him sit beside him.
He calls his daughter, and says to her,
"Damsel, you should become well acquainted
with this knight
and do him very great honor;   495
out of five hundred men there is none better."
When the girl had heard
what her father had commanded,
she was a very happy maiden.
She got up, she calls to him.   500
They sat down far from the others;
both of them were aflame with love.
She did not dare address him,
and he is afraid to speak to her,
except that he thanked her   505
for the present that she had sent him:
he had never valued anything so much.
She replies to the knight
that she was delighted by that,
and that is why she sent the ring   510
and the belt as well,
because she had given him possession of herself;[1]
she loved him with such love
that she wanted to make him her lord.
And if she cannot have him,   515
he may know one thing for certain:
she will never have any man alive.
Now let him tell her his desire in return!

---

1 The verb here, *seisir (de)*, has the technical sense of putting
   someone in formal legal possession of something, usually of land.

"[D]ame," fet il, "grant gre vus sai
520 [D]e vostre amur, grant joie en ai;
[Qu]ant vus tant me avez preisié,
Durement en dei estre lié;
Ne remeindrat pas endreit mei.
Un an sui remis od le rei;
525 La fiance ad de mei prise.
N'en partirai en nule guise
De si que sa guere ait finee.
Puis m'en irai en ma cuntree,
Kar ne voil mie remaneir
530 Si cungé puis de vus aveir."
La pucele li respundi:
"Amis, la vostre grant merci!
Tant estes sages e curteis,
Bien averez purveu ainceis
535 Quei vus vodriez fere de mei.
Sur tute rien vus aim e crei."
Bien s'esteent aseuré;
A cele feiz n'unt plus parlé.
A sun ostel Eliduc vet.
540 Mut est joius, mut ad bien fet:
Sovent peot parler od s'amie,
Grant est entre eus la druerie.
Tant s'est de la guere entremis
Qu'il aveit retenu e pris
545 Celui ki le rei guerreia,
E tute la tere aquita.
Mut fu preisez par sa pruesce,
Par sun sen e par sa largesce;
Mut li esteit bien avenu.
550 Dedenz le terme ke ceo fu,
Ses sires l'ot enveé quere
Treis messages fors de la tere:
Mut ert grevez e damagiez   [col. b]
E encumbrez e [empeiriez];
555 Tuz ses chasteus alot perdant
E tute sa tere guastant.
Mut s'esteit sovent repentiz
Qu'il de lui esteit partiz;
Mal cunseil en ot eü
560 E malement l'aveit veü.
Les traïturs ki l'encuserent

"Lady," he says, "I am most grateful to you
for your love, I take great joy in it;   520
since you have valued me so much,
I can only be delighted;
there will be no neglect on my side.
I am to stay with the king for a year;
he has received my promise of faith.   525
I will not leave on any account
until his war is finished.
Then I will go to my country,
for I do not at all wish to stay
if I may have leave from you."   530
The girl replied,
"Friend, many thanks to you!
You are so wise and courteous,
you will have arranged ahead of time
what you would wish to do with me.   535
I love and believe in you above all things."
They were both reassured;
at that time they spoke no more.
Eliduc goes to his lodging.
He is very joyful, he has done very well: 540
he can often speak to his beloved,
there is great love-play between them.
He put such effort into the war
that he had captured and taken
the man who was making war on the king,   545
and freed all the land.
He was greatly prized for his prowess,
for his good sense and for his generosity;
it had all turned out well for him.
During the time when this was happening,   550
his lord had sent three messengers
to look for him outside the country:
he was greatly oppressed and harmed
and overwhelmed and wronged;
he was losing all his castles   555
and having all his land laid waste.
He very often repented
that Eliduc had left him;
he had had bad advice about it
and had taken the wrong view of him.   560
The traitors who accused Eliduc

E empeirerent e medlerent
Aveit jeté fors del païs
E en eissil a tuz jurs mis.
565 Par sun grant busuin le mandot
E sumuneit e conjurot
Par l'aliance qu'il li fist,
Quant il l'umage de lui prist,
Que s'en venist pur lui aider,
570 Kar mut en aveit grant mester.
Eliduc oï la novele.
Mut li pesa pur la pucele,
Kar anguissusement l'amot
E ele lui ke plus ne pot.
575 Mes n'ot entre eus nule folie,
Jolifté ne vileinie:
De douneer e de parler
E de lur beaus aveirs doner
Esteit tute la druerie
580 Par amur en lur cumpainie.
Ceo fu s'entente e sun espeir:
Ele le quidot del tut aveir
E retenir, si ele peust;
Ne saveit pas que femme eust.
585 "Allas!" fet il, "mal ai erré!
Trop ai en cest païs esté!
Mar vi unkes ceste cuntree!
Une meschine i ai amee,   [f. 156ʳ]
Guilliadun, la fille al rei,
590 Mut durement, e ele mei.
Quant si de li m'estuet partir,
Un de nus estuet murir
U ambedeus, estre ceo peot.
E nepurquant aler m'esteot;
595 Mis sires m'ad par bref mandé
E par serement conjuré
E ma femme d'autre part.
Or me covient que jeo me gart!
Jeo ne puis mie remaneir,
600 Ainz m'en irai par estuveir.

and wronged and spoke ill of him
the lord had thrown out of the country
and sent into exile forever.
He sent to Eliduc out of his great need   565
and summoned him and enjoined,
by the agreement Eliduc made with him
when he took homage from him,
that he should come to help him,
for he needed him very badly.[1]   570
Eliduc heard the news.
It weighed on him greatly because of the maiden,
for he loved her terribly
and she could not have loved him more.
But there was between them no wickedness,   575
fickleness, nor base behavior:
flirting and talking
and giving lovely gifts
was the whole of the love affair
between them.   580
This was her intention and her hope:
she thought to have him entirely hers
and keep him, if she could;
she did not know that he had a wife.
"Alas!" he says, "I have behaved wrongly!   585
I have been too long in this land.
Woe that I ever saw this place!
I have loved a girl here,
Guilliadun, the daughter of the king,
very deeply, and she me.   590
When I must part from her,
one of us must die,
or both, it may be.
And yet I must go;
my lord has sent to me by letter   595
and enjoined me by my oath,
and so has my wife.
Now I must take care!
I cannot stay any longer,
rather it is necessary that I leave.   600

---

1 Eliduc's original lord invokes the oath of homage (literally "being
  someone's man") that Eliduc had sworn him, which was not invali-
  dated by the lord's unjust behavior.

Si a m'amie esteie espusez,
Nel suffreit crestientez.
De tutes parz va malement;
Deu, tant est dur le departement!
605 Mes ki k'il turt a mesprisun,
Vers li ferai tuz jurs raisun;
Tute sa volenté ferai
E par sun cunseil err[er]ai.
Li reis, sis sires, ad bone peis,
610 Ne qui que nul le guerreit meis.
Pur la busuin de mun seignur
Querrai cungé devant le jur
Que mes termes esteit asis
Ke od lui sereie al païs.
615 A la pucele irai parler
E tut mun afere mustrer;
Ele me dirat sun voler,
E jol ferai a mun poer."
Li chevaler n'ad plus targié,
620 Al rei veit prendre le cungié.
L'aventure li cunte e dit,
Le brief li ad mustré e lit
Que sis sires li enveia,
Que par destresce le manda.
625 Li reis oï le mandement
E qu'il ne remeindra nent;
Mut est dolent e trespensez.
Del suen li ad offert asez:
La terce part de sa herité
630 E sun tresur abaundoné.
Pur remaneir tant li fera
Dunt a tuz jurs le loera.
"Par Deu," fet il, "a ceste feiz,
Puis que mis sires est destreiz
635 E il m'ad mandé de si loin,
Jo m'en irai pur sun busoin;
Ne remeindrai en nule guise.
Si avez mester de mun servise,
A vus revendrai volenters
640 Od grant esforz de chevalers."
De ceo l'ad li reis mercié

[col. b]

If I were to marry my beloved,
the Christian faith would not tolerate it.
This goes badly on all sides;
God, how hard the parting is!
But whomever it may harm, 605
I will always do right by her;
I will do all her will
and I will act by her counsel.
The king, her father, has a firm peace;
I do not believe that anyone will attack him further. 610
Because of my lord's need
I will ask for leave before the day
that was set as the end of my time
to be with him in this country.
I will go speak with the maiden 615
and tell her my whole situation;
she will tell me what she wants,
and I will do it as best I can."
The knight waited no longer,
he goes to take leave of the king. 620
He tells and recounts to him what has happened,[1]
he showed and read him the letter
that his lord sent him,
who summons him in his distress.
The king hears the summons 625
and that he will not stay any longer;
he is very sad and troubled.
He offered him much of his wealth:
one-third of his heritage
and treasure made over to him. 630
He will do so much to get him to stay
that Eliduc will be glad of it forever.
"By God," he says, "at this time,
since my lord is in distress
and he has sent for me from so far away, 635
I will go there on account of his need;
I will not by any means remain.
If you have need of my service,
I will willingly return to you
with a great force of knights." 640
The king thanked him for this

---

1 Literally, "tells and recounts to him the adventure."

E bonement cungé doné.
Tuz les aveirs de sa meisun
Li met li reis en baundun:
645 Or e argent, chiens e chevaus,
Dras de seie bons e beaus.
Il en prist mesurablement;
Puis li ad dit avenantment
Que a sa fille parler ireit
650 Mut volenters, si lui pleseit.
Li reis respunt: "Ceo m'est mut bel."
Avant enveit un dameisel
Que l'us de la chambre ovri.
Elidus vet parler od li.
655 Quant ele le vit, si l'apela
E sis mil feiz le salua.
De sun afere cunseil prent,
Sun eire li mustre brevement.   [f. 156ᵛ]
Ainz qu'il li eust tut mustré
660 Ne cungé pris ne demandé,
Se pauma ele de dolur
E perdi tute sa culur.
Quant Eliduc la veit paumer,
Si se cumence a desmenter;
665 La buche li baise sovent
E si plure mut tendrement.
Entre ses braz la prist e tient,
Tant que de paumeisuns revient.
"Par Deu," fet il, "ma duce amie,
670 Sufrez un poi ke jo vus die:
Vus estes ma vie e ma mort,
En vus est tut mun confort!
Pur ceo preng jeo [cunseil de vus]
Que fiance ad entre nus.
675 Pur busuin vois en mun païs;
A vostre pere ai cungé pris.
Mes jeo ferai vostre pleisir,
Que ke me deive avenir."
"Od vus," fet ele, "me amenez,
680 Puis que remaneir ne volez!

and kindly gave him leave.
All the goods of his house
the king puts at his disposal:
gold and silver, dogs and horses,   645
rich and beautiful silk cloths.
He took a moderate amount;
then he told him politely
that he would go and speak to his daughter
very willingly, if it pleased him.   650
The king replies, "I would be delighted."
He sends a youth ahead of him
who opened the door of the chamber.
Eliduc goes to speak with her.
When she saw him, she called him   655
and greeted him six thousand times.
He takes her advice about his situation,
quickly he tells her about his voyage.
Before he had told her all of it,
or taken or asked for leave,   660
she fainted from sorrow
and lost all her color.
When Eliduc sees her faint,
he begins to lament;
he often kisses her mouth   665
and weeps most tenderly.
He took and held her in his arms,
until she recovered from the faint.
"By God," he says, "my sweet love,
bear with me a little as I tell you: 670
you are my life and my death,
in you is all my comfort!
I take counsel with you
because of the faith between us.[1]
I go to my country of necessity;   675
I have taken leave of your father.
But I will do your pleasure,
whatever may become of me."
"Take me with you," she says,
"since you do not wish to stay!   680

---

1 *Fiance* can mean trust or reliance, but also a pledge or promise (of
   marriage, for example), as in the modern word "fiancé(e)." Eliduc's
   words point to the ambiguity of his relationship to the king's
   daughter.

U si ceo nun, jeo me ocirai;
Jamés joie ne bien ne averai."
Eliduc respunt par duçur
Que mut l'amot de bon[e] amur:
685 "Bele, jeo sui par serement
A vostre pere veirement:
Si jeo vus en menoe od mei,
Jeo li mentireie ma fei—
De si k'al terme ki fu mis.
690 Lëaument vus jur e plevis:
Si cungé me volez doner
E respit mettre e jur nomer,
Si vus volez que jeo revienge,   [col. b]
N'est rien al mund que me retienge,
695 Pur ceo que seie vis e seins;
Ma vie est tute entre voz meins."
Cele ot de lui grant amur;
Terme li dune e nume jur
De venir e pur li mener.
700 Grant doel firent al desevrer,
Lur anels d'or s'entrechangerent
E ducement s'entrebaiserent.
Il est desque a la mer alez;
Bon ot le vent, tost est passez.
705 Quant Eliduc est repeirez,
Sis sires est joius e liez
E si ami e si parent
E li autre communement,
E sa bone femme sur tuz,
710 Que mut est bele, sage e pruz.
Mes il esteit tuz jurs pensis
Pur l'amur dunt il ert suspris:
Unc pur rien qu'il veïst
Joie ne bel semblant ne fist,
715 Ne jamés joie nen avera
De si que s'amie verra.
Mut se cuntient sutivement.
Sa femme en ot le queor dolent;
Ne sot mie quei ceo deveit.
720 A sei memes se pleigneit.
Ele lui demandot suvent
Si il ot oï de nule gent
Que ele eust mesfet u mespris

Or if not, I will kill myself;
I will never have joy or happiness."
Eliduc, who loved her most truly,
responds gently,
"Beloved, I am truly bound   685
by oath to your father:
if I were to take you away with me,
I would betray my faith—
until the term that was set.
I swear and pledge to you loyally: 690
if you will give me leave,
and set a term and name the day,
if you want me to return,
there is nothing in the world that will prevent me
provided I am alive and well;   695
my life is entirely in your hands."
She had great love for him;
she gives him a term and names a day
for him to come and take her away.
They showed great sorrow upon parting;   700
they exchanged their golden rings
and kissed one another sweetly.
He went down to the sea;
he had a good wind, he soon crossed over.
When Eliduc has returned,   705
his lord is joyful and happy
and his friends and his relatives
and all the others generally,
and his good wife above all,
who is very beautiful, wise, and worthy.   710
But he was always downcast
because of the love that had captivated him:
he never looked joyful or pleased
by anything he saw,
nor will he ever have joy   715
until he sees his beloved.
He behaves in a very secretive way.
This made his wife heavy-hearted;
she did not know what it meant.
She lamented to herself.   720
She often asked him
if he had heard from anyone
that she had done wrong or acted badly

Tant cum il fu hors del païs;
725 Volenters s'en esdrescera
Devant sa gent, quant li plarra.
"Dame," fet il, "nent ne vus ret
De mesprisun ne de mesfet.   [f. 157ʳ]
Mes al païs u j'ai esté
730 Ai al rei plevi e juré
Que jeo dei a lui repairer,
Kar de mei ad grant mester.
Si li rei mis sires aveit peis,
Ne remeindreie oit jurs aprés.
735 Grant travail m'estuvera suffrir
Ainz que jeo puisse revenir.
Ja, de si que revenu seie,
N'averai joie de rien que veie;
Kar ne voil ma fei trespasser."
740 Atant le lest la dame ester.
Eliduc od sun seignur fu;
Mut li ad aidé e valu.
Par le cunseil de lui errot
E tute la tere gardot.
745 Mes quant li termes apreça
Que la pucele li numa,
De pais fere s'est entremis;
Tuz acorda ses enemis.
Puis s'est appareillé de errer
750 E queile gent il vodra mener.
Deus ses nevuz qu'il mut ama
E un suen chamberlenc mena—
Cil ot de lur cunseil esté
E le message aveit porté—
755 E ses esquiers sulement;
Il n'ot cure d'autre gent.
A ceus fist plevir e jurer
De tut sun afaire celer.
En mer se mist, plus n'i atent;
760 Utre furent hastivement.
En la cuntree esteit arivez
U il esteit plus desirez.
Eliduc fu mut veiziez: [col. b]
Luin des hafnes s'est herbergez;
765 Ne voleit mie estre veüz
Ne trovez ne recunuz.

while he was out of the country;
she will gladly make amends for it 725
before his people, whenever it pleases him.
"Lady," he said, "I do not accuse you
of any fault or misdeed.
But in the country where I was
I pledged and swore to the king 730
that I would return to him,
for he has great need of me.
If my lord the king had peace,
I would not stay here for eight days afterward.
I will have to suffer great trials 735
before I could return.
Never, until I return,
will I have joy in anything I see;
for I do not want to break my faith."
With that the lady let him be. 740
Eliduc was with his lord;
he helped and supported him greatly.
He acted by his counsel
and protected all the land.
But when the time drew near 745
that the maiden had named for him,
he undertook to make peace;
he reconciled all the lord's enemies.
Then he prepared himself to go
and the people he will take with him. 750
He took two of his nephews whom he loved very much
and a chamberlain of his—
the latter had been in on their secret
and had carried the message—
and his squire, no more; 755
he did not care to have any other people.
He made them pledge and swear
to conceal everything he was doing.
He went to sea, he waits no longer;
they crossed over quickly. 760
He had arrived in the country
where he had been most longed for.
Eliduc was very clever:
he lodged far from the harbor;
he certainly did not want to be seen 765
or found or recognized.

Sun chamberlenc appareilla
E a s'amie l'enveia:
Si li manda que venuz fu,
770 Bien ad sun cumand tenu.
La nuit, quant tut fu avespré,
[Ele] s'en [istra] de la cité;
Li chamberlenc od li ira,
E il encuntre li sera.
775 Cil aveit tuz changié ses dras;
A pié s'en vet trestut le pas.
A la cité ala tut dreit,
U la fille le rei esteit.
Tant aveit purchacié e quis
780 Que dedenz la chambre s'est mis.
A la pucele dist saluz
E que sis amis esteit venuz.
Quant ele ad la novele oïe,
Tute murne e esbaïe,
785 De joie plure tendrement
E celui ad baisé suvent.
Il li ad dit que al vesprer
L'en estuverat od li aler.
Tut le jur ot issi esté
790 E lur eire bien devisé.
La nuit, quant tut fu aseri,
De la vile s'en sunt parti
Li dameisel e ele od lui,
E ne furent mais il dui.
795 Grant poür ad ke hum ne la veie.
Vestue fu de un drap de seie,
Menuement a or brosdé,
E un curt mantel afublé.   [f. 157ᵛ]
Luinz de la porte al trait de un arc
800 La ot un bois clos de un bel parc;
Suz le paliz les atendeit
Sis amis, ki pur li veneit.
Li chamberlenc la l'amena
E il descent, si la baisa.
805 Grant joie firent a l'assembler.
Sur un cheval la fist munter
E il munta, sa reisne prent;
Od li s'en vet hastivement.
Al hafne vient a Toteneis;

He prepared his chamberlain
and sent him to his beloved:
he sent him to tell her that he had come,
he has fully followed her command.   770
That night, when it had grown completely dark,
she must leave the city;
the chamberlain will go with her,
and he will come to meet her.
The chamberlain had completely changed his clothes;   775
he goes on foot, every step.
He went straight to the city
where the king's daughter was.
He sought and strove until
he got himself into the chamber.   780
He greeted the maiden
and told her her beloved had come.
When she, all sad and overcome,
heard the news,
she weeps tenderly for joy   785
and kissed him over and over.
He told her that when evening fell
she must go with him.
He had been there all day
and planned their journey well.   790
That night, when it was quite dark,
they left the town,
the youth and she with him,
and there was no one but the two of them.
She is very afraid someone might see her.   795
She was dressed in a silk garment,
finely embroidered with gold,
and had put on a short mantle.
A bowshot from the gate
there was a wood enclosed by a handsome park;   800
below the palisade her beloved,
who had come for her, was waiting for them.
The chamberlain led her there,
and Eliduc dismounted and kissed her.
They showed great joy at their meeting.   805
He had her mount a horse
and he mounted, he takes her rein;
he goes off with her in haste.
He comes to the harbor at Totnes;

810 En la nef entrent demaneis.
N'i ot humme si les suens nun
E s'amie Guilliadun.
Bon vent eurent e bon oré[1]
E tut le tens aseuré.
815 Mes quant il durent ariver
Une turmente eurent en mer,
E un vent devant eus leva
Que luin del hafne les geta;
Lur verge brusa e fendi
820 E tut lur sigle desrumpi.
Deu recleiment devotement,
Seint Nicholas e Seint Clement,
E ma dame Seinte Marie
Que vers sun fiz lur querge aïe,
825 Ke il les garisse de perir
E al hafne puissent venir.
Un[e] hure ariere, un[e] autre avant,
Issi alouent acosteant;
Mut esteient pres de turment.
830 Un des [escipres] hautement
S'est escriez, "Quei faimes nus?
Sire, ça einz avez od vus
Cele par ki nus perissums.   [col. b]
Jamés a tere ne vendrums!
835 Femme leale espuse avez
E sur cele autre en menez
Cuntre Deu e encuntre la lei,
Cuntre dreiture e cuntre fei.
Lessez la nus geter en mer,
840 Si poüm sempres ariver."
Elidus oï quei cil dist,
A poi d'ire ne mesprist.
"Fiz a putain," fet il, "mauveis,
Fel traïtre, nel dire meis!
845 Si m'amie peust laissier,
Jeol vus eusse vendu mut cher."
Mes entre ses braz la teneit
E cunfortout ceo qu'il poeit
Del mal que ele ot en mer
850 E de ceo que ele oï numer

---

1 See the similar lines in *Guigemar*, "Bon oret eurent e süef vent" (l. 194), and *Milun*, "Bon oré orent e suef vent" (l. 508).

they board the ship at once. 810
There was no one but his own men
and his beloved, Guilliadun.
They had a good wind and a good breeze
and the weather was fair.
But when they were about to arrive 815
they met a storm on the sea,
and a wind rose before them
that cast them far from the harbor;
their mast broke and split
and tore away all their sail. 820
They call devoutly upon God,
St. Nicholas and St. Clement,
and upon my lady St. Mary,
that she ask help for them from her son,
that he may save them from death 825
and they may reach the harbor.
One moment backward, another forward,
they were going along like this trying to land;
they were very nearly shipwrecked.
One of the sailors loudly 830
cried out, "What are we doing?
Lord, you have in here with you
her for whom we perish.
We will never reach land!
You married a loyal woman 835
and you are bringing in another to replace her
against God and against the law,
against righteousness and against faith.
Let us throw her in the sea,
then we can soon land." 840
Eliduc heard what he said:
he almost did something terrible out of anger.
"Whoreson," he says, "wretch,
wicked traitor, never say that!
If you could leave my beloved behind, 845
I would make you pay most dearly."
But he held her in his arms
and comforted her as best he could
for the trouble she had at sea
and for the fact that she heard it said 850

Que femme espuse ot sis amis
Autre ke li en sun païs.
Desur sun vis cheï paumee,
Tute pale, desculuree.
855 En la paumeisun demurra,
Que ele ne revient ne suspira.
Cil ki ensemble od lui l'en porte
Quidot pur veir ke ele fust morte.
Mut fet grant doel; sus est levez,
860 Vers l'escipre est tost alez,
De l'avirun si l'ad feru
K'il l'abati tut estendu.
Par le pié l'en ad jeté fors;
Les undes en portent le cors.
865 Puis qu'il l'ot lancié en la mer,
A l'estiere vait governer.
Tant guverna la neif e tint,
Le hafne prist, a tere vint.   [f. 158ʳ]
Quant il furent bien arivé,
870 Le pont mist jus, ancre ad geté.
Encore jut ele en paumeisun,
Ne n'ot semblant si de mort nun.
Eliduc feseit mut grant doel;
Iloc fust mort od li, sun voil.
875 A ses cumpainuns demanda
Queil cunseil chescun li dura,
U la pucele portera,
Kar de li ne partira.
Si serat enfuie e mise
880 Od grant honur, od bel servise,
En cimiterie beneeit:
Fille ert a rei, si en aveit dreit.
Cil en furent tut esgaré,
Ne li aveient rien loé.
885 Elidus prist a purpenser
Quel part il la purrat porter.
Sis recez fu pres de la mer,
Estre i peüst a sun digner.
Une forest aveit entur,
890 Trente liwes ot de lungur.
Un seinz hermites i maneit
E une chapele i aveit.
Quarante anz i aveit esté,

that her lover had a wedded wife
other than her in his country.
She fell on her face in a faint,
all pale, colorless.
She remained in her faint, 855
she did not recover or sigh.
He who is taking her with him
truly believed that she was dead.
He is terribly upset; he got up,
went right to the sailor, 860
and hit him so hard with an oar
that he laid him out flat.
He took him by the foot and threw him off;
the waves carry his body away.
When he had thrown him in the sea, 865
he goes to the rudder to steer.
He so steered and guided the ship
that he reached port, he came to land.
When they had landed safely
they put down the gangway, they cast anchor. 870
Still she lay in a faint,
nor did she have any appearance of life.
Eliduc was terribly upset;
he would die there with her, if he could.
He asked his companions 875
what counsel each of them will give him,
where he should take the maiden,
for he will not part from her.
She will be buried and interred
with great honor, with proper service, 880
in hallowed ground:
she was a king's daughter, she had a right to it.
They were completely at a loss,
they had nothing to suggest to him.
Eliduc thought very hard 885
about where he can take her.
His dwelling was near the sea;
he could be there by dinner time.
There was a forest around it,
it was thirty leagues across. 890
A holy hermit lived there
and had a chapel there.
He had been there for forty years;

Meintefeiz ot od li parlé.
895 A lui, ceo dist, la portera,
En sa chapele l'enfuira;
De sa tere tant i durra,
Une abeie i fundera,
Si mettra cuvent de moignes
900 U de nuneins u de chanoignes
Que tuz jurs prierunt pur li:
Ke Deus li face bone merci!
Ses chevals ad fait amener,   [col. b]
Sis cumande tuz a munter.
905 Mes la fiaunce prent d'iceus
Qu'il n'iert descuvert pur eus.
Devant lui sur sun palefrei
S'amie porte ensemble od sei.
Le dreit chemin unt tant erré
910 Qu'il esteient al bois entré.
A la chapele sunt venu,
Apelé i unt e batu:
N'i troverent kis respundist
Ne ki la porte lur ovrist.
915 Un des suens fist utre passer
La porte ovrir e desfermer.
Oit jurs esteit devant finiz
Li seinz hermites, li parfiz;
La tumbe novele trova.
920 Mut fu dolenz, mut s'esmaia.
Cil voleient la fosse faire—
Mes il les fist ariere traire—
U il deust mettre s'amie.
Il lur ad dit: "Ceo n'i ad mie;
925 Ainz en averai mun cunseil pris
A la sage gent del païs
Cum purrai le liu eshaucier
U de abbeie u de mustier.
Devant l'auter la cucherum
930 E a Deu la cumanderum."
Il ad fet aporter ses dras,
Un lit li funt ignelepas;
La meschine desus covrirent
E cum pur morte la laissierent.

Eliduc had talked with him many times.
He says that he will carry her to him,   895
he will bury her in his chapel;
he will give enough of his land
to found an abbey there,
and will put a community of monks
or of nuns or of canons   900
who will pray for her forever:
may God be merciful to her!
He had his horse brought,
he commands everyone to mount.
But he takes an oath from these men   905
that he will not be betrayed by them.
In front of him on his palfrey
he carries his beloved along with him.
They went straight along the path so far
that they had entered the wood.   910
They came to the chapel,
they called and knocked:
they found no one to reply
nor to open the door for them.
He had one of his men go through   915
to open and unbar the door.
Eight days before this
the holy hermit, the saint, had died;
they found the new tomb.
Eliduc was very sad, he was most distraught.   920
They wanted to make a grave
where he could put his beloved,
but he made them draw back.
He says to them, "Not that, by no means;
rather I will take counsel about this   925
from the wise people of the land,
how I can honor this place
with an abbey or a church.
We will lay her before the altar
and commend her to God."   930
He had cloths brought,
they make a bed for her at once;
they covered the girl on it
and left her as though she were dead.

935 Mes quant ceo vient al departir,
Dunc quida il de doel murir.
Les oilz li baise e la face.
"Bele," fet il, "ja Deu ne place   [f. 158ᵛ]
Que jamés puisse armes porter
940 Ne al secle vivre ne durer!
Bele amie, mar me veïstes!
Duce chere, mar me siwistes!
Bele, ja fuissiez vus reïne,
Ne fust l'amur leale e fine
945 Dunt vus m'amastes lëaument.
Mut ai pur vus mun quor dolent.
Le jur que jeo vus enfuirai
Ordre de moigne receverai;
Sur vostre tumbe chescun jur
950 Ferai refreindre ma dolur."
Atant s'en part de la pucele,
Si ferme l'us de la chapele.
A sun ostel ad enveé
Sun message; li ad cunté
955 A sa femme que il veneit,
Mes las e travaillé esteit.
Quant ele l'oï, mut en fu lie[e];
Cuntre lui s'est apareillie[e],
Sun seignur receit bonement.
960 Mes poi de joie l'en atent,
Kar unc bel semblant ne fist
Ne bone parole ne dist.
Nul ne l'osot mettre a reisun.
Deus jurs esteit en la meisun;
965 La messe oeit bien par matin,
Puis se meteit su[l] al chemin.
Al bois alot, a la chapele
La u giseit la dameisele.
En la paumeisun la trovot:
970 Ne reveneit ne suspirot.
De ceo li semblot grant merveille

But when it came to the parting,[1]
then he thought he would die of sorrow.
He kisses her eyes and her face.
"Beauty," he says, "may it never please God
that I should ever again bear arms
or live or last in this world!
Beautiful beloved, woe that you saw me!
Sweet darling, woe that you followed me!
Beauty, you would already be a queen,
were it not for the love, loyal and true,
with which you loyally loved me.
My heart is most sorrowful for you.
The day that I bury you,
I will become a monk;
every day, on your tomb,
I will make my grief resound."[2]
With that he leaves the maiden
and closes the door of the chapel.
He sent his messenger
to his house; he told
his wife that he was coming,
but he was sad and weary.
When she heard this, she was delighted;
she gets ready to meet him,
she receives her lord kindly.
But she gets little joy of it,
for he never gave a friendly look
nor said a kind word.
No one dared to address him.
He was in the house for two days;
he heard mass early in the morning,
then took to the road alone.
He went to the wood, to the chapel
where the damsel was lying.
He found her in her faint:
she did not recover or sigh.
Thus it seemed a great wonder to him

935
940
945
950
955
960
965
970

---

1 This is very close to a line from *Chevrefoil*: "Mes quant ceo vient al
desevrer, / Dunc comencent a plurer" (ll. 103–04).

2 The word *refreindre* can also mean "to assuage" or "to restrain," and
the multiple meanings may point to the ambivalent image of Eliduc,
as a monk, still lamenting his earthly beloved.

K'il la veeit blanche e vermeille;
Unkes la colur ne perdi   [col. b]
Fors un petit que ele enpali.
975   Mut anguissusement plurot
E pur l'alme de li preiot.
Quant aveit fete sa priere,
A sa meisun alot ariere.
Un jur a l'eissir del muster
980   Le aveit sa femme fet gaiter
Un suen vadlet; mut li premist.
De luinz alast e si veïst
Quel part sis sires turnereit;
Chevals e armes li durreit.
985   Cil ad sun comandement fait.
Al bois se met, aprés lui vait,
Si qu'il ne l'ad aparceu.
Bien ad esgardé e veu
Cument en la chapele entra;
990   Le dol oï qu'il demena.
Ainz que Eliduc s'en seit eissuz,
Est a sa dame revenuz.
Tut li cunta qu'il oï,
La dolur, la noise e le cri
995   Cum fet sis sire en l'ermitage.
Ele en mua tut sun curage.
La dame dit, "Sempres irums,
Tut l'ermitage cerchirums.
Mis sires d[ei]t, ceo qui[d], errer:
1000   A la curt vet al rei parler.
Li hermites fu mort pieça;
Jeo sai asez qu'il l'ama,
Mes ja pur li ceo ne fereit,
Ne tel dolur ne demerreit."
1005   A cele feiz le lait issi.
Cel jur memes aprés midi
Vait Eliduc parler al rei.
Ele prent le vadlet od sei;   [f. 159^r]
A l'ermitage l'ad mene[e].
1010   Quant en la chapele est entre[e]

that he saw her white and red;[1]
she never lost her color,
except that she was a little pale.
He wept in great anguish   975
and prayed for her soul.
When he had made his prayer,
he went back to his house.
One day, as he left the church,
his wife had him watched   980
by a servant of hers; she promised to reward him.
He should follow at a distance and see
where her husband would go;
she would give him horses and armor.
He did as she commanded.   985
He enters the woods, he goes after him,
so that Eliduc did not notice it.
He looked carefully and saw
how he entered the chapel;
he heard the sorrow that he expressed   990
Before Eliduc came out of there,
he went back to his lady.
He told her everything that he heard,
the sorrow, the noise and the cries
that her lord made in the hermitage.   995
Her feelings changed entirely at this.
The lady says, "We will go at once,
we will search the whole hermitage.
My husband needs, I think, to go on a journey:
he is going to the court to speak to the king.   1000
The hermit died a little time ago;
I know, certainly, that he loved him,
but he would never do this on his account,
or express such sorrow."
For the moment she leaves it at that.   1005
That very day, in the afternoon,
Eliduc goes to speak to the king.
She takes the servant with her;
he led her to the hermitage.
When she entered the chapel   1010

---

1   White and red are the ideal colors of a courtly complexion; the
    point here is that the girl retains her beauty even in (apparent)
    death.

E vit le lit a la pucele
Que resemblot rose nuvele,
Del cuvertur l'ad descoveri
E vit le cors tant eschevi,
1015 Les braz lungs, blanches les meins
E les deiz greilles, lungs e pleins.
Ore seit ele la verité,
Pur quei sis sire ad duel mené.
Le vadlet avant apelat
1020 E la merveille li mustrat.
"Veiz tu," fet ele, "ceste femme,
Que de beuté resemble gemme?
Ceo est l'amie mun seignur,
Pur quei il meine tel dolur.
1025 Par fei, jeo ne me merveil mie,
Quant si bele femme est perie.
Tant par pité, tant par amur,
Jamés n'averai joie nul jur."
Ele cumencet a plurer
1030 E la meschine regreter.
Devant le lit s'asist plurant.
Une musteile vint curant:
Desuz l'auter esteit eissue,
E le vadlet l'aveit ferue
1035 Pur ceo que sur le cors passa;
De un bastun qu'il tint la tua.
En mi l'eire l'aveit getee.
Ne demura ke une loee,
Quant sa cumpaine i acurrut,
1040 Si vit la place u ele jut.
Entur la teste li ala
E del pié suvent la marcha.
Quant ne la pot fere lever,   [col. b]
Semblant feseit de doel mener.

and saw the bed with the maiden
who looked like a new rose,
she pulled back the cover from her
and saw her shapely body,
the long arms, the white hands   1015
and the long, slender, smooth fingers.
Now she knows the truth,
why her lord was so sad.
She called the servant forward
and showed him the wonder.   1020
"Do you see," she says, "this woman,
who is like a jewel in her beauty?
She is the beloved of my lord,
on whose account he shows such sorrow.
In faith, I do not wonder at it,   1025
when so beautiful a woman has died.
For pity on the one hand, for love on the other,
I will never be happy again."
She began to weep
and to lament for the girl.   1030
She sat before the bed crying.
A weasel came running:
she had come out from below the altar,
and the servant had struck her
because she ran over the body;   1035
with a staff he was holding he killed her.[1]
He had thrown her into the middle of the floor.
It was only a short time[2]
before her companion came running there
and saw the place where she lay.   1040
She went around her head
and often touched her with her foot.
When she could not make the first weasel get up,
she seemed to make a display of sorrow.

---

1 One could call this weasel "it," since *musteile* is a feminine noun
   regardless of the sex of the animal, or "he" if one assumes that this
   is the weasel's mate; but the translation aims to reflect the density of
   feminine forms in this passage, and the fact that both weasels are
   referred to as "cumpaine" ("female companion," ll. 1039, 1051).
2 A "loee" is actually a measure of distance (a league), but as a
   measure of time it means the time required to walk a league. In this
   formulation—"it did not take but a league until ..."—it implies a
   short time.

1045 De la chapele esteit eissue,
     As herbes est al bois venue;
     Od ses denz ad prise une flur
     Tute de vermeille colur.
     Hastivement reveit ariere;
1050 Dedenz la buche en teu manere
     A sa cumpaine l'aveit mise,
     Que li vadlez aveit ocise,
     En memes l'ure fu revescue.
     La dame l'ad aparceüe;
1055 Al vadlet crie: "Retien la!
     Getez, franc humme, mar se ira!"
     E il geta, si la feri,
     Que la floret li cheï.
     La dame lieve, si la prent;
1060 Ariere va hastivement.
     Dedenz la buche a la pucele
     Meteit la flur que tant fu bele.
     Un petitet i demurra:
     Cele revint, e suspira;
1065 Aprés parla, les oilz overi.
     "Deu," fet ele, "tant ai dormi!"
     Quant la dame l'oï parler,
     Deu cumençat a mercier.
     Demande li ki ele esteit,
1070 E la meschine li diseit:
     "Dame, jo sui de Logres nee,
     Fille a un rei de la cuntree.
     Mut ai amé un chevalier,
     Eliduc le bon soudeer;
1075 Ensemble od lui m'en amena.
     Peché ad fet k'il m'enginna:
     Femme ot espuse. Nel me dist
     Ne unc semblant ne m'en fist.   [f. 159ᵛ]
     Quant de sa femme oï parler,
1080 De duel ke oi m'estuet paumer.
     Vileinement descunseillee
     M'ad en autre tere laissee;
     Trahi[e] m'ad, ne sai quei deit.
     Mut est fole que humme creit!"
1085 "Bele," la dame li respunt,
     "N'ad rien vivant en tut le munt
     Que joie li feïst aveir;

She went out of the chapel, 1045
she came to the herbs in the wood;
with her teeth she took a flower
all of a red color.
Quickly she goes back;
she put it in the mouth 1050
of her companion that the servant had killed
in such a way
that at that very moment she came back to life.
The lady noticed this;
she cries to the servant, "Catch her! 1055
Strike, good man—woe to us if she escapes!"
And he struck, he wounded her,
so that the little flower fell.
The lady gets up, she takes it;
she goes back quickly. 1060
In the maiden's mouth
she placed the flower that was so lovely.
Just a little while she waited:
the girl recovered, and sighed;
afterward she spoke, and opened her eyes. 1065
"God," she says, "how long I have slept!"
When the lady heard her speak,
she began to thank God.
She asks her who she was,
and the girl told her: 1070
"Lady, I was born in England,
daughter of a king of that country.
I greatly loved a knight,
Eliduc, the good soldier.
He took me away with him. 1075
He committed a sin in deceiving me:
he had a wedded wife. He did not tell me
nor ever give me a sign of it.
When I heard his wife spoken of,
I could only faint from the sorrow I felt. 1080
He left me, basely abandoned,
in another land;
he betrayed me, I do not know for what reason.
She is a great fool who believes a man!"
"Beauty," the lady replies, 1085
"there is no living thing in all the world
that could bring him joy;

Ceo vus peot humme dire pur veir.
Il quide ke vus seez morte,
1090 A merveille se descunforte.
Chescun jur vus ad regardee;
Bien quid qu'il vus trova pasmee.
Jo sui sa spuse vereiment;
Mut ai pur li mun quor dolent.
1095 Pur la dolur qu'il menot,
Saveir voleie u il alot.
Aprés lui vienc, si vus trovai.
Que vive estes, grant joie en ai;
Ensemble od mei vus enmerrai
1100 E a vostre ami vus rendrai.
Del tut le voil quite clamer,
E si ferai mun chef veler."
Tant l'ad la dame confortee
Que ensemble od l[i] l'en ad menee.
1105 Sun vallet ad appareillé
E pur sun seignur enveié.
Tant errat cil qu'il le trova;
Avenantment le salua,
L'aventure li dit e cunte.
1110 Sur un cheval Eliduc munte,
Unc n'i atendi cumpainun.
La nuit revint a sa meisun.
Quant vive ad trovee s'amie,   [col. b]
Ducement sa femme mercie.
1115 Mut par est Eliduc haitiez,
Unc nul jur ne fu si liez;
La pucele baise suvent
E ele lui mut ducement;
Ensemble funt joie mut grant.
1120 Quant la dame vit lur semblant
Sun seignur ad a reisun mis;
Cungé li ad rové e quis
Que ele puisse de li partir:
Nunein volt estre, Deu server.

anyone can tell you this in truth.
He believes that you are dead,
he is terribly distraught. 1090
Every day he has come to see you;
I believe indeed that he found you in a faint.
I am, in truth, his wife;
my heart is very sorrowful for him.
Because of the sorrow he showed, 1095
I wanted to know where he went.
I came after him, and I found you.
It is a great joy to me that you are alive;
I will take you along with me
and return you to your beloved. 1100
I wish to make him entirely free,
and I will take the veil."[1]
The lady comforted her so much
that she took her along with her.
She prepared her servant 1105
and sent him for her lord.
He traveled until he found him;
he greeted him politely,
he tells and recounts to him the adventure.
Eliduc gets on a horse; 1110
he did not wait for a companion.
That night he returned to his house.
When he has found his beloved alive,
he tenderly thanks his wife.
Eliduc is very happy, 1115
he was never so delighted in his life;
he often kisses the maiden,
and she him, very sweetly;
they have great joy together.
When the lady sees how they look, 1120
she spoke to her husband;
she requested and sought his leave
that she may part from him:
she wants to be a nun, to serve God.[2]

---

1 Literally, "I will have my head veiled," that is, "I will become a nun."
2 Although Guildelüec is taking the veil for Eliduc's benefit, she still
   has to ask permission; church law stated that a married person
   could not become a monk or nun without the spouse's agreement.

1125 De sa tere li doint partie,
     U ele face une abeïe;
     Cele prenge qu'il eime tant,
     Kar n'est pas bien ne avenant
     De deus espuses meintenir,
1130 Ne la lei nel deit cunsentir.
     Eliduc li ad otrié
     E bonement cungé doné:
     Tute sa volunté fera
     E de sa tere li durra.
1135 Pres del chastel, einz el boscage,
     A la chapele a l'hermitage,
     La ad fet fere sun muster,
     Ses meisuns edifier;
     Grant tere i met e grant aveir:
1140 Bien i averat sun estuveir.
     Quant tut ad fet bien aturner,
     La dame i fet sun chief veler,
     Trente nuneins ensemble od li;
     Sa vie e s'ordre establi.
1145 Eliduc s'amie ad prise;
     A grant honur, od bel servise
     En fu la feste demenee
     Le jur qu'il l'aveit espusee.   [f. 160ʳ]
     Ensemble vesquirent meint jur;
1150 Mut ot entre eus parfit[e] amur.
     Granz aumoines e granz biens firent
     Tant que a Deu se cunvertirent.
     Pres del chastel de l'autre part
     Par grant cunseil e par esgart
1155 Une eglise fist Elidus;
     De sa tere i mist le plus
     E tut sun or e sun argent.
     Hummes i mist e autre gent
     De mut bone religiun
1160 Pur tenir l'ordre e la meisun.
     Quant tut aveit appareillé,
     Nen ad puis gueres targé:

Let him give her part of his land 1125
where she can found an abbey;
let him marry the girl whom he loves so much,
for it is not right nor proper
to keep two wives,
nor should the law consent to it. 1130
Eliduc granted this to her
and gladly gave her leave:
he will do all she wishes,
and will give her some of his land.
Near the castle, in the woods, 1135
at the chapel by the hermitage,
there he has her church built,
her houses raised;
he puts plenty of land and wealth into it:
she will have all that she needs there. 1140
When she has fully prepared everything,
the lady takes the veil there,
and thirty nuns along with her;
she set up her religious life and her order.[1]
Eliduc married his beloved; 1145
with great honor, with proper ceremony
the feast was performed
the day that he had married her.
They lived together for a long time,
there was a most perfect love between them. 1150
They gave alms generously and did great good
until they gave their lives to God.
Near the castle on the other side,
by good advice and with care
Eliduc founded a church; 1155
he put the better part of his land into it
and all his gold and silver.
He put men there and other people
of very good religious life
to sustain the order and the house. 1160
When he had prepared everything,
then he did not delay at all:

---

1 An "order" in this context means the particular set of rules and
practices (e.g., the Benedictine Rule) by which a monastic commu-
nity lives. Although the line might seem to suggest that Guildelüec
sets up a new order, it is likely that she simply established which
rule her community would follow.

Ensemble od eus se dune e rent
Pur servir Deu omnipotent.
1165 Ensemble od sa femme premere
Mist sa femme que tant ot chere.
Ele la receut cume sa serur
E mut li porta grant honur;
De Deu servir l'amonesta
1170 E sun ordre li enseigna.
Deu priouent pur lur ami
Qu'il li feïst bone merci,
E il pur eles repreiot;
Ses messages lur enveiot
1175 Pur saveir cument lur esteit,
E cum chescune se cunforteit.
Mut se pena chescun pur sei
De Deu amer par bone fei
E mut firent bele fin,
1180 La merci Deu, le veir devin.
De l'aventure de ces treis
Li auntien bretun curteis
Firent le lai pur remembrer,
Que hum nel deust pas oblier.[1]

---

1 The scribe wrote this final line just below the last ruled line of the
page in col. a, presumably not wishing to have a single line run over
into the next column, and put a red line around it to link it to the
rest of the column. After the end of this, the last of the *Lais*, the rest
of folio 160ʳ (that is, the entire second column) is blank. The effect,
deliberate or not, is to highlight, at the very end of the *Lais*, Marie's
consistent emphasis on remembrance.

he gives himself over along with them
to serve God almighty.
Alongside his first wife   1165
he put the wife whom he loved so dearly.
She received her as her sister
and treated her with great honor;
she exhorted her to serve God
and instructed her in her order.   1170
They would pray to God for their beloved,
that He should be merciful to him,
and he in turn prayed for them;
he sent his messengers to them
to know how it was with them,   1175
and how each was finding solace.
Each one strove individually
to love God in good faith
and they made a very beautiful end,
thanks be to God, the true divine.   1180
The courtly Bretons of old
made the lai to call to mind
the story of these three,[1]
for no one should forget it.

---

1 Here, once more, the word translated "story" is the resonant term
"aventure."

Appendix A: Speaking Animals

1. From the Anonymous Lai *Melion*, *French Arthurian Literature Volume IV: Eleven Old French Narrative Lais*, ed. and trans. Glyn S. Burgess and Leslie C. Brook (Cambridge: D.S. Brewer, 2007), 436–63, lines 1–22, 37–54, 65–120, 133–226, 323–60, 391–450, 467–592

[One of a number of anonymous Old French lais roughly contemporary with Marie's, *Melion* was probably composed in the late twelfth or early thirteenth century. It survived in two manuscripts (one now burnt) but does not appear in the Old Norse collection. It seems clear that it derives from the same tradition as *Bisclavret*, with which it shares many features, though *Melion* extends the action to Ireland and sets the story in an explicitly Arthurian frame.]

At the time when King Arthur reigned—
He who conquered lands
And who gave magnificent gifts
To knights and to nobles—
He had with him a young knight;   5
I have heard him called Melion.
He was very courtly and noble,
And he made himself beloved of all.
He was in a very great band of knights
And a courtly company.   10
The king kept a very sumptuous household;
It was praised by everyone
For its courtesy and prowess
And its excellence and generosity.
One day they were making their vows,   15
And you may be very sure that they kept them.
This Melion made one vow
Which rebounded on him to great harm:
He said he would never love a maiden,
No matter how noble or beautiful,   20
Who had loved any other man
Or even had spoken of any.

[Melion's vow is reported to the ladies, who say as a result that they will never love him nor even speak to him.]

When Melion heard this,
He was completely downcast;
He no longer wished to seek adventure
Nor did he care to bear arms.   40
He was sorrowful, very unhappy,
And he lost his public esteem somewhat.
The king discovered this, it weighed very heavily on him;
He had Melion sent for and spoke to him.
"Melion," said King Arthur,   45
"What has become of your great sense,
Your prestige and your knightly valour?
Say what's wrong, hide none of it.
If you want land or a manor,
Or any other thing you could have,   50
If it is in my realm,
You shall have it as you desire.
I would willingly comfort you,"
Said the king, "if I could."

[Arthur gives Melion a castle on the coast with beautiful lands and forest attached; Melion is very happy there.]

The country pleased him well,   65
And the forest, which he loved very much.
When he had been there for a year,
He loved the country greatly,
For there was no pleasure he might desire or ask for
That he could not find in the forest.   70
One day Melion went hunting,
He and his foresters.
With him were his huntsmen,
Who loved him truly
Because he was their liege lord;   75
All honour was reflected in him.
Soon they found a huge stag;
Quickly they took and unleashed the hounds.
Melion stopped in a heath
So he could listen for the pack.   80
With him was a squire;
He was restraining two greyhounds in his hand.
In this heath, which was green and pleasant,

Melion saw a maiden
Approaching on a handsome palfrey;   85
The trappings were most splendid.
She was dressed in scarlet silk
Which was sewn well with laces;
Around her shoulders was an ermine cloak,
No queen ever wore better.   90
A pleasing figure, elegant shoulders
And blonde hair.
A nicely shaped little mouth,
The colour of a rose;
She had bright eyes, clear and sparkling: 95
She was very beautiful in her whole appearance.
She came alone without retinue,
And was most elegant and charming.
Melion went to meet her;
He greeted her very politely.   100
"Fair lady," he said, "I greet you
From the glorious one, King Jesus.
Tell me where you were born
And what has brought you here."
She replied: "I shall tell you about it,   105
I shall not tell you a word of a lie.
I am of very high birth
And born of noble lineage.
I have come to you from Ireland;
Know that I am entirely your lover.   110
I have never loved a man other than you
Nor shall I ever love another.
I have heard you greatly praised,
I never desired to love any other
But you alone; never at any time   115
Shall I have love for anyone else."
When Melion realised
That his vows were fulfilled,
He puts his arms around her waist
And kissed her more than thirty times.   120

[*Melion tells his people of the event, marries the lady with great
ceremony, and lives happily with her for three years, during which they
have two sons.*]

One day he went to the forest;
He took his beloved wife with him.
He found a stag; they chased it   135

And it fled, its neck lowered.
He had a squire with him
Who was carrying his quiver.
They went on to a heath.
Melion looked into a bush: 140
He saw a huge stag standing there.
Laughing, Melion looked at his wife.
"Lady," he said, "if I wished
I would show you a huge stag:
See it there in the bush."   145
"By my faith," she said, "Melion,
Know that if I do not have some of that stag
I shall never eat again."
She fell from her palfrey, fainting,
And Melion picked her up.   150
When he could not comfort her,
She began to weep bitterly.
"Lady," he said, "For the grace of God,
Never cry, I beg of you.
I have on my hand such a ring;   155
See it here on my ring-finger.
It has two stones in its setting:
No one has ever seen such work;
One stone is white, the other crimson.
You may hear a great marvel of them: 160
You will touch me with the white stone
And place it on my head
When I am undressed and naked,
And I shall become a huge strong wolf.
For love of you, I shall capture the stag   165
And bring some of its meat back to you.
I beg you, for God's sake, wait for me here
And look after my clothing.
I leave you my life and my death:
There will be no recovery   170
If I am not touched with the other stone;
I should never again be a man."
He called his squire,
And ordered him to remove his boots.
He came forward, removed the boots   175
And Melion went into the woods.
He removed his clothes, remained naked,
And wrapped himself in his cloak.
She touched him with the ring

When she saw him naked and undressed.   180
Then he became a huge and strong wolf:
He had got himself into deep trouble.
The wolf set out, running quickly
To where he saw the stag lying;
He set himself to the scent at once.   185
There will be great strife before
He has captured or approached it,
Before he has any of the meat.
The lady said to the squire:
"Now let him hunt for a while."   190
She mounted, tarried no longer,
And took the squire with her.
Straight towards Ireland, her own country,
The lady went back.
She went to the harbour, found a ship   195
And soon spoke to the crew
Who transported her to Dublin,
A maritime city,
Which belonged to her father, the king of Ireland;
Now she had what she required.   200
As soon as she came into the port
She was welcomed with great joy.
We will leave her at this point,
And will tell further about Melion.
Melion, who was chasing the stag,   205
Harried it intently.
He pursued it onto a heath,
And at once he brought it down;
Then he took a large piece of meat from it;
He carried it away in his mouth.   210
He quickly went back
To where he had left his wife,
But he did not find her there;
She had set out for Ireland.
He was very sad and did not know what to do   215
When he could not find her in that place.
But even though he was a wolf,
He retained the reason and memory of a man.
He waited until evening fell.
He saw a ship being loaded   220
Which was to sail that night
And go straight to Ireland.
He made his way there

And waited until night fell.
He took a risk and boarded it,   225
For he cared nothing for his life.

[*Melion arrives in Ireland the next day and escapes the ship, going up a
mountain to examine the countryside. He eats the meat he has brought
and then begins ravaging the livestock. He finds ten wolves to accompany
him and together they terrorize the population, attacking people. Eventu-
ally they are ambushed while resting in a forest: the king and his daughter
come to watch them being hunted. All but Melion are killed.*]

The hunters went back to the city;
The king was very pleased.
The king felt great joy   325
That he had ten of the eleven wolves,
So he had avenged himself well on the wolves:
Only one of them alone had escaped.
His daughter said: "This one was the largest;
He will go on causing grief."   330
When Melion had escaped,
He climbed a mountain;
He was very unhappy and troubled
About his wolves, which he had lost.
For a long time he suffered,   335
But in a short while now he will have help:
Arthur was coming to Ireland,
For he wished to make a peace treaty.
There were conflicts in the land
And he wished to bring agreement to the factions;   340
He wanted to conquer the Romans,
He wanted to lead them [the Irish] in his war.
The king was travelling secretly,
He did not bring very many people;
He brought with him twenty knights.   345
The weather was fine, they had a good wind;
The ship was both splendid and large
And there was a good navigator;
It was very well equipped
And supplied with men and arms.   350
Their shields were hung over the side.
Melion recognised them.
First he recognised Gawain's shield,
And then he noticed Yvain's,
And then King Yder's shield;   355

All this delighted him and was pleasing to him.
He recognised the king's shield easily;
Know truly that he was very joyful because of this:
He was very happy about it and rejoiced greatly,
For he believed he would yet find mercy.   360

[*The ship is blown off course but manages to land; the king, tired, goes to lodgings to rest.*]

Melion did not hesitate:
He went at once towards the ship.
He halted near the castle;
He recognised them very well.
He well knew, if he had no help from the king,   395
That he would die in Ireland;
But he did not know how to proceed:
He was a wolf and could not speak.
Nevertheless he would go forward at once,
And risk his life.   400
He came to the king's door;
He knew all the barons.
He did not stop for a moment,
But went straight up to the king,
Although it might mean his death.   405
He let himself fall at the king's feet
And would not rise again;
Then you would have seen amazement there.
The king spoke thus: "I can see marvels!
This wolf has come here to me.   410
Now know well that he is tame.
Woe betide anyone who touches him or approaches him."
When the meal was ready,
The barons washed,
And the king washed and sat down;   415
The dishes were placed before them.
The king called to Yder
And sat him at his side.
Melion lay at the king's feet
And recognised all the barons well.   420
The king glanced at him frequently.
He gave Melion a piece of bread and he took it;
Then he began to eat it.
The king began to marvel at this;
He said to King Yder: "Look!   425
You can be sure this wolf is tame."

The king gave Melion a piece of meat
And he ate it gladly.
Then Gawain said: "My lords, look:
This wolf is completely unnatural."   430
All the barons said amongst themselves
That no one had ever seen such a well-mannered wolf.
The king had wine brought
Before the wolf in a basin.
The wolf saw it and drank some;   435
You may be sure that he wanted it very much,
For he drank deeply of the wine,
And the king watched him closely.
When they had risen from the meal
And the barons had washed,   440
They went out on to the shore.
The wolf was always with the king;
He did not know anywhere he could go
Where he could be separated from him.
When the king wanted to retire,   445
He ordered his bed to be prepared;
He went to sleep, he was very tired,
And the wolf went with him;
No one could make him leave him;
He went to lie at the king's feet.   450

[*The king of Ireland hears that Arthur is coming and goes to meet him at
the harbor; they embrace, mount, and ride to the city together.*]

The king mounted his palfrey
And took good care of his wolf;
He did not wish to leave him behind.
All the time Melion was at his stirrup.   470
The king was very happy to see Arthur,
The retinue was large and magnificent.
They came to Dublin
And dismounted at the great palace.
When the king went up into the keep,   475
The wolf held him by the skirt of his robe;
When King Arthur was seated,
The wolf placed himself at his feet.
The king looked at his wolf;
He called him near to the table.   480
The two kings sat together;
The retinue was splendid,

The barons waited on them very well:
In all parts of the dwelling
They were served lavishly.   485
But Melion looked around;
He noticed in the middle of the hall
The man his wife had taken away with her.
He knew that he had crossed the sea
And had gone to Ireland.   490
He went to seize him by the shoulder:
The man could not keep him at bay;
Melion attacked him in the hall.
He would soon have killed and destroyed him
Had it not been for the king's servants,   495
Who saw the great commotion;
From all parts of the palace
They carried sticks and cudgels.
They would certainly have killed the wolf
When King Arthur cried out: 500
"Woe betide anyone who touches him," he said, "in faith!
Know that this wolf is mine."
Yder, son of Yrien, said:
"My lords, you are not doing right at all;
If he had not hated him, he would not have touched him,"   505
And the king said: "Yder, you are right."
Arthur moved away from the table,
And went right up to the wolf.
He said to the servant: "You will confess
Why he seized you or you shall die at once."   510
Melion looked at the king;
He gripped the servant and he cried out.
He begged the king for mercy,
Saying that he would tell him the truth.
At once he told the king   515
How the lady had brought him with her,
How she had touched Melion with the ring,
And taken him there to Ireland.
All this he said and made known,
Just as it had happened.   520
Arthur addressed the King of Ireland:
"Now I know well that this is true;
I am very happy about my baron.
Have the ring brought to me
And your daughter, who took it away;   525
She has played an evil trick on him."
The King of Ireland left there;

He went into his chamber,
Taking King Yder with him.
He cajoled and persuaded his daughter so much 530
That she gave him the ring;
He brought it to King Arthur.
As soon as he saw the ring,
Melion recognised it well;
He went to the king, fell on his knees 535
and kissed both his feet.
King Arthur wanted to touch him,
But Gawain would not permit it.
"Good uncle," he said, "don't!
Take him to a chamber 540
In absolute privacy
So that he is not shamed in front of people."
The king called Gawain,
And he took Yder with him;
He led Melion to a chamber. 545
When he was inside, he closed the door.
He put the ring to Melion's head;
His face appeared like a man's,
All his body changed.
Then he became a man and spoke. 550
He let himself fall at the king's feet;
They wrapped him in a cloak.
When they saw him shaped as a man,
They felt very great joy.
The king wept for pity over him 555
And weeping he asked him
How it had happened to him;
Through misfortune they had lost him.
He had his chamberlain sent for,
And had rich clothing brought to him; 560
He dressed Melion and turned him out well
And took him into the hall.
Through the dwelling they marvelled
When they saw Melion coming.
The king brought his daughter. 565
He presented her to King Arthur,
To do with as he wished,
Whether to burn her or have her torn to pieces.
Melion said: "I shall touch her
With the stone, nothing will stop me." 570
Arthur said to him: "Don't!

For the sake of your beautiful children let her be."
All the barons begged it of him;
Melion granted their wish.
Arthur remained there   575
Until the war was settled.
Then he set out for his own land,
Taking Melion with him;
He was very glad, he rejoiced at it.
He left his wife in Ireland.   580
He commended her to the devil;
She would never again be loved by him
Because she had mistreated him so badly,
As you have heard in the tale.
He never wished to take her back,   585
He would like to have let her burn or be dismembered.
Melion said: "It will never fail to happen
That he who believes his wife completely
Will be ruined in the end;
He should not believe all she says."   590
The Lay of Melion is true,
As all the nobles say.

2. From Gerald of Wales, *The Topography of Ireland*, trans. Thomas Forester, rev. and ed. Thomas Wright (Toronto: In Parentheses Publications, Medieval Latin Series, 2000), 44–45, with emendations in brackets

[Gerald of Wales, also known as Giraldus Cambrensis or Gerard de Barri (c. 1146–1223), was a cleric of Welsh and Norman descent who served as royal clerk and chaplain to King Henry II of England from 1184 to 1196. He wrote several Latin prose works on the history, conquest, landscape, and marvels of Ireland and Wales following his travels there in the 1180s and 1190s. In this passage he recounts the tale of a pious werewolf, one that recalls elements of *Yonec* as well as *Bisclavret*.]

Chapter XIX. Of the prodigies of our times, and first of a wolf which conversed with a priest.

I now proceed to relate some wonderful occurrences which have happened within our times. About three years before the arrival of earl John in Ireland, it chanced that a priest, who was journeying from Ulster toward Meath, was benighted in a certain wood on the borders of Meath. While, in company with only a young lad, he was watching by a fire which he had kindled under the branches of a spreading tree, lo! a wolf came up to them, and immediately addressed them to this effect: "Rest secure, and be not afraid, for there is no reason you should fear, where no fear is." The travellers being struck with astonishment and alarm, the wolf added some orthodox words referring to God. The priest then implored him, and adjured him by Almighty God and faith in the Trinity, not to hurt them, but to inform them what creature it was that in the shape of a beast uttered human words. The wolf, after giving catholic replies[1] to all questions, added at last: "[We are people from Ossory. Every seven years, through the curse of a certain saint, namely abbot Natalis, two people from there, a man and a woman, are forced into exile from their own forms and dwellings. Leaving the human form entirely, they take on that of wolves.] At the end of the seven years, if they chance to survive, two others being substituted in their places, they return to their country and their former shape. And now, she who is my partner in this visitation lies dangerously sick not far from hence, and, as she is at the point of death, I beseech you, inspired by divine charity, to give her the consolations of your priestly office."

At this word the priest followed the wolf trembling, as he led the way to a tree at no great distance, in the hollow of which he beheld a she-wolf, who under that shape was pouring forth human sighs and groans. On seeing the priest, having saluted him with human courtesy, she gave thanks to God, who in this extremity had vouchsafed to visit her with such consolation. She then received from the priest all the rites of the church duly performed, as far as the last communion. This also she importunately demanded, earnestly supplicating him to complete his good offices by giving her the viaticum.[2] The priest stoutly asserting that he was not provided with it, the he-wolf, who had withdrawn to a short distance, came back and pointed out [a small bag,] containing [a handbook and] some consecrated wafers, which the priest carried on his journey, suspended from his neck, under his garment, after the fashion of the country. He then entreated him not to deny them the gift of God, and the aid destined for them by Divine Providence; and, to remove all doubt, using his claw for a hand, he tore off the skin of the she-wolf, from the head down to the navel,

---

1 That is, replies in keeping with "universal" (*catholica*) Christianity; this is before any division into Protestant and Catholic sects.

2 The *viaticum* (Latin: 'food for the journey') is a name for the Eucharist or Communion wafer when given to someone at the point of death as part of the last rites. The ceremony the priest performs here is the same one referred to in *Yonec* l. 186.

folding it back. Thus she immediately presented the form of an old woman. The priest, seeing this, and compelled by his fear more than his reason, gave the communion; the recipient having earnestly implored it, and devoutly partaking of it. Immediately afterwards, the [skin rolled back by the he-wolf returned] to its original form.

These rites having been duly, rather than rightly, performed, the he-wolf gave them his company during the whole night at their little fire, behaving more like a man than a beast. When morning came, he led them out of the wood, and, leaving the priest to pursue his journey, pointed out to him the direct road for a long distance. At his departure, he also gave him many thanks for the benefit he had conferred, promising him still greater returns of gratitude if the Lord should call him back from his present exile, two parts of which he had already completed.

3. **Peire d'Alvernhe, Poems,** *Lyrics of the Troubadours and Trouvères: An Anthology and a History*, **ed. and trans. Frederick Goldin (Gloucester, MA: Peter Smith, 1983), 163–69, with minor emendations**

[Peire d'Alvernhe was a troubadour of the later twelfth century, roughly contemporary with Marie de France; very little is known about him, though his poetry was greatly admired and Dante praises him in *De vulgari eloquentia* He wrote in Old Occitan (also sometimes called Provençal), and this pair of poems, about a lover and lady who send messages by way of a nightingale, echoes *Laüstic* and *Milun* as well as some of the love conventions we see in other lais.]

a. "Nightingale, you will go for me"

"Nightingale, you will go for me
to see my lady in her residence,
and tell her how things go with me,
and let her tell you truly of herself,
and send here   5
how she fares,
but let her think of me,
let her not
for any reason
keep you there with her,   10

"so that you do not soon return to tell me
how she is and how she acts,

for I have no brother and no kin
I so long to hear about."
Now gaily   15
goes the bird
straight to where she rules,
thrusting forth
unafraid,
until it finds her banner.   20

When this bird of noble lineage
saw the beauty of her come forth,
it commenced its sweet song,
as it is wont to do toward evening,
then falls silent,   25
sings no more,
strains its wits,
how to tell,
without confusion,
the things she might deign to hear.   30

"The one who is a faithful lover to you
made me come
to your domain to be his singer here,
to bring you pleasure;
I shall know   35
when I see
some sign from you
what I shall tell him.
Now if I hear anything
that tells him to act with discretion,   40

"if I bring something back to rejoice him,
you should have great joy for that,
for no man ever born of mother
could ever wish such good for you.
I shall fly away,   45
shall soar
with joy wherever I come—
No, I shall not,
I have not yet
said how I would judge in this.   50

"For this I shall be an advocate:
whoever puts her hope in love,

she must never feel unrushed
while there is still a chance for love.
The white turns quickly   55
into dark,
like a flower on the branch;
and a woman is nobler
who acts
before other things compel her."   60

b. "The bird has held a straight path"

The bird has held a straight path
there where I sent it,
and she sends me a message
to answer what he said of me.
"Your sweet discourse,   5
be assured,
has given me much pleasure.
Now you must listen,
for you must tell him
the things that lie in my heart.   10

"It is cruel pain to me
that my friend took himself away,
for I never knew another joy
that gave me so much pleasure.
Too quick   15
was the parting.
But if I were confident,
he would get
more kindness yet;
so there is regret in me.   20

"For I love him so with my whole heart
that always, when I go between sleep and waking,
I have one guide with him together:
play and pleasure and joy and laughter.
The content I have   25
in silence and peace
no creature knows,
while he lies
in my arms,
until he is transfigured   30

"He was always my pleasure,
since I saw him and before I saw him
and I do not wish that I had won
another man of greater lineage.
My mind   35
is firm.
They cannot cause me pain,
wind nor ice,
nor summer
nor heat nor cold.   40

"Honest love has a way
like honest gold, when it is pure:
its virtue is refined
when there is virtue in the one intent on it.
And have faith   45
that friendship
perpetually exalts;
exalted
and beloved
is he of whom joy is foretold.   50

"Sweet bird, you will go for me
to his dwelling, when the morning comes,
and tell him with an honest tongue
how I wait on his desire."
Sped on,   55
it returned,
extraordinarily
instructed,
eloquent
with good news [*aventura*].   60

Appendix B: Love Relationships

1. From the *Roman d'Eneas*, ed. Aimé Petit (Paris: Livre de Poche, 1997), pp. 496–514, lines 8109–458, and pp. 528–42, lines 8718–982. Translated by Claire M. Waters, with reference to the translations of Noah Guynn, *Allegory and Sexual Ethics in the High Middle Ages* (New York: Palgrave Macmillan, 2007), 51–92

[After a scene in which the princess Lavine is urged by her mother to yield to the love of Turnus, the whole town goes to the battlements to survey the Trojans, who are under the leadership of Eneas; everyone is in agreement that they are an exceptionally handsome group and that Encas in particular is outstanding in nobility and looks. In this passage Lavine is wounded by love and laments her "sickness" and suffering in a way reminiscent of Guigemar; her situation also recalls that of Guilliadun in *Guildelüec and Guilliadun* when she finds herself falling in love with a foreigner, and her mother's reaction echoes that of the queen in *Lanval*.]

Lavine was up on the tower,	
she looks down from a window;	8110
she saw Eneas who was below,	
she looks intently at him above all.	
He seemed to her both handsome and noble.	
She has heard how	
they praise him throughout the city	8115
for both prowess and beauty;	
she noted him well in her heart.	
Right there as she was watching,	
Love wounded her with his dart;	
before she moved from that place	8120
she changed color a hundred times.	
Now she has fallen into the snare of Love,	
like it or not: she must love.	
When she sees that she cannot escape,	
she turned all her heart	8125
and all her thoughts toward Eneas.	
Love for him has wounded her greatly;	
the arrow has run her through the heart	
beneath her breast.	
The damsel was all alone,	8130
she ran to close the door of the chamber,	

came back to stand at the window
where she received the mortal blow.
...
She cries out, weeps, sighs and shouts;
she does not know who does this to her
nor who so changed her heart;
when she can speak, she laments,
"Wretch," she says, "what is wrong with me?   8145
Who has captured me? What is this?
A moment ago I was quite well,
now I am all faint and weak.
I feel a fire in my body
but I do not know for whom I am so inflamed,   8150
who changed my heart
and for whom I am entirely lost,
from which my heart feels a mortal pain—
unless it is that hidden evil
that my mother was telling me about yesterday;   8155
I do not know if it is love, or what it is called,
but all it does is make me feel terrible.
I believe, so far as I can tell, I am in love,
from now on I am at its beck and call;
I feel the ills and the sorrow   8160
that my mother told me come from love.
Where is the relief,
the box with all the ointments?
The queen told me yesterday
that Love brings its medicine   8165
and that it always cures its wounds.
...
Many another man have I seen
who never meant anything to me.
One does not love whatever one sees!
I would be in a sad case
if I could not look at a man   8215
without having to love him:
either I would love an incredible number
or I would look at very few.
Have I done wrong because I saw him?
Will Love not have mercy on me?   8220
He wounded me with one look,
he struck me in the eye with his dart,
the golden one that makes you love:
he ran it straight into my heart.

I believe that I alone am wounded,   8225
and Love has led me astray.
The Trojan does not feel it,
my life is nothing to him,
he does not deign to look this way;
Love has touched him, I believe, with the dart   8230
that is made of lead and leads to hate;
for which I will die of sorrow."

[*Lavine laments further, and considers the danger that her mother will
perceive her love.*]

"Love, you have troubled my heart;
soothe me just a little.
It seems to me that I am changed   8295
and turned pale and wan.
My mother knows a great deal of such matters,
she will perceive well
by my face, by my complexion
that I am overtaken by love.   8300
If she asks me what is wrong
and whether I love, what will I say to her?
How can I hide it from her?
She will see me change color,
shake, tremble, and faint,   8305
and sigh, blush, grow pale;
if I hide it from her, she will know well
by the signs that she will see.
I do not wish to lie so as not to tell her
that I love, nor will I hide it from her.   8310
If she asks me afterward 'who?,'
how will I name to her that man
whom she has so strictly forbidden me?
Should she know the truth,
she will kill me, but what do I care?   8315
No other remedy is worth anything to me,
nor do I expect to have any other comfort
from these torments but death.
I have begun this undertaking too foolishly,
I should have done it otherwise: 8320
I should not turn my love
toward Eneas this way
without Turnus having it just as much."

[After further lament and internal debate, Lavine must reckon with her mother, to whom she eventually discloses the truth. The queen is displeased.]

"What have you said, you utter fool?
Do you know to whom you have given yourself?   8620
This wretch is of such a nature
that he does not care for women at all.
He values quite a different trade:
he doesn't want to chase a doe,
he loves male flesh;   8625
he will prefer to have a servant boy
than embrace you or any other woman.
He does not know how to fly a female bird
nor to pass through the little wicket gate;
he really loves a young man's ass.   8630
Trojans are brought up this way.
You have chosen most foolishly:
have you not heard how badly
he treated Dido?
Never did a woman have any good of him,   8635
nor will you have any, I believe,
from a traitor, from a sodomite.
He'll throw you over any time;
if he has some debauched boy,
it would be just fine with him   8640
if you were to do it with his lovers;
if he could draw them in through you,
he wouldn't find it so outrageous
that he should make such an exchange:
that the young man should have his pleasure with you   8645
if he would then suffer the same himself:
he will gladly let him mount you
if he can then have a turn on him.
He does not love coney fur.[1]
There would soon be an end to this world   8650
if all the men who are in it
were like this throughout the world:
no woman would ever conceive,
there would be a great dearth of people;

---

1   There is a pun here on "con," which means both "rabbit" and the female
    genitalia.

no one would ever have a child,   8655
with that the world would come to an end."

[*Finally, after her mother's departure, Lavine decides to take matters into
her own hands by sending Eneas a message.*]

"I must know, I believe,
whether he will love me if I love him:
I shall write it all in a letter,
I shall send it to him, on the page,
my whole condition, the depths of my heart;   8825
I shall seek out a messenger
through whom I can send him the writing.
He will have it in just a little while;
before tomorrow night I shall know my situation."
Then she got up from the window   8830
and went straight in search of ink and parchment,
and wrote to him all in Latin.
    These letters tell what was in the note:
she sent, first of all, greetings
to Eneas her dear friend,   8835
and then said that she loved him so
that nothing meant anything to her any more,
nor would she ever have rest or relief
if he did not think of her at once.
She revealed to him all her desire,   8840
and depicted well on the parchment
how love of him
greatly torments and distresses her, so that she is dying of it.
With great sweetness she asks him
that he take pity on her   8845
and assure her of his friendship.
When she had written what she wanted,
she folded the letter very tightly;
she began to think to herself
about whom she could trust,   8850
by whom she could send it;
she did not know what was the wisest counsel.
She went to the window,
put her head out, looked outside
and saw that Eneas was coming   8855
toward the city, as he used to do;
she was most joyful and happy.
He stopped a bowshot away,

close to the tower, on the other side;
because of the truce, no one paid attention.   8860
     The maiden took the letter,
she wrapped it around the shaft
of a barbed arrow
with the writing turned to the inside;
she bound it tightly with a thread.   8865
She called one of the king's archers.
"Friend," she said, "quickly shoot this arrow for me
to those soldiers
who are down there below that tower;
they are keeping watch around there all day;   8870
I believe that they are spies.
If the truce were broken,
they will have seen and looked well
at where there is less strength
and what is hardest to defend,   8875
and they hope to capture us that way."

[*The archer shoots the arrow, which falls near the soldiers; one of Eneas's men brings it to him.*]

He looked at the letter and detached it;   8915
the maiden watched him.
     Eneas looked at the writing,
he saw and understood everything the letter said:
that Lavine loved him dearly
and that he was assured of her love,   8920
for she would never take another lord.
He saw everything she sent,
he was very happy about it, he hid it well:
he did not wish his people to know
nor for any of them to perceive it.   8925
He turned back toward the tower;
Lavine saw that he was looking,
she kissed her finger and reached toward him,
and Eneas understood well
that she was sending him a kiss;   8930
but he does not feel nor know
what sort of kiss it was;
he would like to know very much.

2. From *La vie de saint Alexis*, ed. Maurizio Perugi (Geneva: Droz, 2000), 167–69, lines 11–75. Translated by Claire M. Waters

[Two noble Roman fathers plan their children's marriage. On the wedding night the husband, Alexis, establishes a chaste marriage with his new bride, leaving her with his ring and sword, like Yonec and his lady, and goes to live in poverty. This is one of the very oldest literary texts in French that survives complete; it was composed in the mid-eleventh century.]

After that time in which God came to save us,	
our ancestors became Christian;	
and there was a lord of the city of Rome,	
a rich man, of great nobility:	
I tell you because I wish to speak of a son of his.	15

Eufemiens, as the father was called,	
was a count of Rome, one of the best who was there;	
the emperor loved him above all his peers.	
He took a worthy and honorable wife	
from the best nobles of the whole country.	20

They lived together a long time.	
It weighed on them greatly that they had no child.	
They both called fittingly on God:	
"Oh heavenly king, by your commandment,	
give us a child who will be to your liking!"	25

They prayed to him with such great humility	
that he granted fertility to the wife:	
he gave them a son, and they were very thankful.	
They had him redeemed through holy baptism:	
they gave him a good name according to Christian belief.	30

He was baptized, and named Alexis.	
She who bore him sweetly nursed him,	
then his good father sent him to school:	
he learned his letters so well that he was thoroughly prepared;	
then the child goes to serve the emperor.	35

When the father saw that he would have no more children	
except this one alone, whom he loved so dearly,	
then he thought about future times:	

now he wants his son to take a wife in his lifetime,
so he obtained the daughter of a nobleman. 40

The girl was of very high lineage,
the daughter of a count of the city of Rome;
he had no other child, he wanted great honor for her.
The two fathers came together to talk:
they want to bring their two children together. 45

They name the terms of their marriage;
when it came time to do it, they did so nobly.
Lord Alexis married her handsomely,
but this was a situation which he did not want at all:
his desires were turned entirely toward God. 50

When the day passed and night fell,
the father said: "Son, go to bed
with your wife, as God in heaven commands."
The youth did not wish to make his father angry;
he goes into the chamber with his noble wife. 55

When he saw the bed, he looked at the maiden,
then he remembered his heavenly Lord,
whom he holds dearer than any earthly thing.
"Ah, God!" he says, "such strong sin oppresses me!
If I do not flee now, I greatly fear lest I shall lose you." 60

When they were left quite alone in the chamber,
Lord Alexis began to address her:
he greatly denigrated mortal life,
and showed her the truth of the heavenly;
but it seemed long to him before he could leave there. 65

"Hear me, maiden: take as your spouse the One
who redeemed us with his precious blood.
In this world there is no perfect love:
life is fragile, there is no lasting honor;
this ugliness turns to great sorrow." 70

When he had explained all his thoughts to her,
then he commended to her his sword belt
and a ring; he commended her to God.
Then he left the chamber of his father:
in the middle of the night he fled the country. 75

3. From Marie de France, *Les Fables: Édition critique*, ed. and trans. Charles Brucker (Paris and Louvain: Peeters, 1998), 194–200. Translated by Claire M. Waters

[While most of the stories in the *Fables* or *Ysopë* have animal protagonists, Marie also tells a few with human characters. The ones below are very similar to *fabliaux*, a comic genre that emphasizes wit, trickery, reversal, and often—as here—adultery, usually on the part of the wife. *Equitan* is often compared to this genre.]

a. "The Wife and Her Lover"

This story tells of a peasant who looked
into the door of his house: he spied.
He saw another man in his bed,
taking his pleasure with his wife.
"Alas," he said, "what have I seen!"   5
Then his wife replied to him,
"What have you seen, beloved sir?"
"Another man, it seems to me,
held you in his arms on the bed."
Then the lady said, very angrily,   10
"I know well," she said, "I have no doubt,
that this is your old foolishness:
you want to take a lie for the truth."
"I saw it," he said, "so I should indeed believe it."
"You're a fool," she said, "if you believe   15
everything you see to be the truth."
She takes him by the hands, she leads him with her
to a vat full of water;
she makes him look into the vat.
Then she begins to ask him   20
what he sees inside, and he tells her
that he sees his own image.
"So then," she said, "you are not
inside the vat with all your clothes on,
even if you see what looks like that.   25
You should not put your faith
in your eyes, which so often lie."
The peasant said, "I'm sorry!
Everyone should rather believe and know
what his wife tells him is the truth   30
than what these lying eyes see,
which fool him with their sight."

By this example we are given to understand
that intelligence and craft are worth much more
and are more help to many people   35
than their goods or their family.

b. "Another Wife and Her Lover"

I want to tell here about another peasant
who saw his wife going
toward the forest, her lover along with her.
He went after them. The man ran off
and concealed himself in the woods,   5
and the peasant came back very angry.
He rebuked and upbraided his wife;
and the lady asked him
why he spoke to her this way.
Her husband replied   10
that he had seen her lecherous lover,
who did him shame and dishonor,
going with her toward the forest.
"Sir," she said, "if you please,
for the love of God, tell me the truth!   15
You thought you saw a man
going with me? Don't hide it from me!"
"I saw him," he said, "enter the woods."
"Wretched me," she said, "I am dead!
Tomorrow, or even today, I will die!   20
It happened just the same way to my grandmother
and to my mother, for I saw it:
a little before their deaths,
it was openly known
that a young man was escorting them,   25
and that he had nothing else to do with them.
Now I know well that my end is near;
send, sir, for all my kin,
and let us share out our goods!
I dare not remain in the world any longer;   30
I will enter a convent
with all of my share."
The peasant heard her, he begged for her mercy.
"Let it be," he said, "my dear!
Do not leave me like this!   35

It was a lie, what I saw."
"I dare not," she said, "remain here any longer,
for I must think of my soul,
above all because of the great shame
about which you have made such a big fuss.   40
I would be reproached forever
for having behaved basely toward you
if you do not swear me an oath,
so that our relatives can witness it,
that you did not see a man with me.   45
Then swear to me on your faith
that you will never speak a word about it
nor ever reproach me for it."
"Gladly, lady," he replies.
They go to a church together;   ·   50
there he swore to her as she wanted
and even more than she had put in.
This is why people say, as a proverb,
that women know how to deceive;
the crafty and the untruthful   55
know one trick more than the devil.

4. From Béroul, *Tristan et Iseut: Les poèmes français. La saga norroise*, ed. and trans. Daniel Lacroix and Philippe Walter (Paris: Librairie Générale Française, 1989), 80–82, lines 1271–1305. Translated by Claire M. Waters

[This is the earliest surviving account of the famous story of the fated lovers Tristan and Yseult (or Isolde), probably from around the mid-twelfth century; nothing is known about its author, Béroul, and the poem survives, incomplete, in only one manuscript. Like Marie's *Lais*, it was written in octosyllabic couplets. In this scene, the lovers and Tristan's faithful tutor Governal have just fought off a crowd of lepers to whom Yseult had been handed over by her husband, King Mark, as punishment for the accusations of adultery leveled against her by members of his court. The three flee to a forest, also the meeting place of the lovers in *Chevrefoil*.]

Tristan goes off with the queen;
they left the plain, and toward the forest
go Tristan and Governal.
Yseult rejoices; now she feels no pain.

They are in the forest of Morrois;   1275
that night they sleep on a hill.
Now Tristan is as secure
as if he were in a castle or behind a wall.
Tristan was an excellent archer;
he knew well how to make use of his bow.   1280
Governal had taken one
from a forester who had it
and two feathered,
tipped arrows along with it.
Tristan took the bow, he goes into the woods.   1285
He sees a roe-buck, he nocks an arrow and shoots it,
he wounds the deer badly in the right side.
It cries out, leaps high and falls down.
Tristan took it and comes back with it.
He makes a shelter: with the sword he has   1290
he cuts branches and makes a roof of leaves;
Yseult covers the floor thickly.
Tristan sits by the queen.
Governal knew how to cook;
he makes a good fire from dry brushwood.   1295
The cooks had a lot to do!
There was neither milk nor salt
in their lodging at that time.
The queen was extremely tired
from the fear she had experienced: 1300
she became drowsy, she wanted to sleep;
she wanted to sleep beside her beloved.
Lords, so they lived for a long time
in the depths of the forest;
for a long time they were in that wasteland.   1305

Appendix C: Prologues and Epilogues

1. **From Marie de France, *Les Fables: Édition critique*, ed. and trans. Charles Brucker (Paris and Louvain: Peeters, 1998), 46–48, 364–66. Translated by Claire M. Waters**

[Marie's *Fables* or *Ysopë*, perhaps composed in the 1180s, is a collection of short narratives with morals at the end, many of which feature animal protagonists. The Prologue and Epilogue both have features that recall elements of the Prologue of the *Lais*.]

[Prologue]

Those who are learned
should apply themselves studiously
to the good books and writings
and examples and sayings
that the philosophers devised   5
and wrote and remembered:
they would write for the sake of morality
the good proverbs that they heard
so that those who set themselves to do well
would be able to improve themselves;   10
so the ancient fathers did.
Romulus, who was emperor,
wrote to his son and told him
and showed by example
how he could guard himself   15
so that no one could trick him.
Aesop wrote to his master,
knowing him and his nature well,
some fables that he had composed
and translated from Greek to Latin.   20
Many people were amazed
that he put his intelligence to such a task;
but there is no fable of folly
that does not contain some philosophy
in the morals that follow after   25
where the whole burden of the stories is.
To me, who must put them in rhyme,
it was not at all becoming to relate
many words that appear there;

but nevertheless one urged me   30
who is the flower of chivalry,
of learning, of courtesy;
and when such a man has asked me,
I do not wish in any way
to fail to put my labor and effort   35
to doing all I can at his request,
whoever may think ill of me for it.
So I will begin the first
of the fables that Aesop wrote
that he sent and told to his master.   40

[Epilogue]

At the end of this writing
that I have composed and presented in French
I shall name myself for the sake of remembrance:
Marie is my name, I am from France.
It may be that many clerks   5
would wish to claim my labor for themselves.
I do not wish anyone to attribute it to them:
she acts foolishly who forgets herself.
For love of Count William,
the most valiant in any realm,   10
I undertook to make this book
and translate it from English into French.
People call this book "Esopë,"
which he translated and had put into writing;
he turned it from Greek into Latin.   15
King Alfred, who loved it dearly,
then translated it into English,
and I have rhymed it in French
as correctly as I could.
Now I pray to almighty God   20
that I may apply myself to such work
that I can deliver my soul to him.

2. **From Marie de France, *Saint Patrick's Purgatory* (*L'Espurgatoire seint Patriz*), Nouvelle édition critique, trans. Yolande de Pontfarcy, ed. Karl Warnke (Paris and Louvain: Peeters, 1995), pp. 74–76, lines 1–30, and p. 278, lines 2297–2302. Translated by Claire M. Waters**

[*St. Patrick's Purgatory* recounts the existence of a cave in Ireland that offers an entrance to Purgatory; those who enter can be purged of their sins. The main part of the story tells of a knight, Owein, who undertakes this penitential adventure.]

[Prologue]

In the name of God—may he be with us
and send us his grace
I wish to put into French and in writing,
as the book tells it to us,
in remembrance and in memory,   5
the pains of Purgatory
that God wished to show to St. Patrick,
the place where one would enter it.
A worthy man asked it of me some time ago;
therefore I have now undertaken it,   10
to set myself to this labor
out of reverence and honor for him,
And if it pleases him and he would wish it
(may he always welcome me in his kindness)
I will say what I have heard about it.   15
Dear father, now listen:
although it is the case that I wish
to cause many people to gain
great benefit and to improve,
and serve God better and fear him,   20
I would never have undertaken this
nor set myself to this task
were it not for your request,
which is sweet and dear to my heart.
I have heard and seen little on this matter;   25
on account of what I have understood,
I have greater love for God
and a greater wish to serve him, my creator.
Therefore I wish to reveal
and bring to light this writing.   30

[Marie's Epilogue]

I, Marie, for the sake of memory,
have put into French the book of the *Purgatory*,
so that it may be understandable
to laypeople, and suitable for them.   2300
Now let us pray to God that by his grace
he make us clean of our sins. Amen.

3. **From Marie de France, *Life of St. Audrey: A Text by Marie de France*, ed. and trans. June Hall McCash and Judith Clark Barban (Jefferson, NC: McFarland, 2006), lines 1–16, 29–31, 4611–25**

[St. Audrey or Etheldreda was a royal Anglo-Saxon woman who founded the monastery of Ely, in eastern England, after escaping the threat of worldly marriage. Marie's *Life* relies on Latin materials about the saint that were composed by about 1190, as well as additional material on her miracles that may have reached Marie in either oral or written form; the *Life* was probably composed in the 1190s or the very early thirteenth century. Its Prologue and Epilogue have a number of similarities with other works signed "Marie."]

[Prologue]

For a good work and for a good purpose
should each person use his time.
It would be wise
for everyone to remember
what he is made of, who made him,   5
and whither he shall return.
People who do good are honored
and loved by God and also by the world.
Since the soul will [one day] leave the body,
earthly possessions are worth very little   10
if one has not shared them for the sake of God
nor in this life been a worthy person
whose good works outweigh his misdeeds,
pride, and evil vices.
Saved is the one who during his lifetime   15
has merited grace and fellowship of God.
…
I have undertaken to write this book

in honor of Saint Audrey the queen   30
whose goodness has never faded nor diminished.

[Epilogue]

Now I have finished this book,
told and translated into French
the life of Saint Audrey
just as I found it in Latin,
along with the miracles I have heard.   4615
I do not wish to let anything be forgotten.
Therefore I beseech glorious,
precious Saint Audrey
to hear me out of compassion
and to give aid to my soul,   4620
as well as to those for whom I pray:
may she help them through her mercy.
One is indeed foolish who forgets herself:
here I write my name 'Marie'
so that I may be remembered.   4625

4. From Chrétien de Troyes, *Cliges*, *Les romans de Chrétien de Troyes II*, ed. Alexandre Micha (Paris: Honoré Champion, 1957), pp. 1–2, lines 1–42. Translated by Claire M. Waters

[Chrétien (c. 1130–c. 1190), a continental cleric and poet who was a contemporary of Marie, was the most influential author of chivalric (particularly Arthurian) romance in the Middle Ages. The prologue of his romance *Cliges* shows a concern for remembrance like Marie's, though couched in different terms: he provides a list of his works to date. He also, like her, acknowledges his debts to classical literature, particularly the poet Ovid, while also making the famous claim that excellence in chivalry and learning had, over time, moved from Greece to Rome, to end at last in France—the movement known as *translatio studii et imperii*, the transfer of learning and power.]

He who wrote of Erec and of Enide,
and put Ovid's *Commandments*
and *Art of Love* into French,
and wrote *The Shoulder Bite*,
as well as about King Mark and the blonde Yseult,   5
and about the transformation of the hoopoe

and the swallow and the nightingale
begins a new story
of a young man, of the lineage of King Arthur,
who lived in Greece.   10
But before I tell you anything about him,
you will hear the life of his father,
where he was from, and of what lineage.
He was so worthy and bold of heart
that to win renown and praise   15
he went from Greece to England,
which was then called Britain.
This story that I wish to tell and relate to you
we find written down
in one of the books of the library   20
of my lord St. Peter at Beauvais;
the story, which bears true witness to the history,
was taken from there:
for that reason it is more to be believed.
Through the books that we have   25
we know the deeds of the ancients
and of the world that once was.
Our books have taught us
that Greece was the first paragon
of chivalry and learning.   30
Then the height of chivalry and learning
came to Rome,
and has now come to France.
May God grant that it be retained there
and that the place will so enhance it   35
that the honor that is now lodged there
will never leave France.
God had lent it to the others:
for no one says a word any more
about the Greeks or the Romans;   40
talk of them is set aside
and their lively spark has been extinguished.

5. From Wace, *Roman de Rou, History of the Norman People*, ed. and trans. Glyn S. Burgess (Woodbridge: Boydell, 2004), 13 (lines 1–42)

[Wace (c. 1100–after 1171) was born on the Channel Island of Jersey, between France and England, and educated at Caen in northern

France. In the 1160s, at the request of Henry II, he began to compose a history of the Normans, dating back to their ancestor Rou or Rollo (c. 845–c. 930), that would substantiate their claims to the English throne. Both Henry II and his queen, Eleanor, could trace their lineage to Rollo, and Wace emphasizes both of them and their patronage in his prologue.]

One thousand, one hundred and sixty years in time and space had elapsed since God in His grace came down in the Virgin when a cleric from Caen by the name of Master Wace undertook the story of Rou and his race; Rou conquered Normandy, like it or not, against the arrogance of France which still threatens them—may our King Henry recognise and be aware of this. He who has very little income has very little benefit from it. But largesse has now succumbed to avarice; it cannot open its hands, they are more frozen than ice. I do not know where largesse is hidden, I can find no sign or trace of it. He who does not know how to flatter has no opportunity or place at court; many people are forced to await their turn. It was not at all like this in the time of Virgil and Horace, nor of Alexander, Caesar or Statius; then largesse had strength and virtue.

I want the subject of this first page to be King Henry, who took as his wife Eleanor, a lady of noble birth; may God inspire both of them to good works!

They do not let me waste my time at court; each of them rewards me with gifts and promises. But need, which sails and rows swiftly, often presents itself and often forces me to make pledges in order to obtain money. Eleanor is noble and both kind and wise, and she was queen of France at a young age. Louis took her as his wife in a marriage of great power and they went on a lengthy crusade to Jerusalem; each suffered great hardship and pain there. On their return, the queen, on the advice of the barons, was parted from him on grounds of consanguinity. But this separation did her no harm; she went to Poitiers, her native home, of which she was the family heir. King Henry, who held England and the coastal land between Spain and Scotland, from shore to shore, took her as his wife and made a rich marriage. People often talk of him and his courage, and of the evil-doers he destroys, like birds trapped in a cage. No baron in his land owns so much property that, if he dares infringe the peace, whether in open country or in woodland, he is not shamed through mutilation if he can be caught, or who does not leave his body or soul behind as hostage.

6. Prologue of Denis Piramus, *Life of St. Edmund* (*La vie seint Edmund le rei*), ed. D.W. Russell (Oxford: Anglo-Norman Text Society, 2014), pp. 67–69, lines 1–78. Translated by Claire M. Waters

[Denis Piramus, probably a monk at the Benedictine abbey of Bury St. Edmunds, composed his *Life of St. Edmund* around 1190–93, drawing on Latin and English sources. His Prologue suggests that there is competition between writings aimed at spiritual edification and those intended for secular entertainment, and it emphasizes the greater worth of the former—including, of course, his own text. This Prologue is of interest both for its view of the contemporary literary scene and particularly for its mention of "dame Marie" and her lais.]

I have, like a sinner, badly misspent
my life in a most foolish manner,
and have spent too much of my life
in both sin and folly
when I would spend time at court with courtly people   5
and write *serventeis*,
little songs, rhymes, and greetings
between lovers and their beloveds.
I took great trouble to make such verses
so that I might be able to bring them [i.e., lovers] together   10
and so that they might be joined together
so they could achieve their desires.
The Devil made me do this,
and so I now consider myself to have been mistreated:
I will never jest any more.   15
My name is Denis Piramus;
my lovely days of my youth
are going away, and I am drawing toward old age:
it is right indeed that I should repent.
I will put my efforts to another task,   20
which is much better and more worthy of note.
May God help me in spirit,
and the grace of the Holy Ghost
be with me and offer help!
  He who composed *Partenopeus*   25
and who made the verses and rhymed them
took great care to speak well,
and he spoke well of this matter:
how the material of fables and lies
resembles a dream,   30

for it could never be.
Yet he is considered a good craftsman,
and his verses are greatly loved
and praised in rich courts.
And Lady Marie also,   35
who made and arranged in rhyme
and composed the verses of lais
that are not at all true,
and yet she is greatly praised for it,
and the rhyme is loved everywhere,   40
for counts, barons and knights
love it very much and hold it very dear;
and they love the writing greatly
and have it read and take pleasure in it,
and so they often have them retold.   45
The lais were accustomed to please ladies;
they gladly and willingly hear them,
for they are according to their taste.
Kings, princes, and courtiers,
counts, barons, and vavasours   50
love stories, songs, and fables
and pleasant poems that are enjoyable,
for they take away and cast out thought,
sorrow, envy, and trouble of heart,
and they cause anger to be forgotten   55
and take away thought from the heart.
Since they and you, lords, all
love such work and such pleasure,
if you wish to listen to me
I will tell you, in good faith,   60
a pleasant thing that is worth a good deal more
than those others that you love so much,
and is more enjoyable to hear,
for it can cure souls
and protect the body from shame.   65
One should indeed listen well to such a story:
one had much better attend to good sense
than waste time on foolishness.
I will tell you who are sensible
a pleasant thing in verse, so true   70
that nothing could ever be more true,
for our ancestors saw it well,
and we, afterwards, from generation to generation,
have seen well that it is true,

for in our time many a miracle
has come to pass from this work.
That which one sees, one should believe,
for it is no dream nor fantasy.

7. Prologue to the Old Norse Translation of the *Lais*, *Strengleikar: An Old Norse Translation of Twenty-one Old French Lais*, ed. [and trans.] Robert Cook and Mattias Tveitane (Oslo: Kjeldeskriftfondet, 1979), 5–9

[This Prologue contains a section original to the Old Norse version, which emphasizes the value of the past as a model for the present, before turning to a translation of Marie's own prologue—though one that, as noted in the Introduction (pp. 37–38), shifts her emphasis in some subtle ways.]

It pleased us to inquire about and examine the deeds of those who lived in olden days, because they were skilled in their arts, discerning in their reason, clever in their counsels, valiant with weapons, well-mannered in the customs of the court, generous with gifts, and most famous for every kind of nobility. And because many marvelous things and events unheard of in our time took place in olden days, it occurred to us to teach men living and those to come these stories, which men of great learning made about the deeds of those who lived in olden days, and which they had written down in books as an everlasting reminder, as entertainment, and as a source of great learning for posterity, so that each man could amend and illumine his life with the knowledge of past events, and so that that will not be concealed in later times which happened in the remote past, and so that everyone might consider with full knowledge and strive with all his strength, and accomplish and achieve with every opportunity to prepare and improve himself for the kingdom of God by means of fitting behavior and good deeds and a holy life's end. For deeds and nobility and every kind of goodness, which embellished and adorned the lives of those who pleased God and those who in olden days earned fame and favors by means of achievements in this world—these things are disappearing more and more as the days of this world march on.

This book, which the esteemed King Hákon had translated into Norse from the French language, may be called "Book of Lais," because from the stories which this book makes known, poets in Brittany—which is in France—composed lais, which are performed on harps, fiddles, hurdy-gurdies, lyres, dulcimers, psalteries, rotes, and other stringed instruments of all kinds which men make to amuse themselves and others in this world. Here ends this prologue, and next comes the beginning of the lais.

It is not fitting that all those to whom God has given wisdom and knowledge and the eloquence to make these known should hide and conceal God's gift within themselves; rather, it is proper that they reveal to others with good will that which it pleased God to grant them. Then they will bear leaves and blossoms like the most splendid tree, and as their goodness becomes known through the improvement of others, so will their fruit become fully ripe and nourish other people. It was the custom of wise and well-mannered men in olden days that they should set forth their learning, so to speak, in dark words and deep meanings for the sake of those who had not yet come, that these should explicate in lucid discourse that which their for[e]bears had said and probe with their intelligence whatever pertained to the elucidation and correct understanding of the teachings which philosophers, sages of long ago, had made. As time and the lives of men wore on, man's art and attentiveness and acumen increased in many kinds of ways, so that the most learned men in every country began expressing themselves in the language of their country. And it is quite fitting that those who want to preserve their lives faultless be always considering and working at that which may make themselves beloved and which may instruct others from their own knowledge. For this reason I thought of making some good story and of translating it from French into Latin, that most might be comforted by that which most could understand. But the lais which I have heard, which were composed in Brittany about the strange adventures that took place in that land, I wanted to translate and tell to others, because I had heard very many things which I certainly want to tell. And I want to leave out nothing of what I can recall to my memory in honor of a courteous king whom God gave to us and endowed with wisdom and might, good fortune, and an abundance of manifold and renowned goodness. Thus I frequently think of gathering all the songs into one book to give to you, my lord and gracious king. If you like them, I am glad that my work pleases and satisfies such a wise chieftain and the courteous clerks of his court and his gracious retainers.

Appendix D: Historical and Legendary Accounts of Britain and the Normans

1. From Geoffrey of Monmouth, *History of the Kings of Britain*, ed. Michael A. Faletra (Peterborough, ON: Broadview, 2008), 122, 171

[These excerpts from Geoffrey's (c. 1100–55) immensely influential legendary history depict two key moments in Britain's linguistic and military contacts with other groups: the British ruler Vortigern's initial encounter with the Saxon princess Renwein and, from a later section, the glories of Arthur's court and his conquest of Norway. The first begins just after Vortigern has made a fateful grant of land to the clever Saxon war-leader Hengist, who builds a castle there; Hengist begins by fighting for Vortigern as a mercenary but eventually turns on him, beginning the Anglo-Saxon takeover of Britain. The second excerpt follows Arthur's defeat of the Anglo-Saxons in the southern and central parts of Britain and of the Scots and Picts in the north to establish himself as ruler of the whole island, after which he turns to wider imperial conquests.]

… In the meantime, the Saxon messengers had returned from their mission, bringing eighteen ships full of the choicest soldiers. They also brought with them Hengist's daughter Renwein, whose beauty was second to none. After their arrival, Hengist invited King Vortigern to his house to inspect the new fortress and fresh soldiers. Coming there in secret, the king praised how quickly the castle had been erected, and he retained the soldiers who had been invited. Once the royal feast had been served, the girl Renwein came out of her chamber carrying a goblet of wine. Approaching the king, she curtsied and said: "*Lauerd king, Waesseil!*" When Vortigern saw the girl's face, he marveled greatly at her beauty and grew inflamed with desire for her. Then he asked his interpreter what the girl had said and how he should answer. The interpreter explained: "She called you 'lord king' and honored you with a word of greeting. You should answer '*Drincheil.*'" The king said, "*Drincheil*," and commanded the girl to drink. He then took the goblet from her hand, kissed her, and drank. From that day until the present time it has been the custom of the table in Britain that whoever drinks should say "*Waesseil*" to his fellow. And whoever receives the drink next should say "*Drincheil.*"

… King Arthur then invited all the bravest men from the far-flung reaches of his domains to join his household. In this way, he was able to cultivate such refinement in his court that people far and wide sought to emulate it. Every young nobleman was tempted to hang himself unless he could dress or bear arms like the knights of King Arthur's court. The fame of Arthur's great generosity and prowess then spread to the furthest ends of the earth, and great fear beset the kings across the sea that Arthur would invade them and seize the lands under their rule. Spurred on by these concerns, they refortified their cities and towers and built castles in strategic locations so that, in the event that Arthur attacked them, they would have a safe refuge. When Arthur learned of these things, he rejoiced at being universally feared, and he desired to submit all Europe to his rule. So he prepared a fleet and sailed first to Norway, hoping to bestow its crown upon his brother-in-law Loth. Loth was, in fact, the nephew of Sichelm, the king of the Norwegians, and should have inherited the throne when Sichelm died. But the Norwegians refused to accept him as their king, setting up a certain Riculf in his place. They believed they could fight off Arthur from within their fortified cities. At that time, Loth's son Gawain was only twelve years old and had been placed in the service of Pope Sulpicius, from whom he received his arms. When Arthur landed on the shores of Norway, as I had begun to say, King Riculf came out to meet him with all the people of his land, and they did battle. After much blood had been shed on either side, the Britons finally prevailed. Making one final advance, they were able to kill Riculf and many of his men. Once they had achieved this victory, they put the Norwegian cities to the flame and scattered the inhabitants with great ferocity until they had subdued not only all of Norway, but Denmark as well, to Arthur's rule.

2. **From an Anonymous Anglo-Norman Verse Chronicle,**
   Chroniques anglo-normands. Recueil d'extraits et d'écrits
   relatifs à l'histoire de Normandie et d'Angleterre pendant
   les XIe et XIIe siècles, **ed. Francisque Michel (Rouen:**
   Édouard Frère, 1836), 95–98. Translated by Claire M.
   Waters

[This excerpt from a chronicle account of the Norman and Anglo-Norman kings of England tells of the unlucky demise of William Rufus (r. 1087–1100), second son of William the Conqueror. Its emphasis on the shortcomings of rulers and on the *aventures* that can accompany hunting makes for an intriguing comparison with Marie's *Lais*.]

William Rufus, who was king,
behaved himself badly;
he was a despicable and wicked man,
very cruel and wild,
arrogant and proud,   5
and, above all else, avaricious:
he taxed bishoprics and abbeys,
treated Holy Church vilely,
mistreated rich and poor people,
held the land to ransom as much as he could.   10
He held bishoprics and abbeys vacant
in his hands for many years;
he did not want to grant the election
of a bishop or abbot
in response to either request or argument   15
unless it was paid for with a bribe.
Prebends and churches
that clerks had once possessed
he refused to give without money;
he commonly had them sold off.   20
The law was not followed in his time
unless the case was made with money.
His friends gold and silver
were the judges throughout the land.
The man who was most corrupt   25
and knew best how to squeeze money out of the people
was his dearest friend
and his intimate adviser.
On account of his great outrages
God took harsh vengeance on him.   30
For one night, when he was in bed,
a horrible dream came to him:
that he was in a church
and fought with the cross;
he had gnawed the cross with his teeth   35
and completely devoured the right arm of it.
In the morning, when he got up,
he told the dream to his men,
at which many were frightened
and greatly astonished;   40
but a wise man who was present
earnestly begged the king
to think deeply
and confess his sins,

to do penance with a good heart 45
and mend his ways henceforth—
for pitiless death
spares no mother's son.
The king, who was hard-hearted,
took this counsel lightly; 50
he speedily sent for dinner,
he said he wanted to go to the woods.
The wise man said at once:
"Sire, hear mass before you go;
for no purse will be diminished by almsgiving, 55
nor any day shortened by hearing mass."
The king wanted to hurry;
quickly he sat down to his dinner.
He was served venison,
wonderfully fattened and in good season. 60
Then the king spoke
to the aforementioned wise man:
"Now, see this venison,
which is fat and in good season.
You may be sure, I tell you, 65
that the beast never heard a mass:
yet it is no less valued
nor less delicious to eat."
After dinner the king mounted his horse;
he entered the New Forest. 70
He soon found a deer
that had wandered off by itself.
Gracefully it passed before him;
it showed no sign of fear.
The king quickly commanded 75
the man who carried his bow—
a young man born in France,
called Walter Tyrel—
"Shoot the devil before it gets away!
it has lived long enough, and it's nice and fat." 80
Walter aimed an arrow at the beast,
and the arrow pierced the king through the middle.
There, by the Evil One, he died,
when he had reigned almost thirteen years.
His men carried him away 85
and buried him at Winchester.

Appendix E: Courtly Life and Pursuits

1. From Wace, *Roman de Brut, A History of the British: Text and Translation*, ed. and trans. Judith Weiss, rev. ed. (Exeter: University of Exeter Press, 2002), 265–67 (lines 10521–620)

[In addition to composing his *Roman de Rou* for Henry II (see Appendix C5), the Jerseyman Wace translated Geoffrey of Monmouth's *History of the Kings of Britain* into French verse, often embellishing it with further detail. This passage describes the courtly feast that follows King Arthur's formal coronation and depicts his court as the epitome of noble behaviors, pastimes, and gift-giving—though Wace seems to enjoy particularly the less elevated behavior brought out by games of chance.]

Beyond all the surrounding realms, and beyond all those we now know, England was unparalleled for fine men, wealth, plenty, nobility, courtesy and honour. Even the poor peasants were more courtly and brave than knights in other realms, and so were the women too. You would never see a knight worth his salt who did not have his armour, clothing and equipment all of the same colour. They made their armour all of one colour and their dress to match, and ladies of high repute were likewise clothed in one colour. There was no knight, however nobly born, who could expect affection or have a courtly lady as his love, if he had not proved himself three times in knightly combat. The knights were the more worthy for it, and performed better in the fray; the ladies, too, were the better and lived a chaster life.

When the king rose from his meal, everyone went in search of amusement. They went out of the city into the fields and dispersed for various games. Some went off to joust and show off their fast horses, others to fence or throw the stone or jump. There were some who threw javelins and some who wrestled. Each one took part in the game he knew most about. The man who defeated his friends and who was prized for any game was at once taken to the king and exhibited to all the others, and the king gave him a gift of his own so large that he went away delighted. The ladies mounted the walls to look at those who were playing and whoever had a friend quickly bent her eyes and face towards him. There were many minstrels at court, singers and instrumentalists: many songs could be heard, melodies sung to the rote and new tunes, fiddle music, lays with melodies, lays on fiddles, lays on rotes, lays on harps, lays on flutes, lyres, drums and shawms, bagpipes, psalteries, monochords, tambourines and choruns. There were plenty of conjurors, dancers and jugglers. Some told stories and tales, others asked for dice and backgammon. There were some who played games of chance—that's a cruel game—but most played chess or at dice or at something better. Two by two they joined in the game, some losing, some winning; some envied those who made the most throws, or they told others how to move. They borrowed money in exchange for pledges, quite willing only to get eleven to the dozen on the loan; they gave pledges, they seized pledges, they took them, they promised them, often swearing, often protesting their good intentions, often cheating and often tricking. They got argumentative and angry, often miscounting and grousing. They threw twos, and then fours, two aces, a third one, and threes, sometimes fives, sometimes sixes. Six, five, four, three, two and ace—these stripped many of their clothes. Those holding the dice were in high hopes; when their friends had them, they made a racket. Very often they shouted and cried out, one saying to the other: "You're cheating me, throw them out, shake your hand, scatter the dice! I'm raising the bid before your throw! If you're looking for money, put some down, like me!" The man who sat down to play clothed might rise naked at close of play.

In this way, the feast lasted three days. When it came to the fourth, a Wednesday, the king gave his young men fiefs and shared out available domains. He repaid the service of everyone who had served him for land: he distributed towns and castles, bishoprics and abbeys. To those who came from another land, for love of the king, he gave cups and war-horses and some of his finest possessions. He gave playthings, he gave jewels, he gave greyhounds, birds, furs, cloth, cups, goblets, brocades, rings, tunics, cloaks, lances, swords and barbed arrows. He gave quivers and shields, bows and keen swords, leopards and bears, saddles, trappings and chargers. He gave hauberks and war-horses, helmets and money, silver and gold, the best in his treasury. Any man worth anything, who had come to visit him from other lands, was given such a gift from the king that it did him honour.

2. From *The Life of William Marshal*, partly included in *William Marshal: The Flower of Chivalry*, ed. Georges Duby, trans. Richard Howard (New York: Pantheon, 1985), 102–04

[This anonymous thirteenth-century verse text tells of William Marshal (c. 1146–1219), a close advisor to Henry II and his sons Henry the Young King (who predeceased his father), Richard I, and John, as well as regent for the young King Henry III. He was regarded in his time as an exemplar of chivalric behavior and values and particularly renowned for his skill as a fighter in tournaments. The excerpt below conveys the chaos of such events.]

... [There was] Grand clangor and great noise.
All were eager to strike home.
Here could you hear the clash
of lance against lance, the pieces
falling so thick upon the ground   5
the horses could not charge.
Great was the press on the plain.
Each troop shouts its war cry ...
Here one might see knights taken
and others coming to their rescue.   10
On all sides were horses to be seen
running and sweating with dread,
each man eager to do all he could
to win, for in such enterprise
prowess is quickly seen and shown.   15
Then would you have seen the earth shake
when the young king said: "Enough,
charge, I shall wait no longer."
The king charges, but the count [his brother Geoffrey, Count of
     Brittany]
stood fast and wisely did not move ...   20
Those then who were about the king
thrust forward with such eagerness
they paid no heed to their king.
So far forward did they rush
that they hurled the others back—   25
it was no retreat but a rout,
when they had forced them to a stand
among the vines, in the ditches.
They went then among the vinestocks
which were thick and heavy on the ground   30
and there the horses often fell.
Quickly stripped were those who fell
and taken captive, and pitiful ...
Count Geoffrey with his banner
charged in such strange fashion   35
when the king came, that all those
who should have been with him were scattered.
Thereupon the king, as he rode up,
could in no place manage to join

with their company, for the enemy fled 40
and was fiercely pursued the while,
some eager to fight well and nobly,
others eager to win spoils.
Thus was the king in great alarm
to find himself thus separated. 45
Upon his right he saw a troop
of enemy soldiers. They might be
forty knights, at the very least.
Holding a lance in his hands
he ran and charged upon them 50
and so hard struck against them
that his lance broke itself therewith
as if it had been made of glass.
And the enemy abounding there
soon seized him by the rein. 55
They ran upon him from all sides
whereas it so happened that the king
had none of all his fighting men
but his Marshal who followed him
closely, for he was in the custom 60
of being at hand, in case of need ...
And William too, William of Préaux,
who on that day had been captured
and separated from his group,
dressed beneath his tunic 65
in a coat of mail concealed
and an iron cap upon his head,
and no more nor less than that.
The others were holding in their hands
the king, each of them striving hard 70
to strike off his helmet ...
The Marshal then came forward
and flung himself upon them.
So hard he struck, before, behind,
so bravely he showed them his mettle 75
and so drove and so dragged
that he managed to tear away
the headstall of the king's horse
and with it all the harness, pulling ...

3. From an Anglo-French Hawking Manual, *Three Anglo-Norman Treatises on Falconry*, ed. Tony Hunt (Oxford: Society for the Study of Medieval Languages and Literature, 2009), 42–44, lines 1–64. Translated by Claire M. Waters

[The author of this treatise both emphasizes its status as a translation and insists on the courtly nature of hawking: it is only for the *courtois*, not for the *vilain* (a peasant or, more generally, a person who is of low behavior or status). He draws attention in several ways to the problem of the "nature" of hawks and humans.]

I saw by the title of this treatise,
which is elucidated here in French,
that it is no fable or lyric poem,
nor a song made out of flattery;
rather it is drawn from authorities   5
and translated from natural philosophy.
French is not for everyone,
but only for the courtly,
for if a peasant understood it
he would go mad immediately.   10
One who is lowly should not hear about it;
rather I advise that he move along
and hear what is suitable to him
and what his nature seeks out.
Custom never wishes to see   15
a peasant associate with the courtly
nor can nature ever make it so
that two contraries should be together.

Now hear what great benefit
you may take from it [the treatise], and great pleasure,   20
but first hear the reason
for which it was made, and in whose name.
There are two causes, one may note,
for which it is made, that it is good for:
in order to heal goshawks and sparrowhawks,   25
fully treat and teach them,
and to see their temperament
from which there comes to them both evil and wickedness;

of molting, and of every concern
that is appropriate to their nature.   30
Samson, who puts his efforts into this [treatise],
presents it to Count Simon,
for no man in his country
is so worthy of it, it seems to him.
They [hawks] are valuable to him, they are dear to him   35
more than to any other knight,
for he holds them in great regard,
and wishes to do them good in return.
Therefore a very needy clerk
chose him as the most courtly,   40
for no one would ever compose in French
for a miser or a wicked man.

Now I shall speak about giving remedies
and the doctrine of keeping [hawks].
Let one who fully puts all his effort into this   45
first inquire into their nature,
for just as we see with ourselves
that we vary in nature—
some humble, some proud,
others wrathful and envious—,   50
if we see ourselves vary,
well may we prove, by reason,
that these creatures vary
according to their behavior and their natures.
We are formed of the same material,   55
except that God held ours more dear,
for with his own Holy Spirit
he set his breath to the face of man.
In his likeness, in his image
he made us: so says holy scripture.   60
Birds, beasts he brought to life
from the bone of man whom he loved more,
but their liveliness
rightly varied from man's.

Appendix F: Textual Variants

The following is a list of textual variants, keyed to line numbers in the relevant lai. Square brackets in the text mark every instance where I have diverged from the reading of Harley 978 (apart from such matters as word division and capitalization), with one exception: a superscript cross+ indicates a place where I have omitted a word or words from Harley 978 without making a substitution (and where therefore there are no brackets). The notes below give the details of the original readings to be found in the manuscript. For those not familiar with the conventions of recording such textual variants, they work as follows: the number given is the line number, followed by the form of the word or words as it appears in the text in this book (without any square brackets, to avoid confusion); if there is more than one correction to a line, they all follow that line number. The word or words after the single right bracket are those that appear in Harley 978 (without modification of i/j or u/v, unlike the text in this book). So if the word(s) after the bracket were substituted for the word(s) before the bracket in the text, the reading would be that of Harley 978. In a few cases I have added a brief explanation or "(see footnote)." In the latter case, there will be a footnote to the line in question that explains something about the original reading or the change I have made. The abbreviation "*om.*" for "*omitted*" after a right bracket means that Harley 978 does not include this word or words; "expuncted" refers to a letter or letter with a dot below, which indicates that that letter was to be deleted.

Prologue

1 escience] en science   26 ceo] *om.*   28 comencai] comencerai
40 Nes] Ne   50 kes] ke

Guigemar

24 une] un   33 vaillanz] uaillant   48 dune] dunez   58 nule]
nul   97 resort] resorti   113 quisse] quiisse   127 guarir] guarire
142 seit] sest   146 vert] unt (corrected to "vert" above the line)
158 or] oi   217 est] *om.*   218 ne] nel   234 la] de   235 mise]
om.   241 le] les   277 oste] ost   282 Arestut sei] Arestuz ele
287 I] V   299 main] maine   300 sein] seine   323 n'eusse] neus
328 ceste nef] cest nef i   344 vus] ws   348 doinse] doins
362 s'est] cest   del] el   420 la] le   424 pale] pal   427 matin]

matin est   474 Turt] Tur   484 s'il] si ele   mustrast] mustrat
480 s'esloinast] sesloinat   481 s'enferté] sa fierte   483 plaie] plai
489 jolivent] lo liuent   496 eimoit] ennoit   515 Femme] Perme
jolive] laliue   516 lungement] lungeme   518 usé] usee
536 Fu] Fui   538 ki ne] lu   539 roe] ioie   541 avenu] uenu
557 aseurez] aseuretz with the –t- expuncted   563 Il] Ele
607 Tute] Tant   629 ad] lad   637 si] sil   658 mise] mis
673 neierai] mettrai   685 bort] port   693 guerreiot] guerrot
697 s'estot] se sestot   709 mise] mis   724 uverra] auera
732 desliez] depeceiz   733 metreit] meteit   738 trenche] tresche
740 n'en] *om.*   776 Dunt] Dunc   798 a] *om.*   800 mie] *om.*
827–28 De la… est avenu] (see footnote)   831 entra] entrai
839 cuneue] cuniue   849 destreiz] destrei   864 Ki guereiot] Si
guereient   874 au prendre] a preutre

Equitan

5 Des] Les   8 hum] *om.*   9 Un en] Vent   10 ne] nai   12 de]
des   17 metent] met   nun] nu   34 uvrat] muat   78 afolez]
afoleez   110 dreite] dreit   117 Sire] Si de   120 sui] sei
123 a] *om.*   124 de vus] vus de   127 entrelaissiee] entrelaissie
143 ame] amez   hautement] hatement   144 a] *om.*   145 dute]
dut   146 requide] requid   163 novelier] noulier   169 m'otrei]
mustrei   184 en] *om.*   209 plura] plurt   228 nul] *om.*
256 se] *om.*   274 des] de   284 fu] feu   298 e] *om.*   300 cil] il

Le Fresne

26 Ki] Kar   39 cele] cel   96 cunfortouent] cunfortent   114 la]
le (see footnote)   121 chief] chive   126 orent] erent   129 une]
un   130 chestun] chescun turn (see footnote)   158 aresteue]
arestee   181 Icele] Icel   229 Le] La (with –a expuncted; see foot-
note)   235 ele] *om.*   266 sejur] serur   345 mesavenu] avenu
346 prudume] *om.*   348 serurs] serur   355 Li] Le   379 Entur]
Entra   449 ceile] ceil   486 fui] fu   502 il] ele

Bisclavret

12 forés] forest   37 si] sil   96 revienc] revinc   105 preiee] preie
123 li] l   254 seumes] sumes   313 nees] neies   314 si viveient]
sovient

Lanval

8 destruieient] destruient   20 des] de   56 veues] veu
58 Laciees] Laciez   61 uns] un   73 enveic] enveit   91 kis] ki
112 venue] venu   124 ne savriez] nosiriez   156 a la] al
162 une] un   190 amené] mene (with a- added above the line)
198 dotaunt] sotaunt   202 hummes] humme   221 De si] Dici
225 esteit] *om.*   233 amené] mene (with a- added above the line)
235 revunt] revient   240 le rei] Lanval   252 parlemenz] par les
mains   n'ert] ni ert   303 part] parte   306 l'out] out   319 la]
om.   323 la] tant   333 ostel] chastel   344 parolt] parlot
358 sun] a lur   384 Que] C (rather than the usual Q with suspen-
sion mark, the scribe has written a C, or the beginning of a Q
without the second stroke)   hum] *om.*   puisse] puis   393 esfor-
ciee] esforcie   410 fole] fol   434 nus] nuls   446 hum] bien
448 une] un   459 perl] perde   466 par] pur (in its usual abbrevi-
ated form)   467 revunt] revait   482 s'amie] amie   505 avum]
averat   539 vindrent] viendrent   570 si chevel] sun cheval
574 li] lui   604 veue] venue   608 li] lui

Deus Amanz

3 enfanz] amanz   41 asaierent] asuerent   59 ful sui
61–62 Li otria … mercie] *om.* (see footnote)   123 riches] riche
deniers] divers   132 tut] tant   134 baillié] chargié   139 tute]
tele   156 hummes] humme   165 A sun] E a   193 escriereent]
escrireent   202 li] l   229 kis] lur   234 E] Ke

Yonec

17 trespassez] trespensez   27 enserree] enserreie   34 une] un
61 en] a   en esveil] asueil   83 gelus] glut   99 blamees] blamez
167 li] lui   207 avient] avint   209 Ne m'en puis] Nen enpuis
230 k'il] ki   233 a] *om.*   249 estez] esteiez   260 l'ad] ad
289 apparailliees] apparailliez   290 enfurchiees] enfurchiez
329 la] *om.*   338 k'el] kil   345 sentier] sentir   355 est] *om.*
376 le] *om.*   380 une] un   421 n'en] ne   458 Ens … per] El
nun ni osa humme trouer (see footnote)   481 vallez] vallaz   her-
berja] herla (see footnote)   497 Coverte] Covert   roee] roe

Laüstic

5 russignol] reisun (see footnote)   7 En] Un   10 forz] forez
49 estreit] estreite   59 reverdi] reverali   89 delite] delit
96 laçun] larcun   100 pris] prise

Milun

1 cuntes] cunte   15 Mut] Amez   28 plest] plust   32 N'en] Ne
47 liee] lie   48 otriee] otrie   60 faite] fait   62 U] *om.*
65 que] quei   93 n'en] ne   106 atendu] tendu   109 les] ses
118 baillent] baille   133 eu] *om.*   182 il] ele   185 huchiée]
huchie (see footnote)   190 En] E   276 remant] remeint
342 apelouent] apelent   371 E] *om.*   390 des] de   420 Cil
raveit] Ia laveit   430 Deusse] Devreit   453 fui] fu   454 fui] fu
489 De] Les   498 nului] nul liu   521 l'] *om.*   525 liee] liez
528 tute] tut

Le Chaitivel, ou Quatre Dols

7 i] *om.*   22 cil] cil le   49 sens] prisens   83 vespré] vespres
125 feruz] perduz   155 a] *om.*   162 poet] poeit   185 penser]
pener   196 Ja] *om.*   197 amera] amerai   198 perdra] perdrai
213 peine] peint

Chevrefoil

55 Se] De   65 espier] atendre   85 a] *om.*   100 l'] *om.*

Guildelüec et Guilliadun, ou Eliduc

39 li] le   73 gardent] gardoent   89 i] *om.*   97 per] pere
197 cum] (The manuscript is damaged at this point, so that only the
first part of the –m is visible and there is a gap before "jo")
209 entrez] venuz   261 Chevals] Chevalers   334 apelé] apelee
336 alée] alé   338 cheïe] chei   361 Seure] Seur   413 del suen]
de scien   422 chevalier] chamberlenc   446 Kar jeo] Kieo (with
an abbreviation mark on the ascender of the K; though it is not the
standard abbreviation for –ar, the context suggests that this is what is
meant)   479 a] *om.*   500 Dresciee] drescie   519–21 Dame...

Quant] (The upper left corner of this folio is torn away; the brackets in these three lines reconstruct the missing letters.)
554 empeiriez] damagiez   608 errerai] errai   673 cunseil de vus] de vus cunseil (with correction marks below "de" and "cunseil" to indicate that the order should be switched)   684 bone] bon   772 Ele] *om.*   istra] eissi   827 Une] Vn   une] un   830 escipres] deciples   957 liee] lie   958 apareilliee] apareillie   966 sul] sus 999 deit] dit   quid] quide   1009 menee] mene   1010 entree] entre   1083 Trahie] Trahi   1104 li] lui   1150 parfite] parfit

Works Cited and Select Bibliography

Works of Marie (de France)

Brucker, Charles, ed. and trans. *Les Fables*. Paris and Louvain: Peeters, 1998.

Burgess, Glyn S., and Keith Busby, trans. *The Lais of Marie de France*. 2nd ed. London and New York: Penguin, 1999.

Ewert, Alfred, ed. Marie de France: *Lais*. Oxford: Basil Blackwell, 1965.

Hanning, Robert, and Joan Ferrante, trans. *The Lais of Marie de France*. Grand Rapids, MI: Baker Books, 1978.

Harf-Lancner, Laurence, trans., and Karl Warnke, ed. *Lais de Marie de France*. Paris: Librairie Générale Française, 1990.

McCash, June Hall, and Judith Clark Barban, ed. and trans. *The Life of Saint Audrey: A Text by Marie de France*. Jefferson, NC: McFarland & Company, 2006.

Pontfarcy, Yolande de, ed. and trans. *L'Espurgatoire seint Patriz*. Louvain and Paris: Peeters, 1995.

Rychner, Jean, ed. *Les Lais de Marie de France*. Paris: Honoré Champion, 1983.

Slavitt, David R., trans. *The Lays of Marie de France*. Edmonton, AB: Athabasca UP, 2013.

Spiegel, Harriet, ed. and trans. *Fables*. Toronto: U of Toronto P, 1987.

Warnke, Karl, ed. *Die Lais der Marie de France*. 2nd ed. Halle: Max Niemeyer, 1900.

Other Primary Sources

Burgess, Glyn S., trans. *The History of the Norman People: Wace's Roman de Rou*. Woodbridge, UK: Boydell, 2004.

Burgess, Glyn S., and Leslie C. Brook, ed. and trans. *French Arthurian Literature Volume IV: Eleven Old French Narrative Lais*. Cambridge: D.S. Brewer, 2007.

Chrétien de Troyes. *Arthurian Romances*. Trans. William W. Kibler and Carleton W. Carroll. London and New York: Penguin, 1991.

Cook, Robert, and Mattias Tveitane, eds. *Strengleikar: An Old Norse Translation of Twenty-one Old French Lais*. Oslo: Kjeldeskriftfondet, 1979.

Geoffrey of Monmouth. *History of the Kings of Britain*. Trans. Michael A. Faletra. Peterborough, ON: Broadview P, 2007.

Hopkins, Amanda, ed. and trans. *Melion and Biclarel: Two Old French Werwolf Lays*. Liverpool: U of Liverpool, Department of French, 2005.

Koble, Nathalie, and Mireille Séguy, ed. and trans. *Lais bretons (XIIe–XIIIe siècles): Marie de France et ses contemporains*. Paris: Honoré Champion, 2011.

Lacroix, Daniel, and Philippe Walter, ed. and trans. *Tristan et Iseut: Les poèmes français, la saga norroise*. Paris: Librairie Générale Française, 1989.

Petit, Aimé, ed. and trans. *Le Roman d'Eneas*. Paris: Librairie Générale Française, 1997.

Piramus, Denis. *Vie seint Edmund le rei*. Ed. D.W. Russell, with Kathryn A. Smith. Anglo-Norman Texts 71. Oxford: Anglo-Norman Text Society, 2014.

Wace. *Roman de Brut: A History of the British. Text and Translation*. Rev. ed. Ed. and trans. Judith Weiss. Exeter: U of Exeter P, 2002.

Wogan-Browne, Jocelyn, and Glyn S. Burgess, trans. *Virgin Lives and Holy Deaths: Two Exemplary Biographies for Anglo-Norman Women*. London: J.M. Dent, 1996.

Works Cited and Further Reading

Alter, Robert. *The Art of Biblical Narrative*. New York: Basic Books, 2011.

Auerbach, Erich. "The Knight Sets Forth." *Mimesis: The Representation of Reality in Western Literature*. Trans. Willard R. Trask. Princeton, NJ: Princeton UP, 1953. 123–42.

Badel, Pierre Yves. "La brièveté comme esthétique et comme éthique dans les Lais de Marie de France." *Amour et merveille. Les Lais de Marie de France: Études*. Ed. Jean Dufournet, with the assistance of Pierre Yves Badel. Paris: Honoré Champion, 1995. 25–40.

Bartlett, Robert. *England under the Norman and Angevin Kings, 1075–1225*. Oxford: Oxford UP, 2002.

Bloch, R. Howard. *The Anonymous Marie de France*. Chicago: U of Chicago P, 2003.

Boyd, Matthieu. "The Ring, the Sword, the Fancy Dress, and the Posthumous Child: Background to the Element of Heroic Biography in Marie de France's *Yonec*." *Romance Quarterly* 55.3 (2008): 205–30.

Bruckner, Matilda Tomaryn. *Shaping Romance: Interpretation, Truth, and Closure in Twelfth-Century French Fictions*. Philadelphia: U of Pennsylvania P, 1993.

———. "Speaking through Animals in Marie de France's *Lais* and *Fables*." *A Companion to Marie de France*. Ed. Logan E. Whalen. Leiden and Boston: Brill, 2011. 157–85.

Bullock-Davies, Constance. "Marie, Abbess of Shaftesbury, and Her Brothers." *English Historical Review* 80 (1965): 314–22.

Bumke, Joachim. *Courtly Culture: Literature and Society in the High Middle Ages*. Trans. Thomas Dunlap. Berkeley and Los Angeles: U of California P, 1991.

Burgess, Glyn S. *The Lais of Marie de France: Text and Context*. Athens: U of Georgia P, 1987.

———. *Marie de France: An Analytical Bibliography*. London: Grant and Cutler, 1977.

———. *Marie de France: An Analytical Bibliography. Supplement 1*. London: Grant and Cutler, 1986.

———. *Marie de France: An Analytical Bibliography. Supplement 2*. London: Grant and Cutler, 1997.

———, with the assistance of Giovanna Angeli. *Marie de France: An Analytical Bibliography. Supplement 3*. Woodbridge, UK: Tamesis, 2007.

Butterfield, Ardis. *The Familiar Enemy: Chaucer, Language, and Nation in the Hundred Years War*. Oxford: Oxford UP, 2009.

Crane, Susan. "Anglo-Norman Cultures in England." *The Cambridge History of Medieval English Literature*. Ed. David Wallace. Cambridge: Cambridge UP, 1999.

Donovan, Mortimer. "Priscian and the Obscurity of the Ancients." *Speculum* 36.1 (1961): 75–80.

Faletra, Michael A. *Wales and the Medieval Colonial Imagination: The Matters of Britain in the Twelfth Century*. New York: Palgrave Macmillan, 2014.

Freeman, Michelle A. "Marie de France's Poetics of Silence: The Implications for a Feminine *Translatio*." *PMLA* 99.5 (1984): 860–83.

Gaunt, Simon. "Romance and Other Genres." *The Cambridge Companion to Medieval Romance*. Ed. Roberta L. Krueger. Cambridge: Cambridge UP, 2000. 45–59.

Guynn, Noah. "Hybridity, Ethics, and Gender in Two Old French Werewolf Tales." *From Beasts to Souls: Gender and Embodiment in Medieval Europe*. Ed. E. Jane Burns and Peggy McCracken. Notre Dame, IN: Notre Dame UP, 2013. 157–84.

Hamesse, Jacqueline, ed. *Les Prologues médiévaux*. Turnhout: Brepols, 2000.

Hollister, C. Warren. "Anglo-Norman Political Culture and the Twelfth-Century Renaissance." *Anglo-Norman Political Culture and the Twelfth-Century Renaissance.* Ed. C. Warren Hollister. Woodbridge, UK: Boydell, 1997. 1–16.

Kinoshita, Sharon. "Colonial Possessions: Wales and the Anglo-Norman Imaginary in the *Lais* of Marie de France." *Medieval Boundaries: Rethinking Difference in Old French Literature.* Philadelphia: U of Pennsylvania P, 2006. 105–32.

———, and Peggy McCracken. *Marie de France: A Critical Companion.* Cambridge: D.S. Brewer, 2012.

Knapton, Antoinette. "À la recherche de Marie de France." *Romance Notes* 19 (1978): 248–53.

Krueger, Roberta L. "Marie de France." *The Cambridge Companion to Medieval Women's Writing.* Ed. Carolyn Dinshaw and David Wallace. Cambridge: Cambridge UP, 2003.

———. "Questions of Gender in Old French Courtly Romance." *The Cambridge Companion to Medieval Romance.* Ed. Roberta L. Krueger. Cambridge: Cambridge UP, 2000. 132–49.

Leicester, H. Marshall. "The Voice of the Hind: The Emergence of Feminine Discontent in the *Lais* of Marie de France." *Reading Medieval Culture: Essays in Honor of Robert W. Hanning.* Ed. Robert M. Stein and Sandra Pierson Prior. Notre Dame, IN: Notre Dame UP, 2005. 132–69.

Maréchal, Chantal. *The Reception and Transmission of the Works of Marie de France, 1774–1974.* Lewiston, NY: Edwin Mellen, 2003.

McCash, June Hall. "La vie seinte Audree: A Fourth Text by Marie de France?" *Speculum* 77.3 (2002): 744–77.

McCracken, Peggy. "Translation and Animals in Marie de France's *Lais.*" *Australian Journal of French Studies* 46.3 (2009): 206–18.

Meecham-Jones, Simon. "Introduction." *Writers of the Reign of Henry II: Twelve Essays.* Ed. Ruth Kennedy and Simon Meecham-Jones. New York: Palgrave Macmillan, 2006. 1–24.

Mercier, Emilie. *Bisclavret: Un film d'Émilie Mercier d'après le 'Lai' de Marie de France.* Trans. Françoise Morvan. Roubaix: Les Films du Nord, 2011.

Minnis, Alastair J. *Medieval Theory of Authorship: Scholastic Literary Attitudes in the Later Middle Ages.* 2nd ed. Philadelphia: U of Pennsylvania P, 2009.

Nichols, Stephen G. "Marie de France's Commonplaces." *Yale French Studies Special Edition, Contexts: Style and Value in Medieval Art and Literature.* Ed. Daniel Poirion and Nancy Freeman Regalado. New Haven, CT: Yale UP, 1991. 134–48.

Pickens, Rupert T. "BnF, nouv. acq. fr., 1104: Marie de France and 'Lays de Bretagne.'" *'Li Premerains vers.' Essays in Honor of Keith*

Busby. Ed. Catherine M. Jones and Logan E. Whalen. Amsterdam and New York: Rodopi, 2011. 341–56.

Pontfarcy, Yolande de. "Si Marie de France était Marie de Meulan ...." *Cahiers de civilisation medievale* 38 (1995): 353–61.

Potkay, Monica Brzezsinki. "The Parable of the Sower and Obscurity in the Prologue to Marie de France's *Lais*" *Christianity and Literature* 57.3 (2008): 355–78.

Rector, Geoff. "Courtly Romance, the Vernacular Psalms, and Generic Contrafaction." *Viator* 45.2 (2014): 117–48.

Rikhardsdottir, Sif. "The Imperial Implications of Medieval Translations: Old Norse and Middle English Versions of Marie de France's *Lais*." *Studies in Philology* 105.2 (2008): 144–64.

Rossi, Carla. "Brevi note su Marie de Meulan ([c.] 1000–1060), un'improbabile Marie de France." *Critica del testo* 7.3 (2004): 1147–55.

———. *Marie de France et les érudits de Cantorbéry*. Paris: Classiques Garnier, 2009.

Short, Ian. "Denis Piramus and the Truth of Marie's *Lais*." *Cultura neolatina* 67.3–4 (2007): 319–40.

———. *Manual of Anglo-Norman*. 2nd ed. Anglo-Norman Text Society Occasional Publications Series, no. 8. Oxford: Anglo-Norman Text Society, 2013.

———. "Patrons and Polyglots: French Literature in Twelfth-Century England." *Anglo-Norman England XIV*. Proceedings of the Battle Conference 1991. Ed. Marjorie Chibnall. Woodbridge: Boydell Press, 1991–92. 229–49.

Silvestre, Hubert. "'Quanto iuniores, tanto perspicaciores': Antécédents à la querelle des anciens et des modernes." *Recueil commémoratif du 10e anniversaire de la Faculté de Philosophie et Lettres* (Université Lovanium de Kinshasa). Louvain: Éditions Nauwelaerts; Paris: Béatrice-Nauwelaerts, 1968. 231–55.

Spitzer, Leo. "The Prologue to the *Lais* of Marie de France and Medieval Poetics." *Modern Philology* 41 (1943–44): 96–102.

Stein, Robert M. *Reality Fictions: Romance, History, and Governmental Authority, 1025–1180*. Notre Dame, IN: U of Notre Dame P, 2006.

Taylor, Andrew. *Textual Situations: Three Medieval Manuscripts and Their Readers*. Philadelphia: U of Pennsylvania P, 2002.

Whalen, Logan E. *Marie de France and the Poetics of Memory*. Washington, DC: Catholic U of America P, 2008.

———, ed. *A Companion to Marie de France*. Leiden and Boston: Brill, 2011.

Wogan-Browne, Jocelyn, ed. *Language and Culture in Medieval Britain: The French of England, c. 1100–c. 1500*. York: York Medieval Press, 2009.

———, Thelma Fenster, and Delbert Russell, ed. and trans. *Vernacular Literary Theory from the French of Medieval England: Texts and Translations, c. 1120–c. 1450*. Cambridge: D.S. Brewer, 2016.

Permissions Acknowledgements

Burgess, Glyn S., editor and translator. Excerpt from *The History of the Norman People: Wace's Roman de Rou*. Woodbridge: Boydell Press, 2004. Reprinted with the permission of Boydell & Brewer Ltd.

Burgess, Glyn, and Leslie Brook, translators. Excerpt from *French Arthurian Literature. Volume IV: Eleven Old French Narrative Lays.* Cambridge: D.S. Brewer, 2007. Reprinted with the permission of Boydell & Brewer Ltd.

Cambrensis, Giraldus. Excerpt from *The Topography of Ireland*, translated by Thomas Forester (1881), revised and edited by Thomas Wright. Toronto: In Parentheses Publications, Medieval Latin Series, 2000.

Cook, Robert, and Mattias Tveitane, editors and translators. Excerpt from *Strengleikar. An Old Norse Translation of Twenty-One Old French Lais*. Norsk Historisk Kjeldeskrift-Institutt, Norrøne tekster 3. Oslo: Grieg, 1979. Reprinted with the permission of The National Archives of Norway.

Duby, Georges. Excerpts from *William Marshall*, copyright © 1985 by Georges Duby. Reprinted in Canada, the United States, and the Open Market with the permission of Pantheon Books, an imprint of the Knopf Doubleday Publishing Group, a division of Penguin Random House LLC. All rights reserved. Any third party use of this material, outside of this publication, is prohibited. Interested parties must apply directly to Penguin Random House for permission.

Faletra, Michael A., editor. Excerpt from Geoffrey of Monmouth, *History of the Kings of Britain*. Peterborough, ON: Broadview Press, 2008.

Goldin, Frederick. Excerpts from *Lyrics of the Troubadours and Trouvères: An Anthology and a History*. Copyright © 1973 by Frederick Goldin. Used by permission of Doubleday, an imprint of the Knopf Doubleday Publishing Group, a division of Penguin Random House LLC. All rights reserved. Any third party use of this material, outside of this publication, is prohibited. Interested parties must apply directly to Penguin Random House for permission.

From the Publisher

A name never says it all, but the word "Broadview" expresses a good deal of the philosophy behind our company. We are open to a broad range of academic approaches and political viewpoints. We pay attention to the broad impact book publishing and book printing has in the wider world; for some years now we have used 100% recycled paper for most titles. Our publishing program is internationally oriented and broad-ranging. Our individual titles often appeal to a broad readership too; many are of interest as much to general readers as to academics and students.

Founded in 1985, Broadview remains a fully independent company owned by its shareholders—not an imprint or subsidiary of a larger multinational.

For the most accurate information on our books (including information on pricing, editions, and formats) please visit our website at www.broadviewpress.com. Our print books and ebooks are also available for sale on our site.

broadview press
www.broadviewpress.com